WITHDRAWN
WRIGHT STATE UNIVERSITY LIBRARIES

COMPREHENSIVE TEACHER INDUCTION

Comprehensive Teacher Induction

Edited by

Edward Britton

*National Center for Improving Science Education/WestEd,
San Francisco, U.S.A.*

Lynn Paine

*Michigan State University,
Lansing, Michigan, U.S.A.*

David Pimm

*University of Alberta,
Edmonton, Canada*

and

Senta Raizen

*National Center for Improving Science Education/WestEd,
Washington, U.S.A.*

KLUWER ACADEMIC PUBLISHERS
DORDRECHT / BOSTON / LONDON

LB
1729
.C66
2003

A C.I.P. Catalogue record for this book is available from the Library of Congress.

ISBN 1-4020-1147-4

Published by Kluwer Academic Publishers,
P.O. Box 17, 3300 AA Dordrecht, The Netherlands.

Sold and distributed in North, Central and South America
by Kluwer Academic Publishers,
101 Philip Drive, Norwell, MA 02061, U.S.A.

In all other countries, sold and distributed
by Kluwer Academic Publishers,
P.O. Box 322, 3300 AH Dordrecht, The Netherlands.

Printed on acid-free paper

This work was supported by the National Science Foundation in Washington, DC, grant #REC9814803.
The opinions expressed herein are those of the authors, not the Foundation.

All Rights Reserved
© 2003 Kluwer Academic Publishers
No part of this work may be reproduced, stored in a retrieval system, or transmitted
in any form or by any means, electronic, mechanical, photocopying, microfilming, recording
or otherwise, without written permission from the Publisher, with the exception
of any material supplied specifically for the purpose of being entered
and executed on a computer system, for exclusive use by the purchaser of the work.

Printed in the Netherlands.

"Life is a bath; all paddle in its great pool;
some sink, some swim." (Seneca, 1st Century AD)

Contents

Preface xi

Chapter 1 Introduction 1

Chapter 2 Entering a Culture of Teaching: Teacher Induction
in Shanghai 20
Lynn Paine, Yanping Fang and Suzanne Wilson

Chapter 3 Co-operation, Counseling and Reflective Practice:
Swiss Induction Programs 83
*Senta Raizen, with Mary Ann Huntley and
Edward Britton*

Chapter 4 Help in Every Direction: Supporting Beginning
Science Teachers in New Zealand 141
*Edward Britton, with Senta Raizen and
Mary Ann Huntley*

Chapter 5 Being and Becoming a Mathematics Teacher:
Ambiguities in Teacher *Formation* in France 194
David Pimm, with Daniel Chazan and Lynn Paine

Chapter 6 Guiding the New Teacher: Induction of First-Year
Teachers in Japan 261
Michael Padilla and Joseph Riley

Chapter 7 Making Sense of Induction: Looking across
International Cases 296

Appendices A: Notes on Data Collection 337

B: Swiss Induction Practices by Canton 351

C: The French *Mémoire Professionel* 357

Notes by Chapter 364

Glossary of Terms 376

References 386

Book Contributors and Project Advisors 395

Index 399

Detailed Chapter Contents

Preface xi

       Audiences xiii

       Acknowledgements xiii

Chapter 1: Introduction 1

    1. Case studies within countries 6

    2. Case-study methods 8

    3. Book conventions and organization 14

    4. Some opening thoughts 19

Chapter 2: Entering a Culture of Teaching 20

    1. Starting up: induction through the eyes
       of Teacher Li Mei 20

    2. Exploring Shanghai as a system for teacher induction . . .24

    3. Experiences that guide the beginner: induction
       as a varied process supporting core goals 38

    4. Acquiring the wisdom of practice: learning
       with and through curriculum materials 50

    5. Talk as a medium for induction: immersion in
       public conversation about and scrutiny of teaching 58

    6. Multiple stakeholders supporting common
       goals: building variation into a system 69

    7. Conclusion 79

Chapter 3: Co-operation, Counseling and Reflective Practice 83

    1. Supporting the first two years of teaching 83

    2. The general study context 91

    3. Teacher education 93

    4. Who is a beginning teacher? The job market
       for teachers 103

5. Responsibilities of middle-school teachers 105

6. Swiss induction: individual and professional
    growth go together 109

7. The training of counselors and mentors:
    not just experienced teachers 130

8. Research and evaluation: making a system reflective . .133

9. A summary of main induction features 136

Chapter 4: Help in Every Direction **141**

1. Introduction 141

2. The national context for local teacher induction 146

3. Expectations and resources for teaching
    the science curriculum 160

4. Diverse support providers: a repertoire
    of support activities 168

5. Enabling factors supporting induction
    within the culture of the educational system 184

6. A summary of New Zealand's main induction features . .186

Chapter 5: Being and Becoming a Mathematics Teacher **194**

1. 'One foot in the classroom': a week in the life
    of a *stagiaire* teacher 196

2. A brief interlude on two key terms 200

3. Some observations about the system of national
    education in France 203

4. How to become a mathematics teacher 213

5. Settings and occasions for *stagiaire* learning 218

6. Some specific elements of the mathematics
    teaching terrain 237

7. Looking more generally 244

8. What is valued by the system .258

Chapter 6: Guiding the New Teacher 261

    1. Yoko Matsubara's first year 261

    2. An overview of Japan's educational system 265

    3. Pre-service teacher preparation in Japan 267

    4. Becoming a teacher 270

    5. Characteristics of today's beginning teacher
       induction training program 275

    6. Program evaluation and the politics of induction 293

    7. Concluding remarks 295

Chapter 7: Making Sense of Induction 296

    1. Why induction? 299

    2. Whom does induction serve?
       Who is (or gets to be) a new teacher? 314

    3. What is induction? What is the 'curriculum
       of induction'? 318

    4. Who provides the needed knowledge and activities?
       Whose knowledge is it? Where does it reside? 324

    5. Induction as complex systems: articulation and
       co-ordination 327

    6. Some concluding thoughts 331

Preface

This book provides a detailed examination of how systems located within five countries shape the early career learning of beginning teachers. It describes, discusses and analyzes comprehensive teacher induction found within France, Japan, New Zealand, Shanghai and Switzerland. We refer to the phenomena we observed as induction 'systems' because they are ambitious, substantial and established: all beginning teachers in these various locales are served; there are no unfunded mandates; these systems have been in place for 10–25 years. Nevertheless, they are still evolving, undergoing review and change – they are dynamic systems. While sharing such similarities, these systems also present striking contrasts in their purposes, policies, program design and the specific activities that constitute them.

These induction systems operate within countries having both centralized and decentralized education systems, and within large jurisdictions as well as smaller ones. Although we primarily looked at beginning mathematics and science teachers of the lower secondary grades, many aspects are relevant to novice teachers of all school subjects at these grade levels, and some structures and insights are germane to the induction of elementary teachers as well.

We have tried to strike a balance between fostering ideas that could be useful elsewhere, while providing sufficient context and detail to discourage wholesale implementation without adequate adaptation. We were alert to the seductive appeal of simple borrowing of specific practices, programs and even policies. Yet, as individuals with daily involvement with and commitment to teacher development in North America, we also appreciate the desire for 'lessons' that might emerge from international study.

We offer four reasons for attending to this volume on teacher induction. First, induction is coming to the forefront of contemporary educational issues. At the time of writing, the IEA (International Association for the Evaluation of Educational Achievement) is hoping to undertake a large, multi-country study of teacher education, likely including attention to induction. The OECD (Organisation of Economic Co-operation and Development) is interested in studying teacher development internationally as well. In addition, at the outset of the study which forms the basis for much of this book, we conducted phone interviews with international colleagues in a dozen countries (many of whom were involved in the Third International Mathematics and Science Study – TIMSS). Most reported that, in their setting, there was limited or no teacher induction but that they wished this situation were different.

Second, these comprehensive teacher induction systems expand considerably a sense of what induction can and even should be. They target broad and diverse goals involving varied providers and articulated activities, going beyond the important but limited support afforded by more common forms of induction, such as orienting teachers to school facilities and procedures for helping them manage pupil behavior. The studied systems also help novices gain more understanding of and skill in how they might teach their subject(s), how to think and talk about their emerging practice, how to assess pupil learning and understanding, how to work with parents and colleagues, and much more. To accomplish such diverse goals, these systems necessarily involve multiple providers drawn from different parts of the educational system to work with both novices' and the systems' sense of need.

Third, examining induction permits an exploration of key aspects of teacher preparation from a number of perspectives. In particular, it allows us to see teacher preparation in a new way, to understand its contribution to teacher formation differently. Reciprocally, knowing about teachers' prior preparation is essential for making sense of what occurs in teacher induction in each setting.

Finally, this study enlarges the body of research on teacher induction. It drew on the extended and repeated observations of multiple sets of eyes, with observers having listened to insider perspectives, but was undertaken with an outsider's gaze. Each study chapter is written with sufficient depth that a reader can gain an understanding of the complexity of practices and contexts that constitute and foster induction there. Much prior writing in English offers the valuable vision and experiences of individual stakeholders in teacher induction. Rarer, however, are studies that provide empirical, external perspectives on induction programs, their design or actual implementation. Research-based articles commonly only provide in-depth studies of particular induction practices or single locales, or surface contrasts across multiple settings.

One project advisor noted:

> Despite the importance of this period of professional learning [induction], it has often been overlooked by researchers [...] impeding the development of an empirically-grounded theory.

While we do not claim to provide such a theory in this book, we do attempt to move beyond description, especially in Chapter 7 where we take a long and hard look across the cases reported in the earlier chapters. Our intent is to make the book more than the sum of the individual cases, with a view to reframing and re-orienting questions and underlying thinking about induction. Individually and collectively, these cases challenge certain conceptions of induction, its purposes, its clients and what might be called the 'curriculum of induction' that should be available for early career learning.

Audiences

This book is intended for several groups of professionals interested in or involved with beginning teacher induction.

- *Researchers* who study teacher induction or professional development, teacher learning, educational policy, teacher education and comparative education – particularly in mathematics or science education. Similarly, faculty in university departments or colleges of education who teach courses related to the above areas or graduate students researching these or related issues will find much here.
- *Education leaders* who establish policies (at national, regional or local levels) for the funding or specification of teacher induction and certification or who provide educational leadership and administration for teacher induction programs at any of these levels. This book examines and explores policies concerned with deciding whom induction should serve and what resources (both material and cultural) are necessary for its success. Administrators overseeing induction programs will become better informed about the types of resources, individuals and organizations that can be used to achieve specific but wide-ranging purposes and goals.
- *Professional developers, school system staff or teacher leaders* who design and implement programs for beginning teachers. This volume presents an opportunity for professional developers to step back and inform themselves further about how others have approached questions of induction, in order to reflect on the fundamentals of what they are trying to accomplish. It might stimulate the possibility of change in their induction programs' design and in the nature of activities that can best address the perceived needs both of their beginning teachers and of the system itself.

Acknowledgements

We want to thank key people and organizations who helped make this book (and the study upon which it draws heavily) a reality. Their assistance enabled us to collect, analyze and come to understand the data reported within its pages. Our financial sponsor was the Division of Research, Evaluation and Communication of the U.S. National Science Foundation (NSF award #9814083). In particular, we are grateful to the NSF REC program officers Larry Suter and Elizabeth VanderPutten whose efforts on our behalf went beyond the administration of our grant to the providing of helpful feedback as the study progressed.

We also wish to acknowledge here the two institutions who supported the day-to-day functioning of this work over three years – the National

Center for Improving Science Education (NCISE) and Michigan State University. They afforded us the time to focus on this study and provided good, critical colleagues from teacher development and from mathematics and science education to encourage and enhance our thinking about these areas. In addition, we appreciated the extensive administrative support provided as we engaged in this complex study. Rachelle Painchaud-Nash prepared the manuscript for publication with skill and graciousness. We are pleased this book has been published by Kluwer Academic Publishers, in conjunction with the Communications department at WestEd, NCISE's parent organization.

From the outset of the study and throughout its duration, our expert advisors generously made time in their schedules to help shape our work: Deborah Ball, Rodger Bybee, Sharon Feiman-Nemser, Robert Floden, Willis Hawley, David Imig, Glenda Lappan, Jean Miller, Jay Moskowitz, Jack Schwille, Gary Sykes, Michael Timpane, Gerald Wheeler and Arthur Wise. (For their individual affiliations, see the *Book Contributors and Project Advisors* section at the end of this book.)

We particularly want to thank our co-authors – Dan Chazan, Yanping Fang, Mary Ann Huntley and Suzanne Wilson – who as study-team members played critical roles in data collection and/or analysis and writing. In addition, we especially thank Suzanne Wilson for reading each draft chapter to provide feedback that enriched both our thinking and our communication. We are pleased that Michael Padilla and Joseph Riley agreed to include in this book an account of their research on teacher preparation and induction in Japan, a study jointly funded by the U.S. National Science Foundation (NSF award #9700667) and Japan's Ministry of Education.

In each case study, the assistance of particular colleagues or new acquaintances within the country significantly enhanced the depth and quality of our data collection and analysis. We cannot adequately convey our gratitude to all of these individuals in this brief space. Finally, we thank the many teachers and other professionals who made their precious time available for interviews or permitted us to observe them at work. We especially appreciate the generosity of time, attention and spirit of the beginning teachers who, despite being immersed in their initial practices and unique challenges as beginners, enabled us to understand their first teaching experiences and the induction programs that were offered to enhance them.

Edward Britton
Lynn Paine
David Pimm
Senta Raizen

September, 2002

Chapter 1

Introduction

Beginning to teach involves both starting a new job and entering a new way of life. There may be more or less ceremony (of welcome or initiation) at the school where one starts; there may be formal or informal procedures intended to aid or ease the challenges of this beginning. There may be nothing in evidence at all. Whether officially inducted or not, new teachers begin teaching every year, all over the world.

As its title suggests, this book is concerned with teacher induction, a topic of growing interest around the world. However, in North America at least, much of the discourse about and practice of induction frames it as a rather straightforward solution to a simple problem. If, for instance, we look across the ever-increasing number of U.S. programs now requiring induction for beginning teachers (currently in more than thirty states), the universe of practice seems remarkably narrow: mentoring predominates and often there is little more.

'Mentoring' has come to stand for an automatic remedy to a problem that tends to remain unexamined. It is variously seen as insufficient experience of the exigencies of teaching, inadequate information about local practices and customs in the particular school or incomplete knowledge of various sorts required for teaching. While the surface analyses vary somewhat, they all share the common presumption that the novice arrives lacking something, arrives equipped with a particular *deficit*: 'induction' – here, meaning the assistance of a mentor – is somehow to make up for this deficiency.

However, induction is not simply the filling in of gaps. Teacher induction can be – and in some places is – far more than the mere orientation of beginning teachers at the start of the school year or the provision of on-going practical support throughout the school year. Induction programs can recognize that even fully prepared beginning teachers need to learn (and can use help in learning) more about teaching. This is so, even though they could not have learned these things before starting to teach – hence neither they nor their teacher preparation programs can be said to have failed in this regard. Induction can go beyond immediate teacher support and survival to assist beginners to learn more about how to: assess pupil

1

E. Britton et al. (eds.), Comprehensive Teacher Induction, 1–19.
© 2003 Kluwer Academic Publishers. Printed in the Netherlands.

understanding; craft a lesson; develop a repertoire of instructional practices; gain a deeper knowledge and broader awareness of subject-matter issues; work with parents; and more. Given this claim, we argue it is important to recognize there are many possible goals for induction and we can imagine systems as being more or less *comprehensive* in their attempts to attend to them. One could imagine an underlying continuum. Figure 1 illustrates possible distinctions between what we have termed 'limited' and 'comprehensive' teacher induction.

Program Feature	Limited Induction	Comprehensive Induction
goals	focuses on teacher orientation, support, enculturation, retention	also promotes career learning, enhances teaching quality
policies	provides optional participation and modest time, usually unpaid	requires participation and provides substantial, paid time
overall program design	employs a limited number of *ad hoc* induction providers and activities	plans an induction system involving a complementary set of providers and activities
induction as a transitional phase	treats induction as an isolated phase, without explicit attention to teachers' prior knowledge or future development	considers the influence of teacher preparation and professional development on induction program design
initial teaching conditions	limited attention to initial teaching conditions	attention to assigned courses, pupils, non-teaching duties
level of effort	invests limited total effort, or all effort in few providers, activities	requires substantial overall effort
resources	does not provide resources sufficient to meet program goals	provides adequate resources to meet program goals
levels of the education system involved	involves some levels of the system, perhaps in isolation	involves all relevant levels of system in articulated roles
length of program	one year or less	more than one year
sources of support	primarily or solely uses one mentor	uses multiple, complementary induction providers
conditions for novices and providers	usually attends to learning conditions for novices	also provides good conditions and training for providers
activities	uses a few types of induction activities	uses a set of articulated, varied activities

Figure 1:   Key features of limited versus comprehensive induction programs

The figure begins with goals, because tackling more comprehensive goals necessitates other features of comprehensive systems. In other words, addressing more (and more diverse) needs of both beginning teachers and the educational systems they inhabit requires more effort, more resources, greater participation by all sectors of the educational system, more kinds of people, more kinds of activities, more time in the year, a longer period of time, and so on. The list of induction program features presented in Figure 1 is drawn from the set of systems described in this book. No individual system exhibits all of the features listed in Figure 1, yet examined together these systems support the possibility of such a continuum.

This book, then, predominantly based on a three-year international study which examined systems for early career learning within four countries, is about comprehensive and *systematic* forms of teacher induction. The study allowed us to expand thinking about induction, to understand better some complexities at the very heart of induction and to reframe a conceptualization of induction itself. There are other ways of viewing induction beyond the elimination of deficits, ways that force a rethinking of fundamental questions about what induction is. These include asking why induction is considered important (and for whom), what induction entails, how it is to be organized and provided, when it is to occur, where it should take place and who should be involved (both as provider and recipient).

Simple (or fundamental) as these questions are, by problematizing tacit assumptions about induction, we have found approaches which can generate new insights into the nature of and hence the possibilities for induction. These questions also encourage us to see induction as something which can itself be talked about in both pedagogic and curricular ways. In short, we argue that it is important to rethink both induction and a 'curriculum' of learning to teach.

What are some of these ways of conceiving induction? Our initial viewpoint was significantly influenced by Sharon Feiman-Nemser's framework for seeing induction variously as a phase in learning to teach, as a process of enculturation and as a formal program for beginning teachers (see Feiman-Nemser *et al.*, 1999a). Further informed by our emerging cases as our study developed, we came to see induction in terms of four broad categories, somewhat differently specified from Feiman-Nemser's. These categories conceive of induction as:

(1) a *process* for learning;
(2) a particular *period* of time;
(3) a specific *phase* in teaching;
(4) a *system*.

The induction *process* supports teachers' further acquisition of skill and knowledge, as well as the development of certain habits of mind – teacher *learning* that can only occur in the course of teaching itself, or at least alongside and in conjunction with actual day-to-day teaching. This conception situates *learning* at the center of the induction process, rather than either training or mere orientation. The dominant North American metaphor for induction has been one of 'support', a frame which does not necessarily involve any learning whatsoever on the part of the novice (Gold, 1996; Feiman-Nemser *et al.*, 1999b).

Induction is also that *period* of time, early in the teacher's career, during which this skill and knowledge in some sense must and certainly can best be learned. Undoubtedly, the induction period can be much longer than the first weeks of school and may well continue over more than a year. Prior studies, both within North America (e.g. Feiman-Nemser, 2001) and internationally (e.g. Moskowitz and Stephens, 1997), have indicated how induction can be viewed as a specific period in the teacher development continuum – and Feiman-Nemser's research additionally examines the central tasks of learning to teach at different stages along this continuum. One example of the salience of period, as is discussed in Chapter 5, is that teachers in their first year of teaching in France are, in fact, identified by a distinct title – that of *stagiaire* teacher – one which speaks directly to them being institutionally framed as residing in this period.

Induction is further frameable as a *phase* within the continuum of a teaching career, one when teachers have to make the difficult transition from student to teacher, face concrete problems they have only studied academically before and begin to construct a personal practice within a particular structured setting. The induction phase can only be understood fully in relation to what comes before it and what comes after – it is to complement novices' teacher preparation and can instill reflection on teaching that promotes continuous learning throughout their careers (see Figure 2).

Teacher Preparation	INFLUENCES	Teacher Induction	PROMOTES	Professional Development

Figure 2:   *Phases of teacher preparation, teacher induction and professional development*

At all phases, at different times, at various levels and to varying degrees, individuals will be working on subject-matter knowledge, pedagogic content knowledge, teaching. They will be affected by various policies, program designs and providers' activities. In all of these phases, they will be involved in continued reflection and learning.

For example, as is discussed in Chapter 4, novice biology teachers in New Zealand frequently need assistance with their common assignment to teach integrated science in the lower grades of secondary school. While strongly prepared in their specialty subject, biology teachers have not customarily studied much (if any) of the chemistry, physics, earth science and astronomy they must teach in this general science course.

Lastly, induction in the settings we studied is also more than a single practice, such as 'mentoring', or a loose collection of relatively unconnected practices. Induction can constitute a *system*, one that is characterized by complexity, interconnectedness, variety, co-ordination, responsiveness and dynamism. Comprehensive induction systems go far beyond support or assistance, using a variety of co-ordinated means tailored to perceptions of the novices' and the general educational systems' requirements.

The case studies reported in this book problematize tacit North American assumptions about induction, generating new insights into the nature of and hence the possibilities for induction. In short, we argue that it is important for those involved in prescribing, designing or providing teacher induction programs to rethink induction and the curriculum of early teacher learning.

Why is induction so important to study and re-conceptualize? There is a growing international realization that launching beginning teachers on the road to learning more about teaching is an investment that can yield enhanced instruction throughout a career lifetime, affecting the quality of what hundreds, even thousands of pupils will learn in conjunction with each teacher. In some countries, though strikingly in only one of those we studied, an additional or alternative goal of induction programs is to *retain* beginning teachers in the profession. For example, a phenomenon of the U.S. educational system perceived as wasteful is that large numbers of teachers who embark on this career soon quit. Ingersoll (1999) documents how the situation is especially acute for mathematics and science teachers. (Interestingly, in Switzerland, teachers leaving the profession after training are seen as enriching society as a whole and so are not seen as a loss or waste there.)

At the outset of this chapter, we talked about beginning to teach as an entry into the new. This book offers novel ways of exploring that entry from a number of viewpoints, including understanding the *processes* for new teacher learning, during this specific *period* of time, in this *phase* connected both to what has gone before and to the upcoming life that is opening in front of these novices. Lastly, but most significantly in some ways, we have chosen to examine *systems* for this early career learning, systems that are necessarily and historically embedded in the social and political cultures of the nations they inhabit.

1. Case Studies within Countries

This book is mostly based on a study of induction at sites within four countries which have rich images of and vigorous approaches to fostering new teacher development. Turning to cases internationally encourages thinking beyond the familiar – both at the practical level of how one does induction, as well as at the conceptual level of what induction is and hence could be. We examined comprehensive induction policies, programs and actual activities – induction *systems* – within France, New Zealand, Shanghai [1] and Switzerland. Additionally, colleagues at the University of Georgia carried out a more limited investigation of teacher induction in Japan, which is reported in Chapter 6.

We conducted case studies of induction systems in order to gain a holistic understanding of them. Reading such case studies will invariably raise questions about 'methods' – among them the researchers' backgrounds and selective biases, the choice of cases and specific foci within them, the nature and amount of fieldwork carried out – particularly so in a collective research study involving multiple researchers working across national boundaries. We discuss these below in the subsequent section and provide more detail about data collection in Appendix A.

Research goals and questions

Our primary study goal was to understand each system of beginning teacher development, training and support in its full complexity – policies, programs and practices – as well as interactions among them. Within each national setting, we explored the following questions.

- What are the purposes of and rationales for induction?
- What does induction entail?
- How is it organized and provided?
- When does it occur?
- Where does it take place?
- Who is involved, both as provider and recipient?

In addition to these general topics, we also sought to answer the following.

- To what extent does the educational system aim to assist, develop or assess beginning teachers?
- What is the 'curriculum of induction', i.e. what is the system trying to 'teach' beginning teachers?
- What is the typical image or framing of mathematics or science teaching into which novices are being inducted?

Further, to the extent we were able to as outsiders, we wanted to understand these induction systems as firmly situated within and predominantly supported by their educational, economic, cultural, historical, political and philosophical contexts. As a research team, we do not feel individual policies or practices make sense without this contextual frame. Therefore, we aimed to understand these and similar issues.

- How does induction fit within the country's educational system as a whole?
- What resources does it require?
- How do general societal beliefs and customs influence the view and treatment of beginning teachers?
- How did this induction system begin and how has it changed over time?
- How has politics shaped who is inducted and who provides induction?
- What are the philosophical underpinnings of the induction system?

Because we see induction as a phase, we needed to understand its relation to that which came before and that which followed. We therefore also investigated these two overarching questions.

- How does beginning teachers' prior preparation influence their induction program?
- Is the teacher induction program consistent with and does it promote the professional development in which novices may participate afterwards?

More specifically, understanding the following four aspects of teacher preparation is essential for appreciating the baseline knowledge and experiences that beginning teachers bring with them at the outset of their first year of teaching.

- What mathematics and/or science do prospective teachers learn? How well does their post-secondary, subject-matter education prepare them for the school mathematics or science taught in lower secondary school?
- What and where do prospective teachers learn about teaching content knowledge?
- What is the nature and extent of 'student teaching'?
- Does the educational system screen out teacher candidates deemed 'inadequate' during their entry to teacher preparation itself, during the preparation program, during the teacher induction program or some combination of these?

Looking forward, we additionally wanted to understand how induction connects (if indeed it does) to learning throughout a teacher's career.

- Does the induction program focus early career learning in a way that promotes continued learning through professional development programs?
- Does the professional development program build upon the induction program?

7

What our study is not

At this point in the book, we need to provide a few caveats about what this study is not. Except in New Zealand, the research is not of induction for entire *countries*, but rather of induction as it occurs at several sites *within* each country, although some components or elements of what is evident may be nationally specified (e.g. in France). Therefore, what appears here is not necessarily generalizable across the entire country in which the particular sites are located. While our resources did not permit a longitudinal study, we made a number of visits to each site over greater than a two-year period, thereby meeting with more than one year's cohort of beginning teachers. Lastly, our research was not an evaluation study in any sense.

In addition, although the research involved sites within several countries, it was not an international comparative study in the classic tradition of using a common template to investigate questions across countries, in order to compare them in uniform ways. Pursuing the complexity in our study goals precluded use of a single case-study design that would work for all the different systems; there was no uniform 'research protocol'. Likewise, there are no tables that force-fit characterization of each system according to various features of induction. We drafted such tables, but decided their value was outweighed by the hazard of oversimplifying comparisons among systems.

All this is not to say we failed to look beyond individual cases. We argue that by looking *across* cases, it is possible to recognize themes or underlying continua where previously there was only particularity. By doing so, we were also able to be surprised by contrasts that encouraged us to think in new ways or to ask different questions of our data. The result of this cross-case examination can be found in the concluding chapter of this book.

2. Case-Study Methods

We employed case-study methods because we wanted to understand teacher induction in its complexity, within the critical frames of its educational and cultural contexts. Each of Chapters 2–5 has been organized to highlight what we see as some of the unique features of the system and the program. While organizing questions infuse our work – for example, about the 'curriculum of induction' and the policy system which requires it to be 'taught' – the actual writing of the chapters was done in ways that we hope give some integrity to the case as a case, rather than as simply a collection of isolated (and comparable) 'variables' of induction. The cases go considerably beyond a study of induction policy at an administrative level. As we detail more specifically below, our study additionally looked at programs and practices, exploring them through observations, interviews and a detailed examination of in-country documents.

In the first sub-section below, we discuss our experiences, expertise and viewpoints about international research, a requisite discussion for considering what particularities we bring to this book and the research upon which it is based. The next sub-section explains how our exploratory inquiries about induction in many countries led to the selection of places where we conducted in-depth case studies. The closing sub-section outlines the types and substantial amounts of data upon which Chapters 2–5 are based.

Researchers' stance

Comparative education has a long and not entirely illustrious history of looking beyond one's national borders at educational practices and institutions 'abroad'. As researchers, we were mindful from the start of the dangers of armchair travel, of the potential to create 'others' of those we studied, others about whom simple generalizations could be made. We were also alert to the seductive appeal of simple borrowing of practices, programs and even policies. Equally, we do not wish to pretend we were 'insiders', with both the strengths and weaknesses that can bring. [2]

Each case study has many facets and is too complex to be told in a straightforward, linear fashion. We were aided in this by our being a group of scholars from different fields. The four main authors of this book all work in anglophone North American research settings, in one or more of these fields: mathematics education, science education, teacher education, comparative education. Mathematics educators studied beginning mathematics teachers and science educators studied beginning science teachers. In each country, we made sure that at least two researchers from the team were involved in data collection on at least one of the visits, to create the possibility for plural interpretation within the study team.

All of the book's authors have experience conducting international research, as well as previous experience observing teaching and conducting interviews with pupils, teachers and teacher educators. In the non-English language settings of our study – France, Shanghai and Switzerland – case studies were led by researchers with prior experience of that country's educational system; case leaders were also fluent speakers and readers of the relevant languages. The lead authors for France and Switzerland have European backgrounds and the lead author of the Shanghai study, although U.S. born, has spent more than twenty years studying aspects of education in mainland China and Taiwan, which resulted in a lessening of cultural distance. When other team researchers were present on site visits, translators were employed or, on occasion, interviews took place in English.

Insiders played a vital role as they helped us consider site selection during our first exploratory visits, acting as key informants and revealing and offering their practices, experience and insight. Colleagues from each country appreciably informed and oriented our work, the initial design of the study and the fieldwork itself – but data analysis and writing were our own responsibility. As drafts of cases emerged, however, we did solicit feedback from insiders within each country. Advisors from the U.S. scholarly and policy community also shared their comments with us. We have tried to ensure that some of the range of differing perspectives is directly visible to the reader. Ultimately, however, this is our work which provides our perspectives on induction within these settings. While benefiting from good access to insiders and having some helpful prior knowledge of the countries involved, we are nevertheless outsiders to each case and, as such, bring both the freshness and the experiential and intellectual myopia of outsiders faced with new and unfamiliar situations.

Selection of countries, foci and locales

We chose four countries for an in-depth study of teacher induction based on exploratory inquiries about induction in a dozen countries. One impetus for our study was the concern that TIMSS (the Third International Mathematics and Science Study), although it incorporated a new curriculum analysis to complement the traditional test of pupils' knowledge and videotaped teachers in three countries, still had collected only limited information about the preparation, characteristics and practices of mathematics and science teachers. Thus, an overarching context of this study of teacher induction was addressing gaps in international understanding about teachers. We had selected a dozen countries for initial exploratory work, chosen because they had average or better TIMSS performances, and/or our TIMSS colleagues, international literature or prior direct knowledge suggested that interesting teacher induction systems might already be established in these places.

A particularly important source of information was two companion studies carried out in the mid-1990s, wherein Moskowitz and Stephens led self-studies of teacher induction systems by member countries of the Asia-Pacific Economic Co-operation (APEC) grouping and Darling-Hammond and Cobb led similar studies of teacher preparation (Moskowitz and Stephens, 1997; Darling-Hammond and Cobb, 1995). Our preliminary work entailed a series of structured telephone interviews with in-country experts on mathematics and science teaching or educational policy and teacher development, many of whom were TIMSS colleagues or referrals by them. After transcribing these first interviews, we asked interviewees to check their accuracy and then conducted follow-up interviews.

By means of analysis of these exploratory data and with guidance from our Advisory Board, we selected a *set* of countries for further study that had these main characteristics: a range of interesting and substantial induction practices; sufficiently established programs and policies to have a robust existence; some diversity with respect to geography and type of educational system – all of which would help make the study results relevant to a wide international audience.

These criteria ensured that the teacher induction program in each selected country has been developed for ten or more years: induction policies, programs and activities vary greatly among the set of countries; the set includes both centralized and decentralized educational systems, and both small and large countries; the countries are located in Asia, Europe and the South Pacific. Among the countries not selected, some induction efforts were minor rather than substantial, while certain other countries were using interesting approaches to induction, but those programs were early in their development. For example, because the Taiwanese government had just required teacher preparation institutions to maintain a supporting relationship with their graduates during their first years of teaching, higher education institutions were only beginning to develop on-line vehicles for doing this (Hsiung and Tan, 1998).

A chapter about Japan is included in this volume on a different basis. Prior research had already documented that Japan has substantial teacher induction programs (Nohara, 1997). Further, Michael Padilla, Joseph Riley and other faculty at the University of Georgia were already seeking to develop a deeper understanding of science teacher preparation there and, to a lesser extent, science teacher induction (Padilla *et al.*, 1999). After establishing a general collaboration with us, these researchers heightened their attention to teacher induction and their work is included as Chapter 6. Because limited resources precluded both an in-depth study in Japan and an on-going, specific collaboration between the projects, the Japan research could not include all of the aspects we discussed in our four case studies presented in Chapters 2–5.

We focused the study in each country on either mathematics or science teachers, because resources limited us to studying primarily one or the other per country. We examined:

- mathematics teacher induction in France and Shanghai;
- science teacher induction in New Zealand and Switzerland.

Although the cases emphasize understanding the subject-specific induction of beginning lower secondary teachers, the cases also generate strong, parallel understandings about induction of teachers in other school subjects.

11

This volume describes teacher induction at specific sites or locales *within* each of the four countries chosen and does not attempt to characterize the universe of teacher induction for the entire country, with the partial exception of New Zealand. Because the fieldwork there involved fifteen schools in two of this small country's three largest metropolitan areas, where a majority of the nation's population resides, this case study comes closer to representing teacher induction for the whole country. In contrast, for example, research in Switzerland focused on three of its twenty-six cantons, places where induction programs were long-standing and substantial. Each case chapter elaborates on how specific sites were chosen within the relevant country.

Fieldwork

Before briefly describing our fieldwork methods, we note the role that prior literature played in the study and how it is used in this book. As mentioned above, existing research about teacher induction in different countries influenced our exploratory research and case selection, particularly the earlier work led by one of our project advisors, Jay Moskowitz. Any literature specific to a country is drawn upon in the appropriate chapter.

Further, we used more general but seminal literature about teacher induction to diversify our notions of induction, develop research questions and draw out specific issues we might encounter. For example, the body of work by another of our study advisors, Sharon Feiman-Nemser, especially influenced all aspects of our study, particularly the three in-depth case studies of teacher induction in the U.S. that she and colleagues were conducting during the same time period as our international research (Feiman-Nemser, 2001). Because presenting extensive case studies already pushed us to the space limits of a single book, however, we do not engage here in extensive discussion of the general literature on teacher induction.

Each in-country study included the following types of data collection, which are further described within the methodological appendix:

- in-country interviews – employing different semi-structured protocols for interviewing informants: for example, beginning teachers, mentor teachers, school administrators, teacher education faculty, induction program directors and seminar or course providers, and educational policy leaders;
- document analysis – obtaining, translating when necessary and analyzing key documents from each country, such as policy documents, published resources for beginning teachers, school syllabi for science and mathematics curricula in the middle grades, syllabi for induction courses;

- observations of 'induction' events – for example, attending post-lesson conversations between new teacher and mentor, facilitated meetings for beginning teachers, public demonstration lessons, training sessions for mentor teachers;
- observations of instruction – observing mathematics or science lessons taught by beginning and more experienced teachers;
- observations of teacher preparation – observing classes at institutions of higher education;
- observations of the informal life of schools.

In addition, some sites afforded the following:

- surveys of teachers' views and experiences;
- attendance at policy meetings.

Researchers made at least three field visits per case, for at least ten days per visit and more often for two or three weeks at a time. While certainly not exhaustive, this extensive data collection permitted in-depth analyses. Additionally, the protracted period of time over which our visits took place allowed for extensive iterative analysis of the data, with subsequent visits both informed and influenced by the outcome of our detailed examination of the results of earlier ones.

In each of our case studies, two or more researchers collected data during at least one of the field visits, collectively involving two to three person-months of fieldwork. As a result, a second team member had some direct experience with each location, which enriched both within-case and cross-case analysis.

In most countries that we initially considered or subsequently selected for study, the whole continuum of a teacher's career (initial preparation, the phase we are calling 'induction' and continuing professional development thereafter) was undergoing some review and reform. As a brief example, during the initial exploration of potential countries for our case studies, colleagues in the U.K. reported that while almost no formal teacher induction programs existed then, a national specification of an induction program was about to be enacted. Three years later, as we complete our work, a national law requires schools to provide beginning teachers with a mentor and a 90 percent teaching load.

Hence, it is important to understand that the information reported in Chapters 2–6 is but a snapshot of a changing reality. Almost all the fieldwork was completed by spring 2001. These analyses, therefore, do not take into account any subsequent developments.

3. Book Conventions and Organization

This book presents case studies of comprehensive induction in several locales within four countries around the world (Chapters 2–5), including description and analysis of the induction systems. Chapter 6 reports on a smaller-scale study of science teacher induction in Japan. Chapter 7 discusses key themes about comprehensive induction systems that are drawn from analyses across the set of cases. Although reading any case by itself or several cases in any order will be informative, reading the cases in the order presented should both enhance understanding of the themes in Chapter 7 and prompt additional insights about both contrasts and similarities among countries' induction systems.

Before providing a rationale for the sequencing of Chapters 2–5, we describe here our usage of a few non-English terms that are crucial to understanding induction in a particular country and our handling of some key English-language terms such as 'induction' or 'beginning teacher'. The general usage of such terms in conversation or writing at this point in time is quite vague, with multiple, conflicting meanings ascribed to them. This book may help fuel a need to develop a more extensive, precise vocabulary of terms in the field of teacher induction.

Definitions and usage

Especially in a setting involving a foreign language, translating foreign terms into familiar English ones can, at times, mask important differences. These can be variations of both tenor and categorization, making one perceive a phenomenon as the same, without exploring to what extent the underlying notions and their accompanying framing are indeed similar or different. As Raymond Bourdoncle (1994) observed about a meeting between members of the French Science of Education Research Association and their German counterparts:

> We immediately had a problem: we did not mean exactly the same thing when we said 'Bildung' in German and 'formation' in French. And 'training', the English equivalent, is again subtly different. As we build the world with our words, we are not living in an exactly similar world, even if we are in the same European Community. (p. 12)

In consequence, we have deliberately left a few key terms and notions in the original language, illustrated by the examples below, in order to signal their particular difficulty in being rendered into English.

> *banzhuren* (from Shanghai), often broadly translated as 'class director' or 'homeroom teacher';

Standortbestimmung (from Switzerland), loosely translated as "determining where I stand" or "determination of status";

formation (from France), referring to "the process of shaping a member of a profession", but it is also the main term used to describe the work done to produce a teacher, a notion that neither 'education' nor 'training' captures, the two common but frequently misleading translations used in English translations.

The *Glossary* at the end of this book details elements of the meaning and connotation of these and other terms we have kept in the original.

However, we have nevertheless tried to limit the use of foreign language terms in this book. In doing so, we had to make some hard choices, because there are subtle and sometimes quite significant shades of meaning attached to terms or expressions referring to similar things. Although adopting specific conventions may seem to be a technical problem, behind each term there is a richness of relationships, goals and practices that make the choice of equivalent terms difficult. Hence, at times, we have chosen to use one term to refer to a range of expressions used in the various countries for similar goals and practices; at other times, we use alternative terms as they refer to distinctive activities or roles.

The following English terms are found frequently in this book. We have tried to maintain consistent usage of them among the chapters.

Beginning teacher, novice

These terms are used quite flexibly and interchangeably throughout the book to refer to teachers who participate in a given country's induction activities. In some instances, an eligible teacher may have had several years' teaching experience as a substitute teacher, teaching at another level or teaching in another state or even country. Nevertheless, these teachers are also referred to as beginning or novice teachers, along with a teacher completely new to teaching. Within some case discussions, however, we use the local term: 'new teacher' for Shanghai (the literal translation from Chinese) or *stagiaire* for France (which marks the status of the individual as one who is undertaking a professional practicum – known as a *stage* – prior to confirmation as a permanent member of the profession).

Country reference

Although only selected sites within a country were studied, for convenience we often refer to the case or country as a whole (though it is always 'Shanghai' rather than 'China'). For example, the Swiss case study is largely based on three German-speaking cantons. Yet, in the general discussions in this chapter and in Chapter 7 about similarities and contrasts among countries, we refer to 'Switzerland' or 'the Swiss case' unless a specific canton is noted.

Induction

We use this word expansively to refer to widely varying processes, policies and goals in the contexts of the different sites. In Switzerland, for example, the German term is *Berufseinführung*, literally "a leading into the profession", and entails development as a person as well as a professional. In New Zealand, induction is referred to as 'Advice and Guidance' or AG, the name of the national government's induction program.

Induction providers

This term refers to institutions or individuals who finance, plan or carry out induction activities. For example, the department heads and administrators of individual schools in New Zealand provide the induction program. For France, we use 'induction provider' to refer to special institutions (known as the IUFMs) and individuals associated with them (known as *formateurs*) created some ten years ago expressly for working with prospective and novice teachers. For Switzerland, the term refers to any of the cantonal governments, the pre-service institutions, the free-standing centers for continuing teacher education and the schools, all of which may provide induction services.

Induction systems

We use this term because the countries' induction policies, programs and practices are so substantial, complex, co-ordinated and robust that we construe them to comprise 'systems'. Induction providers in the relevant countries do not always use the term 'system' for their induction programs, nor even necessarily perceive them to constitute a system.

Middle grades

The level of schooling we mainly studied within each country comprised the 'middle grades': that is, when elementary school is completed and when classes begin to be taught by specialist mathematics and science teachers, whether or not there is a separate type of school dedicated to this age range.

In Shanghai, middle grades refers to the *chuzhong* (lower secondary school) which houses grades 6–9. In Switzerland, the middle grades are found in the lower secondary school (predominantly, in the *Mittelschule*), which covers grades 7–9. In New Zealand, we use the term 'middle grades' to refer to grades 8 and 9, the 'junior secondary' years in the secondary school that covers all grades 8–12. Finally, in France, as in Shanghai, 'middle grades' refers to the *collège* (grades 6–9), a separate lower secondary school.

Student/pupil

In order to avoid potential confusion between prospective teachers as students and the *school* students whom the novice teachers are teaching, the word 'student' is used throughout the text solely to refer to prospective teachers during their pre-service education. The word 'pupil' is used to refer to children and youths in schools.

We

In the Preface and Chapters 1 and 7, 'we' refers to the main book authors Britton, Paine, Pimm and Raizen. Within the individual country chapters (2–6), 'we' refers to the named authors listed at the beginning of each chapter.

Case studies and their sequencing

Each case chapter starts with one or more vignettes that bring to life a beginning teacher's induction activities over the course of a day, a week or even a year. These vignettes introduce some of what induction takes place but also foreshadow issues about induction that are discussed later in the chapter. The rest of each chapter covers these main aspects of teacher induction, although the way and order of discussing them vary:

- an overview of the education system within which induction operates, including an account of typical mathematics or science teacher preparation;
- a description of the intended mathematics or science curriculum and teaching;
- the policies, programs and practices of teacher induction;
- factors enabling or constraining teacher induction.

In Chapters 2–5, we sequenced the cases to maximize juxtapositions of particular system features that called into question our initial beliefs and conjectures about induction and that forced us to re-conceptualize our views. So that each case can be understood alone, however, we almost never make any reference within a case to any other country.

Shanghai's approach to induction (Chapter 2) reflects a robust system articulated across three policy/administrative levels. This is a complex yet coherent system, one deeply grounded in the philosophical roots of schooling and the broader society. In examining how beginning mathematics teachers enter the profession in Shanghai, one is struck by the powerful pull of culture.

Switzerland also represents a full system (Chapter 3), but one that rests on and embodies very different philosophical underpinnings from those of Shanghai. In addition, given the traditions of direct democracy and the decentralized nature of policy found there, Swiss induction varies considerably by canton, with the approach in each of the three cantons studied involving a highly complex system of programs and practices. Contrasting with the Shanghai chapter's focus on mathematics teaching, this case provides a window on the development of beginning lower secondary science teachers, including a particular view of science in the middle grades.

Both New Zealand and Switzerland are small countries, yet have quite different approaches to supporting the growth of new teachers. In the New Zealand case (Chapter 4) on science teacher induction, we see a national mandate that is implemented in every school through a highly decentralized school system that has no intermediate administrative levels. Induction programs began over 25 years ago and continue to evolve and grow in scope and funding.

France (Chapter 5) poses yet another contrast. Here we find another centralized system, yet in this case an intermediate institution (the IUFM within the regional Academy) has been created for the *formation* of beginning teachers. Unlike New Zealand, where induction has a long history, the story of France's new 'induction' system is more recent, being only some ten years old. The traditional cultural power of mathematics in the school system and in the curriculum stands out, along with the diversity of tasks a first-year teacher is paid to carry out.

Chapter 6 reports on part of a study carried out by Michael Padilla and Joseph Riley through a separate grant. Their study of induction was more limited, but it allows us to examine induction there from the perspective of science teaching, connecting subject-matter teaching to teacher development in ways that other literature on Japan's induction system has not.

Since induction in Switzerland, Shanghai and France has not figured strongly in the current English-language literature on teacher development, the principal activities, actors and institutions that support beginning teachers' learning as well as the organization of them will likely represent approaches new to many readers. Teacher induction in New Zealand and Japan, however, has been a focus in some important international research on new teacher induction by APEC (Moskowitz and Kennedy, 1997; Nohara, 1997).

But in contrast to the APEC studies that involved 1–2 weeks of fieldwork, the results of the 8–12 weeks of independent fieldwork discussed in this book provide new insights into and updates on both policies and programs, and, especially, a more detailed look at how induction practices actually play out for teachers in schools.

4. Some Opening Thoughts

We foreshadow here some themes that are explored within and across the following chapters, first by returning to the four aspects of induction raised at the beginning of this introduction. Teacher induction, as observed in these different countries, comprises a process for learning, a period of time, a unique phase in teaching and a system: the cross-case analysis and discussion in Chapter 7 elaborates on these elements of our work. However, although the nature of international work forced us to remain at a descriptive level initially, precisely because of its relative unfamiliarity, our subsequent iterative analysis led us to ask new and more fundamental questions.

The concluding chapter is, therefore, organised around the following 'revised' reframing questions: why, rather than what, is induction? Whom does induction serve, i.e. who is considered to be a beginning teacher? What is the 'curriculum of induction', i.e. what do the systems aim for beginning teachers to learn and what processes and activities are undertaken to support that learning? Who provides the knowledge to cover such comprehensive induction curricula, whose knowledge is it and where does that knowledge reside?

As a final orienting thought, we caution that whenever people look at an educational system different from their own, they often have one of two polarized responses. The first is to see only the *unfamiliar*, the different or the strange, and therefore reject the unknown as irrelevant to 'our' setting. With respect to France, a reader might say, "Our teachers are not civil servants and never will be" or "We believe in teachers' individual freedom to go where they choose. What do we have to learn from a system that assigns teachers to their first job?" Or, in response to the case of New Zealand, "We will never get 20 percent release time for our teachers, so we can just ignore what they do there".

The second pole is to see only the points of *similarity*. This response brings with it the comfort of recognition, but it can drain the genuinely new of its novelty. For example, someone might say, "They use mentors and we already use mentors, so there's nothing to learn from this case", even though the differences in what induction programs mean by the term 'mentor' can far exceed the similarities.

Bearing these pitfalls in mind, we believe that looking beyond the familiar allows us to come to explore induction in new ways. Ultimately, this process should also help us to see our own practices from a fresh perspective, while at the same time raising questions about how induction might be otherwise.

Chapter 2

Entering a Culture of Teaching: Teacher Induction in Shanghai

Lynn Paine, Yanping Fang and Suzanne Wilson [1]

1. Starting Up: Induction through the Eyes of Teacher Li Mei

Li Mei is an energetic, cheerful woman who feels that teaching "is the hardest job under the sun, but the happiest". [2] In her second year of teaching lower secondary mathematics, she teaches thirteen periods a week (the average load for most lower secondary teachers in Shanghai): six each to two different sixth-grade classes and one to an elective 'activity class' *(huodong ke)* that is geared at strengthening and deepening pupils' interest in mathematics and helping them develop 'divergent' ways of thinking that stretch beyond the textbook. Her load is like that of most teachers in her school.

In addition to her instructional work in mathematics, Teacher Li [3] devotes much energy to her work as a *banzhuren* ('class director'). In that role, she manages the study and extra-curricular lives of the forty-eight pupils in one of the sixth-grade classes she teaches for mathematics: her duties in this role are to help nurture what she terms the 'all-round development' of each pupil and the class as a collective. Formally, she monitors morning exercises, mid-morning eye exercises, lunch hours and study halls, as well as organizing weekly class meetings. Informally, she attends to the personal and academic needs of her charges.

Teacher Li's days start early, as she comes to school by 7:00, a half-hour before her pupils arrive for their morning review work. If she is not teaching a class, she spends most of the day in her office, which she shares with a number of other teachers, correcting pupil assignments and meeting with individual pupils. As a *banzhuren*, she also spends time following up on issues related to individuals in her class, consulting with the pupils' teachers of other subjects, helping pupils organize activities and monitoring the maintainance of their classroom, and doing of their work.

E. Britton et al. (eds.), Comprehensive Teacher Induction, 20–82.
© 2003 *Kluwer Academic Publishers. Printed in the Netherlands.*

At 12:45, there are physical exercises; afterwards, there is a break – pupils and teachers can rest and take a nap (something commonly undertaken as a brief after-lunch activity in offices and schools around the country). During this rest period, as a *banzhuren* Teacher Li may be found in her class's room, although in her effort to help develop leadership skills and self-management in the pupils she sometimes relies on the pupil leaders to supervise free time, opting to stay in her office, rather than the classroom.

In the office, she blends mathematics teaching work and dealing with her concerns for pupils' personal, social and academic problems, as pupils pop into the office with "small issues" – questions, concerns or triumphs to share.

> I never plan my lessons in the office; I plan on Saturday and Sunday at home. In the office, I have to deal with pupils' problems. They come to my office and report all kinds of things that require me to deal with them immediately.

Teacher Li does not leave school until 6:00. In fact, she never really leaves school, since she lives in an apartment on campus. But she prefers to leave her weekday nights free of schoolwork. Watching TV and doing other things give her a chance to "re-energize" for the next day. Apart from lesson preparation, she does no other schoolwork on Saturdays and Sundays.

Teacher Li's busy days blending mathematics-focused and *banzhuren* work have their parallels in her weekly routines. On Mondays, during the school day, she takes part in weekly meetings of all the *banzhuren*. The group discusses the past week's activities of the various grades and the school as a whole, announces activities and assigns work for the coming week. Tuesdays include weekly meetings of both the 'lesson preparation group' (*beikezu*) and the 'teaching research group' (*jiaoyanzu*). Both of these groups involve other mathematics teachers in the school.

The lesson preparation group meeting starts at 1:30 and varies in length, depending on what the group needs to accomplish; all three of the sixth-grade mathematics teachers (and occasionally a fourth, who is a part-time instructor) attend. This year, Ms. Li chairs the lesson preparation group. Their meetings provide a time to discuss "where we've reached in our teaching so far, plan lessons together, share our teaching experiences and how pupils have learned, discuss how to assess pupils and analyze exam results". Teacher Li finds this group especially important for it gives her, as a beginning teacher, a chance to ask older teachers how to teach.

Her teaching research group involves all the mathematics teachers in the school, regardless of the grade level they teach. She sees those meetings as occasions to focus on "bigger issues of teaching" – like new reforms in instruction or assessment. These meetings also offer Teacher Li the opportunity to attend activities outside of her school, for she sometimes observes teachers' classes at other schools or attends district professional development events.

For Teacher Li, a graduate of a teacher education program at one of the local universities (Shanghai Teachers' University), teaching requires a combination of knowledge and skill for which pre-service education provided valuable preparation, but which ultimately has to be learned on the job. As a mathematics department graduate, she feels she had a solid preparation in the content she teaches, but views this university-acquired knowledge as largely theoretical.

Entering teaching, moving from "my student role to a teacher role", involved some areas that were "unfamiliar". She needed help, for example, in learning how to "teach a class" and "prepare a lesson". Her student teaching practicum gave her some opportunity to learn about these teacher tasks, but once she began work as a full-time teacher, she realized that she also needed to understand pupils and to develop skill in managing and communicating with them.

While she had studied psychology as part of her university preparation, she now feels a grounded understanding of pupils is not something one can learn well "in a short time", even though it is a "crucial part of teaching". Despite her brief foray into teaching as part of her practicum, it was not until she had her own classes that she "really understood" much of what was being talked about in her undergraduate courses: for example, her role as a schoolteacher in helping pupils both acquire knowledge and become better educated people.

> The university laid an important foundation for our subject-matter knowledge, but to be a good teacher, you need to learn on the job. The knowledge learned in university is relatively theoretical. I can say that I mastered my student-teaching life in school well, but really being together with pupils and facing pupils can only be learned when doing my own real work.

> Now all my energy is on pupils. I was a student before, but now – as the teacher – my energy is on pupils. Now I am a teacher facing my pupils. I did student teaching practice before. It was a short period of training [one month], during which I learned how I was to write a lesson plan, teach a lesson, but learned nothing at that time about how to manage pupils. When we went to a secondary school to do student teaching, we taught classes but never connected with the pupils and did not know about their happiness, anger, sorrow and joy. Only after I formally entered my teaching position did I start to know about pupils and I can say that I spend most of my days with my pupils.

As a beginner, Teacher Li wanted support in learning how to "connect" to pupils, how to "attract" them to the lesson, focusing their energies on learning (and thereby averting discipline problems) and encouraging active participation. These became important subjects of her first year of learning on the job.

In that initial year of teaching, Teacher Li felt surrounded by help of many kinds, provided by many people. She had an assigned mentor in the school, another lower secondary mathematics teacher, who came with more than thirty years of teaching experience. They worked together in the same lesson preparation group, regularly planning lessons jointly and discussing teaching and pupils' learning in great detail. But they also met alone as a pair.

After she taught each class, Teacher Li would bring her lesson plan to her mentor, telling her about what had (and had not) worked. Each week, they also found time to analyze the week's successes and identify places that needed work, asking about and exploring, in the words of her mentor, "all the areas in the past week that hadn't succeeded; where were there failures, and why were they failures, and where were there successes".

In addition to her mathematics teaching mentor, Teacher Li also had a mentor supporting her in learning about what being a *banzhuren* entails. During her first year of teaching, Teacher Li worked as an assistant to a teacher who was a *banzhuren* for that year and was mentored by her. By the time of our observation, in her second year, Teacher Li had taken on full responsibility for that work.

In her first year, she had also found others in the school who offered guidance – the principal (also a mathematics teacher), the head of the teaching research group and other teachers. Outside the school, she also took part in district-organized induction programs, as all first-year teachers are required to do. She found talks there given by "expert teachers" to be useful; they gave her ideas she could "apply" and offered encouragement and inspiration. Finally, she continues to spend time in this her second year observing others' teaching. She studies how teachers teach a lesson, how they motivate pupils to learn and how to attract their attention. Li believes that each teacher has a unique style and she is working on developing her own.

As we have already noted, Li Mei's teaching is marked by a keen interest in maximizing pupil participation. In one lesson we observed, for example, she encouraged pupils to wave their hands vigorously and even call out "me, me" as they completed tasks, so they could be called on, go up to the board or have their work checked. Her lesson on multiplying fractions ended with a lively game, with pairs of pupils running to the board to pull 'fruit' (containing solutions to multiplication problems) off a cardboard tree.

Part of this lesson design reflects her view of her learners. She is mindful of the fact that her pupils are active eleven- and twelve-year-olds. Lower secondary school is, in her mind, a "special time" and her pupils have particular developmental characteristics and needs. Part of her commitment to active learning also reflects the focus of mathematics reform in Shanghai, with significant discussion about the need to connect mathematics to pupils' lives and to increase their participation in class through the choice and design of tasks. These tasks are often focused on what are considered the crucial aspects of a particular topic and, as Li plans a lesson, she is careful to start by looking at the municipal teaching materials and reference guides, to focus on what are commonly seen as the lesson's 'important' and its 'difficult' points (notions we return to later in this chapter).

Teacher Li spends much time preparing on her own, before sharing that lesson plan with others – her official mentor as well as others who unofficially mentor her – and revising it before she teaches it. And she has many opportunities to get feedback on her actual teaching, thanks to frequent observation by her mentor, by others in the school and as part of participation in what are called 'open' lessons [4], as well as teaching competitions organized by the school and the district. All these events create occasions for talk about her teaching. Observation of new teachers by school and district personnel is a key part of the evaluation process that ultimately allowed Teacher Li, and other novice teachers like her, to move from the provisional status they occupied during their first year to the permanent status they are awarded at the end of this first, induction year of teaching.

2. Exploring Shanghai as a System for Teacher Induction

Teacher Li teaches in an ordinary secondary school in Shanghai. She is a second-year teacher in a municipal system that recognizes 'young' teachers, those in their first five years of teaching following permanent certification, as distinct from more experienced teachers. Shanghai's personnel policies for teachers, as well as its teacher development policies, recognize three basic categories of teacher: 'young', 'middle-aged' or 'middle' and 'old' or 'senior' teachers.

A fourth category – 'backbone' (*gugan*) teachers, who carry particular leadership roles in school – is not age-defined. (In fact, many young teachers are 'backbone' teachers.) There are different assumptions made about the work and development needs of these different categories of teachers. 'New' teachers – teachers in their first year of teaching – are yet another category still, and are not combined with 'young' teachers in personnel reports, because they are still provisional teachers who have not yet been converted to permanent status. [5] ('New' teacher is the term we will use most often in our discussion of induction practices in Shanghai.) At the time of our observation, in the early fall of her second year, Teacher Li had just completed her year of 'new teacher training' (*xin laoshi peixun*) or, less commonly called, 'education for entering the profession' (*ruzhijiaoyu*) – what we here refer to as *induction*. [6]

In participating in this 'training' program over the previous school year, she was like all first-year teachers in Shanghai. Her living at the school, preferring to plan only on weekends, particular sources of support, the experience and approach of her mentor, and even her own teaching style, among other things, are not, however, necessarily found in the reports of all the new teachers we interviewed. But her day, her training before coming to teaching, her assessment of what she needs to learn and how she can best learn these things all reflect the general pattern we found among the new teachers we interviewed in four districts in Shanghai. Like Teacher Li, these novices enter teaching through a system of induction and a broader system of education that reinforces certain kinds of learning and creates particular learning opportunities.

Why begin with such a lengthy vignette about a beginning teacher, rather than a description of the induction system or programs themselves? In the case of Shanghai, we find that the story of induction is, in fact, a story that can be told in multiple ways. One can tell it as a narrative of policy aimed at beginning teachers and its implementation in particular programs and activities. But one can also describe it as a collection of experiences as lived by a newcomer to teaching – experiences that, as in the case of Teacher Li, are significantly shaped not only by formal induction policies and specific activities targeted for novices, but also by a broader set of supports and a system-wide orientation to professional development.

In the account that follows, we juxtapose these two induction narratives – a description of a particular induction system, together with its parts and programs, and stories of new teachers and their opportunities to learn. Such learning is an intricate challenge, reflecting a complex system, structure and teaching culture. Here, we provide an examination of four major features of the induction experience – the policies, programs and practices – of Shanghai:

- induction as varied practices concentrated around a central core of goals;
- induction as focused on curriculum;
- induction as immersion in a culture of public scrutiny and talk about teaching;
- induction as a process involving multiple stakeholders and allowing for variation amidst coherence.

In order to understand these four themes, we first offer an introductory description of the educational system, the induction policy itself, its articulation with pre-service education and the links to the culture of schools.

An overview of the system

Teacher Li is a single teacher learning to teach in an enormous city (Shanghai), which itself represents a sizable educational system. With about fourteen million residents, Shanghai has the administrative authority of a province within China's national system and is organized into administrative sub-units, called *districts*. At the time of our study, Shanghai had twenty districts, which between them comprised urban, suburban and rural areas. In 1997, the city had a large population of pupils (over 1.87 million in the K–12 system) and teachers (more than 105,000 working full-time): of these, 37,856 teachers worked at the lower-secondary level (Shanghai Jiaoyu Weiyuanhui Shizichu, 1998).

Shanghai's educational system is a multi-tiered one and each level is involved in induction. At the top of Shanghai's formal education bureaucracy sits the Shanghai Municipal Education Commission. It has several bureaus, three of which are particularly relevant here: the Teacher and Staff Training Section, the Teaching Research Section and the Office of Shanghai Curriculum and Teaching Material Reform Commission (see Figure 1).

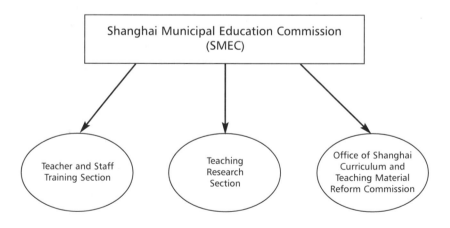

Figure 1: *Relevant sections of the central educational bureaucracy that affect new teacher induction*

The Teacher and Staff Training Section makes policies for K–12 teacher promotion and in-service professional development, of which 'new teacher training' is a component. The Teaching Research Section designs foci for district and school research projects and also grants and approves municipal research projects on 'basic' education (grades 1–9). The Curriculum and Teaching Material Reform Commission co-ordinates efforts to design curriculum, textbooks, teacher reference materials and pupil workbooks; it also pilots curriculum reform experiments and engages in research related to implementing curriculum reform.

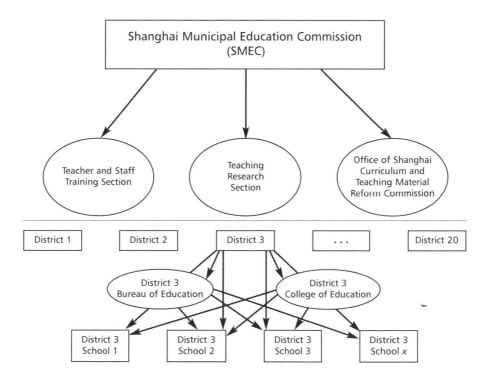

Figure 2: Administrative levels within the Shanghai educational system

As Figure 2 suggests, the second tier of the system consists of the districts and, for our story, there are two large institutions within each district that are of interest due to their impact on the lives and learning of new teachers. One is the Bureau of Education, the administrative office subordinate to the Municipal Education Commission, which handles teacher personnel issues. The other educational institution at the district level is the particular College of Education, a multi-faceted institution which, among other things, has primary responsibility for teacher professional development. The Bureau is, thus, the administrative arm and the College is the education and training arm, of the educational work of the district. Teacher Li's chances to observe teaching in other schools, as well as her much-appreciated opportunities to hear 'experts' lecture on education issues, are arranged by her district's College of Education.

As we examined policies in place at the municipal level and the information collected across the city by the municipal authorities, we also interviewed and observed teachers and professional development programs from throughout the city. However, in order to obtain a more systematic understanding, we concentrated our data collection in four districts that represent a range in economic level, educational achievement and teacher demographics. These districts are Pudong, Songjiang, Xuhui and Zhabei. (We address some of the variation we observed across districts in section 6.) In each district, we interviewed people at both the Bureau of Education and the College of Education, as well as at a range of schools, and in particular observed and interviewed young and new teachers and their mentors.

The third tier of the educational system is the school itself. [7] Nine years of education is compulsory in China and Shanghai traditionally adopted a 6–3 system: six years of elementary school followed by three years of lower secondary. In the 1980s, however, as population growth led to more crowded elementary schools, the sixth grade was moved to lower secondary and is considered the 'preparation class' (*yubeiban*). Today's lower secondary schools enroll pupils from the 'preparation class' through to ninth grade, with pupils aged 11–15. (As an artifact of earlier patterns, grades 7–9 are still referred to as the *first* to *third* years of lower secondary school respectively.)

Lower secondary school is no longer selective, although that is a relatively recent phenomenon. Thus, while pupils entering this level of school no longer take admissions tests, schools continue to have their reputations of relative academic quality based in part on histories of having been more or less selective. Pupils have to take a high-stakes municipal examination for promotion to upper secondary school and results of this examination determine the kind of school (termed 'key' or 'ordinary', in terms of their academic excellence, as well as 'vocational' or 'comprehensive') a pupil will enter. Educators and the public both make distinctions among lower secondary schools as the result of schools' relative performance on these tests.

While these features of schooling reflect long-standing views of schools as sorting mechanisms, Shanghai's schools today are in the midst of significant educational reform – structural, curricular and instructional. There is considerable pressure to de-emphasize education as a sorting system and instead foster the system's capacity to support many kinds of development for all its pupils.

Lower secondary schools [8] tend to be physically separate from upper secondary schools, although a reform from an earlier era had pushed to build consolidated secondary schools and a few remain in terms of campuses housing both lower and upper schools. Recent curriculum reforms created a lower secondary course arrangement that provides pupils with a core set of required courses, some 'activity courses' (such as a mathematics 'interest group' or club) and, for eighth and ninth graders, an elective option intended to deepen individual interests and strengths.

Mathematics is a required class for all pupils each year; pupils also have opportunities to take mathematics activity classes. The mathematics curriculum is untracked; all pupils of the same grade level study the same content. Lower secondary pupils have an average of 26 periods a week of required subjects and an additional number of periods of activity classes (including study hall, school and class activities, interest groups, physical education and 'social practice' activities [9]). The daily schedule includes mornings with four classes of forty-five minutes each, with a ten-minute break between each class and a longer, twenty-minute break between the second and third period. After lunch, there are three classes, each separated by a ten-minute break.

From Teacher Li's vantage point, her school is the immediate locus of activity, community and professional development. The district exerts some visible influence on her activity as a new teacher, chiefly through the formal induction events and evaluation process in which she is required to participate. The Shanghai Municipal Education Commission does not figure directly in any of her conversations about her work and learning. However, its presence – for example, through the curriculum materials and teachers' guides it develops – is also a factor in the formal demands on her as a new teacher, including her own sense of what she needs to learn and the support she has for that learning.

Induction policy

Clearly, the municipal authorities, the district and the school are all important elements in Shanghai's induction story. Thus, whether or not it figures prominently in her own interpretation of her actions, Teacher Li's experiences as a new teacher are shaped, in part (like those of the other new teachers we learned about) by the system-wide cultural and organizational practices related to teaching in Shanghai. Her experiences are also very much a product of a formal induction policy that the Shanghai Municipal Education Commission created over a decade ago. This formal induction policy is an important component of the story of the municipal educational system in Shanghai.

Shanghai has a particularly strong approach to teacher induction, building new formal policy on top of long-standing school practices. For several years prior to a specific municipal policy being created, both secondary and elementary schools had formal induction programs. Plans often involved a contract or individualized program for the first-year teacher, comprising mentoring (with specified expectations and goals, some set by the school and others jointly agreed on by mentor and novice), an on-going novice teacher forum for research and study, and 'competitions' among new teachers (through demonstration teaching, for example).

In many places, where schools were able, beginning teachers had lightened loads. However, some school principals were opposed to this particular practice on principle, saying new teachers need to understand and be able to cope with the full range of responsibilities. Learning to do so was an important aspect of induction.

Around 1985, Shanghai's Municipal College of Education [10] began to offer courses to probationary teachers. These first-year teachers had some support in their schools (through mentors), but the College developed a course in an effort to be responsive to new teachers' needs. The content focused on helping the new teachers familiarize themselves with teaching materials and with each curriculum's 'important', 'difficult' and 'hinge' points (see section 4). These are seen as building blocks for teachers' understanding of what to focus on, why it is important, how it may affect the ways they teach and how pupils learn particular content. This College's faculty also worked to create opportunities for beginners to observe good teachers teach and attempted to develop specific work attitudes in the novices. In addition, faculty members visited schools to observe new teachers. The College only did this for a few years, then stopped about the time the Shanghai Municipal Education Commission established formal regulations for the support of new teachers.

Now a more formalized system for induction has been developed and instituted, specifying the period of induction: new teachers are given one year of probationary status during which – by Education Commission mandate – the district and particular school each provide support to the new teacher. Schools provide mentors; the district provides training. The three main areas [11] for novice teacher development specified by Education Commission policy (Shanghaishi Jiaoyu Weiyuanhui Shizichu, 1998, p. 75), are:

- *education and professional ethics* (chiefly understood as learning about relevant regulations, appropriate professional behavior and ethics);
- *education and teaching theory* (focused primarily on helping the new teacher learn to become a *banzhuren* and "developing class activities

responsive to the pupils' psychological development and successfully carrying out class director responsibilities");
- *education and teaching practical skills* ("mastering the curriculum guidelines and content to develop an instructional plan that meets pupils' actual situations").

The policy identifies rough allocations of time for the first two categories: a minimum of thirty hours/periods (over a year) for each of the first and second categories, although the specification for how to use the required hours is vague. Similarly, the policy specifies that a mentor must work with a novice teacher for at least a year and the 'guidance and training' by the mentor should involve at least two hours each week. But, here too, decisions about how to use that time are unspecified.

Zhang Yuhua, head of the Teacher and Staff Training Section of the Shanghai Municipal Education Committee, explained that induction is understood within the larger continuum of teacher development. (Clearer and more systematic structures were simultaneously developed for the professional development of practicing teachers.) For new teachers, their preparation draws on and is designed to take into account pre-service education, induction-specific programs and career opportunities available to all teachers and to those teacher leaders seen as 'backbone' teachers.

Induction practices vary depending on the learner, as schools and districts provide support to all novices, but tailor or supplement it for teachers who come without formal pre-service training and for teachers who early on show signs of being outstanding. Teacher Li, as a graduate of a teacher education program, experienced an induction situation that reflects the most common arrangement. There are two required avenues in which novices must participate to support their learning.

First, each new teacher is required to work with a mentor. Policy requires that the mentor and novice have a handbook (which is unique to each district); there are standards for their work together; they keep a record of their activity and of the novice's growth. Mentor/novice pairs are required to engage in weekly observations of one or two classes throughout the year. (Observations might include the pair observing a third teacher, the novice observing the mentor or the mentor observing the novice.) Summary and reflection are also required components of their work together.

Mentors are chosen by the school and are teachers in the school. They tend to be teachers who are regarded as strong, with the ability to articulate their reflections on practice and connect their teaching to principles. Mentor compensation is quite limited in material terms – typically only 50 *yuan* (at the time of our study, less than US $7), although schools with resources can augment that. But interviewees reported that mentors found the recognition an honor and the task rewarding. In addition, promotion policies for senior teachers (to be discussed in section 6) now make mentoring, when done well, advantageous to a teacher's application for senior status. [12]

Second, training units in the city provide programs for new teachers and novices are required to spend significant time in their first year – typically a half-day most weeks for much of the year – participating in these programs. The units identify common needs through interviews and counseling and, on that basis, organize special lectures and workshops for beginning teachers. These tend to be very applied in orientation. The most common unit offering induction training appears to be district-level Colleges of Education. But the Education Commission recently authorized an additional arrangement – school-based training – in which a school gets approval to offer induction training to teachers from outside their school. [13]

Special arrangements are made for new teachers who arrive without prior formal teacher preparation (those from non-teacher education institutions). Various approved training centers in the city offer four courses which must be taken: pedagogy, psychology, subject-area methods and being a class director. Subject-area methods courses alone meet for a minimum of forty periods.

Education Commission policy clearly stipulates which levels of the system are responsible for assessment of which aspects of the probationer's knowledge and performance: ideological education and ethics are to be assessed at the school level by relevant administrators and teachers, while subject-matter pedagogy and the principles of being a *banzhuren* are to be assessed by the district in a manner it determines. General pedagogy and general psychology are assessed via a written municipal test. Finally, teaching skills and practice are to be assessed and standards determined by the district.

The policy also specifies under which conditions a probationer can have their probationary period extended, which circumstances are grounds for outright failure (if they have failed the professional ethics and ideological education portion of their training) and which allow the probationer to re-test in a subsequent round (if they have failed the Mandarin spoken-language component or educational theory). Teachers who do not meet the assessment standards at the end of their first year are delayed (and potentially prevented) from moving from provisional to permanent status.

Connections to pre-service education

Shanghai's formal induction policy is a response to many factors, not least of which are the traditions of pre-service education. The connections between the induction system as it is established in schools through the formal policy and the experiences of prospective teachers in pre-service education is a second important component to the story.

Teacher-training universities have been blamed for their strong emphasis on academic disciplinary training and their limited attention to pedagogy. Criticized for years, this tradition reflects a long-standing belief that teachers cannot be prepared by university programs alone: graduates become teachers and learn to teach only after they enter teaching positions at schools and learn by and from doing the job. Our interviews with officials and educators responsible for supporting new teachers revealed a general consensus that, upon completing teacher education programs, new teachers are regarded as "semi-finished products". No one seemed to think that initial teacher training, by itself, could be sufficient to launch a new teacher. Yet there was some difference of opinion about whether the weaknesses of current teacher-education graduates are inevitable (a reflection of the complexity of teaching as a practice and the ways one comes to develop that practice) or largely a function of poorly executed pre-service education.

Institutional arrangements

The institutions engaged in preparing Shanghai's lower secondary mathematics teachers have recently faced substantial challenges. Traditionally, teacher education in Shanghai involved a large mix of types and levels of institutions with separate and overlapping missions. Some concentrated almost exclusively on pre-service, others on in-service, while a third group worked in both realms. Similarly, secondary teacher training schools, two- and three-year teacher education colleges and four-year colleges and universities all contributed to Shanghai's teacher development work. These institutions reflected quite varied institutional cultures and were administered and funded by separate divisions of government. (Some, for example, were administered by the municipal government, while an institution such as East China Normal University was a 'national' university whose resources and regulations stemmed from China's central Ministry of Education.)

Institutional reorganization occurred in the 1990s. As a result, the city's six major teacher training institutions were merged into either Shanghai Teachers' University or East China Normal University. Since 1998, these two universities have become the major institutions supplying Shanghai's teachers. Shanghai Teachers' University prepares elementary and lower secondary teachers (that is, teachers of 'basic education'), while East China Normal University prepares upper secondary teachers.

However, institutional reorganization is not the only challenge to pre-service education. Previously, prospective secondary teachers were mainly Shanghai young people trained in one of the two teacher-training universities (four-year teacher education institutions). Labor policies and regulations restricting internal migration prohibited non-residents of Shanghai from being appointed to public-sector jobs in Shanghai, including teaching. The labor system used to be organized by 'job allocation' (*fenpei*), one in which central labor bureaus assigned individuals jobs, rather as a labor market of individuals and employers seeking matches. Under this system, only graduates of Shanghai teacher-training colleges and universities were assigned teaching jobs; graduates of other types of colleges were assigned to other sectors of the economy.

But recent changes in the labor market and in regulatory policies have made it both possible and desirable for graduates of institutions without teacher education programs as well as for teachers from outside Shanghai to find positions in Shanghai schools. As a result, new teachers joining Shanghai's schools no longer come solely from Shanghai teacher education institutions.

Instead, beginning teachers additionally come from comprehensive universities [14] and from outside Shanghai. In 1996, 1,230 beginning and experienced teachers came from other provinces to teach in Shanghai, while 273 new teachers graduated from Shanghai's comprehensive universities. At 1,503, these two sources between them contributed a number of teachers almost equal to the 1,635 graduates from Shanghai Teachers' University and East China Normal University combined who entered teaching that year (Wang, 1998, p. 256).

Pre-service curricula

These changes have posed challenges for the major pre-service providers. Yet, despite some program adaptations, the general curriculum of teacher education remains largely unchanged. Similarly, while Shanghai Teachers' University and East China Normal University both have distinctive histories, cultures and current missions, the two universities share generally common approaches to pre-service education. Primarily discipline-based, teacher education programs also require pre-service teachers to take three education courses that focus on educational psychology, general pedagogy and subject-specific pedagogy and to undertake limited practicum experience (varying in length, but typically about eight weeks in schools). [15]

Figure 3 below indicates the balance of time among subject-matter preparation, pedagogy-related coursework and the practicum for mathematics majors at Shanghai Teachers' University, the major provider of Shanghai's lower secondary mathematics teachers. [16]

Total		Subject Matter		Pedagogy		Practicum	
Teaching Hours	Credits	Teaching Hours	Credits	Teaching Hours	Credits	Teaching Hours	Credits
3132	189	1386	82	846	47	Length: (1/2 year) 8 weeks now	18
As a % of Total		44.25	43.39	21.01	24.87		9.52

Figure 3:   Time devoted to subject matter, pedagogy and practicum in mathematics education at Shanghai Teachers' University

Tight connections to schooling

Institutionally, pre-service education and induction are separate. They are offered by different providers (the teacher education universities for the former, the schools and districts for the latter). Responsibility for overseeing their programs and assessing their work is also located in different institutions. There is no formal responsibility for pre-service teacher educators to be involved with their graduates once they become new teachers, nor to monitor or support their work. There is also no regular system of follow-up or evaluation as teacher education graduates go into schools.

Yet, one can argue that the link between pre-service mathematics teacher education and the early years of work and learning (induction) of a beginning teacher in Shanghai is a tightly coupled one. While pre-service teachers get limited time in schools, in their university coursework they begin to study the curriculum that they will be teaching. Central to their work as future teachers is their developing understanding of what are called the 'important' points (*zhongdian*), 'difficult' points (*nandian*) and 'hinges' or 'hinge' points (*guanjian*) of teaching particular content. In their mathematics methods classes, pre-service teachers have the opportunity to learn about these points and to become familiar with the curriculum and its pedagogical requirements and implications.

For example, prospective teachers might study curriculum materials for seventh grade, in which they would learn to recognize that a specific element of content such as first-order, single-variable inequalities will include within it an 'important' point for teaching (the solution methods of a first-order, single-variable system of inequalities and the three properties of inequalities) and something that pupils will find 'difficult' (forming a solution set). They will also be encouraged to see that a way into learning about this – a 'hinge' for pupils' coming to understand – is to have pupils master ways of indicating the solution set on a number line. We see this as the beginning development of what Ma (1999) has called a "profound understanding of fundamental mathematics" (p. xxv) and of the related pedagogical content knowledge (Shulman, 1987).

This particular knowledge of curriculum and instruction was regularly mentioned in our interviews with both teachers and administrators as among the most significant things new teachers need to learn. Admittedly, their formal exposure to sites of practice (i.e. classrooms) is limited. Yet engagement with and development of analytic skills and knowledge of practice – this pedagogical content knowledge – begins in the university, well before new teachers take on their first-year teaching jobs. It is reinforced during the practicum and then intensively focused on beyond pre-service training during induction, because these distinctions have currency far beyond the university. For Teacher Li, recognizing the role of 'important' and 'difficult' points was something she first paid attention to in her coursework at Shanghai Teachers' University, but it took on new meaning for her, and required more serious attention, as she began her own lesson planning as a new sixth-grade teacher.

From this vantage point, there is a seamlessness in the pre-service to in-service trajectory that may be missed if one only looks at formal curriculum regarding practica. At the same time, we heard alternative perspectives in our interviews. Certainly, one of the most vocal was a reform-oriented school administrator, who explained why he had recently hired two young lower-secondary mathematics teachers whose training had *not* been in either of Shanghai Teachers' University's or East China Normal's mathematics departments, but in a pre-service program for intending elementary teachers. From his point of view, teacher education is out of step with schools and teacher preparation serves as a conservative force by emphasizing disciplinary knowledge to the exclusion of attention to pupils' learning. He sought out graduates of elementary teacher education programs for their greater understanding of and attention to pupils. While his view was perhaps the most adamantly expressed, we heard others echo the sentiment that mathematics teacher education was "out of step" with new reforms, especially in relation to the schools' need to reach all learners and mathematics curriculum changes that encourage more 'real-world' connections.

Characteristics of lower secondary schools: collaboration around curriculum and instruction

A third critical feature of the educational system that one needs to understand entails the characteristics of Shanghai's schools themselves. A key reason why pre-service education takes seriously the importance of introducing intending teachers to school curricula is because the municipality-wide curriculum is so central to the work of teachers and schools. [17] Traditions of teaching as exam-driven and text-centered (only a single text per grade in mathematics for the whole of Shanghai) give formal curriculum materials and official curriculum goals tremendous power. The role of exams, as well as the way they are constituted, results in a tight coupling between the curriculum and actual school practices.

This closeness also encourages certain common features of school organization [18], which themselves have significant consequences for how beginning teachers work and learn. One is the allocation of time within the school day. Teacher Li's daily and weekly schedule is typical of lower secondary mathematics teachers in Shanghai. She actually spends relatively few hours instructing in the classroom, yet she dedicates a good deal of her time – both in and out of school – to studying the curriculum materials, including inquiring into their use and planning her own instruction while using them.

Recall that in planning her lesson, she first concentrated on understanding the particular 'important' and 'difficult' points. Interviews with other teachers reinforced this. For many teachers, the solo work of planning, as well as the group discussions around teaching, requires attention to these basic curricular/pedagogical building blocks. Similarly, much conversation in teacher offices, in the lesson preparation groups and in some teaching research groups, focuses on pupil examination issues – both how to assess and how to interpret assessment. Time is allocated for this work, for schools take these curricular and assessment issues very seriously, seeing them as matters that require both study and inquiry. This becomes part of what it means to be a teacher and hence part of what new teachers are learning about when learning to teach.

Given the fact that this is work that is seen as shared – with a common curriculum and common assessment – to support such work schools set aside not only time but space for joint work among teachers. Teacher Li spent more of her day in her office than she did in her classroom. This too was a theme we heard across our interviews and across types of schools. [19]

The professional work life of lower secondary teachers in Shanghai appears to be one that is highly social. Like Teacher Li, when teachers are not in their classes teaching, they are often meeting with pupils in their office, talking with other teachers in formal meetings of one kind or another, or chatting informally with colleagues. The isolation, and accompanying 'sink or swim' metaphor now so familiar to many Western descriptions of teaching, fails to capture the induction experience of young teachers in Shanghai. [20]

In fact, any portrait of a new teacher's world in Shanghai would have to include a map of the school, giving prominence to the teachers' office and exploring the web of relations – the nature and extent of contact – with others in that office. One teacher whom we shadowed called the office a "beehive", highlighting its intensity, busy-ness and even the transitory quality of its life.

Whether it is a beehive or, as Ross (1993) suggests, a family, the images of teachers and the community they build in Shanghai's schools is one that is central to understanding induction there. In the sections below, we highlight four major themes and their attendant challenges that emerge from our data of Shanghai's induction experience:

- induction as a variegated process supporting core and common goals;
- induction as shaped by the organization and content of the curriculum;
- induction as immersion into a community of practice publicly talking about teaching;
- induction as variation within a system.

3. Experiences that Guide the Beginner: Induction as a Varied Process Supporting Core Goals

Induction in Shanghai is clearly more than a single policy or practice. In fact, induction in Shanghai is many things. Certainly, the formal policy requires both district and school activity and its focus includes ideological education, educational theory and practical training. Yet, when put into practice, as viewed from the experience of participants (new teachers, mentors or other induction providers), Shanghai's provision is remarkable both for its richness and its diversity.

By the former, we mean that a new teacher like Teacher Li has access to multiple sources of support. These include different people: for Teacher Li, these were her subject-matter mentor, her class-director mentor, her principal, the teaching research group head and experienced teachers from other schools. These people help her focus on different tasks of teaching and varied dimensions of knowledge and skill: subject-matter instruction, lesson planning, assessment, classroom management, pupil support, analysis of curriculum and teaching, becoming skilled at observation and reflection, and more. And their interactions occur in different venues and rely on varied forms: in her own classroom and those of others in and out of her school, in meetings both in and out of school, in small and large conversations, in one-time only events and in on-going conversations and inquiry.

For all its richness, this array of relationships made available to Teacher Li still does not capture the full range of induction support, which is summarized below.

School-based:

- school-based mentoring in subject-area teaching;
- school-based mentoring in working with pupils (as *banzhuren*);
- school orientations in the summer for teachers from a single or many nearby schools – with administrators, experienced teachers and second-year teachers talking about very specific issues related to teaching, working with pupils and families, school goals, etc.;
- pairing up new and older teachers to make visits to pupils' homes before the school year starts;
- contracts or formal agreements related to the goals and work of novices and mentors;
- ceremonies welcoming new teachers, assigning mentors or celebrating the end of a year's work and collaboration, with participants reflecting on a year's learning and/or collaboration.

District-based:

- district-level workshops and courses aimed at new teachers;
- district-organized teaching competitions for new teachers;
- district-provided mentoring;
- a district hot-line for new teachers (with subject specialists on hand at assigned times to answer phoned-in questions);
- district awards for outstanding novice/mentor work.

Occurring at both school and district, often in co-ordinated sequence:

- peer observation – of mentor/novice, of other teachers in the school and other schools;
- 'public' or 'open' lessons (*gongkaike*) – observed by the novice or with a group of novices (and others), typically with a public debriefing and discussion of the lesson afterwards;
- 'report' lessons (*huibaoke*) – in which a new teacher is observed, subsequently comments on the lesson and then receives criticism and suggestions from others;
- 'talk' lessons (*shuoke*) – presentations, in which a teacher (new or experienced) talks through a lesson and provides justification for its design (but does not actually teach it);
- inquiry projects/action research studies done by new teachers with support from others in the school or district teaching research section or induction staff;
- a district- or school-developed handbook for new teachers and mentors.

This range of learning opportunities is itself impressive. As the list suggests, it includes activities that are school-based, others that are primarily organized by the district, as well as ones that require co-ordination of both levels. We did note certain patterns, however, and highlight three common elements below – work with mentors, competitions and seminars – that illustrate some key features of the location, focus and goals for induction.

Mentors

The vast majority of teachers we interviewed placed tremendous emphasis on their work with their mentors. As was the case with Teacher Li, working with mentors involved frequent interaction, with observations of each other's teaching as well as the teaching of other staff, a chance to share lesson plans and seek advice about planning, and an opportunity to talk over more on-going concerns. Many novices talked about encountering things they had never thought about and how they saw the hardest thing they face as their lack of experience.

Time and again, novices claimed that the most important thing they needed to do in learning to teach was "gain experience" and that this is something that is facilitated by their close work with their mentors. A common claim was that working with mentors allowed novices to accelerate their learning and that really good mentors could catapult novices into more advanced learning than they could otherwise do on their own. [21]

But by these remarks mentors and novices did not simply mean that new teachers needed to acquire their own experience. One district administrator, in a conversation with us and several school teachers, talked about the ways in which new teachers "learn the experience of experienced teachers": that is, through conversation and inquiry, an experienced teacher could actually hand over her or his experience – like a legacy – to a novice.

One young teacher was trying to describe what she meant by "learning from experience", when the male administrator chimed in:

> Generally speaking, beginning teachers should learn from older teachers. But how experience should be learned does not mean that we take experiences one, two, three and follow them. No. Instead, it is through these activities, the teaching activities [...], planning lessons. [...] She [the young teacher present] discussed with the older teacher how to amend and improve the lesson she had planned. In such moments, the new teacher uses the experiences of the older teacher even before teaching.

> Therefore, the teacher who just talked [in this interview] about her public lesson is no longer reflecting her own labor, but the work of a lesson preparation group or a teaching research group. At this moment, she learned how to grasp her teachers' experiences; it is in these activities of preparing and giving the public lesson where the experience is grasped. But when you ask a teacher what exactly the experience is, this teacher probably would not be able to articulate it.

When we asked if the idea that "learning experience" could be described as the more experienced teacher "handing a cup of tea" to the beginner, he continued:

> I mean both: that is, one kind of learning is imitation. The mentor teacher shows her how to teach a lesson, the novice takes the mentor's lesson plan and teaches according to it. And the other is through the common joint activities in the process of which the elements of the mentors, including the novice's colleagues, are incorporated but presented through his or her own behavior. If there is no reflection, it likely becomes mere imitation. If there is reflection, it would probably be digested and become her own.

Mentors vary in how they work with their protégés. In one case, the mentor asked the novice to observe him each day and he observed her daily as well. From this novice's perspective, she "had no experience", so she "had to rely" on her mentor's. As she observed him, she studied his language, how he taught 'difficult' points, how he encouraged weak pupils. She took notes and they met daily to talk. He provided specific advice – for example, correcting her language – and made pedagogical suggestions, such as encouraging her to allow pupils to make some mistakes and to learn to see those as windows of opportunity (for both her learning and that of the pupils).

The particular intensity of this arrangement was not typical; much more common were mentors who observed weekly, with the frequency shifting over the course of the year. Nonetheless, learning from the mentor's experience, spending a great deal of time together, the offering of very specific suggestions by mentors, and mentors and novices making their teaching open to each other were common features of mentoring practice.

Teaching competitions

But mentors were not the only important sources of support for the novices. A second feature often mentioned by many novices was their participation in some public demonstration of teaching and the importance of their developing lessons for others to observe and provide a critique. We provide more detail in a subsequent section about the many different ways in which new teachers have opportunities to engage in *public* conversation about and scrutiny of teaching, but here we simply describe the role of one such activity, teaching competitions.

Districts organize these competitions with the goal of motivating new teachers and encouraging serious study of and preparation for teaching, as well as identifying and honoring accomplishment. The competitions take place at multiple levels. Schools have in-school competitions, in order to select candidates whom they wish to nominate for the district-level competition. And in getting ready for these competitions, new teachers go through extensive preparation, working alone and with their mentors and colleagues – especially their teaching research and lesson preparation groups – to select the most appropriate content and pedagogy.

One successful competitor explained how he participated in the district's 'talk' lesson competition for beginning teachers. The event Teacher Wang participated in, typical of these competitions, had three elements: a 'talk' lesson in which teachers have ten minutes to talk through how and why they would teach a topic they have chosen; a multimedia section, with five minutes for contestants to use and describe how they would use technology to help pupil thinking; finally, a five-minute section demonstrating 'blackboard skills', something this teacher (as well as many others we interviewed) stressed as very important.

The 'talk' lesson is evaluated in the following terms:

- the contestants' reasons for choosing the lesson;
- how they organize this topic to help pupils' learning;
- the appropriateness of their methods and approaches (contestants must submit lesson plans);
- their ability to talk through the content and their use of language/ effectiveness of language and demeanor (how the teachers present themselves).

For this young teacher, the time frame was actually quite short: the competition at the district took place only two weeks after it was announced. But, during that time, Teacher Wang worked closely with his mentor (spending a couple of hours together) to choose the topic he might teach, then prepared and, after making his presentation at the school level, was chosen to represent the school at the district level. He then undertook intensive preparation for the next level, choosing a new topic (that he felt, having initially developed the previous one, would be more suitable to show an exploratory approach to teaching). He studied other teachers' lesson plans and went back to his teacher education university to borrow some books. He gave a trial presentation of the 'talk' lesson, as well as enacting this lesson, teaching it for a full period to his own pupils.

About six other mathematics teachers from his school and the teaching research group head came to observe both the 'talk' lesson and the lesson itself and, following the latter, raised questions and discussed it for half an hour. At the district level, teachers were judged by a panel of five faculty from the College of Education and teaching research leaders from across the district. Teacher Wang's lesson, like that of all contestants, was videotaped, so that the district could compile and draw on an archive of such lessons.

After the process was complete, Teacher Wang felt that this had been a "concentrated opportunity to learn". It offered a "kind of pressure", but what was most important to him was the preparation it had entailed, as well as the chance it afforded him to work on his 'basic teaching skills'. As he put it, new teachers do come with strengths, but "not basic teaching skills – they need to work on these". The way teaching competitions for beginners are designed – both the focus and the evaluation criteria – stress these skills.

This experience, according to Teacher Wang, focuses on how a teacher organizes and understands teaching materials as well as one's 'thinking about teaching' (*jiaoxue sixiang*, a bit like one's teaching philosophy or stance) or what one uses to guide one's process of teaching. As such, the process emphasized core elements of teaching that are seen as central for beginners to learn early in their career – basic skills (like blackboard use, handwriting, questioning style), but also skill and understanding related to thinking about and enacting curriculum and pedagogy.

Significantly, this new teacher, like so many we interviewed, made a point of explaining that expectations for new teachers are not the same as those for their more experienced colleagues. The competition makes this clear; the criteria for new teachers are very different from what would be used as evaluation criteria in the equally common teaching competitions for experienced teachers.

Seminars

A third prevalent activity, one that, like mentoring and teaching competitions, highlights some of the core goals for beginning teacher learning, involves district-provided seminars. Each district offers a set of workshops, seminars or courses for its first-year teachers. It was clear from our interviews that districts varied in the emphasis they placed on them, their format(s) and particular issues addressed.

Across the board, however, there appeared to be some attention given to supporting beginners' subject-specific teaching, as well as more general issues related to teaching, management, professional responsibilities and ethics. One district provider, whom we call Mr. Gao, described one session he runs for new secondary (both lower and upper) mathematics teachers in his district. This session emphasizes the integration of theory and practice, building on novices' experiences and encouraging reflection and research.

> For the new teachers, I offer one session [...] I ask what difficulties they have had since they started teaching. Thirty-odd teachers attend and I let them talk. One teacher says there is a gap between the teacher's work and the experience of the pupils, the knowledge that the pupils have mastered. Some say that mathematics

> knowledge is really abstract: how do you make abstract knowledge clear? Others say there are a lot of different levels of pupils in the class and how do you motivate pupils to take the initiative and be active in their own learning? [...] How do you motivate them in actively overcoming the difficulties in mathematics? You want a good atmosphere, but sometimes the class is disorderly.
>
> There are lots of questions like that.
>
> My class is about the art of mathematics teaching. It is not that I talk about the art of mathematics teaching. These teachers have studied theoretical stuff in the university, so I have them first discuss these problems and then I organize them into groups to consider what they can do.

Mr. Gao then describes how a teacher complains that pupils still make mistakes, despite the teacher's stressing of a particular point in class. When he asks for an example, a teacher says that when the empty set equals the set containing the empty set is written in class, he says this is wrong, but the pupils make the same mistake in their homework.

> So then I ask new teachers to discuss why pupils would make these mistakes. Then someone comes up with the idea that pupil learning has a repetitious quality. Thus, teachers need to repeat things. This is one teacher's analysis of the problem. Another teacher says that different pupils attend to different things. For some pupils, when they attend to everything, there is something that gets lost. And some pupils, although the teacher has emphasized correcting the mistake, end up attending to the incorrect response rather than the correct one. So by means of these kinds of issues that come up with the new teachers, I help them use theoretical knowledge of education and psychology so they can see its relevance to these problems.

He follows this kind of discussion with an invitation for teachers to talk about their successes and to give examples.

> The reason I choose this approach to working with the new teachers is for them to talk about the hard things and to reflect on their own difficulties and their own feelings. By having them bring their difficulties to the surface, I have them decide what they should be working on in their professional development. And the reason for bringing up the success is to offer a kind of encouragement.
>
> Then I give them an assignment. They have to write a case: I want them to choose a pupil and observe the child and watch as that pupil changes and grows. Also, I ask them to write down their feelings about their teaching. I do this because I feel many new teachers and teachers who have taught for decades don't know how to reflect on their teaching. And if you can't reflect, you can't

improve. Without that, they lose certain resources they need to make headway. As teachers, we not only have to transmit knowledge: even more importantly, we have to study [literally, "research"] our learners: that then allows us to enrich our theories.

Mr. Gao's goal is to encourage novices to "use what they had learned in the university to help them analyze what they are seeing in their teaching". He relies on conversation, guided inquiry and what he calls the "early stages" of research to help teachers develop a grounded professional practice.

A different provider, Ms. Tan, working in a demographically very different district, organizes her support of new mathematics teachers in another way, yet many of her goals are quite similar. She meets repeatedly with secondary mathematics novices throughout the year, initially getting to know them and their preparation. Then, about one month into the school year, she gives a series of lectures on special topics, including, among other things, how to plan a lesson, how to teach a lesson, how to construct exam questions [...] and the 'knowledge points'. [22]

Ms. Tan observed, "To be a teacher, you have to be able to develop test questions and analyze text materials". The topics change in response to the learning needs of the new teachers and the information they have available.

> After the mid-term exams, we get everyone together again and we look at how all their classes did and compare that with their school as a whole. The mid-term is given by the school itself. You see what differences there are, the gaps between my class and the score of others in the school, and you try to understand the reasons. And then we get the teachers together mid-way through the year to talk about their learning opportunities and what they have been learning. They talk about where they have had difficulties and problems. They also talk about some successes they have had: for example, what about the weaker pupils in your class?

> I will help them understand the reasons why the weak pupils are doing poorly and I give them some guidance about how they can compensate. After this session, I go and listen [23] to each new teacher's lesson. After I listen to the class, I give them face-to-face guidance. If there is a district-level public lesson or a research lesson, then the new teachers have to go. If there are any city-level demonstration lessons, I will take them to some. [24]

This particular district has mathematics specialists, like this interviewee, serving as district-level mentors to the new teachers, who observe each novice several times each semester. While Ms. Tan's involvement with the teachers is more intensive than that of Mr. Gao (the first district specialist described above), in both cases, the district resource people are seen as just that – resources to help beginners develop professional knowledge and skills.

It is expected that these district-level providers combine theoretical work with close knowledge of practice and that they communicate this in ways that are meaningful to teacher learners early in their career. Furthermore, in both instances, the district mathematics specialist encourages inquiry into and reflection upon the teacher's own practice.

Supporting core goals

We have only highlighted three induction activities here – work with a mentor in the school, teaching competitions and district subject-specific seminars. They are common elements across districts, yet not the only such ones. We introduced them as critical examples of a broader array of offerings. This rich mix of learning opportunities, reflected in the small set described here, tends to draw on varied forms of and purposes for support: guidance, demonstration, joint inquiry, encouragement and assessment. In addition, the variety of induction opportunities also tends to emphasize certain core content for new teachers to learn and master.

For Teacher Li, induction is many things – activities, relationships and opportunities. Li Mei's particular collection of relationships and opportunities to learn (as well as their relative significance or weight) is determined, in part, by the choices she makes; but it is also significantly influenced by her school, her district and her teacher preparation background. This was the case for all the new teachers we met. We heard about varying constellations of activities, as well as considerable variation in the relative value of particular associations or occasions. [25]

Despite this variation, there appears to be a relatively clear consensus about the goals for induction – both in terms of what new teachers need to learn and how they best learn these things. Four themes emerged as we interviewed and observed Shanghai educators. These are the need for new teachers to get support in:

- learning routines;
- acquiring pedagogical content knowledge;
- coming to understand pupils better;
- gaining reflective skills.

In this regard, varied as the experiences are, there appears to be some coherent sense of what teaching is about and what needs to be learned, once in school.

The list of core or common goals says much about an implicit theory of teacher learning. Consider, for example, the emphasis on 'teaching routines and basic skills'. When asked about what falls within this category, informants mentioned blackboard use, planning a lesson, teaching a lesson, homework, assessment, home visits and working with parents. These were seen as fundamentals for any teacher, which beginners must master early in their work to have any chance of success in the classroom. Significantly, these were also seen as generic topics and actions, ones which *all* new teachers could learn through direct instruction, guidance, on-going mentoring and effort. In many schools and districts, these topics were prominent in the before-school orientation for new teachers which many schools organize, for these fundamentals needed to be discussed before the school year even starts.

The three other areas – familiarizing oneself with the curriculum, understanding pupils and developing reflective skills – clearly receive attention throughout the year in both school- and district-level programs and activities. We heard repeatedly about the importance for a beginner of "familiarizing oneself with the curriculum and teaching materials". Obviously a subject-specific activity, the support for this occurs through work with mentors, the teaching research group, the lesson preparation group, in the many public lesson activities and in varied district sessions. (See below for more extended discussion.) The emphasis on the curriculum reflects long-held approaches to teaching that stress the importance of text and textual knowledge, which positions the teacher's authority as resting on mastery of that knowledge (Paine, 1990).

In contrast, understanding pupils – another commonly described learning goal for new teachers – reflects a more recent effort in Shanghai's education reform: as one common phrase framed it, the intent is 'to teach not books, but learners'. The reformers' calls to make learning active, to have education promote individual growth and to encourage creativity place demands on new teachers' learning in at least two ways.

As beginning teachers, they need to learn how to manage a class in ways that support each pupil's growth socially, academically, personally. For Teacher Li, the need to understand pupils is a crucial one early in her career and it has relevance not only to her classroom instruction but also her work as a *banzhuren*.

> It is not about managing pupils, but rather inducting and educating pupils. The job of a *banzhuren* is the job of a class director, because pupils are not people I manage, not like the relationship between the superior and the subordinate in a business company, but rather a relation between teacher and pupils. I will teach what I have learned to pupils and they are going to learn it. So it is not management, but teaching them knowledge. Then, inducting them in how to conduct themselves – educating them how to behave in the world. To do the job of teacher well can only happen through learning from your teaching.

But as beginning mathematics teachers, they also need to learn how to organize mathematics instruction in ways that involve all pupils, that encourage their active participation and sense-making. Experienced and novice teachers alike talked about the importance of learning about pupils – as individuals, as members of a class and as learners of mathematics. With regard to the latter, novices frequently talked about the need to learn how to prepare a lesson not simply by preparing the material but by "preparing the pupils". By this, they meant preparing the lesson by taking into account one's pupils as learners with particular strengths, certain weaknesses and diverse experiences.

One young teacher, in her fourth year of teaching, described how she had shifted in her understanding of how she needed to focus on pupils: "I might have thought more about knowledge when I prepared my lessons at the beginning. Now I think more about how to cultivate pupils' abilities." She was surprised to find that some of her pupils were "high in scores but low in ability".

> They could remember the knowledge but did not know how to solve problems themselves [...] I did not realize this at the beginning. I was only concerned about how I could present my lessons clearly to pupils. Later on, I found pupils forgot the knowledge they'd learned.

As she learned more about pupils and consulted her mentor, this teacher came to approach her teaching differently.

These three goals – acquiring basic teaching skills, familiarizing oneself with the curriculum and understanding pupils – are ones respondents readily mentioned. The fourth we identified – reflection – was less commonly noted explicitly, but was present nevertheless, as a subtext of many of the induction activities. In mentor–novice collaboration, for example, a standard practice is for the novice to provide periodic reflections to the mentor. In one school, beginners had to observe their mentors weekly and every two weeks they had to write and give their mentors a written reflection on their own teaching. 'Report' lessons, required of all new teachers, include as a standard component the novice's reflection on the lesson.

Similarly, district providers regularly described activities that encourage first-year teachers to reflect both on their teaching itself and on the process of their learning about teaching. In short, while not explicitly stated – and thus not exactly comparable with the other three goals – reflection nevertheless seems to be a powerful skill that those organizing induction activities seek to support in their charges.

In sum, for Teacher Li, like other new teachers in Shanghai, induction involves a range of activities in and out of the classroom, in her own school and elsewhere. These activities vary in their focus and frequency. Looking across the activities, one sees a combination of encouragement, demonstration, guidance, collaboration and study by and assessment of the new teacher. Yet together these activities make explicit some content that should be learned – content that says a great deal both about how teaching is viewed and about how people think teachers learn to develop their practice.

Activities to guide and train: challenges in the process

Clearly, induction in Shanghai is not 'sink or swim', but a kind of 'guidance' and 'training', both of which are the key words most often used in Shanghai to describe what we are calling induction. The focus of this guidance and training is, as we have argued, clear and consistent, while the processes and forms are quite varied. What are some of the implications of this situation? What challenges are associated with interpreting induction as 'guidance and training'?

In both cases – guiding or training – there is a sense that the goals, the target outcomes, are known and that more experienced others can help and, indeed, are necessary for helping the beginner to reach them. In that sense, the induction approach of Shanghai draws on traditional didactic assumptions about learning. Induction does not begin from a wish to create a new kind of teaching, but from a desire to develop strong teachers in the existing mold of their older, experienced and successful colleagues. Some might see this as an inherently conservative process. Perhaps it is. One challenge, therefore, one in fact noted by some of our respondents, is the difficulty of helping new teachers develop reform-minded practices in a context of induction, constructed as it is in this setting.

Certainly, such a position does not presume that new teachers are the best authority on what they need in terms of learning to teach. Induction, here, ascribes perhaps less of an active role to the learner (the new teacher) than other arrangements might encourage. While new teachers can seek out all manner of support, those officially responsible for their support are seen as guides whose very experience can help to shorten the period of transition new teachers inevitably face. There is an unspoken assumption that guides know where the novice needs to head.

At the same time, the varied cast of characters involved, and the range of issues, skill and knowledge that they are helping the new teachers to develop or master, reflect the complex and rich culture of teaching which is distinctive in Shanghai. This complex character shapes the host of activities and relationships that comprise teacher induction and leaves considerable room for creativity and responsiveness, as well as the possibility of poor quality (a lackluster mentor, a mediocre seminar). Assuring a certain quality in such a large endeavor becomes, necessarily, a challenge.

4. Acquiring the Wisdom of Practice: Learning with and through Curriculum Materials

Induction in Shanghai, however, is more than a rich and varied set of induction-specific activities – for, in some ways, the life of Teacher Li and other new teachers is a lot like the life of all Shanghai teachers. The teaching culture in Shanghai, with its research groups and collective lesson planning, common curriculum and municipal assessments, is one in which *all* teachers learn to engage in joint work to support their teaching and personal learning, as well as the learning of their pupils.

Indeed, as we listened to young teachers talk about their own development, images of joining a community of practice stood out. In any setting, induction is part of the stream of teaching. In Shanghai, that stream has teacher learning at its heart, both structurally (with a vast array of learning opportunities and resources) and in the assumptions about the nature of the work (teaching).

Both these ways of seeing induction – as entering a community of practice and as part of a larger stream or system of teacher learning – in some general way apply to induction in any setting. But, in Shanghai, it is significant that the enculturation process, the joining of a culture, is organized in a staged way specifically designed to support the beginner's learning. For the beginning mathematics teacher there, the process encourages a growing understanding of what teaching is and how one develops and improves one's practice.

Two particularly fruitful sites for examining this enculturation are in new teachers' work with curriculum materials and their gradual immersion into the public conversation about and scrutiny of teaching. We examine the former in the remainder of this section and the latter in the next.

Learning the 'important', the 'difficult' and the 'hinge' points of mathematics teaching

Teacher Li's days include much attention to the textbook and teaching reference materials. Indeed, these represent key tools in the process of learning and new teachers in Shanghai rely heavily upon them. As Teacher Li's description of her process of planning an individual lesson suggests, using these tools involves certain analytic frames, ones that she was initially encouraged to develop as a mathematics major at Shanghai Teachers' University.

For Teacher Li, and other new mathematics teachers, these frames – the 'important', 'difficult' and 'hinge' points in school mathematics – are picked up, reiterated and elaborated through the daily study of teachers, informal conversations among teachers (including mentors and others) and formal meetings in lesson preparation groups. These frames help teachers learn to think about both mathematics itself and the pedagogical and learning implications of mathematics.

What constitutes 'important', 'difficult' and 'hinge' points – all terms used frequently in interviews and found in the curriculum materials themselves – is complex. Different people provided somewhat varying definitions. But, at a general level, individual responses tended to highlight the features present in the response of a Curriculum and Teaching Material Reform Commission member.

'Important' points are related to the knowledge system/structure of knowledge. They represent the most basic, crucial parts. It is assumed these are the same for most pupils, having more to do with the structure of the discipline than individual variation among learners.

'Difficult' points are based on what pupils have trouble learning, but this will vary with pupils and schools. But these are not completely independent of the 'important' points either.

'Hinge' points are specific and key pieces of understanding, strategies or solution methods through the mastery of which pupils can overcome the 'difficult' points and get at the 'important' points.

As Gu Lingyuan, Deputy Director of Shanghai's Academy of Educational Sciences and a pivotal figure in mathematics education reform, explained:

> Every chapter and every section has its important and difficult points, and every unit and lesson has its hinge points. [...] For factorization, the important points are two factorization formulae. The difficult points are not how to use the formulae in standard ways, but rather how to use the strategies and skills to do the problem. The key to breaking through (or the hinge point) is how to promote the factorization skills up to the level of methods.

Teachers learn about these various 'points' through and in the teaching reference materials (a kind of detailed teachers' guide to the textbook), the standard document accompanying the curriculum materials. The Curriculum and Teaching Material Reform Commission provides some model lesson plans, on the assumption that teachers can learn more effectively by starting with example lessons.

An administrator at the Commission explained, "But there is more than one way to approach a lesson, and so we have come over time to make these reference materials vaguer and to try to encourage teachers to consider different ways of thinking of approaching the content".

A content analysis of one passage in the teachers' reference guide to the pupil textbook shows the wealth of supports these guides offer teachers. The teaching guide indicates for each section of each chapter what the learning goal is: to know, understand, master or apply particular content. 'Important', 'difficult' and 'hinge' points are explicitly labeled as such and, typically, are discussed. In the teachers' guide to the first-semester, seventh-grade text, for example, a brief write-up of what the 'important', 'difficult' and 'hinge' points of the content of the entire text is provided. Then, within each section, a more fine-grained analysis is provided.

For instance, in the chapter on first-order systems of equations in two unknowns, the closing paragraph of the introduction states:

> The most important part of this chapter is how to solve systems of linear equations in two unknowns and that the method of elimination may be difficult for pupils. The key step in this method is to ensure, for one of the variables, that the absolute values of the coefficients should be equal, so that adding or subtracting the equations eliminates this variable. Remember to make the pupils understand how and why you should eliminate one variable and then substitute the value from the other back into the original equation to find out the solution. (Shuxue Jiaoxue Cankao Ziliao, 1998, pp. 27-28)

Such annotation helps new teachers sort the instructional wheat from the chaff, to understand what their substantive priorities should be, as well as how to focus their pedagogical attention. Additionally, commentary throughout the reference guide is intended to make the teacher aware of how the content of a particular lesson connects to other knowledge: that is, to the previous content on which this particular teaching is based. In so doing, the guide helps teachers to see links in substantive knowledge: it also delves into theoretical knowledge of mathematics. In these ways, teachers get support for deepening their own understanding of mathematics.

In the section on the graph of a linear equation in two unknowns, the guide explains:

> The textbook intentionally combines the solutions of linear equations in two unknowns with concepts of the rectangular co-ordinate system and ordered pairs to demonstrate the mathematical idea of linear equations graphically. (p. 27)

But the commentary also helps teachers think about the relationship between this knowledge and pupils' learning. It regularly mentions what pupils already know relative to the content being taught. It suggests pedagogical considerations related to how the knowledge in this lesson connects to pupils' prior knowledge, discussing motivational issues related to learning particular content.

We see several of these features in the 'analysis of materials and teaching suggestions' provided to teachers for the section on systems of linear equations in two unknowns and their solutions. We provide the passage in its entirety:

> The related knowledge that pupils already have: the concepts of 'variable' [or 'unknown'] and 'order', the solution to the equation and transformations of the equation.
>
> *The concepts of linear equations and their solutions.* The textbook uses real-life examples to introduce related concepts and to encourage pupils' interest, and [teachers] obtain solutions to the practical questions by discussion during the class, so that the pupils are able to accept new concepts concretely and graphically.
>
> During teaching, in order to make pupils understand the concepts of systems of linear equations in two unknowns better, let them review linear equations in one variable based on the concept of 'variable' and 'order of the equation'.
>
> There are two levels for understanding the solutions of linear equations in two unknowns: the first level starts with practical problems and then obtains limited numbers of positive integer solutions. The second level starts with abstract problems involving linear equations in two unknowns and then enables pupils to know that there are unlimited numbers of solutions for any single linear equation in two unknowns and helps them understand the concept of 'solution set'.
>
> In the previous edition of this textbook, we defined the solution set of a linear equation in two unknowns as "all possible solutions of one linear equation in two unknowns comprises a set and we call this set the solution set of this linear equation in two unknowns". But we found it was difficult for pupils if they had not learned about solution sets before. In this edition, we change the definition to "all solutions of a single linear equation in two unknowns comprise the solution set for this linear equation in two unknowns".
>
> When we solved $2x + y = 10$, we used a table to show its solution set. During teaching, instructors can give values of x and let pupils find the corresponding values of y. This method has pupils understand the relationship between the two variables and that there are unlimited possible solutions.
>
> Have pupils answer the first exercise question in this chapter orally in the class and let them discuss exercise 4 in class too. Give counter-examples for wrong answers. (p. 29)

Tools for teacher learning

These materials, crammed with information on pupils' prior knowledge, more or less powerful instructional strategies and insights into lessons learned from past experience are key for any teacher. Further, the examination system reinforces their importance, since the curriculum, which these guides expand upon and explain, is the foundation for high-stakes, grade-twelve examinations for university entrance, where mathematics is one of only three key required subjects given particular emphasis. For new teachers like Teacher Li, however, these teaching reference materials become an especially vital individual tool, as well as being the texts that organize much of their interaction with other teachers.

These materials serve as resources for new teachers to learn about many crucial dimensions of teaching: mathematics itself, how pupils learn and developmental issues related to pupils' learning of mathematics, how teachers can reason about pupils' prior knowledge, 'important' and 'difficult' points in content and pedagogical moves that support pupil learning. The reference guides provide both warrants and common language that support teacher learning about the teaching of mathematics.

Furthermore, the materials support communication about teaching, and are themselves the product of a long-term conversation among Shanghai's mathematics educators, written iteratively, with authors self-consciously reflecting on what has and has not worked in the past. The materials thus represent shared knowledge about a specific and specified curriculum that is located in and among teachers. They are, to paraphrase Shulman (1987), the wisdom of practice, the products of teachers' and administrators' individual and collective inquiries into how and what instructional materials best support pupil learning. Thus, these materials comprise an important heritage that new teachers must gain access to and a certain mastery of, if they are to join this community of practice.

In a way, Shanghai's mathematics curriculum itself comes to act as a teacher of teachers. This seems especially true for beginning teachers like Teacher Li. Across many different levels of participants in the educational system, a common answer to our question about what new teachers need to learn or do was "to familiarize themselves with the teaching materials". Much of the conversation among teachers – between novices and mentors or among teachers in their lesson preparation or teaching research groups – centers on examining the teaching materials and discussing teaching particular textbook content. Curriculum analysis becomes a key induction activity, one carried out across different settings.

Gu Lingyuan claims that, few Chinese teachers "sink", but "few excel". His explanation for the high survival rate among new teachers points directly to the curriculum supports discussed above. For him, the presence of the curriculum outline (the Shanghai Municipal Education Commission-developed curriculum frameworks) and the practice of "curriculum analysis" together make a difference.

New teachers in any setting need to learn how to think about and work with curriculum. In Shanghai, learning to develop a "curricular vision" (Zumwalt, 1989) that allows a teacher to think deeply about both the what and the how of teaching is essential, especially given the centrality of the common curriculum. At the same time, by having a clear curricular vision as an entire municipal system, Shanghai offers its new teachers a setting where they do not have to invent everything anew. [26] Thus, new teachers are encouraged to develop a shared understanding of what teaching is, what one should pay attention to and how one can approach teaching in ways that support pupil learning; they use the curriculum materials to anchor their collegial conversations and their learning.

Yet the system – like teaching – is always under scrutiny; for the wide-spread assumption is that the system, much like teachers, can and must learn. It is not surprising, then, that another Shanghai mathematics scholar argues that the very structures of 'important' and 'difficult' points impede the possibility for new ways of thinking about mathematics teaching. This researcher claimed that one would have to "blow up" these categories in order to achieve genuinely new approaches to teaching mathematics in school. This point highlights a central tension in induction and professional learning. While structures can help support learning – especially for novices – they can also obscure vision and act as conservative forces. This is a tension that, across all levels in Shanghai, mathematics educators face.

Learning to teach in a period of reform: challenges for induction

This picture is complicated further by considerable curricular reform in Shanghai in recent years. Consequently, new teachers there learn to teach in a dynamic setting. Zhang Minsheng, the Deputy Director-General of the Shanghai Municipal Education Commission, argued to us that "of all the reforms in Shanghai's education, the most important is the reform of the elementary and secondary curriculum". That reform is understood, he went on, to include "teaching materials, pedagogy and assessment". In an article published a couple of years previously, he had written:

> Crucial to the reform of the basic [compulsory, grades 1–9] education is *suzhi jiaoyu* [often translated as 'quality education']. (Zhang, 1998, p. 6)

As this term is understood, quality education challenges traditional, examination-oriented education and is best defined in terms of its contrast with academic, promotion-driven schooling. The two hallmarks of quality education are a commitment to educating *all* children (not just those heading to further education) and educating the *whole* person (and not just advancing the cognitive abilities needed for university admission).

As the reform is new, and its vision of reformed practice not fully specified, quality education poses a particular challenge to new teachers in Shanghai. Themselves educated in schools with an emphasis on academic advancement (what gets described as 'promotion-driven schooling'), these new teachers are expected to learn to teach in ways that they have not necessarily experienced themselves as pupils and to do so from more experienced colleagues who are also in the process of having to reinvent their own teaching practice. In understanding the kind of practice new teachers are expected to develop, educational reform becomes both a goal and, because of its uncertainty, a challenge.

There are parallel challenges within the teaching of subject matter as well. Reforms in the mathematics curriculum are equally far-ranging and pose challenges for new and experienced teachers alike. These mathematics reforms may heighten the importance of the teachers' reference guide, as teachers are being asked to teach mathematics in a way that they themselves have not previously experienced. As a result, the "instructional goals and instructional design [of the curriculum materials] were especially designed" with new teachers in mind, according to Zhang Fusheng, Deputy Director of the Curriculum and Teaching Material Reform Commission.

Shanghai's lower secondary mathematics curriculum is a new one. Shanghai is now undertaking its second major cycle of reform (which is in an early stage and not yet implemented city-wide) with the first cycle having begun in 1988. The initial push for reform (what became the first cycle) was motivated by a desire for a big change from traditional mathematics teaching, moving away from focusing entirely on large amounts of content, emphasizing instead helping pupils to learn mathematics well.

By 1991, schools began to use the new materials. The new curriculum structure in mathematics for lower secondary pupils includes both required and elective courses, as well as some mathematics-focused, extra-curricular activities. Electives represent a small part of the whole. This first cycle is a considerable change from what preceded it, but it is judged "still not perfect", especially in the links between the curriculum and 'real life'. The second cycle, among other things, aspires to address some of these problems.

For lower secondary, there is an effort to strengthen the 'basic quality' of algebra and the logic of geometry. Across K–12, there is a goal of strengthening the links to 'real life' and strengthening the 'practical aspects' of mathematics education. One curriculum reformer explained:

Now the curriculum is divided into three stages. In the first two stages, the emphasis is on observation and experimentation that require generalization and induction, not on rigorous proof. Logical proof is introduced in the last stage. Of course, the requirement for pupils' logical proof ability is lower than before. [...] In the past, we cut off the original sources and the practical applications of mathematical knowledge. Mathematics became formulae and theorems. We didn't care where it came from, where it will be applied or how useful it is.

This last comment echoes a theme we heard repeatedly in interviews with mathematics educators and curriculum reformers. Gu Lingyuan, Zhang Fusheng and their mathematics education colleagues used a common metaphor of "a fish cooked without head and tail". While a complete mathematics process goes through three phases – abstraction from the world, symbol manipulation and application back to the world – teaching and learning the middle phase alone (as critics say mathematics teaching in Shanghai traditionally did) separates mathematics education from both reality and its history, and mathematics knowledge becomes both cut-and-dried and fragmented. [27]

A university mathematics educator claimed that, in the past, people felt that if you give pupils the structure and system of mathematics knowledge, they could do applications. People believed application could not come before pupils had learned that abstract system of thinking. Today, university mathematics educators argue that mathematics education should now emphasize both 'application' and the 'basics'.

The current new reform effort seeks to restore the 'head and tail' of mathematics knowledge, by introducing into the curriculum opportunities to learn about where mathematics comes from and where it goes in the service of human life. This also represents a new understanding of mathematics, one which views mathematics as a form of knowledge that not only trains abstract, logical and systematic reasoning, but also nurtures creativity. It views mathematics knowledge as not only useful for school (academic) learning, but also for application to real-life settings.

The main line of systematic foundational mathematics knowledge, which is the essence of the traditional Chinese mathematics curriculum, is to be kept but streamlined (Gu *et al.*, 1997; Shanghai Zhongxiaoxue Kecheng Jiaocai Gaige Weiyuanhui, 2000). This strategy, they reason, will allow pupils to learn about the 'whole fish'. It seems that Shanghai's mathematics education community is endeavoring to seek a balance among nurturing creativity, making mathematics relevant to life and keeping the basics. This is referred to as "tradition plus reform".

The efforts of Shanghai mathematics educators over the past decade to create a substantial reform of what a mathematics education comprises and how it is taught might eventually lead to this coherent mathematics education community changing and perhaps becoming multiple communities. Our observations in classrooms across schools and districts, however, coupled with our interviews, suggest that even in the wake of Shanghai's mathematics education reform, there still seems to be a vision of teaching that can be characterized as a dominant theme with variation. Indeed, one teacher educator suggested:

> Older teachers endeavor to balance solving problems and teaching for understanding. But because of the pressure of the examinations, school principals and other teachers tend to think that a good teacher is one whose pupils are more successful in competing in the promotion exams and higher-education entrance exams. Therefore, a novice tends to be more narrowly focused on solving problems – and not problem solving [he laughs] – instead of teaching for understanding.

Even granting the possibility of more diverse approaches to the teaching of mathematics, our interviews suggest that the official curriculum framework, textbook and teaching reference materials – reinforced by the examination – remain in a primary place, one that defines what mathematics teaching is. It has the potential to act as a conserver of dominant practice.

The centrality and specificity of the curriculum materials mean that even pre-service teachers have early exposure both to the materials and to the frames of viewing teaching which are embedded within them. In the mathematics methods courses, for example, teacher education students begin to learn about 'important' and 'difficult' points in teaching. But we found consistent evidence that the most serious engagement with these frames occurs as individuals make the transition from student to teacher. In their first years of teaching, novice teachers find concentrated study of these materials a crucial activity for their professional development.

5. Talk as a Medium for Induction: Immersion in Public Conversation about and Scrutiny of Teaching

Up to this point, we have focused primarily on the content of curriculum materials, for they provide new teachers with much guidance about what to teach and how. But the curriculum materials are important in another way, as they also serve as the primary context for new teacher learning: that is, they provide occasions for public conversation about teaching. The presence of commonly-used teaching reference materials, as well as their organization and content, leads to curriculum analysis being both a central task of teaching and a primary activity of induction. They provide a focus for much of the substantive interaction in induction activities both in and out of school.

While the curriculum materials help define what teaching in classrooms should be, analyzing curriculum – as a professional skill – is not something the novice has to learn solo. Because of the nature of teachers' work, the spaces and times of their work life and the assumptions about teaching, this task occurs in a steady stream of public conversation.

Furthermore, public conversation about teaching – and its attendant scrutiny of practice – extends far beyond talk of curriculum. Crucial to the process of new teacher learning, and closely associated with the central tools of teaching, is the constant talk – what one teacher described as "bee-hive" activity – that characterizes the days of teachers' school lives. Thus, because it is part and parcel of teaching, public conversation also becomes a vehicle to support induction. And because educators in Shanghai take a developmental perspective, induction is organized to allow the newcomer to make a gradual, supported entry into that conversation.

As the opening vignette of Teacher Li's life suggests – its time, affiliations and space arrangements – there are many opportunities in the regular week of any teacher to engage in public conversation about teaching. For new teachers, this feature of the Shanghai teaching community creates possibilities for novices to engage in what Lave and Wenger (1991) would call 'legitimate peripheral participation'. In the weekly meetings of the lesson preparation groups, the teaching research groups, the class director groups and in the teachers' offices, the beginning teacher has multiple opportunities first to listen to more experienced others talk about teaching and then gradually to join in.

These conversations offer opportunities for new teachers to hear and develop ways of talking about the content and processes of teaching, about how one makes judgements and decisions, about notions of learning and about mathematics itself. Teachers vary tremendously in their reflectiveness and skill in articulating their reasons and thinking behind their teaching. Yet the novice teacher, in these regular conversations, has multiple opportunities both to listen and to be encouraged or pushed to develop skill and understanding. Finally, these conversations also highlight for new teachers what their colleagues think teaching is all about, what teachers need to pay attention to and what the goals of teaching should be. As such, these are occasions for developing fundamental professional knowledge and skills.

Teacher Li's experience in this regard seems somewhat representative of the teachers we interviewed. The opportunity to be part of a lesson preparation group and a member of a teaching research group at the school, the chance to be a participant in school- and district-level 'open' lessons and having a base in a teaching office were all important to her learning. We consider each of these in turn.

Participating in lesson preparation groups

Teacher Li worked closely with her lesson preparation group and found the opportunity to talk with teachers there especially important, since she could check her pace and understanding of the text, as well as "ask older teachers" about teaching her subject. Her lesson preparation group was a place where teachers "analyze important and difficult points", as one of her mathematics colleagues explained, and engage in detailed and "concrete" discussions about their teaching. Through these conversations and others with experienced teachers in the school with whom she could have frequent interaction, "their experience became mine".

The notion of developing expertise and sharing experience is clearly present for other teachers as they talked about the benefit of such planning group conversations. Another young teacher, in a different school, explained that she turns to her lesson preparation group as she is preparing a lesson, in order to ask:

> How am I to do this lesson better? For example, when I graded pupils' workbooks, I found many pupils made mistakes on the same problem. What might be the reasons for the problem? Is it a problem of my teaching or is it a pupil-thinking problem? We will discuss it and figure out some methods to deal with it.

In yet another school, we observed a regular lesson preparation group meeting of the seventh-grade mathematics teachers. The meeting was relatively short, slightly more than half-an-hour in length, but was a lively, fast-paced, freewheeling conversation among eight teachers, including two novices. The teachers, sitting at their desks in a shared office, were looking closely at their textbook as they discussed what and how to teach. Much of the conversation focused on the solution to a problem of inequalities involving a mixed number ($3^{6}/_{7}$) and how to engage their pupils in converting to improper fractions. The teachers spoke rapidly, offering ideas, questions and experience.

The novices were not officially treated differently; they asked questions and gave their views. But there was also a clear pattern throughout the meeting as the novices voiced their concerns, expressed unfamiliarity with how pupils might respond to particular content or tasks, got clarification and drew on the prior teaching and insights of more experienced others.

The experienced teachers in the room freely passed out advice, but there was a give-and-take that suggested that the novices themselves should ultimately decide how they would teach their own lessons.

For example, one teacher suggested, for a particular problem, "convert it to an improper fraction and then indicate it and 12 on the number line and see the distance between them". But a young teacher worried out loud that "this makes it very complicated [...]". The other teachers took turns explaining why it is worth making a number line to help pupils understand this. But rather than this be solely an opportunity for the young teachers to learn how to teach something, other teachers also raised questions, asking what sort of number line works best for this kind of problem.

In the end, the meeting served as an occasion for the teachers both to agree collectively on content and to think aloud about different teaching approaches and their justification. It also afforded the young teachers a chance to get explicit advice (as when one of the older teachers quickly noted, "Young teachers need to pay attention to this"). Over the course of this brief meeting, the novice teachers had the opportunity to watch (and join) teachers discussing and solving mathematics problems and to consider how pupils learn some content and how different pupils react differently. Members of this particular group explained that the lesson preparation group had, in effect, constructed itself as serving multiple purposes, one being the induction of new teachers.

Being a member of a teaching research group

Teacher Li, like all beginning teachers, is also a member of her teaching research group. That group similarly provides a forum for discussion of teaching and, hence, for the novice, a special opportunity to learn. The discussions vary. Part of the mission of teaching research groups is to support the development and discussion of 'open' lessons (in the school and the district); another part of the group's mission is to explore more general issues in teaching and educational reform.

Sometimes, teachers discuss articles about mathematics education reform. As the head of Teacher Li's teaching research group explained, they discuss "teaching method as well as teaching content, [since] the content has changed a lot. The text changes a lot." At many schools, we heard about classroom research projects that teaching research groups were undertaking, such as focusing on questioning styles, cross-curricular teaching, and so on. Teacher Li especially valued the way in which her teaching research group created opportunities for her to observe others teaching and "to look at their style and think about how to make it mine".

Learning from public lessons

As a part of that opportunity to observe public lessons, Teacher Li and other Shanghai beginning teachers can enter yet another conversation about teaching, this one being the public discussion that follows any 'open' lesson. One new teacher said participating in a public lesson was:

> very useful, especially the discussion in the last part of it. After listening [what we would call observing the class], discussing the class is very useful.

When probed about which aspects were useful, she explained:

> They will talk about the important and difficult points that pupils easily make mistakes on. Because we [beginning teachers] lack experience, we don't know where pupils will flounder. And also, we can learn teaching methods.

The talk itself appears to provide newcomers with lessons in how to think and talk about teaching. No one assumes that the novice watching and taking part in this conversation has the same skill at participating or the same depth of experience as the older teachers. Typically, in these public conversations about a demonstration lesson, novices are keen listeners, perhaps providing some small comments after others with more experience and higher status have contributed. But in this listening, the beginning teacher has ample opportunity to hear teachers describe the content of their teaching, reflect on what teaching is, reflect critically on practice, discuss what learning is, make instructional decisions and use evidence and other warrants for their decisions and judgements.

The observer sees teachers engage in self-reflection and critique, as well as others take on the role of "critical colleague" (Lord, 1994). Given this and the emphasis placed on 'open' lessons, it was not altogether surprising that at one 'open' lesson debriefing we attended, young teachers from the school who themselves had been unable to observe the lesson in question were nevertheless encouraged to attend the discussion; they were told that the discussion would still be helpful to them. They were even asked to comment during the discussion. Since they could not comment on the lesson itself, their comments inevitably focused on observations about the conversation. In this way, beginners learn not only about the content and processes of teaching, but also about a professional stance of reflection and inquiry, as well as professional talk.

One lower-secondary, mathematics teaching research group meeting combined the discussion of two 'open' lessons during a single meeting. The contrast of the two teachers reflecting on their lessons and the uptake of other group members in the discussion illustrated how much variation exists across teachers and across schools in the content and quality of such reflections. Here, two teachers contrasted sharply in their ability to articulate grounds for their teaching and insight into their pupils' learning.

At the crudest level of comparison, one teacher could only muster six sentences to describe her teaching and rationale while the other spoke in paragraphs, explaining her goals, what prior understandings the pupils brought, how she thought about her teaching in relation to (but not bounded by) the textbook's requirements, the contrast between her plan and what she ultimately did, the skills required for this teaching, her appraisal of her effectiveness and her concerns about what is appropriate learning for her pupils. Throughout, she modeled a form of questioning of her own actions that reflected a deep interest in improving her teaching through self-examination.

At first blush, the contrast between these two teachers is striking. At the same time, what struck us as impressive as outsiders was the very publicness of this conversation. 'Open' lessons, and the conversations that follow them, make teaching open to a community of teachers. Teaching thus becomes community property, not owned privately by one teacher but shared by all. Even this imbalanced discussion allowed participants to think concretely about what it means to talk about one's teaching. For new arrivals to this community, these conversations hold tremendous power: they help new teachers learn to think about teaching and to reflect on their teaching. The conversations also help new teachers acquire the language and norms of public conversation about teaching.

It is also important to remember that these conversations are a natural part of the fabric of any teacher's work life. We observed that the standard expectation at a school was that each teacher, new or experienced, must observe at least eight lessons a semester: some may be within one's own school, some may take one out of the school to another school. Yet the minimum of eight (and with mentor–novice arrangements, it typically was a much higher number for first-year teachers) means that all teachers frequently enter others' classrooms and join in talking about and listening to others talk about mutually-observed teaching. The very frequency of this increases the novice's potential for learning quickly shared norms related to talk, analysis and reflection.

Offices as sites for teacher talk and learning

Finally, offices appear as an important site in which additional talk occurs and, for the beginning teacher, one which offers more scope for legitimate listening and gradually increasing participation. In one office we observed, two mathematics teachers, while grading pupil homework quickly between classes, spent the majority of the time simultaneously grading and having an informal conversation. These comments might look incidental and certainly had none of the preparation or formality of an 'open'-lesson debriefing. Nevertheless, like those debriefings, it provided teachers with a chance to talk about how to solve a problem, how to teach it, even why one might not want to do exactly what is recommended in the teacher's guide.

Time and again, novices whom we interviewed talked about the large amount of time they spend in their offices. These offices offer not just a place to plan lessons, mark papers and tutor individual pupils, but they also provide, among other things, a flexible and responsive site for learning about teaching through direct questioning of others and the unpressured listening in on informal conversations about work.

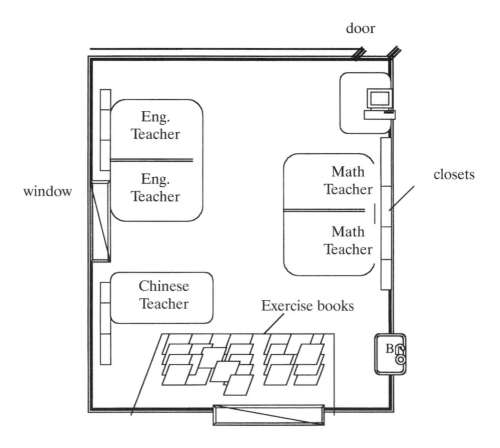

Figure 4: *Map of the sixth-grade teachers' office in Lanting Lower Secondary School in Shanghai*

The maps in Figures 4 and 5 indicate some of the range of office arrangements we observed. Whether all the teachers for one grade level are together or only some portion of the teachers, the novices find themselves in work spaces that inevitably connect them to others with shared interests – teaching a certain cohort of pupils, teaching the same subject matter – but also others with greater depth of experience. Work is visible there. Teaching, already treated as a public act in other ways (like the 'public' lessons), is once more and continually opened to others' eyes, ears and minds.

Classrooms

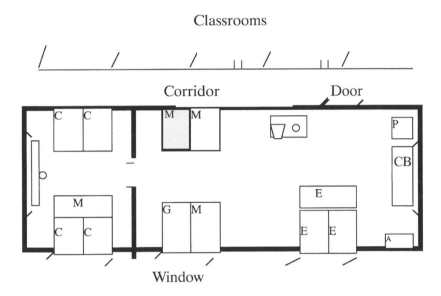

Legend: M: a math teacher   C: a Chinese teacher   E: an English teacher

G: Geography teacher (not usual, the only teacher of a minor subject in the office)

P: Phone   A: Air conditioner

CB: Cabinet

Shaded desk is the desk for the novice. The other three mathematics teachers are all experienced senior teachers.

Figure 5:   Map of the sixth-grade teachers' office at Shanghai Attached #7 Lower Secondary School

Public conversation and public scrutiny as opportunities

All of these sites – the lesson preparation group, the teaching research group, public lessons and the office – clearly create regular occasions for new teachers to obtain additional support, sometimes formally, sometimes less so. These sites, as ordinary aspects of the culture of teaching in Shanghai, are places where experienced teachers inquire and continue to learn while also, in the course of that work, welcoming and socializing their newer colleagues into schools and the culture of teaching. But the novice is the beneficiary of more than this general culture of teaching that places great value on collective examination of teaching and articulating ideas about practice.

Induction itself, through the formal requirements put in place by the Shanghai Municipal Education Commission and the districts, as well as school-level practices, creates special occasions for new teachers to begin to join this conversation. These occasions reflect the shared assumption that learning to teach is a staged task that involves repeated and varied opportunities for guidance and assistance.

Recall the range of core induction activities that require beginners to engage in public conversation about teaching. Certainly, the mentor and novice rely heavily on regular talk about their teaching, but other key induction activities widen the circle of conversation. Beginners have to observe a certain number of other teachers' lessons and, hence, at the minimum, listen to the public debriefing. This activity, like mentoring, occurs throughout the year. But as the year proceeds, expectations rise. The beginner needs not only to be able to observe thoughtfully (and must hand in notes or reflections on some of these observations as part of the year-end assessment), but also be able to articulate and enact a vision of teaching.

The 'report' lesson (a public lesson specifically designed for new teachers to demonstrate their learning of subject-matter instruction and their ability to reflect and critically comment on their own teaching), the 'class meeting' (*banhui*) they must hold to demonstrate their skill as a *banzhuren*, and teaching competitions, typically at the end of semesters, are all scheduled at points in the year to push the new teacher (at the same time that they provide interim assessments of the novice's progress).

The ways in which these activities are organized reveal that, while serving some assessment function, they are very much intended as learning opportunities. Guidance and support are provided along the way. Even the idea of a 'trial' lesson before the actual 'open' lesson implies the staged process at work. Recall Mr. Wang, the teacher who had won a district teaching competition. That process – of working with his mentor, with his teaching research group, of developing a trial lesson before the final one –

is quite similar to the process we heard about repeatedly as teachers told us about their public or 'report' lessons. Teacher Li, for example, having initially prepared for her 'open' lesson and vetted it with key colleagues, taught the lesson to one class, received a critique of it from members of her teaching research group, revised the lesson and only then taught it as the actual 'open' lesson, this time to her other class of pupils at that grade level.

Following that public lesson, there was a detailed conversation about the class. In this discussion, as in each discussion of this kind we were able to observe, comments moved between very specific attention to details of the teaching (e.g. the size of a chart, the color of chalk) to far broader discussion about teaching (e.g. what constitutes reform-minded mathematics teaching, what one can expect of sixth-grade pupils). In learning to talk (and participating in talk) about the specifics of practice, the principles that undergird it and the dilemmas one must reason through, beginners are developing professional knowledge and skills.

To a person, teachers acknowledged that this sort of public performance puts some pressure on them. But the comments of one teacher were somewhat typical: she claimed that, "after the first five minutes, it's not so nerve-wracking and is more like an ordinary class". At another school, a group of young teachers explained that during the first three to four weeks of the term, school administrators observed them. During the first semester, a new teacher has to give a public mathematics lesson and a public 'class meeting', to which the district people come. "This gives pressure but motivation", observed a teacher in another district. While both observing public lessons and giving one's own public lesson are valuable, "being observed and listened to is more helpful, because I can find my own short-comings and give myself more pressure".

There was great consensus on the value of feedback at these sessions. Teachers reported they "welcome" comments: said one, "it's very important to my improving". The winner of a teaching competition explained that the more the participants come from a diverse set of schools, the more likely the conversation stresses the positive, but that, if the debriefing is internal, the discussion moves more quickly to point out the problems and shortcomings in the teaching since, according to him, that is where one can get the most learning.

Certainly, some of the sessions we observed involved quite pointed and elaborated comments. In one session, a young teacher, after she had explained her goals for the lesson and her sense of how it went, received extensive extemporaneous comments from two different mathematics specialists from the district, as well as briefer comments from her principal and others attending. The first district specialist spoke at length about problems with the way she had organized the lesson (a review of fractional expressions), analyzed patterns in pupils' mistakes and how she handled them, commented on her language use and explained principles he has for blackboard use (and criticized hers in the process).

Of this last aspect alone, he said:

> Another suggestion [...] I think a mathematics teacher, if she wish-es to give a good lecture, besides what I have said about this class, she should be conscious about the art of writing on the board, the art of designing the board writing. That means what I am going to write on the board is not whatever I want, wherever there is a space, wherever I could draw. The relatively ideal [board writing] is one in which one is able to know what you have mainly lectured about today by looking at your blackboard, even if the person just stopped by right before the class is finished.
>
> When starting to write on the blackboard, one should consciously realize all the content that needs to be kept from the beginning to the end. What content will be needed when I do the summarizing? What could be erased, for the spacing? I also have mentioned to your principal if the classroom is going to be equipped with a pro-jector, some writing or technical procedures can be presented from the projector. The blackboard then can be used to keep the most important content.
>
> Now the blackboard appears very messy to me. It's not easy for pupils to read either, right? You can't even find a place to write. You can't touch pupils' stuff because their work will have to be lec-tured about later. Therefore I suggest like this it's necessary to have a certain level of board writing and design skill. Actually, this should have been roughly done when you were preparing this class. It is just a suggestion.

The debriefing that continued included further comments from this speaker, as well as responses from the teacher observed and additional speakers. The intensity, seriousness and blending of principle and practice were not equally present in all the sessions we observed, but it seems clear that these open conversations, connected to 'open' lessons, play several important roles.

The induction year involves a gradual process of inviting beginning teachers to look hard at their own and others' teaching, to develop ways of analyzing, articulating and effectively communicating with others about the goals and processes of their practice. Through the assisted performance they take part in, which follows a longer process of legitimate peripheral participation in a broad conversation about teaching, new teachers not only develop knowledge and skills about teaching but also habits of mind. These encourage the teacher to see teaching as something that is worthy of serious scrutiny, that can be jointly constructed and that benefits from the critical eyes of colleagues.

Through this process, novices come to see teaching as more of a collective enterprise than a privatized act. One new teacher, in describing her experience in working closely with her teaching research group to develop her lesson she (successfully) took to a district competition, claimed that "this was a collective achievement". She had come to see that "behind a lesson is a collective".

Much of induction – particularly highly-valued informal practices – takes the sharing and gaining of experience as both the goals and the forms of teacher learning. But here one sees the dilemmas inherent in induction in a period of reform of practice. If one is to improve by exchanging experience, but experience reflects what has occurred in the past, not what one might anticipate for a new and different future, the exchange-centered foundation of professional development is, necessarily, both constrained and constraining.

6. Multiple Stakeholders Supporting Common Goals: Building Variation into a System

One solution to the inherent conservatism of such school-based induction involves many different individuals, reflecting different vantage points. Shanghai's induction policy requires just that. We turn now to a feature of induction which flows from this situation: the interplay of central policy and local variation.

For Teacher Li, induction is both a set of varied activities and the opportunity to join, with increasing involvement, a culture of teaching, one that has a shared focus – the curriculum – and a common language. From her perspective, the policy of induction is less prominent than the programs and practices. Yet the very complexity of these programs and practices depends upon a robust policy, one that puts in place a system of inter-linking parts that simultaneously support a central task yet allow for variation. Shanghai's approach strongly supports the interaction of culture and system. In this section, we explore the challenges of making support for new teachers a system-wide reality, doing so in ways connected to and building on culture.

Shanghai's induction is highly systematic; it works on several connected levels. The formal induction policy lays these out, but also allows sufficient latitude for details to be worked out in the process of implementation. Induction simultaneously relies on at least three levels, but each has its unique function.

Roughly speaking, policy setting and co-ordination is the central level's responsibility. The district Bureau of Education is to establish a plan for training and set standards for evaluation, while additionally inspecting the induction plan at the school level. It is also to hold up outstanding examples of mentoring and other induction support for dissemination. The district College of Education is to oversee and organize induction training and guidance, as well as organize evaluation and record keeping. The school, identified in the policy document as the "main base for new teacher training" (Shanghaishi Jiaoyu Weiyuanhui Shizichu, 1998, p. 79), is similarly obliged to develop an induction plan, to provide mentoring and to develop plans for and carry out documented evaluation of the novice's learning and the mentor's mentoring (see Figure 6).

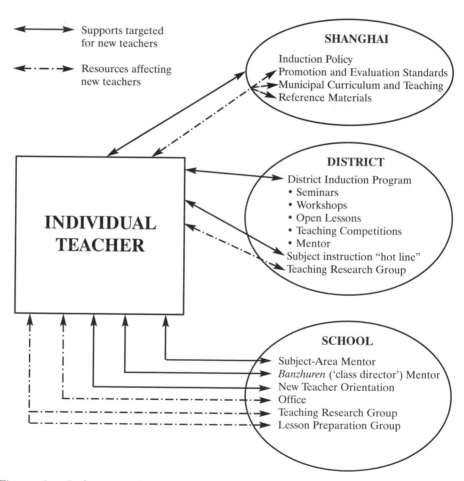

Figure 6: *Induction of beginning middle grades mathematics teachers in Shanghai*

In order to carry out the induction program, multiple stakeholders are involved. For so many people to be involved in induction, there needs to be both co-ordination of and meaningful articulation among the various parts and participants. Co-ordination of induction of some kind occurs at each level. It is not simply a matter of people working at different levels – central, district and school: additionally, within each of those levels, the various programs, activities or policies require the involvement of different groups of people.

Certainly, at the central level, the Education Commission Teacher and Staff Training Section is directly involved. But the section responsible for teaching research and the Commission for Curriculum and Teaching Material Reform also have a clear connection to new teachers through their work with districts and schools. Similar patterns are evident at the district and the school, where teaching research staff, as well as mentors, administrators and others are all involved in the training of beginning teachers.

Central guidance from policy and incentives

The central (Shanghai Municipal Education Commission) level guides the policy's implementation through a structure of incentives and rewards, over and above the simple (but important) regulations it issues. Consider, for example, how its treatment of mentoring not only makes mentoring a piece of induction but also encourages a kind of mentoring that goes beyond replicating the work of the mentor to ground the learning of the novice in theory and principles.

As Zhang Yuhua, the head of the Education Commission's Teacher and Staff Training Section, explained:

> If the mentoring is "experiential imitation" (*jinyanxing de mofang*), the mentor gets no credit [towards promotion]. If the experience is raised to the level that it recognizes and reflects a theory or theories, we give credit. Experiential imitation, for example, is when I write this way and you follow me in the exact way; I do an experiment and you do another following me. For this, no credit. But, when I do an experiment, and there is the question, "Why do I do this experiment?", then I have to study a theory or theoretical model. This is given credit. [...]
>
> In the past, our old teachers mentoring the young teachers were a model of experiential imitation. Now through this measure [i.e. a new policy giving credit only for mentoring if it is theoretically grounded or oriented towards research], the old teachers are gradually led into recognition that mentoring new teachers should not be just imitating experience. So, this measure played a role getting them to do this.

From the Education Commission's point of view, the success of induction policy rests in part on its articulation with other policies. Zhang Yuhua set the incentive structure for mentoring in the context of broader policies of professional development (which include grades and rankings for experienced teachers).

> When we say this, we do not mean training new teachers exists by itself. All these policies have come together as a whole set. That is to say, we have a general continuing education system, in which for senior-rank teachers, there are 540 professional development/study hours required, of which 300 hours are for theme-based research. Through such research, it is intended that all senior-rank teachers have certain research projects. [...] Therefore, in mentoring, this provides sources for theoretical support.

The role of districts and the variation they afford

Having a central policy, embedded in a broader policy, is important for Shanghai's induction. Yet for it to succeed and be sustained in Shanghai, as in any system, induction policies must be developed which are responsive to local conditions.

Here, districts provide a distinctive way in which induction can be both coherent yet varied. Shanghai's districts make possible a system which is distinctive in being neither top–down nor bottom–up. Instead, the district offers great possibility for connecting top and bottom in support of a common goal. The result is a system which works through the middle.

Working the middle ground

We witnessed one such example during our fieldwork when a district mathematics specialist gave a lecture on 'how to listen to a lesson' to the lower-secondary mathematics teaching research group heads from all the schools in the district. Seventy teachers first observed an eighth-grade mathematics lesson, taught by a young teacher in his fourth year of teaching. Immediately following this, after the pupils had filed out, the district mathematics specialist gave an hour's lecture on classroom-observation-based evaluation.

He sprinkled his comments with references to and examples of teaching he had recently observed, including the lesson his audience had just observed. But his comments, in a pattern that seems common across district mathematics specialists, combined attention to concrete details with principles and conceptual arguments. His talk outlined what to look at and consider when one observes a class, but he consistently would make comments about distinctive issues related to observing lessons of novice teachers.

For example, he noted that 'knowledge consolidation' – one aspect of what he saw as "delivery of knowledge" – tends to be especially important to pay attention to when looking at young teachers' teaching. He claimed that they often feel this is "too easy" and hence "underemphasize it", even though, he argued, it is a crucial aspect of learning. His talk identified not only areas in which new teachers might need particular assistance, but suggested that the observer/evaluator needs to work with the young teacher to "help develop the novice teacher's teaching capabilities in a planned and stage-by-stage manner".

This district specialist works in the middle ground connecting theory and practice. Coming from the district, supporting a vision of teaching endorsed in the mathematics curriculum reforms and speaking to teachers from schools, he works in the middle terrain between the academic, theoretical or policy center and individual school. And by connecting his work on improving teaching to his more focused comments on supporting new teacher development, he connects induction to the stream of teacher learning.

While the sea of teachers in the room reminded us of the size and scope of this large community, the presentation focused on clear goals for teaching. Finally, this lecture was to be the first in a series the district was organizing to support school leaders in their work with and induction of new teachers. In short, the lecture reflected a high degree of articulation between levels of the system, the induction program within the broader system of teacher professional development and induction with curricular reform.

Similarly, while the central policy indicates roles for each level of the system to participate in assessment, it is clear from interviews that the district plays a key role in supervising the evaluation process. Teachers failing to pass the assessment at the end of their first year seemed very rare. In 2000, in Pudong District, for example, only about ten out of the cohort of five hundred probationers were not able to pass on time and their delayed transition to regular status tended to be because they had not attended required district workshops or had not submitted required work associated with their training program.

In Songjiang District, an official explained that:

> Every new teacher has to do certain things, the report lesson, turn in lesson plans, analyze test results. They have to write something that relates to some specialized topic and we evaluate them on these dimensions and on their pupils' test scores. These new teachers can be ranked as outstanding, some who might not pass and the vast majority fall in the middle. It is very rare that someone doesn't pass. One reason this doesn't happen is that there is this intensive mentoring and the district also requires the school mentor to eval-

73

uate the novice both semesters. The mentor has to go and listen to classes: we give very clear directions to the school level, so it is very rare for a teacher not to pass, as the school is working very hard.

Districts were quite similar in having few instances of teachers not passing their probationary period and the explanation given in Songjiang seems to resonate with what we learned elsewhere. But in evaluation, as in other aspects, we found variation in how induction operates on the ground. Clearly, induction in Shanghai is a system that assumes local conditions and needs vary, and hence the details of how the system's policies will operate (or even what they are in terms of actual curriculum, for example) will get worked out at the middle and lower levels.

Maximizing variation

It seems that part of the effectiveness of the Shanghai induction policy is its ability to maximize variation: that is, rather than see variation as an instance of policy failure, officials at the central level talked about the need to build variation into the policy. Zhang Yuhua described the way variation comes into play:

> We have a common requirement for every district: what the common criteria for a qualified teacher are. These criteria serve as a basis for evaluating and approving initial professional rank [upon transition from probationary to permanent status]. The second basis is the Teacher Certificate promulgated by China. For a teacher to obtain the certificate, we have some work requirements that are common for teachers in Shanghai. Beyond this, every district, every school works on the basis of its own characteristics. What kind of teachers it wants to train determines the kind of mentors it matches with the new teachers. So this reflects an individuality requirement. The common requirements are complementary to the individual requirements.

This illustrates the pivotal role of districts, operating in the middle between central expectations and local conditions:

> What we have is a uniform standard for evaluating teaching. In implementation, the districts create their own features themselves.

The district appears to have a significant role in defining expectations for school-based mentoring and in creating external support for new teachers. Faculty and administrators from what was formerly the Shanghai Municipal College of Education suggest that the district work varies. For example, Songjiang District, a traditionally rural area, has district-level mentors, serving both as subject-matter mentors and *banzhuren* mentors, for each new teacher. Each school also provides a subject-matter and *banzhuren* mentor for each first-year teacher. In effect, then, in this district, one new teacher has four mentors. A consequence of this arrangement is that district-level people work with a cohort of new teachers – across the district – over time. At times, this means that the district-level mentor goes to individual schools; at other times, all of the new teachers associated with that mentor gather at one central place. [28]

Zhabei District, on the other hand, is a historically poor district that is making the transition to being 'on the rise'. The hallmark of its school improvement programs has been a school-based reform called 'success education' *(chenggong jiaoyu)*. This program shifts the focus of schooling from educating a small number of successful pupils to do well on examinations to trying to provide education for all pupils by starting where the learners are. The district's induction program is also heavily school-based. The role of district courses and enthusiasm for discussing them both seemed small.

The district personnel played a role – as thoughtful expert – in a seminar we observed that was convened by Zhabei #8 Lower Secondary School as part of their school-based training site program (a professional development course on mathematics teaching, based at and run by the school, offered to teachers throughout the district). The time allocation during this particular session, focusing on problem design, involved individual teachers taking part and presenting mathematics problems or exercises they had designed, guided by a master mathematics teacher from the school and the district mathematics education professional developer.

The image was that the school took the lead and the district actively supported. The district personnel clearly had worked closely with school people over years to develop jointly many of the ideas that permeated the approach to teacher development (including new teacher development) in the district – but induction had a distinctly school-based emphasis.

This contrasts with Pudong District, a rapidly growing new urban area, which has the largest number of new teachers. In fact, in some schools, almost the entire staff is made up of new teachers. In this district, there is an energetic champion of teacher induction efforts. Instead of investing in district mentors, Pudong has invested in district new teacher curriculum planning and courses. There is now a district-wide curriculum for new teachers with a formal framework (that has undergone revision over the past two years).

The director of the program talked about induction in terms of a coherent program. Laid out in a grid organized along categories of learning goals for new teachers, the plan provides a comprehensive schema for describing what new teachers need to learn, where they get opportunities to learn this, when in their induction year this learning should take place and how that learning is to be assessed. From this perspective, school-level support is subsumed under the district's plan, rather than being separate from it. In just the past two years, Pudong has moved to become even more systematic in its district program, developing a 'handbook' for new teachers (a kind of record of their work and learning) and revising the district-level new teacher curriculum.

Xuhui District, a more developed and affluent community, offers yet another contrast. When we asked district personnel about teacher induction, they pointed to three different sections in the district College of Education: Training Section (*peixunbu*), Teaching Research Section (*jiaoyanshi*) and the Teaching Program Office (*jiaowuchu*). Each plays some part in activities that can involve the new teacher. In this district, it appears that teacher induction is not treated as a function separate from all teacher development. Rather, it is folded into teacher research and curriculum work.

New teachers who come without any prior teacher preparation participate in specific activities organized by the teaching program office, but the vast majority of new teachers – those coming with some pre-service education – get most of their district-level induction support through the other two offices (and general professional development activities and courses organized by them), rather than in induction-specific seminars.

All districts provide support to new teachers; all take some responsibility for assessing them. And all are mindful of Shanghai's policy directives regarding the goals of induction. Where there is variation, it is around a core of givens. Yet the variation, from the ground, does make the experience for the new teacher somewhat different by district (as well as by school). How districts define 'training' varies. Shanghai's Municipal Education Commission delegates responsibility for training to the districts, but does not define what that training is.

Across the districts, there is considerable variation in the definition of training. Some districts conceptualize it as a collection of workshops, others as a more coherent curriculum that unfolds over time; some frame it as individual relationships with mentors, some as belonging to a collective. In addition, where the training is located and who teaches the new teachers varies as well. Furthermore, it appears that the relationship between the district and schools varies for a variety of reasons, including resources within individual schools, the number of new teachers in the district and capacity at the College of Education level, among others.

Policies around induction in Shanghai now take into account the variation among the learners (the new teachers) as well as district-level variation. In terms of variation within the population of new teachers, there are different requirements and program components based on whether one is a new teacher coming with prior pre-service preparation or not (that is, coming directly from some other higher education program). Now, there is also specific training required by the Education Commission for teachers coming from outside Shanghai, even those with prior teaching experience. This training reflects the recognition that Shanghai is its own educational world – with its unique policies, curriculum and reform history, all contributing, policy makers argue, to a distinctive school climate.

Challenges in sustaining systems for induction within teacher development

How induction can be provided in efficient and effective ways is a thorny policy question in any setting. Shanghai's size and diversity make the challenge of creating workable systems for professional development very complex. Shanghai's current solution, one gaining attention nationally in China, has been to shift to a single system of life-long education.

In the 1990s, analysts criticized the inefficient arrangement of two independent specialized systems – one for pre-service preparation and the other for in-service development. Shanghai's original six higher education teacher training institutions – some locally administered, while another was under the central Chinese authority – created a situation of overlap and duplication. There appeared to be an ironic imbalance in resources, with the locally-funded institutions actually better supported than the more prestigious, national East China Normal University.

Another seeming contradiction was the arrangement that had the higher-level university (East China Normal) only providing training for pre-service (B.A.) students, while lower-level institutions with less academically qualified faculty were charged with providing post-B.A. training of experienced teachers. These structural problems were compounded by the city's predicted shift in manpower needs – with greater demand for upper secondary teachers and a sharp reduction in the numbers of elementary teachers needing to be prepared. Facing what they saw as too many institutions, the municipal authorities redesigned the institutional landscape.

Using economy of scale arguments, they moved to reduce dramatically the number of freestanding institutions of higher education and professional development. Arguing that it made better educational sense to conceive of professional development across a continuum, one that would involve the strongest resources in supporting all teachers, the Shanghai government moved to consolidate smaller, lower-status colleges into the leading teacher training universities (Lu, 2000). It redefined the mission of these universities to charge them with the responsibility of providing both pre-service and in-service education.

77

But this transition has, of course, come at some cost. Each of the many kinds of institutions, formally autonomous, involved in teacher training – teacher training schools, colleges of education, teacher training colleges and universities – had distinct identities, came to represent vested interests and possessed unique institutional histories. The culture clash as institutions merged and were redefined is unsurprising, but clearly difficult for some.

Members of the former Shanghai Municipal College of Education complain about the lack of understanding of the real problems of teachers that their new institutional home has, while university faculty reel at the teaching load they are now expected to take on in fulfilling the university's new mission to offer continuing education. Additionally, many feel unprepared for this new kind of work. Yet as the universities have moved into professional development, the delicate middle-ground work of the districts becomes (some argue) more important, while at the same time (others worry) more vulnerable.

In terms of policy and implementation, induction in Shanghai depends on careful articulation of parts. Districts and schools have been able to succeed in providing vital guidance and support to beginning teachers in so far as they have the staff and other resources to do this. We clearly saw cases in which individual schools were poorly prepared to provide the kind of mentors new teachers most needed. Principals talked about the fact that a good mentor is not simply an experienced teacher, but one who is able to reflect articulately on his or her own practice.

In schools with few experienced teachers, choices about who might be a mentor were often especially limited. Apart from this issue, however, schools for the most part seemed to have worked out the resources – especially time – that allow them to give sustained support to new teachers. While they do not have to deal with particularly challenging problems of releasing teachers from classroom instruction time to engage in induction activity, they nevertheless were mindful of the demands the induction program puts not only on the new teacher – having to attend a district seminar, for example – but also on mentors, curriculum heads, teaching research group leaders and others. Yet one teacher explained that all the concentrated resources invested in a beginning teacher should not be seen as an investment in an individual. As he claimed, "This isn't for the teacher, it's for the pupils".

One reason school resource variations may be less problematic is because in some cases districts can compensate for school weaknesses. But there is no comparable back-up for districts and the pressure on districts to find ways to carve out and work the middle ground discussed earlier seems very real, especially in the wake of reconfigurations of higher education and a newly competitive market that district Colleges of Education face from challenges by school-based providers and universities. One college administrator lamented that the College, in its defense, had had to cast itself as a kind of medicine that could cure all ailments – versatile in filling every need.

Where districts have been able to create a successful niche is in their offering some special insider/outsider perspective, with faculty who have both close links to schools and the resources to engage in research. The challenge, they lament, is that "the universities don't see us as being theoretical enough; the schools see us as being too theoretical". A second challenge they face is in providing situated, sustained support to individual teachers and schools while serving hundreds of teachers. Finally, district personnel suggested that, even though much of induction work revolves around learning about practice that can only happen in and from practice, their job continued to be complicated by new teachers coming with pre-service backgrounds that increased the induction needs. In their view, teacher education's continued weaknesses make their job harder.

The experience of the universities and district Colleges of Education in the midst of the reform of professional development highlight fundamental dilemmas about locating and creating knowledge for and about teaching. In district after district, we heard heated remarks about the vulnerability of college faculty, whose academic credentials typically differ from the university faculty. But these comments were always combined with impassioned defenses of particular kinds of knowledge that they felt they have to offer – a blend of insider/outsider understandings.

Equally impassioned remarks came from distinguished university faculty, who bemoaned the lack of a research basis in professional development. Left unresolved in these debates are the more complex questions about what kinds of knowledge are at the heart of professional development, where that knowledge is located and how it is best inculcated and supported in teachers themselves. These challenges were lamented by district staff concerned about new teacher induction programs. But the most serious challenge to induction in Shanghai, say many insiders, is the possibility of induction existing on paper – in formal, perfunctory activity – but not in any vital work that really affects teachers.

7. Conclusion

Induction in Shanghai already has a history. While it continues to change, clarifying its goals, rewards and structures, it seems so much part of the ordinary lives of both new and experienced teachers and schools – no matter how the policy is interpreted – that it seems difficult to believe that induction practices will evaporate or become mere shells of the on-going work.

Perhaps we have this reaction as outsiders. Looking at the system and practices related to induction in Shanghai, we are struck by how induction in a system where on-going teacher learning is a significant part of schooling looks strikingly different from a place where induction is a separate, and lonely, policy. Shanghai's induction demonstrates a tight link between broader cultural practices – around the curriculum, of how teachers talk and look at teaching – and systems for support for new teachers. It appears that the ways in which each reinforces the other gives strength to the induction policies and practices that have developed.

As we examine this setting, we see four dominant features to induction as it has developed and as it is experienced by new teachers in Shanghai. It comprises a highly varied set of activities, aimed at developing a relatively small range of fundamental skills and some specific knowledge. Its focus on curriculum materials helps beginning teachers acquire the wisdom of practice. This is in keeping with broader cultural norms of teaching – which treat teaching as a practice open to scrutiny and collectively shared – to support and make particular accommodations for new teachers which help them develop a common language and joint understanding about teaching. These are both vital for participation in the community of teaching. Induction depends on the interplay of central policy implemented through variation; it requires attending simultaneously to system concerns and cultural practices.

Yet as we look across these four themes, we note some broader points. Shanghai's system reminds us of the need to consider important features of the context when exploring the nature of induction. For example, the fact that we offer here stories of induction into teaching – a profession with a culture, norms, practices and expectations that fundamentally shape the character of that induction – is a non-trivial point. Of the many things this can teach us, whether as outsiders or insiders, is the importance, when inquiring into the nature of induction, of considering the kind of teaching induction is organized to help teachers construct.

This case suggests that focusing our gaze too narrowly on induction without asking about the nature of the profession and the practice it supports may leave us missing important insights into why induction is constructed as it is, with the goals, structures, forms and relationships it has. Similarly, assumptions about how teachers learn prove to be central to how induction is organized and carried out.

Shanghai's approach makes a strong case for recognizing the importance of induction as a phase. The underlying premises for induction in Shanghai suggest that there is crucial and complex knowledge that teachers need to learn early in their practice and that this learning can best be done in, around and through practice.

But seeing Shanghai's induction as a dynamic system, with, for example, tensions as educational reforms attempt a transformation of lower secondary education and of the teacher education system, reminds us of the very real challenges at the heart of induction. The delicate relationships between institutional participants in this story speak to how hard it can be to achieve the comprehensive range of supports that induction calls for.

Shanghai's induction system points out the complex possibilities of having common goals and policies through variation. Its system-wide reach appears to come in part through its ability to respond to differences across the system. Yet achieving this precarious balance of coherence and diversity requires equally delicate institutional arrangements. Finally, the complexities of Shanghai's experience raise the dilemmas inherent in a practice – induction – which has as its joint aims both reproducing the teaching profession and transforming it.

Acknowledgements

This research would not have been possible without the support of many people in Shanghai working in educational policy, research, professional development and teaching. Leadership at the Shanghai Municipal Education Commission provided crucial help as individuals offered their valuable time generously with us. Zhang Minsheng, Zhang Yuhua and Zhang Fusheng each shared their vantage points on induction and mathematics education reform and gave us useful suggestions for the conduct of our study. We thank Gu Lingyuan and his colleagues at the Shanghai Academy of Educational Sciences for their many contributions to this study. They helped facilitate arrangements for three of our four study trips, mobilized districts to compile statistical data for us, were willing to be interviewed repeatedly over the course of our study and offered significant insights based on their own knowledge and research on these issues. Professor Gu's office also helped us locate two graduate students, Bao Jinsheng and Wu Yingkang, who gave us help of all kinds during David Pimm's fieldwork. In addition, Professor Gu and colleagues provided a critical reading of a draft of this chapter, giving us useful feedback.

University faculty, central and departmental administrators and research scholars in many units of both East China Normal University and Shanghai Teachers' University welcomed us each visit, making it possible for us to observe classes and student teaching; they shared curriculum documents, organized faculty seminars and student focus groups, and were willing to be interviewed themselves, many for repeated conversations. We also thank many in the districts – both their Bureaus of Education and their

Colleges of Education – that we studied. Administrators and faculty were generous in letting us interview them over many visits, as well as making possible our rich conversations and observations in their college programs and local schools. Finally, we owe much gratitude to the many teachers and administrators who opened their classrooms and offices to us and reflected on the challenges of teacher learning. While our research agreements preclude us from identifying individuals, these people, too numerous to list, demonstrated intellectual generosity and serious commitments to education and the development of teaching that we deeply appreciate.

Many education scholars and policy officials, while not directly involved in Shanghai education, helped steer us to people, institutions and ideas which proved vital to our work. We thank: Jinfa Cai, Kaiming Cheng, Li Yeping, Liping Ma, Teng Xing, Wang Yingjie and Zhang Linyi.

This chapter reflects ideas developed through many hours of work as a project team. The authors wish to thank Daniel Chazan and David Pimm, as well as Violetta Lazarovici, for the important ways in which they helped develop an approach to the fieldwork, conducted some of that work and supported analyses. Jian Wang, at the University of Nevada-Las Vegas, developed important analyses as well. Others at Michigan State University contributed as interview and videotape translators and analysts: Cheng Haojing, Dai Tiesheng, Li Shuxin, Ni Yongmei, Peng Xioahui, Wu Xiuwen, Zou Zhiwen and Zuo Shengxi. Over the years of our study first Amy Graves, then Jennifer Rosenberger, and finally Darryl Pettway provided crucial staff support, supervised a group of student transcribers and helped keep our project moving forward.

We benefited from thoughtful colleagues who read and commented on drafts of this chapter over many months: Brian DeLany, Robert Floden, Glenda Lappan, Sharon Feiman-Nemser, Catherine Lewis, Jack Schwille, Sharon Schwille, Gary Sykes and Joseph Tobin, as well as the commentary provided by our other advisors, noted elsewhere in this volume.

We thank all these people for helping us investigate and come to inquire about the complex portrait of teacher learning that Shanghai offers. Without their generous and honest help, producing this chapter would not have been possible.

Chapter 3

Co-operation, Counseling and Reflective Practice: Swiss Induction Programs

Senta Raizen,
with Mary Ann Huntley and Edward Britton

1. Supporting the first two years of teaching

We start this chapter with a look at the real lives of two young beginning teachers at the start of their teaching careers. Markus, whom we interviewed, teaches science and mathematics in a middle school (grades 7–9) in the canton of Zurich; Bertila, whose practice group we observed, teaches mathematics and French in upper elementary school (grades 4–6) in the canton of Bern. The practice group constitutes a common approach to induction for elementary and lower secondary teachers: it is a facilitated group of novice teachers from across a geographic area within a canton, who together engage in solving problems arising from their classrooms. Zurich, on the other hand, features a required course as part of induction, before teachers can be fully certified. Though this course requirement is unique, Zurich's use of voluntary counseling reflects induction practices in other cantons in the country.

The stories of these two teachers illustrate the rich variety of activities characterizing the Swiss notion of *Berufseinführung* – the "leading into the profession" – for beginning teachers. Yet a common philosophy undergirds these induction activities: the "leading in" involves deeply experienced colleagues who are specially trained for their counseling and mentoring role; nevertheless, the beginning teacher is seen as an adult learner who has a large say in the content of the induction activities. Most significantly, the emphasis is on the development of the individual as a whole, as well as the development of an effective, self-confident teacher.

Markus's induction experiences

Markus has just started his third year of teaching. He now teaches in the canton of Zurich in a middle school (grades 7–9) of 120 pupils (two classes per grade). He teaches mathematics/geometry, *Man and the Environment*

83

E. Britton et al. (eds.), Comprehensive Teacher Induction, 83–140.
© 2003 *Kluwer Academic Publishers. Printed in the Netherlands.*

(an integrated science, geography and social studies course new in the curriculum), technical drawing and a shop class that involves working with materials and tools. He received his undergraduate training in Philosophy II (Natural Sciences, including mathematics), obtaining a four-year university degree with a major in chemistry and minors in both mathematics and geology. He undertook all his teacher preparation coursework in Zurich.

Markus's practice teaching was done in several cantons, in different types of schools and with pupils from diverse social backgrounds. However, he never worked with ethnic minority pupils, as pupils who are not proficient in German usually attend schools other than the regular middle schools. He had three sets of practice-teaching experiences, the first observing the mentor teacher and teaching a little, the second instance involved teaching with the mentor present and the third planning and teaching lessons on his own.

In general, he found all the practice sessions and related didactics classes helpful [1], acquainting him with problems of real teaching (e.g. what do you do with classrooms unequipped for experiments?) that could then be discussed in the didactics classes. The didactics teachers seemed to him more effective when they worked with direct feedback from the students' practice-teaching sessions. One mentor teacher really impressed him; Markus adopted a lot of his teaching strategies and has also asked this teacher for advice on a number of occasions since starting to teach himself.

Markus found it quite difficult to find the job he was looking for. Positions are scarce for a male teacher with a Philosophy II degree who wants a full-time job teaching mathematics and the sciences. Most experienced science and mathematics teachers are males who work full time and, having found a position to their liking (which takes four years on average), they remain in that same position for the rest of their professional lives (especially in the countryside). Women change jobs more often (they get pregnant, for one thing), more often work part-time and usually teach languages and history (the Philosophy I fields). So women are really in demand for the science and mathematics positions, since there are now so few of them teaching in the technical fields.

Markus has completed a four-week induction course, which is compulsory in the canton of Zurich. He found the course very helpful:

> I was really grateful for the course and its down-to-earth, realistic grounding in actual teaching. It gave me much-needed time to reflect on my work.

The course needs to be completed by beginning teachers within the first two years of teaching. After two years of teaching and completion of the induction course, Markus (as with all teachers in Zurich) has completed the 'beginning' phase and is considered to be a fully licensed teacher by the canton. As he sees it, however, the distinction between beginning and fully-licensed teachers will become less sharp under the canton's proposed new employment provisions, which mandate one-year rather than the traditional four-year contracts for all teachers, not just beginning teachers.

Markus has found no time for other professional development since he started teaching. Informally, however, he has created a community for himself. Ever since graduating from teacher preparation, he has been meeting with ex-fellow Philosophy II students, now teachers themselves, on a voluntary basis three or four times a year (usually on Wednesday afternoons, when Swiss schools close early). The teachers exchange experiences, materials and information on cantonal and school policies, as well as on testing and pupil evaluation. Initially, the meeting was a social dinner, but by their second meeting they had already decided to make it more professionally oriented. Topics concerning teaching are chosen and presented in turn by one of the teachers.

This group has been a great source of support for Markus. Together, the participants plan lessons, get help on instructional problems or undertake work on their curriculum or action-research projects. In the future, he expects to spend four weeks over a period of four years on further education; this will count toward the five percent time allotted to all teachers in the canton for professional development. Markus will probably spend two weeks of that time taking a didactics course in a particular discipline; the other two weeks he will most likely devote to more general pedagogic work.

Before Markus's time, the canton mandated counselors to help with induction during the first two years. This counseling was compulsory and carried out by an experienced middle-school teacher; it also involved evaluation. But a few years ago, this practice of obligatory counseling/evaluation was abolished in Zurich. In part, the tension between the two functions, those of counseling versus evaluation of the beginning teacher, made the counselor's role problematic and led to the policy's demise. Now, during their first two years, beginning teachers have the right to seek counsel voluntarily from any teacher of their own choice.

Some new teachers prefer to work on their own and are glad that counseling is no longer compulsory, while others continue to seek out support and advice. In these latter cases, the counselor observes the teacher's lessons and afterwards discusses them, offering advice. The maximum number of counseling sessions a beginning teacher can apply for is sixteen. A second set of sixteen counseling sessions is possible if specially applied for. The absolute maximum is thirty-two visits. Mostly, however, two visits from a counselor are sufficient to solve a beginning teacher's specific problem.

Although Markus has had no major problems, he wants to make use of the counseling possibilities offered, even though he finds his older teaching colleagues to be skeptical about asking others for help. They tend to want to keep things to themselves and do not understand why a beginning teacher would ask for external professional counsel. When Markus told some of his school colleagues that a counselor was coming to visit his classes (to help him work on a particular part of his practice that he wants to improve), they assumed he must be having some major teaching problems.

> But I and my friends want to open up our classrooms, not just to counselors, but to parents, maybe to talk about their work, or specialists in a particular topic like the environment and others who can help. Although we get wonderful training in didactics and methodology, it is another thing to put what we learned in class into practice, yet we are expected to be competent from the start.

Markus knows counseling really works. One of his friends, a very good teacher, got such a difficult class that she had to apply for counseling. The counselor came to the class four or five times and even came to a parent evening to help out. The teacher learned how to work with these pupils and their parents, and decided to stay. (Markus thinks he read somewhere that, by the end of the first six years of teaching, 40–50 percent of teachers have left the profession.)

The greatest problem that Markus has experienced is the heavy workload. This is aggravated by a mountain of administrative duties: everything from his pupils' absences to their dentist visits must be recorded. What makes it worse is the huge amount of curricular material to work through, especially for the integrated, three-year, middle-school course *Man and the Environment*, which includes a wide range of specific subjects: chemistry, physics, biology, geography, history, art and singing.

Although subject specialists do come in to teach home economics, art and several other subjects, the quality and availability of these specialists varies across schools. His teacher preparation did not prepare him to teach this wide range of subjects and he finds the course requires an excessive amount of time. Rough curriculum guidelines are given by the canton, but the choice of specific subject matter is up to the teacher. This freedom of choice is quite a burden for Markus:

> I think it would be more practical for beginning teachers if we had specific guidelines like we have for mathematics. As it is, I tend to rely for choice of subject matter in teaching *Man and the Environment* on my personal interests and competence, falling back on my own middle-school physics. Even the physics I had in the *Gymnasium* was too abstract.

If Markus had any wishes for himself as a teacher, he would ask for smaller classes. (Swiss classes average 20 or 21 pupils; the maximum is about 28.) Although preparation time is the same whether the class is large or small, grading papers and paying attention to the pupils of a small class and their parents would make a world of difference to him.

Bertila's practice group

> I run out of time to do all the things I plan for my lessons – there is
> so much paperwork to do all the time and then the canton's instruc-
> tional plans really demand a lot.

This is Bertila's big problem as a first-year teacher in the canton of Bern, which she has brought to her practice group. Her problem is echoed by the others in the group. Bertila teaches two key subjects, French and mathematics, to five different grade-six classes 21 periods per week (a full load is 29 periods for the elementary grades). [2]

The 'practice group' is one means of helping her make the transition from her teacher preparation to the full responsibilities of the classroom she faces as a beginning teacher. The group includes four other beginning teachers from different elementary schools (grades 1–6) in the canton. The group has decided to meet for eight sessions, each lasting three hours. Twelve of these hours (half the number of sessions) are supported, i.e. paid substitute teachers are provided so the group can meet during the school day – a contribution from the canton.

The practice group meetings take place in the school, preferably in the classroom, of one of the teachers, who take turns hosting. The group is mediated by a facilitator/counselor, an experienced teacher herself. She has had special training for this role from members of Bern University's Institute of Cognitive Psychology; her particular interest is art therapy. The practice group's meetings always are social occasions; everyone has brought something to drink or eat for the break in the middle of the three-hour session and at its conclusion.

The counselor starts the meeting by asking the teachers which flower they associate with themselves as a teacher. She directs them to stick with the first image that comes to their minds and to think of possible meanings the image could have. Two picture themselves as roses with stems and thorns. Thorns are for protection – a rose needs to be handled with care – the rose smells nice, it is closed and then unfolds, like a person. The rose is also associated with love.

Two others picture themselves as sunflowers, denoting warmth, a sunny disposition, strength, standing tall, being friendly. It is important that the children are happy. The sunflower blooms brightly, strongly, but only for a short time. The core of the sunflower can be used again. Another teacher sees herself as a tulip: planted in winter and blossoming in spring, but it does not flower for long. The tulip has two separate parts (bulb and flower); this teacher does not know if she really wants to teach or take up another career. The counselor talks about imagining herself (when she taught) as a gentian, beautifully blue and strong.

During the next part of the session, Bertila has a chance to share her impressions as a new teacher. The teachers, several of whom already have had a year or more of teaching experience, swap stories in response to questions. What gives you energy? What takes energy? What gives you joy? What do you find difficult?

On the positive side, the teachers talk with pleasure about the spontaneous reactions of the children ("I love this about my job", observes Bertila); surprisingly wonderful moments, like when the children sing in class. The teachers speak of being able to open worlds of possibilities to children, about good days when the children are happy, about parents who are supportive. Two of the teachers who are job-sharing like the way their team-teaching is working out.

But, there are also many problems. Some parents can prove very tiresome, perpetually interfering. The respect teachers once enjoyed does not seem the same as in the past and some of the group feel insecure about how to deal with parents. And Bertila airs her problem with time pressure. One consequence is that she has too little time to pay attention to individual children. As she says: "I can't be everywhere – monitor everything".

She also has difficulties with homework – how much is allowed or should be given? Other teachers feel under continuous obligation to perform at a high level. Work never seems finished and the teachers often trudge home with armloads of work. It is very difficult to find time to relax.

The counselor notes emerging themes. The problems this group is airing are faced by most beginning teachers: time pressure, obligation to perform, dealing with parents. She pursues Bertila's homework problem: "Some children keep on 'forgetting' their assignments, no matter what I do".

The counselor tells them the canton's policy (one hour per week for grades 1–3; three hours per week for grades 4–6; no homework during the weekend). But how do you judge how long homework really takes? Bertila thinks a particular assignment would take 20 minutes, but a pupil reports that "I worked for two and a half hours". Another teacher says parents are always complaining – some say there is too much homework, some say there is too little. The 'homework problem' is an aspect of teaching these teachers were barely aware of as students and that was not dealt with effectively even in their pre-service practice teaching.

The teachers continue to exchange experiences, hints, make suggestions and proposals on how to help children do their homework. One comes up with the idea of using the 'forgetting homework' problem as a theme for her class about learning and work habits and to discuss with the pupils what distracts them and why they take a different amount of time. Other suggestions include stressing the importance of having a place where you *only* do homework and learning to tidy up and have order.

This leads to a discussion about how much time teachers can take to create order in the class. Bertila says she does not want to drill the children, she does not want to be a policewoman. The counselor asks her why not, noting that order can be positive – a help to children. She comments:

> Don't just assume that parents will always provide the structure most children need and desire. Your goal is to solve the 'forgetting of homework' problem and have children learn to be responsible. The development of an intrinsic drive to do this is essential, for the external control of the children is bad, creating a bad climate. Besides, it simply doesn't work in the long run.

Orderly classrooms are stressed in Switzerland's German cantons as being conducive to effective learning and so it is not surprising that the teachers exchange ideas about how to help the children do their homework and keep order. Everyone admits that pupils' poor work habits are a drain on instruction: it takes a lot of time to check for pencils, scissors and other utensils (which are always disappearing anyway). Someone suggests that special hooks to hang up the scissors help, so that the teacher knows exactly when something is missing. Files, colored folders, reserving one hour each week to tidy up, giving pupils time to file their work so they become responsible for their own work and materials are all offered as helpful hints.

The counselor assures the teachers that they are allowed to spend part of the 45-minute lesson establishing order, noting that they should stick to the methods that work for them. She continues:

> The important thing is to be consistent and clear: if teachers are clear about what they want, pupils catch on; if they are ambiguous, pupils notice. Pupils need boundaries, boundaries make them free. Set the boundaries lovingly, but with clarity and strength.

Bertila returns to her concern that she never seems to get to everything she has planned. Another slightly more experienced teacher advises her to relax; she says she also prepares too much material, but notices during the lesson and tries to adjust.

> Find the system by which you get the eighty percent done, consider how much energy you want to expend to get the other twenty percent done and whether the effort is worth it.

The counselor, too, tries to reassure Bertila – observing that after all, she is producing people, not screws. One suggestion to make instructional time more effective is to work with 'learning partnerships', a strategy that involves pairing pupils off. Several teachers report positive experiences with this strategy: working with partners consolidates the good learners' knowledge and gives the teacher time to continue her instructional plan. Sometimes children are better at explaining to each other than the teacher is. The group decides to try and use learning partnerships consciously and share experiences in their next practice group meeting – a kind of small action-research project for this group of teachers.

The last part of the practice group meeting is devoted to a discussion about parent meetings, scheduled for the near future in January. [3] The counselor wants the teachers to think about preparations for these meetings: setting the date, how to begin and end the meeting, practical details, how to structure the specific things they want to talk with parents about. For fifteen minutes, the teachers move around freely and talk to each other about their plans for these meetings. They identify a central issue: what is the purpose of the parent–teacher meeting?

Other issues are also explored: how long should the meeting be? What do you want to know from the parents? Should the child be present or not? Where should the meeting take place – the classroom or the parents' home? (Neither is neutral territory.) Should there be boundaries about where to talk to parents – at restaurants, at casual meetings at the pool, at the store? What 'counts' as a parent meeting?

Everyone agrees that both the teacher and the parents should have the opportunity to express themselves, for children may be different at home and at school. The counselor asks the teachers to consider the meeting's general ambiance – be creative and personal, bring flowers and mineral water. How do you greet the parents and start the conversation? Give the parents a chance to talk first; sometimes, they want to say something so urgently that everything else may be lost till they are able to voice their concern.

What do you do when the conversation threatens to escalate? You might break off the meeting and make another appointment to discuss things in peace and quiet. How do you conclude? Give five minutes notice before the end; use certain sentences to signal that the conversation needs to end; have a watch on the desk.

The practice group meeting concludes with the group deciding (with the counselor's encouragement) that the content of parent–teacher meetings will be the subject for next time. The group sets a date and one of the teachers offers to host the next meeting at her school.

2. The General Study Context

To understand and appreciate the complexities of teacher induction in Switzerland, as mirrored in part by Markus's and Bertila's experiences, it is necessary to understand the larger context in which induction is embedded. Switzerland is a small country. Yet it has 26 independent school systems run by the 26 cantons (states) that make up the Swiss Federation. Given this setting, it would be impossible to describe educational practices for the entire country.

Thus, we attempt to sketch – in broad strokes – the general approach to education in the country, by considering practices in three German-speaking cantons: Bern, Lucerne and Zurich. All three cantons contain both large cities and rural regions. Practices in these cantons vary in interesting ways, due to different histories and policies. Yet the three cantons exhibit a number of commonalities, particularly in their philosophies both of education and of what it takes to help beginning teachers to become successful professionals.

We elected to study these cantons after initial visits to six cantons, recommended to us by Swiss colleagues as worth exploring. While the three cantons we studied in some depth helped us capture some of the similarities and differences in induction practices across Switzerland, they are but a subset of actual practices and need to be treated in that way.

For example, considerable differences exist between the German- and French-speaking cantons with respect to teacher education and induction. Educational authorities in the French cantons believe that teachers emerging from teacher education, which involves rigorous university training in the disciplines they will teach, as well as related didactics courses, are fully capable of taking over teaching responsibilities. We were told in Geneva, the largest French-speaking canton, that support services for beginning teachers did not exist as such. Exploring these differences was beyond the scope of the present study. [4]

The country and some common educational features

According to the TIMSS Encyclopedia (Moser *et al.*, 1997), Switzerland has seven million inhabitants. There are twenty-six cantons (states), of which eighteen are German-speaking (65 percent of the population), seven are French-speaking and one is Italian-speaking. Some 19 percent of the population are immigrants who do not speak any of the three main Swiss languages. [5] By geography and history, the Swiss highly value their independence – as a country, as a canton and as an individual community. The implications for education are profound.

- There is no federal ministry of education. While there are some inter-cantonal institutions, all education decisions and funding are matters of cantonal or local policies and regulations.
- Elementary and lower secondary schools have no principals. There is a teacher-leader or leadership team that facilitates school decision-making by the teaching staff. Schools are tightly tied to their communities; each (or sometimes a group of schools) has its own school board made up of locally prominent or active citizens.
- The country's physical terrain has led to the preservation of many small schools in rural mountain and valley areas.
- Switzerland's direct democracy reaches far down into school policy, with local votes deciding such matters as school structure and, in small communities, even teacher contracts.

After elementary school (grades 1–6), Swiss pupils are tracked into three levels for lower secondary school (grades 7–9), based largely on their teachers' recommendation. The élite, pre-*Gymnasium* track leads directly to the academic pre-university preparation in a senior secondary school known as the *Gymnasium*. (In a few cantons, the *Gymnasium* actually starts at grade 7; in most cantons, it begins at grade 9 or 10.) About 15–20 percent of the lower secondary school cohort constitute this track.

The general lower-secondary track enrols the majority of pupils in an institution known as the *Mittelschule* (literally, the 'middle school'). The third track is technical/vocational in nature. In the cities, this third track is generally filled with immigrant children who need to have more time and help to attain acceptable achievement levels, but in the countryside, the enrollment in this type of school may be as high as 40 percent of the age cohort.

In most cantons, the Swiss lower-secondary school system is in transition, with some cantonal policies moving toward integrating these previously differentiated tracks. There are efforts under way to make the once-clear separation between the pre-*Gymnasium* and the middle-school cohort fuzzier, with some movement of pupils back and forth, with pupils even sharing classes.

In the German-speaking cantons, however, it is still generally true that 15–20 percent of the cohort go on to *Gymnasium* at the upper secondary school level and sit for the *Maturität*, the graduating exam leading directly to university admission without any further entrance examinations. (The élite cohort is somewhat greater in the French cantons and in the cantons comprised of such cities as Geneva and Basel.)

For all pupils, no matter what their track, the critical subjects in grades 7–9 are mathematics, German and French. Pupils' performance in these subjects weigh most heavily in their school reports; these subjects also

comprise the voluntary exams given at the end of grade 9 to demonstrate
pupils' readiness for the *Gymnasium*. Attainment in science counts for
less than in these other subjects. [6]

In the next section, we discuss teacher education and the teaching context in the three cantons we studied in depth.

3. Teacher Education

Here, we summarize teacher preparation practices for all levels of schooling. This is necessary, since the middle grades (the focus of our inquiry)
represent the transition period between elementary and upper secondary
school and thus they need to co-ordinate with both. Moreover, though
grades five and six are still considered part of elementary school, they often
employ specialist teachers for different fields, e.g. languages and mathematics (like Bertila).

The education of teachers in Switzerland is in transition. It is moving
from a split system – extended secondary education sufficing for elementary
school teachers (grades 1–6) and tertiary education for secondary school
teachers – to requiring a tertiary education for all teachers.

In transition: the education of elementary school teachers

Until recently, the *Seminars* (teacher training 'colleges') have been the specific institutions training the elementary teachers in many cantons. They are
considered an extension of the secondary school system, since one used to
be able to start teacher preparation there after only nine years of education
(i.e. after completion of elementary and lower secondary school). This
approach derives from the strong tradition in Switzerland (as in Germany)
of the apprenticeship system. However, some difficulties have developed.
For example, the Swiss elementary teaching diplomas awarded by the
Seminars were not recognized or valued as were teaching diplomas from
other European countries obtained from tertiary institutions. Moreover,
the hope is that content preparation for elementary teachers – considered
weak in some areas – will be improved if their education takes place in a
tertiary institution.

The general idea for the German-speaking cantons is that teacher training will now be done at the professional schools (the *Pädagogischen
Hochschulen*) that are affiliated with or housed within universities. [7]
Zurich is further ahead with this reform: its tertiary-level professional
school is already in place and prospective elementary teachers already
have to attend a special *Gymnasium* prior to enrolling in this school.
Even in Zurich, however, the desire is to enhance the academic level of

professional teacher-preparation institutions, including having the faculty conduct more research and linking the institution to the university.

Beside potentially positive effects, we suspect the changes may lead to some deleterious ones as well: for example, this could lead to breaking the close tie between pre-service education and induction we observed in Zurich, where the pre-service *Seminar* faculty also provide counseling and courses for the beginning elementary teachers they had taught as students a year or two earlier.

In Bern, the proposed changes have been voted through after long deliberation by the canton's parliament. The Bern law and plans as now formulated are quite far-reaching. Even the Center for Continuing Teacher Education, currently a free-standing institution providing professional development and induction services, is not immune from consolidation. It remains to be seen whether the small department of Pedagogy and Didactics at Bern University, currently concerned only with prospective *Gymnasium* teachers, can really absorb or co-ordinate a major part of all teacher education, including delivery of the necessary didactics instruction. A well-informed observer compared this to a mouse attempting to swallow an elephant.

The education of middle-school *(Mittelschule)* teachers

When one considers the rigorous training in both subject matter and peda-gogic content knowledge (didactics) required of middle-school teachers in Switzerland, one can better understand the relative lack of emphasis these areas receive in the induction procedures, as mirrored in Markus's experiences.

University education

All prospective lower and upper secondary teachers must have a *Gymnasium* graduation certificate; it is therefore taken as given that their general school education has been completed. Hence, at the tertiary level, middle-school teachers concentrate on the content and methods for the fields they will be teaching. Prospective middle-school teachers, like all other university students, major at university in either Philosophy I or Philosophy II (though not all Swiss universities use these names). Philosophy I essentially includes all the languages, history, educational and cognitive psychology, clinical psychology and other social sciences. The natural sciences and mathematics make up Philosophy II. The degrees of secondary school teachers and university professors alike carry one of these two designations. (In most cantons, there are special programs and institu-tions for educating teachers of sports, arts and music.)

Zurich serves as an example, as illustrated in Figure 1 below (adapted from Ziegler, 1994, p. 61). When preparing to teach at the lower-secondary level, students must have subject-matter preparation in a major subject (30 semester hours) and two minors (24 semester hours and 14 semester hours). (Bern requires a major and three minors.) For students concentrating in Philosophy II, one of these subjects must be mathematics. These courses are taken at the university and a degree must be obtained.

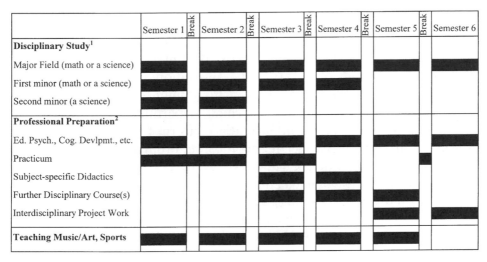

	Semester 1	Break	Semester 2	Break	Semester 3	Break	Semester 4	Break	Semester 5	Break	Semester 6
Disciplinary Study[1]											
Major Field (math or a science)											
First minor (math or a science)											
Second minor (a science)											
Professional Preparation[2]											
Ed. Psych., Cog. Devlpmt., etc.											
Practicum											
Subject-specific Didactics											
Further Disciplinary Course(s)											
Interdisciplinary Project Work											
Teaching Music/Art, Sports											

[1] Provided by university faculty; includes two of the following sciences: biology, chemistry, physics

[2] May include courses to teach grades 7–9 interdisciplinary science, e.g., geology

Figure 1: Zurich preparation of middle-school teachers

In addition, there is professional preparation for teaching, consisting of *didactics* courses that stretch over six semesters. In Zurich, we observed a number of these courses in the teaching of mathematics, physics, chemistry, archaeology and nature study, as well as more general didactics courses (e.g. evaluating the quality of science lessons). The continental concept of didactics education is virtually unknown in North America, and in anglophone countries more generally, and has no simple or ready analogue in these countries' teacher preparation. Didactics in Switzerland consists of the science of teaching, comprising both general principles applicable to teachers' tasks (e.g. how to evaluate course materials or a lesson) and the specifics of teaching a particular subject at a given level.

Didactics classes tend to be much more focused than 'methods' classes in North America, for example; they include both learning theory related to the subject (e.g. common misconceptions and how to address them) and practical applications (e.g. how to conduct a given laboratory demonstration or use alternative curriculum materials). These courses deal quite specifically with teaching strategies for content, use of particular textbooks, conduct of demonstration and pupil labs, presentation of material and ideas put together from the canton curriculum guidelines and appropriate materials, etc.

Didactics courses are both theoretical and practical, but are always focused on classroom practice. In Zurich, these classes are taught in a magnificent grade K–9 school adjacent to the university. The didactics faculty consists of specially qualified teachers with long experience, some of whom also are still teaching pupils in grades 7–9. Some of the more theoretically-oriented didactics courses (for example, educational psychology) are given at the university; the courses aimed more directly at practice are taught in the school.

A didactics lesson

The lesson we observed was in didactics of physics for prospective middle-school teachers. It was a ninety-minute lesson, divided into three segments devoted to different teaching materials and approaches. The first segment dealt with three different computer programs for teaching addition of multiple forces (vector addition). The second segment consisted of a discussion of the structure of the middle-school physics text used in the canton and a closer analysis of one of the chapters to explore how the text's structure can be used to enhance pupils' understanding. The third part of the lesson dealt with what pupils might have learned from an experiment on heat and temperature – a difficult distinction for this age range – that had been conducted the previous day. All three parts of the lesson were continually tied to application in the prospective teachers' future classrooms. We describe the first two parts of the lesson and view it as quite typical of Swiss subject-specific didactics classes.

The teacher started by showing students the goals of the lesson on an overhead (itself a teaching technique). The class then went to the computer lab to look at the three computer programs. The teacher asked them to evaluate the three approaches: a moving diagram of vectors; colliding balls; 'Orbimania', a program that portrays the movement of the bodies within the solar system and provides the velocities, masses and gravitational fields of the sun, earth and moon, and the other planets. The teacher posed leading questions:

> Is this program [the vector diagram] practical? [...] On what level of abstraction is it? [...] Can pupils understand this? [...] Can you give an example of a real problem being illustrated?

A student answered: "No, these are just abstract representations or calculations". The teacher commented further on the vector program:

> The death warrant of a method is if it is too abstract, if you can no longer imagine what kind of problem lies behind the representation, when there is no connection between school physics and the daily physics that pupils can recognize.

The lesson proceeded through evaluating the colliding balls program ("At least you could imagine a billiard game", observed the teacher) and 'Orbimania'. The teacher again asked leading questions: "What kinds of insights could this program give?" Students mentioned that the program could be used to illustrate the movement of astronomical bodies or to explain ocean tides to seventh-graders. The class agreed that this was the best of the three programs for teaching addition of multiple forces. The teacher cautioned that one should always examine and evaluate computer programs before actually using them in the classroom.

The teacher then asked students to discuss in small groups the links between the computer program evaluation they had just completed and a Howard Gardner article (read for homework) on naïve ideas that pupils bring to the classroom. A discussion by students from the different groups followed, facilitated by the teacher's questions.

Student A: There is a conflict between existing naïve ideas formed by everyday experience and scientific knowledge taught in school. If a connection is not consciously made, if the teacher is not aware of the ideas pupils bring to school and addresses them, misconceptions remain isolated from school knowledge.

Student B: Seemingly, pupils think that school knowledge doesn't apply to the outside world, it belongs only to the school environment of exams and problem calculations in the book.

The teacher supported the students' points and encouraged them to expand on them.

Teacher: What is 'everyday physics'? Where does this knowledge come from?

Student C: It's knowledge children have gathered and constructed from their surroundings.

A discussion of the development and location of this knowledge followed. What is derived from experience? How do scientific concepts replace this experiential knowledge?

The teacher affirmed and summarized the discussion.

> Many teachers think children construct their naïve knowledge consciously through their experiences with everyday materials, but, in

fact, models and schemes of how the physical universe works are mostly constructed unconsciously. And these schemes do not match canonical scientific knowledge. If we ignore this experiential 'knowledge' of our pupils in our lessons, physics teaching cannot be successful.

The teacher and students then returned to their science classroom to begin the second part of the lesson, a discussion of the physics textbook with an emphasis on how to use its different components in lesson planning and instruction. The instructional style of this part of the lesson contrasted greatly with that of the computer program evaluations. The teacher explained why it is necessary to understand the intent and structure of the textbook, since the accompanying teacher guide only provides solutions to the problems in the book. He then handed out copies of the book and asked the students to familiarize themselves with the table of contents. The teacher demonstrated the structure of the book with cards on the board (another teaching technique).

Each major physics topic is treated as follows (though not necessarily always in the same sequence).

- Each topic starts with an introductory experiment or demonstration to engage pupils. Example: heating a coin and striking a match. (He has students demonstrate.) Which one grows hotter sooner? It is important in physics to start with something concrete, perceptible. In the book, the experiments indicated with 'V' can be done at home with everyday material. Those indicated with 'V' need special material and should be done in class.
- Explanations and definitions. The explanations are provided in pupil-friendly language, which is very important.
- Exercises. These follow after introductory experiments and explanations, after the *Durcharbeiten* (working through the topic) phase has been completed. The exercises represent the consolidation phase; besides paper exercises of various levels of difficulty, this phase could involve more experiments requiring calculations.
- Application of the concept in the everyday world, in other fields and in technology.
- History of the topic's development.

These last two parts are very important, according to the teacher, and effective instruction requires really good materials and examples for them. The teacher exhorted further:

It is extremely important that the knowledge of the physics lesson is integrated with other fields and school subjects: the environment, geography, history, biology, chemistry and the technical world. In the book, you will find a list that will help you.

As a check on pupils' learning, the book has a part with *Überlegungsaufgaben* (reflection problems), which test whether pupils have understood the essentials of the topic. These do not involve formulaic calculations applied to familiar problems, but being able to explain why a particular phenomenon occurs the way it does. The reflection problems serve as a summing up of the whole topic treatment. Such problems can also be used for assessment purposes.

The teacher has interspersed this lecture with soliciting student questions; there were few. Throughout, he emphasized that the learning process is more important than the text and teaching materials. The model in the book can be used variably, depending on the topic. A teacher should always ask him- or herself: how can I present this concept or clarify it through an everyday example? How can I best address the pre-existing everyday conceptions of the pupils to help them change these into the accepted scientific conceptions?

He handed out a possible timetable to get through the 75 chapters of the book and a schematic of the learning processes for physics lessons: the path from the concrete/factual to the abstract and back to the concrete, distinguishing between pupils' everyday experiences of the world, their everyday concepts and scientific concepts, concluding:

> The book is meant as a help to plan your lessons, not as something
> to follow slavishly. Decide for yourself what parts of each topic
> treatment are useful to you.

This part of the lesson ended with silent, individual work by the students as they selected and analyzed a specific chapter, at the teacher's request. The class then proceeded to the third part of the didactics lesson, a very interactive, hands-on review and discussion of their earlier experiments with heat conductivity.

Project and field experience

In addition to didactics, professional education includes project work, in which the prospective teacher might develop some curricular materials, research pupils' learning of a particular topic or analyze observed teaching strategies by experienced teachers. Also, there are three extended sets of practice-teaching sessions like the ones that Markus experienced. The first set is carried out in pairs, lasts three weeks and consists mostly of observing experienced teachers; it is scheduled between the first and second university semester, with a preparatory course.

The second set of practice teaching sessions also lasts three weeks and is scheduled between the third and fourth university semester. It too is preceded by a preparatory course, in which groups of three or more students design lessons and then teach these lessons to secondary school pupils in turn, while their two colleagues as well as the mentor observe and then discuss the lesson. (Most teacher education programs try to develop the ability in their student teachers to work in teams, as there is a strong belief that teachers in a school should work collaboratively.)

We observed a number of such practice teaching sessions in Zurich. Typically, after each of the student teachers had given their lessons, a whole period (45 minutes) was devoted to discussion. The discussion of each lesson would start with the teaching student reflecting on the lesson, then the two observing students giving comments, before finally the mentor providing feedback. This structure and discourse somewhat resembles Chinese and Japanese practice, in which beginning teachers give exhibition lessons for other beginning teachers and also for experienced teachers to observe and critique. However, the Swiss practice is more limited, in that it is not systematically applied either to beginning or more experienced teachers.

The third set of practice teaching sessions is more extensive still. It is scheduled between the fifth and sixth university semester and lasts for six weeks, when the student teachers are on their own to design and teach lessons in their specialty subject areas. Mentor teachers for the practice teaching may be the same individuals who taught the relevant didactics classes, if the student teacher's practice teaching is in the same school building. In any case, mentors are always experienced teachers in the same field being taught by the beginning teacher.

Early evaluation and selection of prospective teachers

Bern has a quite similar program, which lasts four rather than three years, and is known for its special strengths in science. The Bern University teacher preparation program loses one-third of its students by the end of the first year as a result of their performance either on the content examinations in their chosen subject specialties or from their early student teaching experience. This is an important screening tool, since pupils who have passed the *Maturität* (the *baccalauréat* in the French-speaking cantons), the *Gymnasium* graduation exam, can gain automatic entrance to this as to all other university and professional programs. Accordingly, while the eight-semester program as a whole can be taken part-time and extended, the first-year teaching experience and content examinations must be passed successfully during the first year – and this requirement is strictly enforced. [8]

The eighth semester (final) practice teaching includes a culminating evaluation. The student may choose the type of class (grade, pupil ability level if classes are tracked, and topic). He or she prepares a lesson plan, which will be appraised as part of the evaluation. The observation team includes a representative from the canton (one of the inspectors), the mentor (lower-secondary) teacher and a university faculty member. (A university faculty member generally does 20–30 observations a year for about 10–15 student teachers, as the same faculty member is responsible for the practice teaching sessions in both semesters seven and eight.)

Immediately after observing the lesson, the student teacher and the observation team separately spend 30 minutes reflecting upon the lesson. They then convene and the student teacher has 20 minutes to provide a critique of his or her own lesson, including suggesting ways to address any deficiencies or problems that arose. Following this, the evaluation team presents its own critique and assigns a grade. The grade is for the entire practicum and therefore comprises two parts that receive equal weight: the mentor teacher's grade for the entire teaching period of three weeks and the team's grade for the evaluated lesson. It is extremely rare for a prospective teacher to fail, which is not surprising, since the program should have caught major deficiencies before this point.

The Bern program has a pool of about 300 mentor teachers, of whom about 50 to 60 have had special training and are used regularly. The training consists of 3-4 hours per week for two semesters; it is co-ordinated by two university faculty members whose specialty is teaching the general didactics courses and who call on subject matter specialists as needed. The mentors also are convened for a special one- or two-day workshop that is more specialized by subject. All mentor teachers are compensated, with the amount dependent on the frequency of their involvement; those specially trained earn some Sw.Fr. 7,500 (nearly US $4,500) above their yearly salary.

The education of *Gymnasium* teachers in Lucerne (grades 7–9)

Teachers teaching in Lucerne's cantonal *Gymnasium* (some 2000 pupils) need to get an advanced university degree in their specialty (e.g. mathematics, physics or one of the other sciences), which requires at least 12 and commonly 16 semesters, hence they have a really strong subject matter background. Many teachers at that level also obtain doctoral degrees, which means a total study time of some eight to ten years. In addition to this extensive academic training, teacher education requirements include two semesters of subject-focused didactics and practice teaching and four semesters of more general didactics. At some universities, this professional preparation is then completed by one semester of *Colloquium* (a discussion course).

A beginning *Gymnasium* teacher commented:

> The *Colloquium* was really the most useful part of all the didactics courses. That's because it included beginning teachers already out

101

> in the classroom, as well as us students who already had done their practice teaching. The exchange of experiences and talking about how to solve problems that come up in the classroom helped a lot as I started to teach on my own.

The practice teaching, which is part of the subject-focused didactics courses, consists of about fifty class sessions. Some twenty of these are observations of experienced teachers (generally, observations of the teacher who is supervising the student's practice teaching), while the rest are taught by the student teacher. The beginning teachers we interviewed reported that the teachers supervising their practice teaching provided good models, although occasionally there were disappointing experiences.

Supervising teachers are always present at practice lessons. The practice lesson is always discussed after it is taught, with attention to how the prospective teacher dealt with the pupils, might have changed the content of the lecture, might have presented the content differently to make the lecture more effective, and so on. Discussions range broadly from aesthetics to technical details. Many supervising teachers require the student teachers to write self-appraisals of their teaching.

The beginning teachers we interviewed felt that their practice teaching was only a partial preparation for really taking over a classroom. Although practice teaching was a real challenge, they nonetheless saw it as a welcome novelty compared with the academic work, because it brought them closer to their prospective career, although only partially so. As one beginning teacher said:

> In practice teaching, you concentrate on your lesson and pay attention to the pupils just enough to make the lesson successful. But once you're out in the classroom on your own, you really have to know the pupils, on whom to call, who doesn't raise a hand but should be given a chance. There is much more responsibility but also more satisfaction.

In summary, lower secondary teachers, whether they have prepared to teach in a middle school (including the pre-*Gymnasium* track) or grades 7–9 in a *Gymnasium*, have a thorough grounding in the disciplines they expect to teach. (However, as Markus's experience with the middle-school integrated science curriculum demonstrates, the university disciplinary courses do not always prepare future teachers for changes in the school curriculum.)

These novice teachers also have spent several semesters in their pre-service education studying both general pedagogy and subject-specific didactics – how to teach particular content of all sorts in a coherent and effective manner to the young adolescents they will be facing in the classroom. And third, they have spent considerable time observing science or mathematics lessons in grades 7–9, then planning and teaching such lessons with some of their fellow students, before finally taking over completely a class or course for an extensive period (some six weeks) on their own, albeit with continuing feedback from teacher mentors and university observers. Yet, novices entering the classroom still find themselves unprepared for the many day-to-day and hour-to-hour decisions they must make as they assume responsibility for a full year of their pupils' learning.

4. Who is a Beginning Teacher?
The Job Market for Teachers

Understanding the conditions that shape employment for prospective teachers allows one a better understanding of just who participates in induction activities – to what extent the participants really are completely new to the profession and to what extent they have had previous teaching experience. The educational job market in Switzerland seems very flexible. An individual's salary may come from several sources. One of the teacher leaders we interviewed, working part-time, told us that 10 percent of her salary came from being a practice group leader, 50 percent from teaching and 20 percent from working on curriculum materials.

In fact, many teachers (and even administrators) work part-time by choice, as does this *Gymnasium* beginning teacher in Lucerne (where most teachers start at 80 percent time with 80 percent pay):

> I don't want to teach more than 80 percent time even next year. I don't need the money and teaching 100 percent of the time is very hard – most teachers here don't do it. I need the extra time to find materials, to do research in the library, to prepare my lessons well.

Other teachers work part-time because full-time jobs are not available. Thus, teachers may have entered their career as a substitute or part-time teacher, a preferred mode for women with families (apparently preferred by them and society, but not necessarily by male colleagues who find it hard to compete with them when seeking a full-time job, as Markus found out). There are also assistance programs run by unemployment offices for teachers who cannot find immediate employment. These programs place novices with 'mentor' teachers having handicapped or other children with difficulties and needing help. This provides another avenue for entering the profession. Teacher salaries in Switzerland are relatively high (Moser *et al.*, 1997), which may enable 'getting one's foot in the door' with a part-time job or permit opting to work less than full time.

In a number of areas (although not in mathematics and science), there is a surplus of beginning teachers, which probably adds to the relative frequency of part-time teaching positions. In Bern, in 1999, there were about 500 applicants for teaching jobs (grades 1–9, but particularly 1–6) for only 250 positions. Hence, many beginning teachers accept half-time positions. Some complete their training, but do not go into teaching. Computer- and media-related jobs are attractions. From a societal point of view, the Swiss regard this as productive, since people get a good education when they prepare to be teachers and thus will be contributors to the Swiss society and economy, whether or not they eventually teach in the future.

There are definite career ladders in the teaching profession in Switzerland, even though, at this time, there are no administrative positions available to aspire to in elementary and lower secondary schools. Elementary school teachers can advance to become middle-school teachers, and on to become *Gymnasium* teachers, provided they have undertaken or make up the requisite academic work and acquire the appropriate degree. Teacher pay is higher at each of these schooling levels, presumably commensurate with the greater amount of formal education required. Teaching loads are lower and prestige is higher. And, as one beginning *Gymnasium* teacher told us, who had previously taught at the elementary level, responsibility shifts from developing the whole child to concentrating on one's discipline, which he found much less burdensome.

A less-structured form of teacher advancement is to become a provider of a variety of induction and other professional development activities. Specifically, as described below, practice group leaders, mentors and counselors are trained for their responsibilities; they are relieved in part or in whole from their teaching responsibilities to work with beginning teachers and receive higher remuneration for this work than if they had taught instead. Teachers also have been able to build on their experience to become didactics teachers for prospective teachers. However, this may become a somewhat more arduous career path, as all didactics teaching is being moved into the universities or special professional schools and they will have to acquire advanced degrees beyond their teaching credential.

The number of teachers who have had part-time experience raises the question of who really is a beginning teacher. Also, as noted above, many 'beginning teachers' at the secondary level (perhaps as many as 30 percent) are not really beginning teachers, but have already taught at the elementary level. For economic, workload or status reasons, they have decided instead to go into secondary teaching. Nevertheless, they are eligible or even required to participate in induction programs, especially if coming from another canton or country such as Germany.

5. Responsibilities of Middle-School Teachers

According to the 1995 TIMSS teacher questionnaires, Swiss teachers were quite unusual compared with their peers in other countries in expressing a very favorable perception of the teaching profession, even at the middle grades. This is true for all regions of the country. Salaries for middle-school teachers are high – about double that for nurses, about the same as that for government lawyers and initially even better than those for engineers.

The converse of high salaries is that teaching loads in middle schools are high: 26–27 periods per week for 39–40 weeks per year. Class size is some 24–25 pupils; grades 7–9 technical/vocational school classes are somewhat smaller (about 19 pupils). Since there are about six periods per day, there is no separate planning period, although there are officially scheduled breaks and lunch periods during which teachers meet in a separate teachers' room and often discuss current classroom issues.

Teachers are employed year round. They are expected to do planning during the seven or eight weeks that school is not in session and take four to five weeks of vacation during the same time period. As is true for all employees in Switzerland, a full-time workweek for teachers is 42 hours. Teachers in grades 1–4 are expected to teach 29 45-minute periods; in grades 5–6, there are 28 such periods and in grades 7–9 (non-*Gymnasium*), they teach 27 such periods (or 26 periods if also a class teacher). The remainder of official work-time is to be devoted to lesson planning, correction of tests and homework, administrative responsibilities, interaction with parents, participation in school committees and other school activities, and professional development. The average work time is 1,950 hours per year, roughly 42 hours for 47 weeks. In many cantons, five percent of this total (some 90 hours) is supposed to be used by the teacher for professional development.

Middle-school teachers with a degree in Philosophy II are expected to teach all the mathematics and science in the curriculum for grades 7–9, including the new integrated science/social sciences courses such as *Nature, Man and the Environment* in Bern or *Man and the Environment* in Lucerne and Zurich. An outline for Zurich's course is given in Figure 2 (pp. 106–108), indicating the wide-ranging and inclusive expectations for such courses. Finally, all teachers are also expected to be able to teach sports and either music or art.

Given that the volume of suggestions for the integrated course – none of which is mandatory – requires a teacher to make choices, it is quite possible for pupils in Zurich, for instance, to complete middle school without a single lesson in chemistry or physics. This would hold especially if their teacher did not have a major or minor in these subjects, since, after all, most teachers tend to avoid what they feel underprepared or incompetent to teach. Such a gap would not have happened in the past, when all of the lower secondary science curriculum was more clearly structured by the academic disciplines.

Also, Philosophy II graduates find it hard to deal with the liberal arts aspects of the course, as Markus complained. The possible under-preparation of teachers for handling these integrated courses is partly compensated for by providing special professional development in how to teach them, as we observed in Bern and Lucerne. The cantons also publish support materials documenting relevant literature and curricular materials available to teachers (ZBS, 2000).

In the technical/vocational schools, teachers teach any assigned subject, regardless of their specialty during preparation, although this too is likely to change in the future. Also, schools can be very small in rural Switzerland. Hence, there may be only one teacher for the whole of grades 5–9 (as we found in the case of one participant in Bertila's practice group), who has to teach all the subjects for these grades, regardless of university preparation and degree. Assignment out of field may also happen in a regular middle school, if beginning teachers cannot find a job in their field; but, if so, normally they go back to university for further subject area courses. It is only in the *Gymnasium* that teachers definitely teach their specialty, but it may be their minor, not only their major.

The instructional guide for Zurich covers nine grades, lower and upper elementary (grades 1–3, grades 4–6) and lower secondary school (grades 7–9). Five subject areas are discussed of which *Mensch und Umwelt* (Man and the Environment) is one. The other four areas are Language (German, French, with English or Italian as an elective), Arts and Music, Mathematics, and Sport. Several cross-subject fields are also discussed in the guide, including use of media and information technology, and preparation for career choices. The guide is quite detailed, comprising some 360 pages.

The following summary pertains to the instructional guidelines for *Mensch und Umwelt* from the *Lehrplan für die Volksschule des Kantons Zürich* (Erziehungsdirektion Zürich, 1991).

> The goal of the *Mensch und Umwelt* curriculum and instruction – which includes science – is to have pupils understand that human beings are shaped by their social and natural environment, as well as helping to shape it. As they come to know

---

themselves, others around them and forms of social organization, and learn about the natural environment, pupils also
come to understand that there are boundaries to human
knowledge and understanding. The ultimate goal is to have
young people assume responsibility and actively shape the
future. *Four strands comprise the curriculum. The content goals
of each are briefly summarized below for grades 7–9 only.*

- *The individual and community* [encompassing some 'social studies' in the North American sense] For lower secondary school,
this strand emphasizes the interplay between the individual and
society, and understanding the social compact and rules for living together. Also development of the child into a young woman
or man and integration of mind, body and spirit, and an understanding of one's own values and the values and norms of group
membership.

- *The natural world and technology* The goal is to have pupils
understand natural phenomena around them through carrying
out experiments, making observations, representing data, making comparisons and drawing conclusions. [9] Pupils are expected to learn definitions, symbols and formulas and work with
models as they conduct investigations into the physical and
chemical properties and changes of matter and into the characteristics, functioning and behavior of living organisms.

  Knowledge and concepts to be acquired include the following:
  Physics: Notions of time, volume/mass/density, gravity, electrical
  circuits, energy/work/efficiency, models of atom and nucleus.
  Chemistry: Elements/compounds/mixtures/pure substances,
  decomposition and synthesis, atoms/molecules/ions, water/
  oxygen/carbon dioxide, chemical changes and conservation of
  mass, oxidation/reduction and acid/base reactions, selected
  organic reactions.
  Biology: Development of plants, including growth, propaga-
  tion, photosynthesis, development and growth of animals from
  a single cell, use of nutrients by living organisms, respiration
  and the oxygen/carbon dioxide cycle in plants and animals, cel-
  lular organization of all organisms, selected organ systems of
  humans including circulatory and digestive systems.

  Ecology and the Environment: Energy in nature and in technology, adaptation of living organisms to the environment, food
  chains and food webs, the hydrogen/oxygen/carbon cycles and
  disturbances in the cycles, use and disposal of materials (e.g.
  metals, food, fibers). Also, nutrition and health, personal
  development, human development in general, technological

developments, changes (positive and negative) in the natural environment due to human activity.

Technology: Consumption, use of leisure time, mobility and transportation, generation of waste and waste disposal, toxic materials and pollutants, nature/technology/science. Healthy nature – healthy economy: a paradox?

- *Home, neighborhood, country and the world* [generally equivalent to 'geography' in the European sense, which includes physical, economic, cultural and political geography] This includes orienteering, use of all types of maps (e.g. road, topographic, geologic and weather maps; atlases), bus/train/plane schedules, globes, models. Pupils are expected to understand ratio and proportion, distance and altitude, also day and night, time zones, latitude/longitude (equator, meridians) and different types of climate and climate change. Also included are earth features (mountains, glaciers, deserts, tropical rain forests, grasslands, agricultural belt, etc.), land and the oceans. Also human cultures, styles of living, art and religion as well as economic geography – industry, food production, urbanization. Also developed and underdeveloped countries, especially Europe and the third world, north–south conflicts and inter- and intrastate conflicts.

- *Past, present, and future* [a combination of archaeology, anthropology and history] This includes understanding of sources for documenting past and current cultures, e.g. excavation, historic sites, archives, written and pictorial documents, art and music. Topics to be studied are antiquity (Egypt, Greece, Rome), the middle ages, modern times (discoveries, the Renaissance and humanism, French revolution, formation of nation states, industrialization), current times (imperialism, world war, east–west conflict, north–south conflict). Also includes the biographies of individuals who have made major contributions during these eras. Key concept: the world is 'shrinking' and requires greater co-operation among peoples locally and internationally.

For all four strands of this course, the curriculum guide discusses desired learning goals, provides many suggestions for instructional approaches and specifies a number of topics in greater detail. Religious instruction is interwoven with these four strands to provide the basis for understanding culture and history. (Similarly integrated science and social studies courses are part of the Bern curriculum for grades 1–9 and the Lucerne curriculum for grades 1–6.)

Figure 2: Instructional guidelines for 'Mensch und Umwelt'

6. Swiss Induction:
Individual and Professional Growth Go Together

The three cantons we studied in depth offer several forms of support for beginning teachers, usually combined in various ways in any particular jurisdiction. We describe each form in greater detail below and discuss its use in the specific canton where it is most prominent. First, though, we consider the important underlying assumptions that run throughout all teacher induction across the cantons.

Philosophy: helping adult learners with problems of practice

No matter what the specifics of induction practice are, Swiss cantons share a common philosophy, laid out in Dossier 40A (EDK, 1996), a seminal document produced by the inter-cantonal conference. [10] A pictorial representation of this philosophy is shown in Figure 3.

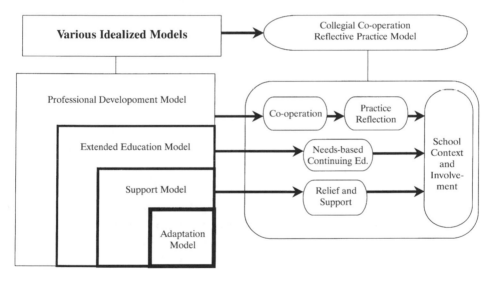

Source: Dossier 40(A) (EDK, 1996)

Figure 3:   Induction model – key elements

Two central assumptions underlie the Swiss induction philosophy, both within and across the cantons we visited.

- Teachers are assumed to be lifelong learners. This is not just rhetoric, but has a physical presence in institutions and staff (present in each canton) devoted to continuing professional development and a policy

presence in the requirement that all teachers spend a certain proportion of their time (e.g. five percent in the canton of Bern) on professional development. Teachers themselves choose how to spend this
time; they are expected to keep a journal on their professional development activities, to be reviewed by the local school board.

- However, induction is not seen as either an extension of pre-service
education or 'just' professional development, for the assumption is
that the challenges faced by the novice teacher in the beginning years
are unique.

From these basic assumptions flow several working principles that characterize Swiss induction practices:

- separation of evaluation from support;
- treating teachers as adult learners;
- a focus on problems arising out of practice;
- seeing induction as a phase that focuses on the development of the
individual as well as the professional;
- special institutional and staffing arrangements.

We briefly discuss each of these in turn.

Separation of support and evaluation

For elementary and lower secondary beginning teachers in Lucerne, induction has been completely separated from evaluation and selection of teachers. The belief is that having to make judgements about beginning teachers
markedly diminishes the likelihood that these teachers will openly air problems and that their group leaders and counselors would consequently be
unable to establish an atmosphere of trust.

Until recently, in Zurich, counseling and evaluation had been combined. Now, however, these obligatory counselor/evaluators *(Begleiter)* who
'accompanied' the beginning teachers for two years and evaluated them, as
well as counseling them, have been abolished. Instead, the beginning
teacher has the right to request assistance for two years or until he or she
has finished the still-obligatory three- or four-week course – see Markus's
vignette. Beginning teachers can request a specific person and, when they
do, they often ask for an experienced older colleague at their school or elsewhere in the canton.

In Bern, while these two functions have been separated in principle, the
counselors/group leaders are often former inspectors and still paid by the
inspectorate (which is responsible for teacher evaluation). These inspec-
tors-turned-counselors received special training for their new function, but
some still retain a few of their former practices, such as giving written
reports to teachers they have observed.

Beginning teachers as adult learners

In all three cantons, beginning teachers have considerable influence on the substance of the help available to them. While certain structures are in place – individual counseling, practice groups, group counseling, classroom observations and subsequent discussion by colleagues or counselor/mentor, individual mentoring, obligatory or voluntary courses, auxiliary help booklets – the problems and concerns actually taken up are largely shaped by the participating beginning teachers. The Swiss philosophy explicitly rejects a 'deficit' model of induction (i.e. that beginning teachers are not adequately trained or competent to do their job) and instead intentionally draws on the strengths of the individual or group to find problem solutions, sometimes bolstered by the counselor's or group leader's experience. This mirrors the philosophy practiced in Swiss professional development generally and in pre-service education as well.

Focus on problems arising out of practice

Given the conscious rejection of a deficit model, there is no obligatory emphasis on content knowledge. Elementary and lower secondary beginning teachers bring their uppermost concerns to the group or individual counselor. While these concerns can (and sometimes do) focus on instructional strategies, they more often concern classroom management, time management, parent conferences, evaluating pupils' work and occasionally dealing with colleagues, school leaders, the school board or the cantonal administrators. The assumption is that induction should focus on the complex decision-making required of teachers day-by-day and hour-by-hour, which cannot be learned during teacher preparation.

There are some settings in which instructional issues are more likely to come up: for example, as a result of classroom observations or requests for individual counseling, especially using experienced colleagues. Special courses are also offered that address instructional issues: for example, a one-week, lesson-planning course offered in Bern in the summer before the start of the school year, popular with both beginning and experienced teachers.

Induction as a developmental phase

Induction is not considered as simply continuing from where pre-service education left off. Teachers are considered fully educated in both content and pedagogy when they graduate from pre-service education. As beginning teachers, they are career entrants facing special challenges. Yet, induction is also considered different from professional development, of which the novice teacher is not yet prepared to take advantage due to confronting the complexities and responsibility of first managing a class. However, as induction helps the beginning teacher to become skilled in this, it can lay the foundations for effective participation in future professional development.

Support for beginning teachers also is different from professional development for mature teachers, in that it stresses development of the whole individual, not just as a teacher, but as a person. Reflection on one's status (*Standortbestimmung* – literally, "determining where I stand") is a crucial part of induction in two of the three cantons we studied; it also is practiced in pre-service education for similar reasons.

Institutional arrangements and shared responsibility

To facilitate the support provided to beginning teachers, the cantons have created special institutional arrangements which make the commitment to induction explicit and visible. In Zurich, this responsibility has traditionally been tightly coupled to the pre-service teacher institutions. In Lucerne, where induction has a long history, there is a separate, quite large building devoted to professional development for the whole canton. A special wing of this building is devoted to induction, including rich resources housed in a media library. In Bern, induction activities for the canton also are housed in buildings with staff devoted to continuing teacher education. In addition, there are other professional development institutions in Lucerne and Zurich that reach out to all the German-speaking cantons.

Responsibility for induction is shared among the schools, the regions (administrative sub-structures) within the canton and the canton itself. Schools take responsibility for general orientation and help new teachers learn how to plan school schedules, work with school staff (ranging from the school housekeeper to the school board), locate new materials, and the like. Beginning teachers are expected to interact with their recent predecessors: for example, by visiting the class before they actually start teaching and learning about the pupils and the history of the class. Regions sponsor practice groups and counseling; cantons sponsor formal courses and provide funding for induction staff and facilities.

While beginning teachers in Switzerland get no lighter or easier assignments than other teachers, they are, like all teachers, expected to spend a certain percentage of their paid time on professional development – induction activities in their case. In addition, the three cantons we studied all pay for the services being provided during school hours and, to the extent specified below, for induction activities carried on outside school hours, such as the practice groups, counseling, and particular courses. Schools are expected to provide their own form of induction to their beginning teachers and there are now offerings – e.g. in Bern – to educate the school leadership in this responsibility and in appropriate approaches.

Induction activities: reflection permeates every level

While we investigated only three of the Swiss cantons in some detail, our preliminary visits made it clear that all of the German-speaking cantons follow similar practices for supporting beginning teachers, with varying emphases. For each practice we describe, we draw on our observations of the cantons where it is most prevalent, without describing the whole range of practices for each canton. Across the portraits of these practices, one sees the variety of activities designed to support new teachers' learning.

Among the types of support we encountered, five were prominent:

- practice groups, with associated classroom observations and discussion;
- *Standortbestimmung* (determining one's status as a teacher and as an individual), a form of support for beginning teachers that springs from the Swiss concern with developing the whole person as well as the teacher;
- individual and/or group counseling;
- courses – 'impulse' courses (put together at little notice) to meet a short-term need, voluntary courses offered on a regular basis, obligatory courses;
- one-on-one mentoring of classroom practice, sometimes done as part of counseling when requested by the beginning teacher or – rarely – by the school inspectorate or the school leadership. Mentoring is the common induction mode for *Gymnasium* teachers.

These practices are supported by training for practice group leaders, counselors and mentors. Each of the cantons also carries out some research and evaluation on its induction activities, used to a greater or lesser degree to revise and improve the offerings for beginning teachers. Appendix B on p. 351 provides an overview of the use of the various induction practices across the three cantons.

The practice group: collaborative reflection and problem solving

Practice groups are a form of structured, facilitated networking to support beginning teachers in effective problem solving. This support mechanism has a long history in Lucerne, going back to 1973 when 'counseling of beginning teachers' first got its start in the canton. Moreover, the Lucerne approach is featured in the inter-cantonal guidelines for induction – Dossier 40A – and has spread to other cantons, as portrayed in Bertila's experience in Bern. We therefore base our description of the practice group on the Lucerne model, which is solidly institutionalized and has been prescribed in this canton for all beginning K–9 teachers since October 1994. The model is elaborated in Vogel and Vogel (1996). Major aspects of this model include the following.

- Joint responsibility between the school and the agency or individuals responsible for induction. Schools should offer induction into their specific context; they should also free beginning teachers from additional school duties and arrange their assignments so they can participate fully in the induction offerings. Induction leaders should provide effective professional development for beginning teachers and ensure proper scheduling for classroom visits.
- A personal counselor and person who looks out for every beginning teacher, usually the practice group leader.
- Collaborative group work as the central element. The group work should be concerned with reflection on practice, forms of co-operation, dealing with stress, etc.
- Classroom visits as a second central element, with feedback and discussion.
- Making connections between theory and its practical applications in the classroom.
- The questions and needs of the beginning teachers as the starting point of the induction activities.

The model operates on two levels. First, there is a professional team (in this case, Fritz and Monika Vogel, the originators of the program, and their staff) that heads the whole set of induction activities and is in charge of the individual leaders of the practice groups. [11] This team institutes continuing evaluation of the activities of the practice groups and other offerings for beginning teachers. The evaluation results are used to improve the groups' effectiveness and to ensure their quality. This is further supported through professional development of individual practice group leaders.

The second level consists of the individual leaders, all active teachers themselves, who provide the key to the quality of the practice groups and other induction components such as classroom visits and individual counseling. These individuals are freed up from some of their teaching for their responsibilities as practice group leaders, get additional pay and are themselves supported by the central team. The leaders are trained for their responsibilities and partake of a wide range of professional development offerings to increase their leadership competence.

There are about six beginning teachers per group, each of whom comes from a school within one of the administrative regions of the canton. The groups may be organized by grade level, by area of instruction not taken up in didactics classes (e.g. German for foreign-language pupils) or by cross-grade and cross-subject areas. In 1998/99, there were twenty-seven such groups for 172 beginning teachers; in 2000/2001, there were thirty groups for 220 beginning teachers, five of which were for middle-school teachers. The groups meet for about 50 hours during the year. (As local schools and communities take on greater responsibility for their beginning teachers' induction, these centrally organized meetings may be reduced somewhat in number and duration.) Thirty hours are devoted to group meetings during instruction-free time (except for the first session, for which beginning teachers get release time); twenty hours are for classroom observation during school hours (also on release time).

Since the emphasis in these groups is on problems arising from practice, visits to observe instruction are critical, both by the beginning teacher to the classrooms of other teachers and to the beginning teacher's classroom. These observations ground the group's reflections in the practice observed. Observations also provide occasions for both feedback and counseling. Practice groups generally conclude with a summary discussion that includes a type of group *Standortbestimmung* (ascertaining the participants' views of themselves at the end of their first year of teaching) and an evaluation of the group's processes and effectiveness, often elicited through a formal questionnaire. In the future, every beginning teacher also will participate in an individual *Standortbestimmung*, to be facilitated by one of the members of the leadership team or the practice group leader.

The addition of summer courses, courses offered during school time as well as on a full-time basis, an extensive media center for teachers, a special series of text booklets dealing with a range of teaching issues and related responsibilities (see Appendix B on p. 351) and individual counseling further strengthen the Lucerne induction system. Figure 4 below represents

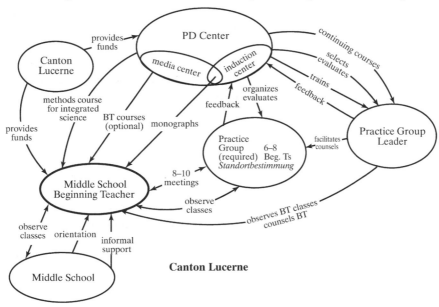

Figure 4: Typical induction components: impact on beginning teachers

Lucerne's multiple induction components as they affect beginning middle-school teachers.

The group leaders. The group leaders are carefully selected for their personal qualities. Each candidate is interviewed by a member of the leadership team of the induction program. Prospective group leaders can take some preparatory courses offered by the Center for Continuing Teacher Education, in which the induction activities and staff are housed. These courses often help both the induction staff and the course partici-pants to decide whether leading a group is an appropriate choice for a spe-cific individual. Once selected, group leaders participate in introductory training, which includes preparation on how to start a new group, generate discussion themes, lead and moderate discussions, conduct observations, provide feedback and conduct counseling sessions.

Every year, each group leader has a personal interview with one of the center induction staff, which serves as a time to reflect on the group, inclu-ding feedback from participants. This reflection also allows leaders to plan 'next steps' based on the needs of group members, as well as their own continuing education. Group leaders are expected to engage in continuing professional development over some ten years. The central induction staff believe that the long-term and permanent building of leader cadres pays off in the effectiveness of the Lucerne practice groups.

Organization and processes of the practice group. During the first meeting of the practice group, participating beginning teachers decide on their sched-ule (e.g. 15 meetings for two hours each, 10 meetings for three hours each) and meeting places. All members pledge to observe the schedule or to be responsible for any necessary changes. The leader arranges with every group member for the classroom visits, providing feedback and counseling when appropriate. More visits than are usually scheduled are possible if desired.

Authenticity and trust are essential qualities of each group. All members, including the leader, must pledge confidentiality. Other commitments that drive the group's work are to make connections between the group discussions and classroom instruction, and to ground themes and issues to be worked on in the needs of the beginning teachers. The leader sets the tone, helps with finding a theme and takes responsibility for making the group effective for each participant. Although the leader facilitates sessions and may share his or her own experiences, the group entails work by autonomous adults. Thus, participants are responsible for their own learning.

The classroom observations. These are seen as key both in induction and in continuing professional development. New teachers have the right to at least two classroom observations by the practice group leader and/or fellow members, up to a total of twenty for the group. Group members visit each other and visits to beginning teachers and experienced teachers outside the group also are possible. Visits usually allow for one hour for preparation and planning, two hours of observing lessons and one hour of discussion afterwards. The pre- and post-sessions can be conducted outside school hours.

Vogel and Vogel (1996) recommend that classroom visits always be related to a theme that the practice group is working on. Optimally, the class will be engaged in a piece of significant work. Written notes of observations serve as documentation for the discussion period, any follow-up counseling and progress between the two observations. The whole process (pre-session, observation, post-session), as with all practice group activities, is subject to evaluation.

Beginning teachers and group leaders alike learn to focus their observations on particular aspects of the class, including teacher and pupil talk, participation patterns and the quality of the discussion (including the teacher's questions, reactions to pupil responses and body language). Observers also look for evidence of a warm classroom climate, how teachers deal with conflicts and difficulties and whether pupils are learning. Feedback is given only when and if the observed teacher requests it and is couched in the language of subjective impression, not scientific analysis or authoritative report. The discussion, especially if the leader has been involved in the observation, can include next steps and possible further professional development for the beginning teacher.

Some problems. Practice groups are time- and energy-consuming. In Lucerne, for example, where practice groups at the lower levels of schooling have been well institutionalized, they have only just been introduced for *Gymnasium* teachers. For these teachers, the main induction approach traditionally has been mentoring. There was intensive recruiting in 1999 and 2000, but the canton ended up with only one or two practice groups for beginning *Gymnasium* teachers. A beginning *Gymnasium* teacher (teaching half-time while completing his studies) commented:

> I was invited to join a practice group at the beginning of the year, but I was much too busy. I still have to complete my university studies, including my dissertation, and I have to prepare for my didactics exam. Besides, I have to plan for three different kinds of classes, eighth-grade geometry, ninth-grade biology and twelfth-grade biology, and I get real help from my mentor, especially in biology.

In Zurich, where facilitated peer groups are voluntary and less structured, teachers we interviewed commented on the large size (nine beginning teachers) making up their group. As one of them put it, "I prefer individual advice. In the group, they never get to my problem."

Two other Zurich beginning teachers said they had dropped out of their practice groups as being too time-consuming, with advice from experienced colleagues in their school proving more valuable. As illustrated by Markus's story, however, this does not preclude teachers from organizing their own informal help groups.

Practice groups have recently been introduced in Bern for all beginning teachers of grades 1–9. The teachers participate in 24–32 hours of practice group meetings, including twelve hours during class time, when substitute teachers are provided by the canton. Participation in the practice groups is free for the first two years of teaching, after which teachers can carry on a group on their own time. One Bern teacher reported on her beginning teacher practice group, which was so successful that it transmuted into one for experienced teachers, with several of the original members still participating. This teacher thought her practice group to be by far the most productive and helpful thing she did as a beginning teacher:

> I was lonely and afraid. I lacked self-confidence and could not defend my methods, even though I could see they worked with my pupils. The practice group I joined helped me immensely in standing up for my own ideas. All of us in the group found it so valuable that we are still continuing, even though the canton isn't paying any more.

We observed a marked difference in the styles of the Bern and Lucerne practice groups. The Bern leaders appeared considerably more ready to come forward with direction and advice than was the case for the Lucerne leaders, who performed their group-leading role more as facilitators than as counselors. This may stem from the fact that the Bern leaders have been drawn from the inspectorate, whereas the Lucerne leaders are or were classroom teachers.

The Standortbestimmung: where I stand as a person and a teacher

Beginning teachers are encouraged to reflect not only on their teaching, but on their status within the teaching profession, most notably in the *Standortbestimmung*. This process is a self-evaluation of self-competence, social competence and competence in one's area of teaching. It is intended to lead to a determination of next steps in self- and professional development, with a number of choices possible (including leaving teaching). Beginning teachers are encouraged to think about the following.

What can I do well?
What are my strengths and competences?
How do I use these personal resources?
What have I learned during this period of professional activity?

Where do I stand now?
What still seems difficult?

This type of self-reflection is common in Swiss industry and administration, as well as in pre-service teacher education. It is mandatory for beginning teachers in Bern and Lucerne, but not in Zurich, and should occur sometime toward the end of their first year. It can take place in the context of personal counseling (usually by the practice group leader) or as a culminating experience during the last meeting of a practice group.

A Standortbestimmung in a practice group. In Lucerne, we had occasion to observe a number of practice groups. As is common, one of these devoted part of its last meeting to a group *Standortbestimmung.* The group consisted of eight grade 7–9 beginning teachers and a teacher leader. First, the group constructed a visible group record consisting of individual responses in the following areas:

energy/use of time in my teaching;
use of free time;
'I as teacher';
social competence;
subject competence;
self-competence;
expectations for the future;
finances;
health.

Each participant rated each area according to his/her own perceptions on a five-point scale from 'happy' to 'unhappy'. The group leader summarized the group picture; the teachers then took turns explaining some of their ratings – both the negative and the positive ones – in each area. As to the future, about half of the participants were committed to teaching as a career; a couple wanted to teach, but not full-time; a couple were staying with teaching for the next year or two but thought they would probably leave for jobs in the (private) 'economy'. [12] The same atmosphere of trust and openness prevailed in the last session of this practice group as had characterized the opening session of Bertila's group. By the very nature of how the practice groups are structured, this supportive and non-judgemental atmosphere is their hallmark, even though each group develops a dynamic of its own.

The individual Standortbestimmung. In the individual sessions we observed, teachers also were asked to reflect on their teaching over the past year. Was it developmentally and instructionally appropriate to their classes? Did they have difficulty with planning, organization and implementation of instruction, including work with individual pupils and evaluation of pupils' work? How did conferences with parents go? Regarding the school as a whole, beginning teachers were also asked to consider the structure of daily school life – teamwork within the school and their contribution to the development of the school. An important component was the beginning teacher's own further personal and professional development: for example, deciding what would lead to a better balance between their teaching responsibilities and satisfying leisure activities (e.g. time and stress management).

Despite our presence, teachers freely aired their personal and family problems and how these meshed or interfered with their professional goals. After having been asked to reflect on how she was doing, one teacher said:

> Work is very central for me. I worked before I was married at all sorts of jobs and enjoyed solving problems. I didn't live while I was just caring for family – go to market, cook, take care of three small children. [Counselor interjects: "Don't undervalue your experience with your own children."] I asked myself, 'Is that all there is?' And then my world went to pieces [when she got divorced ...].

> But I am strong, I don't get depressed. This year, I had too much work, between added family responsibilities and my class that had some special-needs children in it. I make a plan for my lessons, then the kids have problems, a stomach ache, homework not done, unruly behavior. [Counselor: "What are your plans for next year?"]

> I made three applications. We'll see what comes of them. One is for a special education class, but I'm not sure I can really do that all year, even though I have the training. What if I decide on something and it doesn't work out? And I don't want to have to teach physical education or music. My ideal would be to teach school half-time and do art therapy the rest of the time. But I guess I should just stick with my decision and not always look for the ideal [...] Can I come back and talk to you again when I have to decide? [Counselor: "You know you can come back."]

In Lucerne, the school leadership also conducts a type of *Standortbestimmung*, really a performance evaluation, for every teacher every year. It consists of three parts: a self-evaluation by the teacher, observation of instruction by three other teachers once or twice a year and a talk with the school leadership to set goals and review professional development opportunities (*Erziehungs- und Kulturdepartment des Kantons Luzern*, 1998). The schools themselves are evaluated every four years by the canton's inspectorate; the schools are expected to prepare a school profile to identify their strengths and weaknesses, their goals and their strategic planning. Consultant counselors are available to help with these improvement plans (Erziehungs- und Kulturdepartment des Kantons Luzern, undated).

Individual counseling

All three cantons we studied put considerable resources into personal (or sometimes group) counseling for beginning teachers. The counseling is generally available to all teachers as part of their professional development, but a greater number of sessions are free for beginning teachers and especially emphasized for them. The individual counseling often grows out of the practice group, as in Lucerne, or groups are formed on the basis of bringing together beginning teachers within a region having similar needs. The majority of beginning teachers' concerns have to do with the daily life of the teacher.

Some of the most frequently-raised concerns include: organization of instruction, planning lessons and evaluating pupils' work, particularly for the sixth-grade transition decisions. Also, general pedagogic aspects are asked about frequently – conducting a class, unruly pupils, social learning – as well as difficulties with parents or school authorities. Beginning teachers often experience tensions between their ideals and classroom realities. Early counseling, just as with the practice groups, helps beginning teachers resolve these tensions; their subsequent success works as a powerful mechanism to keep them in teaching.

Bern. In this canton, the inspectorate has staff for two kinds of function: inspectors and counselors. The inspectorate deals with all schools up to and including grade nine and also with all upper secondary schools except the *Gymnasium*. Inspectors make sure that schools adhere to the canton's instructional plan and also to the individual school's plan. They additionally arbitrate disputes and settle complaints. There are sixteen inspectors (who all work full time); half are assigned to grades K–9. Each could be responsible for as many as 800–1000 teachers, since there are 5,000 elementary and 2,500 lower secondary teaching positions in the Bern canton, plus additional specialty teaching slots. So it is not possible for the inspectors to observe all individual teachers every year.

The counseling function is carried out by about twenty-five specially trained individuals, available on demand. They typically function for 50–60 percent of the time as counselors and work in schools as teachers for the balance of their time. The work of the counselor with a teacher is completely confidential. This requirement led, in 1996, to the counseling service being completely separated from the work of the cantonal inspectors, although nominally the counselors are still a part of the inspectorate.

Ten percent of all the counseling is requested by a school inspector or the school leadership, the other ninety percent by individual beginning teachers themselves. These requests very often lead to the formation of practice groups, as beginning teachers in the same region often have similar problems. Visits to classrooms by inspectors and/or counselors are compulsory during a beginning teacher's first year. (Because there are not enough inspectors to go around, counselors help with the classroom visits. This introduces some ambiguity as to the support or evaluation role.)

In one Bern region, beginning teachers must have at least six counseling sessions per year; they can ask for as many as twelve or occasionally sixteen. There is no cost for the counselors' services, as counselors are sponsored by the canton. Because working with a counselor is seen as self-reflection and analysis, the beginning teachers' time devoted to getting assistance can be considered part of the five percent of their time allocated for required professional development.

Counseling for experienced teachers is voluntary. When voluntary counseling was first established, there was some reluctance to request counselors because needing assistance was perceived as a stigma (as Markus remarked about his older colleagues). But, now, counselors are getting more and more requests. The demand has reached the point that the counselors are considering combining their assistance to teachers in the same school who have the same needs.

At the first session, the teacher and counselor discuss the ostensible problem. They then negotiate a written contract that spells out what will happen, including diagnosis of problem and possible referrals. Counselors encourage beginning teachers to ask themselves probing questions. What do I need to develop at this point in my teaching? How can I go about doing this? They delve sufficiently into the details of the beginning teachers' concerns to help them ask the right questions and explore where and how to find the means and methods to grow.

In fact, counselors often make referrals to other resources, including the canton's Center for Continuing Teacher Education. Sometimes counselors, while visiting a beginning teacher's classroom, will volunteer help with didactics. Usually, this occurs in a case where an inspector has suggested there are instructional or disciplinary problems in the classroom. Difficulties with complete trust between beginning teacher and counselor may arise when it is undertaken at the request of school authorities.

Zurich. Beginning teachers in Zurich also are entitled to individual counseling, thirty-two hours generally being the maximum. This service is available to them for the first two years of teaching. Mostly, the beginning teachers choose these counselors for themselves, as they have the right to counseling from anyone of their choice who accepts. If they want counseling, but have no specific counselor in mind, the head of induction services in the canton finds a suitable counselor for their particular problem. Although Zurich has not instituted the *Standortbestimmung*, the counseling emphasizes the development of the teacher as individual *and* professional.

We observed classroom visits and counseling requested by some beginning teachers at the upper elementary level (grades 4–6) from their former pre-service faculty advisor. They knew him from their teacher training institution (the *Seminar*), which presently is responsible not only for pre-service education but also for induction and continuing professional development, together with other canton-wide institutions. (But see above for changes in elementary school teacher education, i.e. the likely abolition of *Seminars* in favor of tertiary institutions closely tied the universities.) About 60–70 percent of the K–6 beginning teachers who graduated from this *Seminar* request counseling involving the faculty there. (As in Bern and Lucerne, counselors in Zurich now have no formal evaluation function.)

When this service is requested, a counselor will go to the school to observe and discuss the beginning teacher's practices or the beginning teacher can come to the *Seminar* to meet. The counseling is adjusted to address the individual teacher's needs. After the initial meeting(s), the counselor and beginning teacher together will write a 'contract', which specifies what the program of assistance will be. Resources permit a typical assistance program of six sessions up to a maximum of eight, but there could be more if needed and approved.

An important consequence of the *Seminar* faculty doing the induction support is that all parties speak a common language – the pre-service educators, the beginning teachers and the mentor teachers in the schools. They understand each other's contexts, prior experiences and points of view. But there are some problems in letting the individual beginning teachers be the sole judge about the problems they need help with. A *Seminar* teacher and counselor commented:

> A big issue in elementary science education is whether science gets taught at all. Since science content at this level is a broad topic including social science and geography, teachers who feel less equipped to teach science may emphasize the latter aspects at the expense of science. So, requests for help with teaching hands-on science arise only infrequently during counseling, although the need might be there. [13]

For group counseling, the Zurich counselors are divided regionally according to the seven regions in the canton. They use the requests for counseling to form groups of about five or six teachers which are facilitated by one of the counselors. The group could meet anywhere, including at the *Seminar* but also at a school or a coffee shop. The model is peer networking and support with facilitation, although not as elaborated as the Lucerne practice group concept. The groups formed could also well be a continuation of groups that worked together during their teacher preparation, as illustrated by Markus's experience.

The key *Seminar* induction staff have periodic meetings to discuss their counseling, e.g. particularly difficult problems that arise. These meetings are confidential. The staff also work on the content and philosophy of the voluntary group meetings. We observed a discussion of the origin of 'supervision' groups (not to be confused with the North American concept of supervision of teachers) and the use of 'intervision' groups.

'Supervision', as it is understood in Switzerland, focuses on developing a reflective attitude, on releasing the individual's potential at the professional level. 'Intervision' groups (sometimes called 'co-operative counseling', usually referring to mutual classroom observations) have the same aim as supervision groups, but function without an external guide common to the practice groups. The *Seminar* staff saw it as important to start teaching students to use 'intervision' even before they leave the *Seminar* for their first teaching posts, so as to encourage collegial, co-operative problem solving on their own in the school setting they would enter.

Courses

Professional development is compulsory for beginning teachers in Zurich, in particular the four-week course for lower secondary teachers (three weeks for elementary teachers) that completes the two-year induction period. We found the requirement for such a course to be unique among the six cantons we investigated in our preliminary research; it is a relatively recent requirement for Zurich as well. Participating teachers whom we interviewed, Markus among them, found the course very helpful.

The main organizer of the course is the head of induction for the canton. The course generally is given in February and March toward the end of the beginning teacher's second year; the maximum number of participants in any one section of the course is twenty-seven. Within the course as a whole, mini-courses are given by professors of pedagogy and psychology, and by didactics teachers of school subjects related both to Philosophy I and to Philosophy II. University professors responsible for subject-matter content (e.g. mathematicians, chemists, biologists) also give half-day courses in their disciplinary specialty.

Input of the beginning teachers regarding the course is solicited. Two meetings precede the course to orient participants and allow them to discuss which topics and themes might be of interest. Examples of frequently-requested themes are:

> carrying out a project of their own;
> pedagogy and cognitive science;
> social background of foreign pupils;
> dealing with single parents.

Information provided by the beginning teachers at these pre-course meetings (the first one is in November) forms the basis for the content of the induction course in the early spring.

Although the university and associated K–9 school providing didactics courses prepare middle-school teachers for several cantons, the induction course is only for beginning teachers in the canton of Zurich, for whom it is provided free of charge. The canton also pays for substitute teachers for the beginning teacher's classes. If beginning teachers from other cantons want to enroll, they must pay.

The canton requires that teachers take this course, regardless of whether they were trained in Zurich or in another institution outside the canton. In fact, teachers cannot get a permanent teaching position until they have finished this course; until then, they are on a year-by-year contract. The *Seminar's* or university's current student teachers take over the participating beginning teachers' classes, in order to release the latter for the course. Prior to the course, the student teacher visits the beginning teacher's classroom for a day and also spends an evening with the teacher in preparation for the three- or four-week substitution.

After this experience, the student teachers (who acted as substitutes) still have six or seven weeks in the program when, in part, they will debrief extensively on this final student teaching experience. A faculty member reflected on his experience with the course:

> When we began the induction course, we were prepared for problems to arise when the student teachers were on their own. We thought the schools and parents would be concerned about the prospect of inadequate teaching of their kids. We set up a telephone hot-line with faculty scheduled always to be available for consultation with the student teachers. But everything went smoothly and nobody called. The seven regional school boards in the canton now generally support the course. It's actually mostly some beginning teachers who get anxious and want to visit their own classes, but they get over it and, regardless, it's not allowed.

When signing up for the course, beginning teachers choose from among the groups and topics offered and are given the opportunity to suggest additional topics. They also work on projects. The projects are put together for beginning teachers having similar needs. They work on their projects continuously over the three or four weeks, whenever there are designated block periods for project work. Beginning teachers are put into groups of eighteen to foster interaction and informal networking that lay the groundwork for possible continuing collaboration and support among various members after the course ends.

Each group has three leaders, carefully chosen to bring in different expertise and potential roles. Each leadership team contains an induction counselor from the *Seminar* (for elementary school beginning teachers), a subject specialist (mathematics, science, etc.) and an experienced mentor of student teachers. Although there are some common topics addressed by each group, the treatment of the topics is put in an appropriate context by the various leadership teams.

Participants also have the opportunity to go to a school with the mentor teacher (of the leadership team) to observe something that addresses a need they have expressed. This option is exercised frequently: for example, if participants want help knowing how to assess pupils' learning, they could go and observe some techniques in use in actual classrooms. This example provides a good illustration of an advantage of the induction course – being able to discuss something that is better understood after having considerable teaching experience (versus just practice teaching). Faculty of the induction course have the opportunity to raise issues best suited to this phase in the teachers' development, as well as to repeat some topics that may have seemed abstract to students during their preparation. Sometimes, the novice teachers do not even recognize that they have studied the topic earlier.

Many other types of courses specifically aimed at beginning teachers are offered by the cantons and in cross-cantonal institutions. An example from Bern is the week-long summer course to prepare for the coming school year. Although this course is open to all teachers, it is tailored to the needs of beginning teachers. Participants identify difficulties they might encounter and how to prepare for these together with colleagues, share experiences and materials they have found helpful and form networks of support for the coming year. Various experts are brought in to work with the beginning teachers, but time and support for individual planning also is part of each day's program.

A participating beginning teacher (quoted in the 1998 course evaluation) wrote:

> I felt like a dumb calf and that made me quite unhappy. But then I met other calves in the meadow, which restored my self-confidence.

Mentoring

In the cantons we observed, the main form of induction support for *Gymnasium* teachers is one-on-one mentoring, often provided by the same teacher(s) who supervised the beginning teacher's practice teaching. In Lucerne, where the *Gymnasium* begins at grade seven, a beginning teacher is assigned two mentors, one a school vice-principal in charge of the relevant set of subjects (e.g. mathematics and science) and one a classroom teacher in the same school who teaches the same subject. In the Lucerne cantonal *Gymnasium* (probably the biggest *Gymnasium* in Switzerland), each of the seven vice-principals mentors thirty teachers, including two or three beginning teachers each year who are hired in his or her area of responsibility.

This mentoring includes at least two classroom visits per year and a 45-minute post-lesson discussion, considered crucial. Written protocols for the observations and for the discussion are available for the mentors. In addition, the teacher-mentor observes the beginning teacher as often as one lesson per week, with discussion afterwards. Toward the end of the first year, the teacher-mentor facilitates a formal *Standortbestimmung* with the beginning teacher and provides a written report. On being queried about the focus of the mentoring, a *Gymnasium* teacher-mentor said: "No, subject-matter content is not very important in our discussions – if command of the subject were an issue, the person shouldn't be teaching here."

Mentoring of a ninth-grade biology lesson. The beginning teacher we observed in this lesson has already had teaching experience in a middle school, but as a first-year teacher in a *Gymnasium*, he is assigned a teacher-mentor who provides him with feedback at least twice during the year. The teacher-mentor must write a report for the *Gymnasium's Prorector* (vice-principal) on each of his or her observations and discussions with the beginning teacher. He or she is not relieved of any teaching duties, but is paid about Sw. Fr. 1000 (US $600) per year in extra salary for this additional responsibility.

This is the second time the teacher-mentor has formally observed this beginning teacher: however, during the first observation, the *Prorector* was also present, mostly to observe the mentor who is new to this responsibility. In preparation, the mentor has taken a special course for *Gymnasium* mentors offered at the induction branch of Lucerne's Center for Continuing Teacher Education. He commented:

> I was 'strongly encouraged' to take the course, I didn't really want to. But it turned out to be extremely useful – very intense and strenuous, but I learned a lot even about my own teaching, especially from the videos. I would highly recommend the course to others, not just mentors.

This *Gymnasium* has about 800 lower secondary pupils (37 classes, grades 7–9), is housed in a attractive modern building and is well equipped. For example, the three biology classrooms (each individually equipped for wet labs) are built around a large and well-stocked biology preparation room. A technician does the preparations; she works 60 percent of the time. The same arrangement and technician help holds for chemistry, but physics has no lab and is taught completely theoretically. In general, this *Gymnasium* has an open-door policy; the teachers themselves have requested that they can make three classroom visits to colleagues during the year and have their own classrooms visited three times as well, as part of their professional development.

The biology class has nineteen pupils present, seven of whom are girls. Two 45-minute periods are allotted to this lesson. After reviewing some homework, the beginning teacher launches into the day's topic, evolution. He goes through three different stages of evolutionary theory: first, the spontaneous generation of life from a test tube of dirt; then, Lamarck's notion that improvements developed by an individual during his lifetime (e.g. strong biceps through lifting weights) can be passed on to offspring, followed by Darwinian theory. He shows transparencies, highlighting specifically the observations made that led to the subsequent hypotheses.

The teacher tries to make connections to the pupils' interests. He asks:

> Why is it good for a species to have many offspring? How many children does it take to keep a human population constant? [The pupils say it takes two children – he corrects them; it really takes 2.2 or 2.3.] Do you know what the average number of children per couple is in Switzerland? It's less than two. Can you think why that's so in much of the developed world, but couples have more children in the developing world?

The pupils make quite reasonable conjectures, citing cultural and economic conditions. Then, as instructed, they copy the main points on the overheads into their notebooks. The teacher emphasizes that evolutionary theory does not answer philosophical questions (Why are we here? Where are we going?), but speaks only to the development of the different varieties of life – nor does it say that humans are at the apex of creation.

As the first period concludes, he gives the pupils their assignment for the next 45 minutes (when he will not be teaching, as he will be debriefing with the mentor). He has assembled several different texts, some pro-evolutionary theory, some more skeptical. He wants them to read the texts and then write down their own opinions and justify them. What supports evolutionary theory, what speaks against it? They are to work as individuals, not in pairs or groups.

We retreat to the commodious biology preparation room. The mentor gives feedback, given in the familial *'du'* rather than the formal *'Sie'*. The discussion is highly interactive, with the beginning teacher often responding immediately to specific comments by the mentor. It is obvious that there is collegial respect and even friendship between the two teachers, even though one is more experienced than the other and today they are not simply discussing as colleagues.

As the mentor proceeds, he frequently consults notes he has made using a protocol designed for mentoring purposes. He wonders what prior knowledge the pupils had: for example, do they understand what a theory is? He continues:

> I can understand why you lectured for almost the whole period with a few questions and answers sprinkled in, since you had to lay the foundation for the second period when the pupils were to work on their own. But this is the simplest form of instruction, no constructivism. Also, your media use was very dry, no little film clips, no pictures.

The beginning teacher responds: "I wanted to get the main points across". The mentor also wonders whether the pupils could possibly really have got the whole development of evolutionary theory in a half-hour; that seems like a lot to expect. The mentor continues his critique:

> You started a lot of different topics and almost lost the thread, although you did manage to return to the main point. Too many little side excursions, like the population one, may be confusing for the pupils [... Comment by the beginning teacher, "I wanted to make the topic relevant to the pupils". ...] You have a very good delivery style, animated, good rhetoric – a little too didactic maybe, but the kids seemed engaged. Good class atmosphere, although maybe the kids were a bit loud, especially when they asked just when they would be able to give their oral reports on their own projects before the evolution lecture began. Maybe you should keep a little more distance between them and you.

The beginning teacher readily accepts this and says he wants to see how the pupils do on their own during the second period. The mentor also notes:

> You seemed always to call on the same three or four kids, also you pointed with your finger instead of calling on them by name.

All this is delivered and received in a very positive manner. The mentor also praises the beginning teacher:

> This class wasn't as hectic as the earlier one I observed. The goals were clearer, but the criticisms are still the same.

The beginning teacher sums up:

> I'm annoyed I didn't change more. I'd like more observations and feedback, so I can get a whole profile not just a single snapshot.

Informal interaction activities

The elementary and lower secondary schools we observed all had the equivalent of teacher lounges, used for formally-scheduled breaks mid-mornings and for lunch. Pupils are expected to keep order on their own during these breaks. The time allowed for these periods is long enough and the setting is sufficiently conducive to encourage collegial exchange – sharing of experiences, discussion of difficulties and potential solutions to instructional conundrums. It is not unusual for a teacher to make an appointment with a colleague to talk about a specific concern during break or lunch. Get-togethers after school, as reported by Markus, are also common in many schools, although educational leaders express the opinion that co-operation among teachers within a school needs to be further strengthened.

A fifth-grade beginning teacher in Zurich observed:

> What has helped me the most is talking to some more experienced colleagues in the school. They are really interested in helping me out and want me to succeed. Sometimes, I also call up colleagues in other schools who were students at the *Seminar* with me or we get together after school and compare experiences. The counseling by Mr. X [her advisor from the *Seminar*] also helps. I can always call on him when I have problems.

In the *Gymnasium*, the department as a whole serves as additional support to the beginning teacher. One of these teachers we interviewed in Lucerne, teaching grades 7–9, found the biology preparation room the most productive source of ideas, where his more experienced colleagues in the department gave him advice. As he said:

> While I'm in the biology prep. room putting away the plants and animals I just used for one of my classes, I chat with colleagues there about what materials they use for particular topics. Then I go to the library and look these materials up, and often that gives me new ideas about what to do in my classes.

In our Bern interviews, we not infrequently found groups of teachers who first met formally as a practice group, but then continued to meet of their own accord to solve problems together collegially and informally.

7. The Training of Counselors and Mentors: not just Experienced Teachers

Throughout the cantons, there is recognition that helping beginning teachers develop in their careers takes special training. Although the training for counselors, mentors and group leaders varies, all three cantons invest considerable resources to prepare the individuals involved in induction programs for their roles and responsibilities.

Bern

Since counselors play an important role in inducting new teachers in Bern, it is not surprising that cantonal officials have given considerable attention to the learning needs of potential counselors. When counseling was first introduced, for instance, a special course was offered for former inspectors or experienced teachers who were interested in becoming counselors. As the program was being established, these individuals were required to take a three-year course concurrently with doing the counseling job, in order to launch the program quickly. The course included peer counseling, coaching, 'supervision' (in the Swiss sense, see above), etc.

Now, this course must be completed before entering counseling and a certificate is required to become a counselor. However, no such course is offered in Bern currently, because there are enough counselors for the canton. The Center for Continuing Teacher Education has also twice offered a course to help equip experienced teachers with the means to facilitate practice groups, so the canton now has a cadre of about sixty such qualified facilitators for 14,000 full- and part-time teachers. A course for mentors of beginning *Gymnasium* teachers is planned for 2002; it will be based on the Lucerne course described below.

The University of Bern, responsible for the preparation of prospective *Gymnasium* teachers, also offers several courses for *Gymnasium* mentors. An advanced and quite intensive course we observed consisted of several five-hour sessions held throughout the year, with fifteen mentors and four course leaders. The mentors were already experienced and had been mentoring for several years, but wanted to learn new and more systematic methods of evaluating student teaching and generally how to improve their mentoring.

The course session we observed started with a preparatory discussion among the mentor participants and leaders, which focused on systematic observation and recording of classroom events. The mentors then split into three groups according to their subject-matter expertise, in order to observe a student teacher scheduled to teach a full lesson. Each of the student teachers had formulated three questions ahead of time that he or she wanted the mentors to address in their observations and feedback. The participating mentors also chose particular methods they would use to systematize their observations: for example, observing a particular pupil, observing pupil–teacher interaction, observing pupil–pupil interaction or concentrating on apparently unengaged pupils. The observations were recorded and specific responses to the student teacher's questions formulated.

A subsequent debriefing with the student teacher followed: the course leaders gave clear instructions that the purpose was training for the mentors rather than evaluation of the student teacher. The session concluded with a plenary meeting of the mentor participants and leaders to exchange what they had learned (recorded publicly on the board and on large posterboard sheets) and what they wanted to take up in future sessions. The whole session was very closely planned and structured, while also supporting student teachers as well as the participating mentors. It seemed to accomplish its goal of helping mentors base their judgements of teaching by their student teachers on systematically observed and recorded evidence.

Lucerne

In addition to the intensive training for leaders of practice groups discussed above, Lucerne offers training for mentors of beginning *Gymnasium* teachers, mentioned by the mentor of the ninth-grade biology lesson described earlier. A typical course consists of five full days in November (8:30 am to 5:00 pm, with a couple of evening sessions as well) and two additional days later in the year. Topics taken up during the first two days of the November sequence include views of good instruction, visits to mentors' own classrooms, reflection on their instruction and the provision of critiques of videotapes of experienced teacher and beginning teacher lessons.

The third and fourth days include talks with beginning teachers, observation of their classes and coaching on giving feedback in a sensitive but productive manner, and identifying the needs of beginning teachers based on these experiences. The fifth day is devoted to intensive discussion of the role of the mentor as coach and counselor and how to facilitate conducting a *Standortbestimmung* with a beginning teacher. A protocol is provided for this purpose to reflect the views of both a beginning teacher and the mentor. The November course is followed by a day in February for observation of each other's mentoring and another day in March for case discussions based on the mentors' experiences during the observations and for their evaluation of the course as a whole.

Zurich

Zurich is in the process of developing courses for the counselors of beginning teachers. The plans are to have all leaders of induction services and counselors trained within the next eight years. The courses will cover psychological and cognitive research, didactics and developing expertise in counseling, in personality and in team development. The head of induction services in Zurich is himself taking such a course, which started in the fall of 1999 and is given over two years, in order to get ideas for the planned Zurich course. The course he is taking was initiated by the Conference of Cantonal Education Leaders and is modeled on courses for leaders responsible for developing social workers, which have been in operation for some time already.

8. Research and Evaluation: Making a System Reflective

Among the sites that make up the chapters of this book, the Swiss cantons conduct by far the greatest amount of research and evaluation on their induction programs. In fact, evaluation of programs, individual courses and activities is a common practice throughout the continuum of Swiss teacher education. The main purpose is to obtain feedback for continuing improvement of the programs offered to pre-service, beginning and experienced teachers.

Lucerne

The practice groups in Lucerne have had both internal and external evaluations. The internal evaluations, which have been carried out annually for some ten years, consist of surveys of all the beginning teachers who participated in a practice group, separate surveys of their group leaders, interviews with the group leaders and evaluation by the central staff (see, for example, *Erziehungs- und Kulturdepartment des Kantons Luzern, 1999*).

In 1999, the five main themes taken up in the groups were: managing the classroom and disruptions interfering with instruction, assessing pupil progress, individualized versus whole-class instruction, lesson planning and working with parents. Classroom visits to and by participants took place in all the groups. Nearly half of the participating teachers also availed themselves of one-on-one counseling and one-third undertook an individual *Standortbestimmung*. The central staff sees this low incidence of individual *Standortbestimmungen* as a problem and is considering how to make them more attractive and meaningful, so as to encourage greater participation.

The 1999 evaluation showed that a large majority of participating teachers (about 90 percent) saw the practice group as an ideal means for continuing education – efficient and relevant to their job. They particularly valued classroom visits by colleagues, exchange of experiences and mutual support. They also commented on the competence of the leaders, especially their professionalism, their valuing and treatment of group participants as adults, the sensitive counseling and mentoring, and the concrete, direct feedback. Criticisms centered mostly on organizational aspects, e.g. size and make-up of the group, location and duration (too time-consuming). Certification, which is granted on the basis of at least 95 percent completion of all the practice group activities, was awarded to almost all the participating beginning teachers, indicating high acceptance for the support provided by the practice groups.

The evaluations of the group leaders mostly agreed with those of the beginning teachers. However, a third of the group leaders did not think that the competence of the beginning teachers was much improved, in contrast to the views of the beginning teachers themselves who thought they had gained greatly in knowledge, competence and skills.

A 1998 external evaluation report confirms these positive judgements (Ambauen, 1998). It compared two models of induction support: mentoring in canton 1 (unnamed in the summary) and the practice group in canton 2 (Lucerne). The researcher found that only 17 percent of beginning teachers in canton 1 judged their induction experience to be of high quality compared with 76 percent of beginning teachers who did so in Lucerne. This evaluation, while recommending the Lucerne model for adoption by other cantons, made some suggestions for improvement: tying practical exercises more closely to theoretical work; strengthening work on leadership and relationships; giving more attention to the composition and size of the practice groups.

Zurich

Zurich has also collected a considerable amount of evaluation data, reflecting feedback over several years on its counseling and other induction activities (Zzing, 1999). During the obligatory induction course, questionnaires are used to solicit participating beginning teachers' feedback on how well their preparation equipped them for their teaching practice. Student teachers also get a questionnaire at the end of their pre-service education and a similar one again at the end of their first year of teaching, along with a 'needs assessment' instrument that is used to develop the induction course.

Some of the main problems identified by the beginning teachers were physical exhaustion, the need to strive for perfection, the gap between ideal and reality in the classroom, the time crunch ("it never lets up") and being responsible for the pupils' fate. Also ranked high were lack of professional feedback, fear of pressure and judgement by parents, and problems with discipline and order. Not surprisingly, student teacher responses differed from those of the beginning teachers, especially regarding unanticipated boredom with routine. ("Forty years the same thing?", commented one beginning teacher.)

In particular, beginning teachers commented on 'job shock', especially with regard to class management. This is the one issue that turned out to be substantially worse than they expected as students. Evaluation and assessment of pupils also is a continuing concern and commonly requested as a topic for the induction course. This is especially the case for the beginning teachers having to make placement decisions in the sixth grade. In response, a special course on 'transition' is being offered to all sixth-grade teachers and support for assessing their pupils is offered to all beginning teachers.

The experiences considered to be most helpful by beginning teachers were support by friends and partners (i.e. their social networks), relationship with the pupils (which tends to be very close in Switzerland), exchange with colleagues in- and outside the school and the newly-instituted induction course. Support by the pupils' parents, individual counseling and reduction in school duties were also ranked as being helpful. One of the supports judged as significantly more important by beginning teachers than by pre-service students is the continuous support of the *Seminar* and *Seminar* counselor. As several commented: "The counselor should always be there for me".

The most commonly-used form of support was individual counseling in concert with classroom visits or observations, used by 80–90 percent of second-year beginning teachers, who call on this service more frequently than first-year beginning teachers. However, as an induction leader (and researcher) commented:

> Apparently, beginning teachers are not worried about lesson planning or learning materials. This could be positive feedback: teachers have been well prepared in their teacher training. It can also be seen negatively: beginning teachers are not willing to confront the quality of their lessons and prefer to blame problems on classroom management. In some of the lessons I visited, teachers demonstrated a superficial understanding of the lesson materials. I'd like to see teachers do more research into learning processes.

In contrast to Lucerne, the voluntary, less formally organized practice groups received strikingly low ratings from participating teachers. The schools highly recommend the practice groups as necessary for becoming a good teacher, but even this has not been very successful in encouraging participation. The reasons beginning teachers cited for not participating in these groups were lack of time, enough other kinds of support and sufficient alternative induction activities that were more immediately helpful. Beginning teachers in Zurich appear to prefer individual counseling, because it is more focused.

Bern

Bern also carries out research and evaluation of its induction activities: for example, on the summer planning course. Participants are asked whether they had enough time to address their individual problems and about their reaction to the course both as a whole and to specific parts of it. Their general reaction has been very positive, with 90 percent reporting that they felt considerably helped in their career as a teacher. The plenary forums presenting lecturers were the least well received. Working with colleagues on specific plans for the school year was most appreciated, as was the time for sustained individual work. Comments by participants quoted in the evaluation report included:

> [The course] helped me a lot, because I could always ask for help when I got stuck [with my planning]. I got the most help from colleagues in the special interest group. The course leaders were always there for us in the background without imposing their ideas.

9. A Summary of Main Induction Features

Several themes emerge from our study of Swiss induction.

(a) Beginning teachers are viewed as professionals, sharing in the shaping of their induction experiences. These experiences focus on the development of the person as well as on the development of the professional teacher. Beginning teachers draw on the realities of the classroom to hone reflection on their practice and their collegial problem-solving skills. This starts in student teaching as teams of three students mentor each other, continues for beginning teachers in their practice groups and is carried forward in mutual classroom observations between beginning teachers and experienced teachers.

Observations of classroom teaching continue as part of the evaluation process for all teachers; peer networking supported by facilitators is available both to beginning and to experienced teachers. Schools themselves, although increasingly emphasizing the role of the leadership team, are run on a collaborative basis.

(b) Each of the three cantons offers a carefully crafted array of induction experiences that include formal and informal practice groups, individual and group counseling, classroom observations and follow-on discussions, review of personal and professional status and progress, specially-designed courses and help booklets. Figure 4 above (p. 115) illustrates this array for Lucerne.

Appendix B on p. 351 provides an overview of induction features specific to each canton. In all three cantons, induction services are seen in part as helping beginning teachers to understand their professional development needs, so that they will be able to choose wisely from the canton's and inter-cantonal professional development offerings as they gain in professional experience and personal maturity.

(c) The induction systems in the individual cantons, though they vary in specifics, all rest heavily on reflective practice. Activities and programs are evaluated and feedback is used to make appropriate and sometimes quite sweeping changes. Individuals concerned with providing induction services and professional development see their work as changing and improving.

Taking Lucerne as the strongest (but not unique) example, the leaders and staff think of the whole set of activities for developing teachers as a learning system, one which gathers data about itself consistently and continuously. It then tries to improve on the basis of this information, a form of action research engaged in by all the participants in the induction system.

(d) Human and financial resources are committed specifically to induction programs. All the programs have paid permanent central staff and physical facilities maintained by the cantons; the cantons also pay for the counselors, group leaders and mentors, all of whom receive specific training for their responsibilities. Participation in the induction activities by the beginning teachers is also subsidized by the cantons by means of providing substitute teachers and as part of the professional development hours expected of all teachers and paid for by the cantons as part of their regular salary.

(e) Induction responsibilities are shared among the three types of institutions responsible for a teacher's continuing learning: the schools, the pre-service institutions and the cantonal centers for professional development. This tri-partite responsibility is part of education law in Bern. The connection between pre-service education and induction is most evident in Zurich, where the *Seminar* that educates K–6 teachers is also in charge of induction services, plans the obligatory induction course and provides the counselors – constituted from their pre-service teachers – for beginning teachers.

In Lucerne, the connection is clearest at the *Gymnasium* level, where the mentors for practice teaching are likely to be those who also mentor beginning teachers. Frequently, the *Gymnasium* mentors are trained by the same university didactics faculty who also educate the pre-service teachers. Strong connections are the norm in other cantons as well, particularly since the cantons in Switzerland are quite small and hence people in teacher education are all quite likely to know each other.

In addition to the induction programs of the individual cantons, a number of cross-cantonal institutions offer professional development courses open to all Swiss teachers, e.g. the Center for Continuing Education in Lucerne. This center offers some 100 continuing education courses and activities for lower and upper secondary school teachers from across Switzerland and also provides courses and training for didactics teachers and for whole-school development. The center is supported in part by the cantons and in part by participants' fees.

Some concluding comments

What can we conclude from our inquiries into induction policies and activities in Switzerland, particularly the three Swiss cantons we studied in some depth?

First, looking across the cantons, we observe that *teaching is seen as a complex, difficult – even stressful – job*. Despite rigorous preparation in both subject matter and teaching methods and extensive opportunity for practice teaching, it is broadly acknowledged that beginning teachers still have a lot to learn. They need to acquire further knowledge and skills that can only be learned in context, after assuming full responsibility for a class or a set of courses. Hence, induction does not consist of a monolithic set of policies and induction curricula. In each canton, it comprises a system containing several articulated practices adapted to the context of different types of schools and the needs of novice teachers, who are specified as any teacher (even someone with considerable previous teaching experience) who is new to the given type of school and/or the canton.

Second, we observe that *the induction systems are dynamic*. They are able to evolve and change as needs change. This is demonstrated by the completely altered roles of the counselors in Bern, who previously were inspectors rather than counselors, and in Zurich, where counseling was previously obligatory and now is available on demand by the beginning teacher. In both cases, the change has been from some sort of overseeing of the beginning teachers to engaging them in reflection on their practice with an experienced colleague.

Another example of current change is the balance of responsibilities between schools and the canton, both in Bern and Lucerne. As schools offer more opportunities to beginning teachers for reciprocal classroom observation and collegial interaction around problems of practice, the canton-sponsored practice groups are able to reduce their demands for the number of meetings and observations. Yet another example is the introduction of courses in all the cantons for counselors, leaders of practice groups and mentors of *Gymnasium* beginning teachers.

Third, the *systems* not only *adapt* to the *context* of the schools and the needs of the beginning teacher, but also to *the particularities and changing curricula of Swiss schools*. Thus, since there are many small lower secondary schools, which may have only one beginning teacher in a given year, the practice groups are designed to draw from all the schools within a region of the canton. This also adds to the richness of experiences forming the content of practice group sessions, emphasizing collegiality across schools.

A further example involves the training courses offered to beginning and returning teachers to help with teaching the integrated science and social issues courses recently introduced into the middle-school curricula of Bern and Zurich, for which their pre-service education did not prepare them. Yet another example is Bern's recently introduced and popular summer course devoted to planning for the coming school year, open both to experienced and to beginning teachers.

Fourth, *reflection on one's performance as a teacher and even one's choice of career* is deeply woven into the fabric of teacher preparation and induction. Practice teaching is carefully evaluated during both the first and the last year of teacher preparation. Performance evaluation is conducted mutually between a counselor and the beginning teachers, in the form of the individual or group *Standortbestimmung*, a discussion of where the teacher stands with respect to the profession of teaching and with respect to his or her own personal development.

This process is not designed to 'weed out' poor teachers, but to help each individual discern strengths and weaknesses in his or her practice and to plan further development for the next several years. Indeed, if some decide to pursue other careers, this is not seen as a drain or waste: rather, their knowledge and skills contribute to a well-educated society no matter what their choice of profession.

Reflection is not just demanded of the individual, but also of the system. Evaluative feedback on its induction activities is collected by each canton and Lucerne conducts formal performance evaluations, similar to those for beginning teachers, and with analogous purposes, for the practice group leaders. In each canton we studied, we observed changes being made on the basis of the feedback information gathered from the beginning teachers and their counselors, mentors and other induction staff.

Acknowledgements

Our exploratory visits in Spring, 1999 were arranged and facilitated by Peter Labudde and Armin Hollenstein, both professors at Bern University. Peter Labudde is in charge of the pedagogic and didactics education in science for prospective *Gymnasium* teachers; Armin Hollenstein teaches pedagogics and didactics for prospective secondary mathematics teachers. We are most grateful for their help. We further thank Peter Labudde for his careful review of a draft version of this chapter.

We also wish to acknowledge the considerable help in collecting data and writing up field notes provided by Christine Wassmer, a graduate student at the University of Bern who is fluent in both German and English and who accompanied Senta Raizen to most sites during her November, 1999 field visit.

We particularly wish to thank the many teachers, counselors and practice group leaders, mentors and administrators who allowed us to interview them and observe their induction activities. Especially, we want to thank the heads of induction programs in the three cantons – Jacob Manz in Bern; René Meier and Claudio Zzing in Zurich; Werner Schüpbach, Fritz Vogel, Monika Vogel and Gabrielle Schorno in Lucerne – both for arranging a rich array of visits and interviews and for themselves providing key interviews, background information and documents. The Vogels and Schorno also reviewed earlier drafts of this chapter and provided helpful comments.

Without the hospitality and courtesy extended to us by these individuals, and the many others not named here, our study would have been superficial and impoverished. They deserve much of the credit for the reflection in this chapter of a rich set of policies and practices in support of beginning teachers. Any errors and possible misinterpretations, however, are solely the responsibility of the authors.

Chapter 4

Help in Every Direction:
Supporting Beginning Science Teachers
in New Zealand

Edward Britton,
with Senta Raizen and Mary Ann Huntley

1. Introduction

A common experience of beginning teachers is to encounter new pitfalls at
every turn. However, in many New Zealand schools, beginning science
teachers also find help in every direction. The story below highlights the
kinds of support that a new science teacher, Sarah, receives at her urban
secondary school, serving 1200 pupils from grades 8–12. Like all of the
science teachers in the school, Sarah teaches courses at both lower and
upper grades. It is term two (of four) in Sarah's first year of teaching.

Support throughout Sarah's hectic day

Form (homeroom) period is mostly uneventful today, except for having to
refer a pupil to the Dean of her form for failing again to come dressed in a
complete uniform. Before her first class, Sarah picks up the apparatus and
materials she will need for the lesson's activity from the department's lab
technician, who has prepared everything according to the request slip Sarah
submitted yesterday. She planned this grade 8, general science lesson on
biological classification according to the department's outline.

Sarah begins class with a brief lecture and then has groups of two or
three pupils use a classification key on the supplied biological specimens.
This activity fulfills the national specification and widespread practice of
including science practicals (pupil 'hands-on' tasks) every day. Sarah cannot
imagine accomplishing this without the support of the lab technician. She
was glad to find out about the technician's services during her school orientation. Following the classification activity, she concludes the period with a
whole-class discussion of the relevant concepts.

E. Britton et al. (eds.), Comprehensive Teacher Induction, 141–193.
© 2003 *Kluwer Academic Publishers. Printed in the Netherlands.*

After her second period, general science class for tenth-grade pupils, Sarah goes to the staff room where she grabs a coffee and relaxes during interval (morning break). This pause indeed feels like an interval from Sarah's hectic day, albeit one only fifteen-minutes long. Almost all the teachers are there and Sarah spots Mrs. Hopkins, her science department head. Sarah suggests some alternative specimens for the classification activity and Mrs. Hopkins asks Sarah to remind her to have the laboratory technician order some of them for next year. Sarah is happy to learn that, at the department meeting before school tomorrow, Mrs. Hopkins will lead a discussion on teaching 'Oceans', a four-week unit that all the grade-eight science teachers will begin next week.

Every teacher in Sarah's department, including Mrs. Hopkins, teaches at least one of the integrated science classes that comprise the science curriculum in junior (lower secondary) grades 8 and 9. Mrs. Hopkins believes that pupils in these grades need a good foundation and to be drawn into science.

> So, they need experienced teachers with the most skill for preparing them for the senior science courses. I'd never assign just beginning teachers to the junior grades and just experienced teachers to their science specialties in the senior grades.

Next period is free for Sarah and she is glad to have the time to prepare for her weekly meeting with Mrs. Hopkins. They will be planning Mrs. Hopkins' observation of Sarah's worst class. In term one, Sarah was apprehensive about these observations, because Mrs. Hopkins is also officially appraising Sarah's teaching. But she has been so supportive and constructive that Sarah has chosen this challenging class for the next observation. Speaking of Mrs. Hopkins as well as administrators who observe her, Sarah remarks, "They're here to help, after all. If you don't let them see what your problems are, how can they suggest anything?"

Sarah spends her free period thinking carefully about the most important things that she would like Mrs. Hopkins to notice. She hopes, for example, to get more possible solutions for handling some pupils with chronic behavior problems. Fortunately, as a first-year teacher, she has been spared from being assigned the most difficult pupils in the school. Also, things have improved since her 'buddy' teacher in the next classroom dropped by a couple of times to see the difficulties. He suggested some different questioning strategies to use and Sarah no longer dreads walking into class.

Another source of help was the one-day workshop for beginning secondary teachers that Mr. Bennett (the deputy principal) arranged for her to attend last week at the regional Advisory Service. Sarah heard some good ideas for classroom management and learned about some science resources. But more important than that, she felt "as though a weight had been lifted from my shoulders" when the workshop organizers had participants trade notes with beginning teachers from other schools. Sarah discovered that, "Everyone felt overwhelmed by the job: I was so relieved to know that I wasn't the only one who had been discouraged by classroom management problems".

After teaching one of her grade nine classes during fourth period, Sarah sits with some other beginning teachers in the staff room and relaxes during the thirty-minute lunch period. But they also talk about asking Mr. Bennett (who facilitates the bi-weekly after-school meetings for beginning teachers) to spend time at their meeting this afternoon on further suggestions for writing pupil progress reports. In a previous session, he illustrated some 'dos and don'ts' for writing them. Sarah is heartened to hear that she isn't the only one who was caught off guard recently by the reactions of a few pupils and parents, despite her best efforts to write clear yet judicious remarks. After eating, Sarah hurries to her class to have a little time to prepare for grade eleven chemistry class.

The following class is Sarah's favorite because of her strong chemistry background and the pupils' motivation. She has previous science experience as a chemistry technician in a national laboratory and enjoys bringing real-world applications into both her chemistry and general science courses. Sarah also likes the class because these pupils have elected to take the course. Required to take some science course, they have chosen chemistry over physics, biology or continuing with general science.

She looks forward to the chance to teach the coveted grade twelve chemistry class in the future. However, she is glad that Mrs. Hopkins avoided assigning it to her this year, even though she has a deeper chemistry background than the current teacher. The grade twelve elective is a college-preparatory course that is paced dramatically faster than grade 8–11 science courses and goes into topics in far greater depth.

Sarah also has the last period on Tuesday free, as one of the extra free periods she is entitled to as a beginning teacher. She spends most of the time in the department's resource room, preparing for the 'Oceans' unit that starts next week. Sarah is a little apprehensive about the topic because she did not take any earth sciences course in college. Fortunately, the department's box of resources for this unit is full of possibilities, including a unit outline, lots of handouts for 'hands-on' activities, some lecture notes that other teachers have used and a guide for a weekend field trip to the ocean. Also, the room's library of teacher reference books has more than a dozen titles on this topic.

Sarah feels fortunate this time. Curriculum resources available for a previous unit were skimpy, forcing her to struggle more with exactly what content to teach and how to teach it from day to day. She is tempted to check out one of the class sets of pupil textbooks more often, but that would have felt like failure. Like most New Zealand teachers, Sarah believes good teaching is having pupils doing something, not working through textbooks. Sarah also feels lucky because of a conversation with Glenda, a friend from teacher training who is now teaching at a different school. Glenda's science department provided almost no specifications for any units in the general science classes, let alone lesson plans or handouts for teaching them.

After school, Sarah joins Mr. Bennett and the schools' five other first-year teachers for their bi-weekly meeting. In term one, they got together every week, but during terms two through four they are meeting every other week. The school's second-year teachers also participate today, sharing some things they wish someone had told them in the first year.

Particularly, they urge Sarah and her peers not to fritter away their 20 percent release time on marking papers and planning lessons, while saying that there is not anything wrong with spending the release time in these ways on occasion. But their advice is to take advantage of the opportunity to observe other teachers and to take some courses, because it gets much harder to schedule these things the second year when you have lost the extra free periods.

After hearing comments from the second-year teachers, Mr. Bennett had planned to discuss school disciplinary procedures, but is happy instead to address requests by first-year teachers to discuss further the writing of pupil reports. Before ending the session, he reminds the first-year teachers of some planning they need to do soon: arrange to observe classes of their department head or another science teacher; review the out-of-school course offerings he suggested, especially in light of his offer to cover the afternoons required with a substitute teacher without taking away any of their free periods; schedule an individual meeting with him to discuss how things are going.

Sarah wonders how to work all that into her schedule. She feels that most of the time spent with Mr. Bennett and Mrs. Hopkins is worthwhile and some of it is indispensable. The regional beginning teacher workshop was good and some of the other off-site courses seem interesting. But she still has to teach five classes and four different science courses, as well as be form teacher for a class of eighth graders. Without her release time, sorting out these competing time demands would be impossible. Sarah tries to set her dilemmas aside as she dashes off to help coach the last of soccer practice.

Overview of the chapter and the case

The support Sarah receives is in an important sense something of a 'best-case' scenario, but many urban schools provide fairly similar levels and quality of support. [1] This chapter emphasizes elaboration of these substantial, well-designed and implemented induction programs. However, there is a wide range of provision, so we offer some caveats about ways in which induction programs can prove less successful at many schools.

Later in the chapter, we will describe induction providers and activities – both those illustrated in Sarah's day and some additional ones. First, however, we detail aspects of the educational system most salient to teacher induction, as well as school science curricula and science teaching practices. This is done in order to understand better what beginning science teachers are being inducted into and how these factors shape the needs for teacher support. After providing these contexts, we turn to describing and analysing in detail the induction programs and activities themselves. Finally, we identify and discuss some enabling factors, things outside the ostensible induction program, which also support beginning teachers.

We focused the study on which this chapter is based in secondary schools (grades 8–12), because they best met these study criteria: they encompass some middle grades (grades 8 and 9) and have science teachers teaching science courses. [2] Most secondary instructors teach classes in both 'junior' science (grades 8 and 9) and 'senior' science (grades 10–12). We did not select teachers of grades 6 and 7, since pupils in these grades can be found both in elementary schools (grades 1–7) and in intermediate schools (specifically for these two grades only). The latter are organized similarly to elementary schools – namely placing a class of pupils with a single teacher all day for most subjects.

We primarily observed and spoke with beginning science teachers and those who supported them. However, one third of the novices whom we contacted primarily or entirely taught other school subjects as well. The detail in this chapter's descriptions of induction programs generally apply to *all* secondary teachers, except, of course, aspects of teaching particular to science – such as how to conduct 'hands-on' instructional activities in science practicals.

We visited one rural school and fourteen urban or suburban schools in greater Auckland and Wellington, the two most populated metropolitan areas in the country. Schools in these areas have the country's most diverse pupil populations, both in terms of socio-economic levels and of race/ethnicity. The socio-economic levels of the pupil populations in the visited schools ranged across the entire spectrum, including schools at deciles

1 and 10, and most levels in between. [3] The visited schools were generally larger, all serving at least several hundred pupils and half serving over a thousand. (See Appendix A on p. 344 for more information.)

The data in this chapter are mostly drawn from observations and interviews undertaken at the schools we visited. These schools were identified for us as ones known to have some of New Zealand's best 'Advice and Guidance' programs (the formal name for what we are calling induction). We selected such schools in order to understand better what induction *can* be, given the enabling condition of a policy that both requires and makes time available for it. In order to put these widespread practices in a national perspective, however, we also conducted observations and interviews at regional workshops for beginning science teachers, which bring together participants from schools having induction programs of all levels of effort and quality. These data make clear that some New Zealand novices, particularly those in smaller or rural schools, do not find as much and/or as diversified help as do novices in the schools recommended to us.

2. The National Context for Local Teacher Induction

We provide three types of background information necessary for understanding teacher induction in New Zealand: first, we outline a few features of the general education system; second, we discuss how aspects of science teacher preparation influence the kinds of support that beginners need; third, we explain national policies for teacher induction and the guidance provided to local schools for creating support programs that fulfill them.

The general educational system

About 3.8 million people live in New Zealand on two islands covering 268,000 square kilometers. [4] The country has 350 secondary schools, which range in size from dozens of pupils to a couple with as many as two thousand. About 30 percent of secondary schools are single-sex institutions and over 90 percent require pupils to wear school uniforms. The country is officially bilingual, requires all schools and teachers to address Maori culture in the curriculum and supports some Maori immersion schools. About 17 percent of secondary pupils are Maori and another 7 percent are other Pacific Islanders. Two-thirds of the population lives on the North Island, and three-quarters of this population lives in the greater metropolitan areas of Auckland (the largest city) and Wellington (the nation's capital city).

Since 1989, there are only two levels of governance in the New Zealand education system: the national level and individual local schools. The national Ministry of Education (additionally referred to in this chapter as the Ministry or MOE) interacts directly with every school in New Zealand on policies, funding, etc. For example, even the heavily populated Auckland area has no school district or regional authority to supervise Auckland schools and the Ministry provides funds directly to every Auckland school. Parents of pupils enrolled at every school elect its own Board of Trustees to oversee the administrators' major financial, policy and hiring decisions. While no intermediary levels of governance exist, the Ministry does partially fund regional Advisory Service offices and staff who provide professional development services to schools, including some teacher induction activities. The remainder of the Advisory Service funding comes from individual school payments for requested services.

Legally, parents have the right to send their child to any public school of their choice in the entire nation. Schools can limit enrollment to the capacity of their facilities, but, since 2000, they are now required to accept pupil applicants from their neighborhood *before* opening spaces to pupils from other areas. This policy revision places pressure on prestigious schools to serve neighborhood children as well as élite pupils from elsewhere. Practically, many parents can only afford the time and/or money to get their child to the nearest school, as there are no school buses. However, some parents do consider more than one nearby school and a few go to considerable lengths to get their children into distant, well-regarded schools.

This recent 'free marketplace' model has resulted in fierce school-to-school competition for the best possible teachers and pupils. Principals are now in the business of promoting their school: for example, by developing prospectus documents for recruiting purposes that highlight a school's assets and accomplishments, meeting interested parents or contacting the parents of high-performing pupils. [5] Major newspapers publish school-by-school results of national, standardized examinations such as the School Certificate exams taken in grade 10 and high-performing schools use these results in recruiting both pupils and staff.

The Ministry sets a national salary schedule for all teachers annually, after formal negotiations with the powerful Post-Primary Teachers' Association (PPTA – the secondary school teachers' union) or the comparable union for elementary teachers. This Association estimates that 95 percent of eligible teachers are members (and offers first-year teachers an 80 percent discount on union dues). The Ministry provides salary funds directly to each school based on a complex weighted formula involving school/pupil characteristics.

Some principals view creation of a strong support program for beginning teachers to be an effective recruiting tool that can give them an edge in hiring the best prospective teachers. While the Ministry funds all teacher positions at each school, it does not fill them. Schools compete with each other to recruit and retain teachers. School administrators commonly advertise positions through a national education magazine (the Gazette) produced by the Ministry or a private, national education newspaper which we saw in most staff rooms of schools we visited.

Figure 1 illustrates the relationship of local schools and teachers with the Ministry of Education and two other national, government entities: the Teacher Registration Board (TRB) and the Education Review Office (ERO).

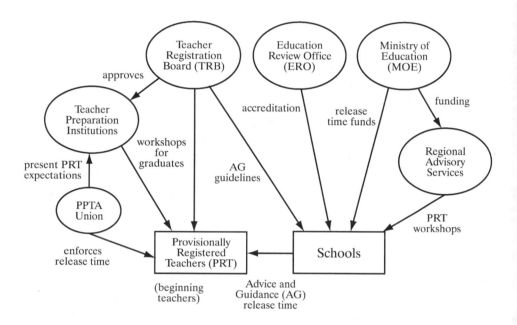

Figure 1:   Aspects of New Zealand's educational system relevant to teacher induction

All prospective teachers must apply to the Teacher Registration Board to become a Provisionally Registered Teacher (PRT). It is illegal for schools (even private schools) to employ unregistered teachers. Schools must create and provide a two-year 'Advice and Guidance' support program (also known as the AG program) for their beginning teachers and the Teacher Registration Board provides publications of suggestions for strong Advice and Guidance programs, as well as actual illustrations.

The Education Review Office re-accredits schools every three years on the basis of site inspections. As part of the inspection, Education Review Office inspectors may ask for documentation related to a school's Advice and Guidance program. Both the Teacher Registration Board and the Education Review Office are legislatively-created entities that collaborate with the Ministry of Education but function autonomously from it. The second sub-section below, on the national induction policy and guidance provided for its implementation, discusses the roles of the Teacher Registration Board and Education Review Office in more detail. [6]

Relationships between teacher preparation and induction

This sub-section discusses four aspects of preparation programs for secondary science teachers:

- how programs screen their candidates and those enrolling;
- how science content preparation is (and is not) aligned with the content of secondary school science courses;
- what practice teaching takes place;
- what expectations the programs give their soon-to-be graduates for the kinds of support they should receive as beginning teachers.

Graduate diploma programs in secondary teaching (the standard secondary teacher preparation) are one year long. A three-year bachelor's degree is a pre-requisite, but, at many institutions, the degree does not have to be in the subject specialty that the student will subsequently teach. [7]

However, it is especially challenging at this time to make generalizations about the specifics of New Zealand teacher preparation programs. Prior to 1996, the government permitted such teacher preparation programs at only seven teacher colleges and universities. In 1996, in keeping with its market-oriented policies begun in 1989, the government 'liberalized' the requirements for teacher preparation programs, so that many additional institutions launched programs; Thirteen institutions now have programs for secondary teachers and twenty institutions prepare elementary teachers. We visited two of the long-standing programs, at Auckland College of Education (ACE, the largest program in the country) and Wellington College of Education (WCE), and additionally a new program at Auckland University (AU). [8]

Screening candidates

Leading teacher preparation programs put considerable effort into screening their applicants. The Auckland College of Education program requires applicants to make at least some visits to different schools before admission – they must include documentation of their school visits in their application to Auckland College of Education and comment on the experiences' effects on their view of and desire to be a teacher. In addition to reviewing extensive applications and candidates' academic backgrounds, faculty interview applicants at length to determine whether they are felt to have the disposition and interpersonal skill needed in teaching. In both the Auckland University and Auckland College of Education programs, three or more people interview the candidates.

The Wellington College of Education program provides groups of 5–6 applicants with an educational issue, asks them to come to consensus during an hour's discussion and observes the session. In addition to faculty present, observers include a union representative, a school-board trustee and an active, experienced teacher. Faculty usually reject at least 10 percent and up to 40 percent of applicants on the basis of the interviews. [9] Wellington College of Education also requires candidates to write a half-hour essay on an educational issue under test conditions. After the first practice-teaching placement, Wellington College of Education faculty counsel about 10 percent of the cohort who are having the most difficulties and some years may encourage up to half of them to leave the program.

These screening functions before and during pre-service education act as a critical quality control within the New Zealand teacher preparation system. As is described later, very few beginning teachers are denied permanent registration at the completion of their induction period. The New Zealand system's stance toward beginning teachers is that they are prepared to be teachers, suited to be teachers and should be supported to become proficient teachers by means of the induction program.

Science preparation

Virtually all prospective science teachers studied their science specialty for two years in senior secondary school and also had had some earlier introduction to the subject in junior secondary as part of the integrated science courses. Using prospective chemistry teachers as an example, they have two years of chemistry in senior secondary school, where the fast-paced, second-year class is limited to college-intending pupils. This grade 12 class is assessed by a national examination and pupils' scores influence their admission to colleges and universities.

Prior to entering or before completing most secondary teacher preparation programs, students are required to have some post-secondary courses in a science specialty. Prospective chemistry teachers at the new Auckland University program must either have a chemistry degree before entry or have completed a third-year university course. The Auckland College of Education requires completion of a first-year college chemistry course. However, because science jobs in industry have been scarce in recent years, the majority of the science cohorts we observed at Auckland

College of Education and Wellington College of Education had prior Bachelor's degrees in science and some had additional industrial experience as laboratory technicians.

All three programs that we investigated required two or more science methods courses: one or more courses focused on teaching integrated science in junior secondary and one or more courses concentrated on teaching a science specialty in senior secondary.

Practice teaching experiences

First-year teachers begin teaching having had 14 to 18 weeks of prior teaching experience from their preparation programs. The Auckland College of Education and Wellington College of Education programs provide three shorter teaching sessions (4–6 weeks each), which allow students to become more familiar with different types of schools. The Auckland University program requires two longer sessions (8 weeks each), which enable student teachers to become more familiar with their pupils and the life of a teacher in a specific school. Programs vary the types of schools experienced by a prospective teacher across the two or three practice-teaching sessions: for example, by using schools having pupils of different socio-economic levels or teaching in both mixed-sex and single-sex schools. Practice teaching placements can lead to jobs later: for example, about 40 percent of the 1999 cohort at Auckland University obtained teaching positions at one of the schools where they had been assigned as a student teacher.

For each practice-teaching placement, all programs ensure that science teachers are assigned to integrated science classes in grades 8–10 as well as grade 10–12 classes within their science specialty. Program staff observe student teachers once or twice during each placement. Two programs ensure that a student's integrated science classes are observed, but one program concentrates all or most of its observations on the senior science classes.

The alignment of college science with school science

Secondary science teachers are typically assigned to teach, every year, some classes of general science (grades 8–10). This means that most teachers end up teaching some science subjects that they probably have not studied in college. The new National Science Curriculum implemented in the 1990s accentuated this misalignment between teachers' content preparation and school science, because it mandated both astronomy and geology strands, which fall outside of any of the more common science majors of biology, chemistry or physics. The head of science teacher preparation at Auckland College of Education explained: "There has long been an expectation of teaching astronomy and geology, but many teachers did not because these science areas were not included in the School Certificate exams [taken at the end of grade 10]". Teacher preparation programs generally do not have any courses specifically intended to broaden students' science content knowledge beyond their major. [10]

However, Auckland University is taking an innovative step to bring the science content of science teacher preparation into somewhat closer alignment with the content of school science courses. The Auckland University secondary science program now requires prospective teachers to take science courses in fields outside their science major (though not astronomy or earth sciences). For example, all prospective biology teachers at Auckland University are required to take two courses, one each on the chemistry and physics most often found in the integrated science classes of grades 8–10.

The approach that Auckland College of Education uses to address alignment is more typical of preparation programs: the science methods class is designed to cross all disciplines and the program requires students to develop a teaching unit on a topic outside of their science specialty. A senior faculty member for science in the Auckland College of Education program clarified the aim of this program feature: "We don't teach content *per se*; we address instructional strategies in their weak areas – pedagogical content knowledge such as dealing with pupil misconceptions".

Educating prospective teachers to expect support

Prior to graduating their students, most teacher preparation programs discuss both teacher registration procedures and the support they should expect to receive as beginning teachers. For example, in 1999, the Auckland College of Education program devoted the entire spring issue of its college newspaper to issues that graduates are likely to face as beginning teachers. The fifteen-page edition contained profiles of six first-year teachers' experiences plus articles by experienced teachers and administrators offering advice on how to make good use of a school's support program for beginning teachers (ACE, 1999). It also encouraged its soon-to-be graduates to pursue union assistance should they encounter difficulties in the first year.

The Palmerston North College of Education provides its graduates with a 160-page guide for beginning teachers in secondary schools (Willetts and Williams, 1990). It provides 2–3 pages of advice on each of 54 topics organized into five sections: *survival* (e.g. controlling stress, discipline procedures), *succeeding in teaching* (e.g. questioning strategies, working with groups), *administration* (e.g. extra-curricular roles, school reporting), *teacher assessment* (e.g. your rights, role of principal) and *wider background* (e.g. school politics, sexual harassment).

Although teacher preparation institutions expend some effort on familiarizing their upcoming graduates with critical aspects of being a beginning teacher, traditionally they have had no role in assisting with these teachers' induction. Until recently, institutions were not in a position to assist graduates because they did not formally keep track of their graduates' whereabouts. While regional Advisory Service staff who offer in-service courses are often housed at teacher preparation institutions, these advisors seldom interact with teacher preparation faculty and the latter generally do not conduct in-service courses.

However, the three teacher preparation programs we studied have now begun one-day professional development workshops for their graduates. With more programs competing for students, leaders of these programs felt that bringing in first-year teachers demonstrated a more comprehensive commitment to their students. Faculty also gained feedback from the first-year teachers on their preparation programs, which was helping the institutions improve these courses.

Teacher unions also foster prospective teachers' expectations of a support program. The Post-Primary Teachers' Association sends representatives to the larger teacher preparation institutions, where they are welcomed to speak to classes of students who are about to graduate and take their first teaching jobs. The representatives provide pamphlets informing beginning teachers of their rights under the national teachers' contract, particularly the right to 20 percent paid release time (PPTA, 1999). The ten-page pamphlet also explains the intended roles of the school personnel who provide an Advice and Guidance program (also known as the AG program) to help beginning teachers develop their knowledge and skill. The publication outlines the functions of principals, Advice and Guidance co-ordinators and department heads in the Advice and Guidance program. It also encourages beginning teachers to contact their local union representative in the event that novices' feel their school's Advice and Guidance program is inadequate (especially if they are not receiving their 20 percent release time) – should they have been unsuccessful in trying to resolve this with their administrators themselves.

We investigated whether principals discussed their schools' induction programs as part of interviewing prospective new hires. Several principals mentioned that they promote their school's Advice and Guidance program as a recruiting tool, emphasizing to prospects that they will be supported. Several beginning teachers reported that knowing whether or not a school had a good induction program influenced their employment decision. [11] But experts on induction also knew of a few extreme instances where prospective teachers offered unofficially to forego release time as an enticement for principals to hire them. Another topic discussed in hiring interviews concerned expectations for involvement in extra-curricular roles. National professional standards for teachers require them to contribute to the school community: for example, by being involved in extra-curricular activities. The Auckland College of Education newspaper offered this comment by a principal:

> Most schools don't expect too much [by way of extra-curricular responsibilities] from their first years. Yet in interviews, some [prospective teachers] promise the earth and set up expectations that they will do extra-curricular functions. It's easy to overload, so don't put a hand up to volunteer for everything. (ACE, 1999, p.16)

National policies for induction, certification and performance

This sub-section covers the following topics:

- characteristics of recent cohorts of beginning science teachers;
- national provision of 20 percent, paid release time for all beginning teachers;
- the guidance schools receive for providing an Advice and Guidance program to support first- and second-year teachers;
- requirements for provisional and then permanent teacher registration;
- new national expectations for beginning teachers' performance.

Who is a beginning teacher?

In recent years, beginning teachers in New Zealand have not necessarily been young. Many beginning teachers are individuals switching careers or are experienced teachers from other countries who are retraining for acceptance within the New Zealand system. Faculty at Wellington College of Education estimated that only 10 percent of their secondary cohort entered the program directly after completing a bachelor degree. The average age of the cohort in preparation at Wellington College of Education was 31 and ranged from 21–59. About half of the cohort at Auckland University consisted of experienced teachers from seven other countries, and the Auckland College of Education and Wellington College of Education cohorts also included some foreign teachers. We encountered former industrial science technicians in five of the fifteen schools visited and several were enrolled in each of the three preparation programs we studied. Because the mature students in the Auckland University program had financial obligations, such as supporting their families, about 90 percent of them were working part-time in addition to participating in full-time study.

Science teachers are better paid than science technicians in industry and teaching positions are currently more plentiful than jobs in science. The Post-Primary Teachers' Association collective bargaining agreement for 2001 set the national annual salary for a beginning secondary teacher who graduated from a teacher training program at $35,500 NZ. Teachers routinely receive a salary step increase each year. After only five years of experience, most teachers reach the maximum salary, which for 2001 is $48,800 NZ. [12] Science technicians from industry can be directly hired to teach, but they will receive a higher salary if they complete a teacher preparation program. This financial incentive ensures that most teachers who are new to teaching in New Zealand have completed a full preparation program. Therefore, the induction system does not need to screen out people who may not be prepared for or suited to teaching.

The main career path for secondary teachers that can advance their salary after the cap at the end of five years of increments is to take on departmental responsibilities and leadership. Department head (head of department or HOD) is a defined position that schools post and advertise nationally. It is common for teachers to apply for department head positions at other schools when no prospect of becoming department head exists in their current school for the foreseeable future. In larger science departments, supplements can be paid for fulfilling more specialized leadership roles in the department, such as heading the group of biology, chemistry or physics teachers. In one of the few schools where an experienced teacher rather than a administrator was leading its induction program, the teacher was paid a supplement for supporting beginning teachers. Some interviewees reported that taking on such roles bolsters a teacher's résumé for any future application to a department head position at another school.

While most beginning science teachers are enthusiastic about their chosen profession, the status of teaching is not necessarily high, as illustrated by this second-year biology teacher's comments about entering teaching after working as a science technician in a national laboratory:

> I decided that teaching was what I wanted to do. But it was kind of hard because you've heard the saying: 'Those who can, do; those who can't, teach'. I've always had the idea that teaching is one of the lower occupations. So, I had to fight all of my own prejudices and thinking: 'Why on earth would you want to be a teacher?' It's ridiculous – a career going nowhere. Now that I've done it, it's perfect for me and I'm glad that I didn't do a Ph.D. in biology. I realized I had two good skills besides science: organizational skills and people skills. So, that made me consider teaching.

Paid release time for a support program

For more than twenty-five years, the Ministry has provided funds that permit schools to make 20 percent paid release time available to every first-year teacher. Since the 1989 school restructuring, the Ministry of Education distributes these funds directly to each school having first-year teachers. Schools' approaches to implementing this statutory requirement varies, but administrators generally assign four classes per day to first-year secondary teachers instead the five classes typically required of other teachers. In terms of time, beginning teachers typically have 3–5 more free periods per week than do other teachers. School personnel with major roles in supporting beginning teachers already have time available for this through other means, which will be explained later. [13]

All of the schools we visited provided the expected release time to first-year teachers. Two schools (one advantaged and one disadvantaged – deciles 8 and 3, respectively) additionally extended 10 percent release time to their second-year teachers, electing to use funds from other budget categories to supplement the dedicated funds received from the Ministry for the release of first-year teachers. While it did not specifically ask whether beginning teachers actually received their release time, a national survey by the Teacher Registration Board reports that 90 percent of beginning secondary teachers felt their support was very good or satisfactory (Mansell, 1996).

In many schools, the people who support beginning teachers remarked on the importance of protecting release time from other demands, such as covering other teachers' classes. One administrator was aghast at the notion of misusing release time: "We never, never, never touch that time: it's inviolate". An administrator in another school reported her policy:

> My duty assistant [who assigns people to cover classes] knows that beginning teachers' release time is sacrosanct. There have been rare, unexpected times that we've had to approach them. But it is such an essential survival mechanism that I can't imagine prevailing upon their release time.

In contrast, administrators at three other schools we visited had on repeated occasions asked or prevailed upon first-year teachers to use release periods to fill in for absent teachers. In two of these schools, however, the Advice and Guidance co-ordinator ran interference with the duty official to ensure this practice was eliminated or drastically reduced. Beginning teachers emphatically felt their release time was crucial, as this novice observed:

> It's really frustrating when you are asked to cover someone's class, because you've really planned to use that time to prepare for

a practical or whatever. So now, what do you do? It's a real pisser. They don't ask you. You just find out in the morning. Sometimes, I've thought: "Oh no! They could have asked for any other period and it would be OK, but not that one!"

National policy also requires each school having beginning teachers to create a two-year Advice and Guidance program to provide support for beginning teachers to develop the skills and abilities needed for permanent registration. In practice, schools devote much more attention to first-year teachers than to second-year teachers. However, even experienced teachers from another country but new to New Zealand are required to participate in a school's Advice and Guidance program. We met teachers with ten years science teaching experience in other countries who were participating in school support programs and attending a regional workshop for beginners.

Schools create Advice and Guidance programs for their beginning teachers: the extent, nature and quality of the programs vary widely. [14] Larger schools that have several or many beginning teachers typically designate an administrator or staff member to be the Advice and Guidance co-ordinator of the school. The Teacher Registration Board issues small booklets of guidance on the characteristics of good programs (TRB, 1994, 1997). The booklets recommend roles and activities for everyone involved in supporting the beginning teacher: principals, Advice and Guidance co-ordinators, department heads, 'buddy' teachers and other school staff. The Teacher Registration Board publications also describe briefly some principles for designing programs. The examples below are drawn from several such publications:

- incorporate induction as an integral part of the school;
- provide for both group and individual assistance;
- provide support that is personal for the individual teacher and of practical use;
- locate a beginning teacher's classroom near the department head or buddy teacher;
- take particularly stressful periods in the school year into account, e.g. first reports to parents or major national examinations;
- involve beginning teachers in the development of their induction pro-grammes;
- document programmes;
- arrange conditions so that support providers can fulfill their roles;
- perceive Advice and Guidance as part of the overall professional development of teachers.

The Education Review Office, when inspecting schools every three years, has until recently mostly asked *whether* schools had developed a beginning teacher support program but did not determine *what* it was. In terms of documentation, a school's Board of Trustees is required to have a written policy on the supervision of beginning and student teachers. Some national officials are encouraging the Education Review Office to initiate greater scrutiny of this school function in the near future. The Advice and Guidance co-ordinator at one school credited a suggestion from the Education Review Office inspection the year before as the impetus for starting bi-weekly meetings for all beginning teachers in his school.

The New Zealand education system's funded induction policy is so long-standing because educators share a cultural belief in the importance and worth of supporting young professionals, which is described towards the end of the chapter in the fifth section on enabling factors. Given the prevalence and depth of this belief, it is not surprising that we could not find a formal program evaluation of its impact; its worth is taken at face value. Clearly, concerns about retaining beginning teachers in the profession is not the primary cause of these policies. Over the course of its twenty-five-year history, induction support has existed during times of over-supply as well as undersupply of teachers.

A 2001 PPTA survey of principals indicates that 26 percent of secondary teachers who began teaching in 1999 had left teaching after two years. Echoing this survey finding, many beginning teachers during our interviews said they did not envision being a teacher in ten years time. Most often, their reasons focused on a perceived degradation of the professional conditions of teaching due to increasing administrative work and curriculum changes. Very few novices mentioned salary as an issue.

Current concerns about teacher attrition has led the Post-Primary Teachers' Association to request an extension of paid release time to second-year teachers, as well as for first-year teachers. The Ministry has agreed to provide 10 percent paid release time for second-year teachers, beginning in 2002. This successful proposal to extend support to second-year teachers is the latest instance of an overall trend of strengthening the national induction policy during its twenty-five year history. As another example, in 1996 part-time beginning teachers employed half-time or more became eligible to an amount of release time proportional to their level of employment.

Expectations for provisional and permanent teacher registration

Up until 2001, students graduating from a teacher education program had to submit an application (along with a $15NZ fee) to the national Teacher Registration Board to become a *provisionally registered teacher*. All schools, including private schools, can only hire teachers who are registered with the

Teacher Registration Board. After two years experience, teachers can obtain a *practicing certificate* (a credential that must be renewed every three years). [15]

The Teachers Registration Board criteria for fully registered teachers address four, broadly conceived categories of teacher characteristics and skills (TRB, 1999, pp. 6-7): professional knowledge, professional practice, professional relationships and professional leadership. A total of twenty-two more specific characteristics are listed for these four broad categories. For example, seven kinds of knowledge expected within 'professional knowledge' include current curricula in subjects taught, pupil character-istics and progress, and appropriate learning activities and assessments. These requirements are applicable to all secondary teachers, regardless of grade level or subject to be taught. There are no additional registration requirements that are more specific to science teachers or to teachers in any other subject.

The authority to recommend a beginning teacher for permanent regis-tration rests with the school principal, who must attest to the teacher's fitness and competence. In practice, the principal consults with and may defer to staff who support the beginning teachers, particularly their depart-ment head. Administrators rarely stop a teacher from gaining permanent registration. Officials of the Teacher Registration Board knew of only about a dozen instances in the last few years. Instead of taking that action, princi-pals would be inclined to extend a beginning teacher's support program to three years and defer making a determination about permanent registration.

However, this option is also rarely exercised. Principals at only two of the fifteen schools visited had used it and only once during the last few years. The Teacher Registration Board has the authority to reject applica-tions for permanent registration, but has insufficient staff to review them for more than administrative purposes, unless some glaring inadequacy appears in an application or other information about deficiency in Advice and Guidance at the school are brought to its attention.

Under terms of the Post-Primary Teachers' Association collective-bargaining agreement with the Ministry of Education, a school cannot ini-tiate termination of provisionally registered teachers until they have taught for a minimum of two years. The intent is to allow beginning teachers two years to develop their competence. In theory, this legislates a school com-mitment to support beginning teachers, helping them to improve because they cannot fire them. However, some schools now use long-term relieving contracts (annual contracts for substitute teachers) to hire beginning teach-ers instead of the traditional practice of hiring them as permanent teachers.

Expectations for beginners' performance

The Ministry's new performance management system that all schools are currently implementing includes specific attention to and singling out of beginning teachers. For example, sample performance indicators for the 'learning and assessment theory' portion of the professional knowledge dimension (MOE, 1999, p. 34) include distinctions among 'beginning' teachers (those provisionally registered), 'classroom' teachers, and 'experienced' teachers (usually those who have taught for more than five years):

- classroom teachers should use an appropriate range of assessment techniques while beginning teachers should be able to do the same, but *with guidance*; further, experienced teachers also should be able to write assessment tasks for use across the department as well as in their own class.

Distinctions made for 'curriculum' include:

- demonstration by beginning classroom teachers that they understand knowledge base(s) underpinning curriculum areas/subjects, while classroom teachers should do the same but also demonstrate awareness of links between curriculum areas.

In addition to 'professional knowledge' illustrated above, there are seven dimensions of performance indicators. These are *professional development* (individual, collaborative and the Treaty of Waitangi [16]), *teaching techniques* (teaching programs/resources/activities, range of teaching techniques, technology and evaluation/reflection on teaching techniques), *pupil management* (managing pupil behavior, response to individual needs, response to diversity, and positive/safe environments), *motivation of pupils* (engage pupils in learning, establish expectations of learning), *Te Reo me ona Tikanga* (Maori pronunciation and protocols), *effective communication* (pupils, staff, families), and *support for and co-operation with colleagues* (effective working relationships, assistance with improving teaching and contribution to wider school activities).

3. Expectations and Resources for Teaching the Science Curriculum

In addition to enabling a beginning science teacher to succeed in general aspects of teaching, another goal of induction is to enhance a beginner's *science* instruction. To set the stage for appreciating the latter, we now address the following two questions.

- What must beginning teachers do day to day to decide on details of what science topics to teach and creating lessons for them?
- What are the typical New Zealand science teaching practices to which novices aspire?

Typical school science courses and staffing

As shown in Figure 2 below, the only science courses offered during the first two years of secondary school – the main focus of our study – is an integrated science course. It includes biology, chemistry, physics and earth and space science.

Grade	Common science courses in NZ schools	Sarah's assignment[i]
8	integrated science	1 class
9	integrated science	2 classes
10	either integrated science or biology, chemistry, physics	1 class, integrated
11	biology, chemistry, physics	1 chemistry class
12	advanced biology, chemistry, physics	none

[i] While this figure indicates that five classes are assigned to Sarah, any specific class will only occur on particular days. Typical secondary school schedules occur over six days with different classes being held each day. This explains the apparent discrepancy with the earlier statement that administrators assign four classes per day to first-year teachers.

Figure 2: *Science courses most commonly offered in New Zealand secondary schools and Sarah's course assignment*

Sarah's teaching assignment illustrates the prevalent New Zealand practice for staffing science courses (true of all fifteen schools visited). Department heads typically assign at least two integrated science classes to every science teacher, as illustrated by the following department head's explanation.

> By and large, we've now made a policy here to say a teacher has three senior science classes and two juniors, or a fair amount of each. If you don't do this, you'll have some of the most difficult pupils [in the lower secondary grades] being taught by inexperienced teachers. If you get your experienced teachers down there, you are sharing that expertise throughout the department, you up-skill the entire staff's ability to teach junior science, and the kids are getting a good guide, someone who is really skilled. I also think it's important for young teachers to get experience teaching senior science early in their career.

National science curriculum framework

In the early 1990s, the Ministry of Education included science as one of seven required school subjects. Over the rest of the decade, the ministry produced national curriculum frameworks for each subject, including publishing upper secondary science frameworks for biology, chemistry and physics, and integrated science for grades 1–12. Figure 3 below illustrates the national framework for integrated science by presenting its goals for physical science.

Achievement Objectives. Pupils can ...

1. carry out simple practical investigations, with control of variables, into common physical phenomena, and relate their findings to scientific ideas, e.g. *energy content of fuels, reflection/refraction, electromagnets, forces and motion....*,

2. describe various ways in which energy can be transformed and transferred in our everyday world, e.g. *rockets, electric blankets, hair dryers;*

3. investigate and describe the patterns associated with physical phenomena – some patterns may be expressed in graphical terms, e.g. *links between voltages and currents, heat and temperature, forces and simple levers;*

4. investigate how physical devices or systems can be used to perform specified functions, e.g. *an arch to support a bridge, a moisture tester for house plants, light-emitting diodes as off/on indicators.*

Possible Learning Experiences (samples, 3 out of 12). Pupils could be learning by:

• making a human shape from cardboard and using a plumb-line to find the position of its centre of gravity;

• describing the pattern of results formed from graphing the effects of applied forces on a spring;

• using electrical meters to make measurements of voltage and current in series and parallel circuits, when wiring circuits to light a model house.

Assessment Examples (samples, 2 out of 6). Teachers and pupils could asses the pupils:

• ability to collect and analyze data from a variety of sources, when the students present a report on local energy resources;

• ability to relate a knowledge of chemistry to their design of a device, when they explain the operation of a moisture detector.

Excerpted from **Science in the New Zealand Curriculum** (Ministry of Education, 1997, pp. 80-81). *Italics are indicated in original document.*

Figure 3:   *National goals for integrated science: physical science objectives, learning experiences and assessment (examples for grades 8 and 9)*

Varying science department course specifications and resources

The general nature of the language of the national curriculum framework affords schools wide latitude in specifying the detailed topics to be taught in grades 8 and 9 and how to teach them. Individual school science departments must devise their own agreements on the curriculum for each integrated science course and they develop detailed course specifications with no external assistance and no practice or requirement of filing their course plans with the Ministry. However, the Education Review Office inspects the quality of course specifications when it reviews a school's program every three years.

For integrated science in grades 8 and 9, science departments typically organize the course into 6–12 units, with each unit spanning 2–4 weeks of instruction. The units collectively sample content from all of the science disciplines. One school's list of unit titles for grades 8 and 9 are provided in Figure 4 as an example of the curriculum at these levels. Science departments vary by school in whether all teachers must teach the same units and whether they must teach them in the same order.

Subject area	Grade 8	Grade 9
scientific skills	laboratory skills	experimental design/investigation
living world	plants, animals, places leaves cells and microscopes	NZ disappearing wildlife plant reproduction diet
material world	nature of matter chemical separations	introduction to chemistry chemical change
physical world	forces machines	electricity light energy
earth and beyond	oceans	earth science

Figure 4:   *Unit titles for integrated science in grades 8 and 9 (sample taken from one secondary school)*

For each unit, departments specify objectives for pupil learning. The resource set for the introduction to chemistry unit, noted above for grade 9, includes the following objectives among nine desired learning outcomes: describe the arrangement of electrons in atoms, recall the formulae and names of common ions and write word equations for simple chemical reactions involving the formation of ionic compounds. Each teacher is expected to address all the objectives, but is free to add objectives if time permits.

Departments, for each unit, compile and regularly update instructional ideas and lesson plans such as the following:

- handouts and instructions for pupil activities;
- sheets for pupil work in class or at home;
- key points for lecture notes;
- activities for assessing pupil learning;
- references to pertinent sections of the department's textbooks;
- background information for teachers themselves about the science content of the unit.

Typically, many staff contribute the contents of these unit folders, normally made available to all staff in the science department's resource room, with teachers offering curricular resources for science topics within their subject expertise. At one school, for example, the physics teacher was credited with adding a lot of resources to the 'Forces and motion' unit within the integrated science course for grade 9, while the chemistry teacher provided extensive instructional materials for the 'Introduction to chemistry' unit in the same course.

Teachers in most schools are free to decide whether or not to use these departmental curricular resources, while adapting or creating their own curricular approaches and resources is looked upon favorably, provided the unit's learning objectives are met. We encountered beginning teachers who took advantage of some of their release time to create their own lessons. One commented: "I made heaps and heaps of lessons because I didn't like the games, worksheets and hands-on activities in the department's boxes". A science department also created workbooks containing homework assignments and sold them to pupils at the beginning of the year for use during the entire grade 8 and 9 integrated science courses. At another school, a science department guide for its beginning teachers included procedures for taking science field trips, for using the services of the science laboratory technician and details on how to request that the technician order scientific reagents and apparatus.

Textbooks play a minor role in most New Zealand science classrooms, serving as an infrequently-used class resource rather than daily medium of instruction. At grades 8 and 9, class sets of one or more textbooks are available for teachers to check out from the department's resource room and use in their classes on a given day; none of the schools observed issued textbooks to individual pupils for their use during the year. The seven textbooks inspected all contained 100–150 pages for a year-long course, but varied in the proportion of pages providing information, instructions for pupil activity or exercises/questions for pupil assessment.

Only two of the fifteen observed classes among five schools had textbooks in the room for the lesson that day. In one instance, the day's activity worksheet cued pupils to obtain a copy of the textbook from the front of the room to look up an answer to one particular question. In the other class, the teacher distributed copies of the textbook to permit pupils to refer to a biological classification key while examining some specimens. During interviews, most teachers indicated that they would bring textbooks to their class on average once every two weeks, considerably less often than this or almost never.

Some department heads reported that a minority of teachers might use textbooks in their instruction several times per week. Many teachers view textbook-based lessons as useful to leave as lesson plans for days when they have to be absent. An education researcher at Auckland College of Education observed: "This lack of emphasis on textbooks partly is a resource issue and partly a philosophical tradition of schools crafting their own curricula".

The quality of a department's course specification and locally developed curricular resources is a strong influence on all teachers, and, particularly, on the beginning teacher. A strong syllabus and rich resources lay out an instructional course of action for beginning teachers and equips them to teach it. In Sarah's school, beginning teachers do not have to spend a lot of time deciding what topics to teach or seeking out guidance to inform such decisions, because unit titles and their topics are specified. In other schools, such as that of her friend, support for the year-long courses are less specific, necessitating beginning teachers working extensively on their own or in collaboration with others to fill in more detail. Departments also vary in the extent to which information is on hand specifying how to teach what topics, which activities to use, what resources are available, and so on.

Science departments found in smaller schools, particularly rural schools, find it more challenging to marshal such specific curricular guides. Any beginning teacher entering a school as its lone science teacher would be very hard-pressed to create a strong science course, if the predecessor did not leave one behind. Advisory Service experts were very aware of small schools where such under-resourced circumstances exist. In a recent comparison of mathematics and science instruction in five countries, the Education Review Office questioned these practices.

> The task of developing class programmes directly from national curriculum statements is both difficult and time consuming. In the overseas countries we studied, it is considered that teachers should not be required to undertake the task alone and that support should be provided in the form of textbooks and teacher guides. (ERO, 2000, p. 102)

Universal 'hands-on' science teaching aided by science technicians

The national science curriculum emphasizes investigation through 'hands-on' experiences, referred to as 'practicals'. This long-standing practice reflects a broader societal outlook that emphasizes leading an active life, especially valuing outdoor activities in nature. Most schools organize science-oriented field trips for all pupils at least once during the year. During our visit, for example, staff at one school took pupils for a weekend astronomy camp while another school planned a day trip to the seashore as part of the middle-grades oceanography unit.

Referring to the practical science emphasis, a refrain heard in many interviews with beginning teachers, experienced teachers, administrators and national experts in science education, the president of the science teachers association for greater Auckland noted:

> It is standard for secondary schools, regardless of their socio-economic status, to have laboratory facilities in multiple science classrooms – such as lab benches, gas, water, electricity, a fume hood – and to have adequate equipment like microscopes and beakers. The amount of hands-on science taught is probably more strongly related to teachers' styles. But there is a New Zealand tradition of teaching science from a practical view, especially in junior secondary. Teachers have pupils do a science experiment almost daily. So, the science-equipped classrooms are not just assigned for the senior biology and chemistry classes, they are for the earlier integrated classes as well.

Indeed, classrooms in each of the schools visited had such facilities and equipment. The schools, of widely varying socio-economic status, also had well-stocked science supply rooms. Hands-on science is emphasized particularly in the integrated science courses of grades 8–9, as one department head explained: "The philosophy of junior science is to be hands-on, more than the senior science classes. So, we make extra effort to schedule junior classes in science-equipped rooms." Over four-fifths of the lower secondary lessons we observed engaged pupils in activities during 70–95 percent of the class period. Activities included investigating a pendulum swing, making precipitates, taking a laboratory practical on a dozen basic tasks such as reading a meniscus level and exploring electric circuit boards. [17]

The existence of laboratory technicians in secondary schools' science departments enables beginning teachers, particularly, as well as experienced teachers, to teach science practicals virtually every day, a requirement of the national science curriculum. Laboratory technicians prepare solutions and equipment, repair apparatus, order supplies, and more. A science specialist at the regional Advisory Service emphasized their importance:

> Techs prepare reagents and deliver them to the science class as requested. I've been in schools with bad techs and it's trouble. If your techs are good, the teachers are not stressed out. If you are doing practicals all the time, you can't be running around having to grab things. They do agar plates [for growing bacteria] and everything like that. They may do all the photocopying as well.

All teachers interviewed (especially beginning teachers) said that they could not imagine functioning without the lab technicians. In a few schools, both lab technicians themselves and beginning teachers reported that the technicians went beyond supplying physical resources: they were also coaches, helping beginning teachers set up and use apparatus, or even showing how to conduct practical science tasks with their pupils. A science department head related that "my lab techs definitely make instructional suggestions to beginning teachers, and I suggest to beginning teachers that they get advice from the techs".

Prevalent practical teaching methods create a steeper learning curve for science novices than instruction relying more heavily on lecture and seatwork. Novices universally express frustration with learning to address the realities of classroom management, such as dealing with pupil behavior. Coping with active learning in science practicals adds several layers of complexity to this general learning challenge: for example, dealing with science safety. Another learning burden is how to use science supplies and apparatus with pupils effectively, which is quite different from having used such things themselves in their college science courses. Fortunately, the existence of science laboratory technicians in schools eliminates the need to learn how to acquire and assemble supplies and having to spend time doing this. But, teachers still face the challenge of learning how to manage instruction with science apparatus and supplies. The following comments by a deputy principal express a common perception that beginning science teachers have a lot to learn about teaching.

> It's important to remember that the universal experience of beginning teachers of needing more time is compounded for beginning science teachers. They have to become familiar with new materials, equipment, facilities, etc., needed for the practicals. Teachers need to run experiments themselves beforehand if they aren't familiar with them in order to see what happens.

One beginning teacher estimated that he had made fifty trial runs of equipment, reagents and apparatus during his first year of teaching. While this was the most extreme occurrence that we heard about, many beginning science teachers felt that conducting dry runs of science activities consumed considerable time.

4. Diverse Support Providers: a Repertoire of Support Activities

We were struck by the variety of the sources of support incorporated into the design of schools' induction programs and how they employ a range of induction activities. One reason we chose to study induction in New Zealand was its contrast with places where induction programs place all or most of the responsibility for assisting beginning teachers on a single mentor or on a couple of people. After describing the diverse support providers and varied induction activities, we distinguish between the support given to first- and second-year teachers, noting that the support received by a beginning New Zealand teacher is not always that prescribed.

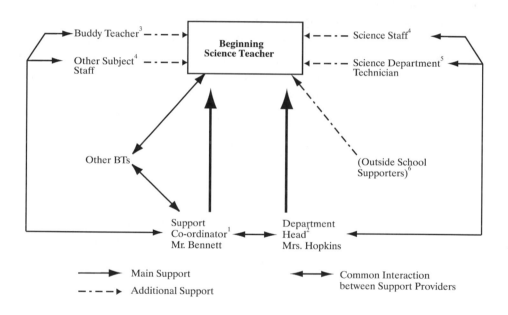

[1] Usually a deputy principal. Sarah's co-ordinator was Mr. Bennett.   REQUIRED
[2] Usually the head of department (HOD) for science. Sarah's HOD was Mrs. Hopkins.   REQUIRED
[3] Usually a young, promising teacher.   OPTIONAL
[4] Usually through faculty coffee breaks, department meetings, or impromptu interactions.   UNOFFICIAL
[5] Depends on disposition of science lab technician.   UNOFFICIAL
[6] Science teachers in other schools, regional advisors, workshops, courses.   OPTIONAL

Figure 5:   *Main and additional support providers for beginning secondary science teachers*

Diverse support providers

In the course of a typical day and week, Sarah benefits from support from many sources, as shown in Figure 5. It includes a comprehensive set of support providers to be found in New Zealand, whether or not they appeared in Sarah's particular story. The science department head (Mrs. Hopkins) and the deputy principal (Mr. Bennett) are Sarah's two principal sources of support. School Advice and Guidance programs assign a main mentor to each beginning teacher. Advice and Guidance guidelines also recommend assignment of a 'buddy' teacher. Additionally, beginning teachers support each other through facilitated peer support meetings.

Although not a formal part of the induction program, several other sources within the school support beginning teachers: other science staff, science department laboratory technicians and staff in other subjects. Beyond the school, regional science advisors and workshops or short courses at colleges and universities also aid novices. The following comments by one second-year teacher illustrates and summarizes the ways in which novices in New Zealand find support in many directions.

> Four people were especially helpful last year. Dorothy [her department head] was brilliant. Any questions and I'd go straight in and ask and she was happy to answer. I still do. The second person was Glenda [her buddy teacher], the biology teacher next door. She was the first line of attack because she was next door. I'd run across to her and she was full of advice. The third was Irene, who helped me with astronomy and geology. Mr Hastings [her AG co-ordinator] absolutely was looking out for me and the meetings he ran for all of us [beginning teachers in the school] were really valuable. Officially, Dorothy and Glenda were assigned to me by Mr Hastings. But, with Irene, it just turned out that she was a lot of help to me too.

Given the level of effort put into teacher induction, it is interesting to note that few opportunities exist for support providers to learn about their roles and even fewer support providers take advantage of what there is. The most common training is indirect: many department heads have received a few days of training at some time during their career from teacher preparation institutions. These sessions focus on how to be an effective supervising (tutor) teacher for students doing their practice teaching. During our study, a national, week-long, between-term course specifically about induction was offered to Advice and Guidance co-ordinators, heads of departments and administrators. It had to be cancelled due to low enrollment. Similarly, the Wellington region's Advisory Service offered a one-time, after-school meeting to discuss induction program issues but dropped it when almost none of the Advice and Guidance co-ordinators expressed interest.

Department heads

In the vast majority of the schools we visited, the primary assigned mentor was the science department head: the few other schools assigned another experienced science teacher. Given that department heads are generally well-regarded as instructional leaders, they are accomplished teachers who have expertise to share with beginning teachers. Administrators provide department heads with release time and a stipend for their overall role; mentoring provisionally registered teachers is considered part of this work.

While the head of department interacts with beginning teachers in many ways in their capacity as supervisors, they also interact with their novice teachers in a variety of ways in their specific role within the induction program. For example, they observe beginners' classes both formally and informally, they hold one-on-one meetings with them, they permit beginners to observe their teaching and they alert them to professional development opportunities outside the school. We encountered many schools where head of department–novice teacher interactions around induction were limited, usually focusing on formal observations of the novices' teaching. But most heads of department and their novices nevertheless viewed the relationship as quite open, with novices feeling their department heads were accessible. In a few schools, the mentoring involvement of the head of department was quite intense, as illustrated by this departmental head's comment about helping a first-year teacher: "In the first term, I must have spoken with him after school for about 30 minutes on four days of the week. This is not uncommon in my experience. The conversations are informal in nature."

Department heads evaluate beginning teachers as well as support them. Although these two roles could theoretically be at cross-purposes, Sarah and other novices as well as department heads whom we interviewed generally did not perceive this to be an actual conflict. This beginning teacher comment illustrates how novices mostly feel free to be open with their head of department:

> I choose a class where I had run out of ideas. The pupils weren't bad, but they weren't as good as I wanted them to be. So, I asked [his department head] to come into that class. I got some really good ideas. I'm still using them today.

Another novice took a while to acquire an openness to being observed:

> I have one class that is a nightmare. I would like to have had the head of department come to observe that class, but it's also human nature to want to avoid having her observe that class. I eventually let her see it late in the year.

'Buddy' teachers

Department heads may not have the personal dynamic to relate well to younger beginning teachers, nor have all the skills or expertise needed to address the range of beginner needs. This potential problem is eased by the fact that a 'buddy' teacher is also usually assigned to a beginning teacher, often chosen to complement the skill and attributes of the department head.

Buddy teachers are usually a secondary source of support and their roles vary. Sarah's buddy teacher helped substantively by observing one of her difficult classrooms and offering her advice on classroom management. An AG co-ordinator in another school had a quite different view of the buddy teacher's role: "I assign a buddy teacher who lives nearby and can give them a ride if need be, bring some work home to them if they're sick, etc." We only heard of buddy teachers in two-thirds of the schools visited.

Advice and guidance co-ordinators

The school's Advice and Guidance co-ordinator is the second main source of support. Deputy Principals usually have the responsibility of running the school's professional development program for all teachers and this includes creating and playing a leading role in the Advice and Guidance program for first- and second-year teachers. The administrators' flexible schedules give them the availability to meet beginning teachers for one-on-one meetings whenever the novices have free periods. In two of the largest schools, administrators appointed experienced, interested teachers as the AG co-ordinator and provided them with stipends, but did not make release time available for their Advice and Guidance role.

More commonly than the Department Head, the AG co-ordinator looks out for the novices' personal welfare: "You've got to be prepared to be a mother hen". The co-ordinator in another school similarly remarked:

> I watch them closely during the first term for ill-health. I had one
> [beginning teacher] who thought that every lesson of every day had
> to be perfect and I could see her literally get sick over it. I told her,
> hey, actually if you teach one perfect lesson a day, that's terrific.

Co-ordinators frequently counsel first-year teachers on what extra-curricular responsibilities to take on, as noted by these remarks made by two such co-ordinators:

> All teachers absolutely must be involved in something as required
> by national guidelines and they should because it gives a whole dif-
> ferent perspective of the pupils. But my recommendation is to be
> sensible about what they can manage.

> I temper their enthusiasm to say 'yes'. I encourage volunteering for limited incidents rather than long-term commitments: for example, being an assistant coach instead of a coach. I show them a pyramid of priorities, with teachers themselves at the top. Care for the caregiver or you won't be able to be of much help to the pupils.

But the Advice and Guidance co-ordinator also addresses more substantive aspects of teaching, particularly at the regular meetings when they convene all the beginning teachers in the school, which will be described in the following sub-section. Through these meetings, beginning teachers themselves become important sources of support for each other. The comment below illustrates how co-ordinators address both the personal welfare of beginning teachers as well as their need to learn more about teaching.

> I gave them some information on stress and some strategies to deal with it, and on being a good colleague. I said it's important for you to timetable in some time for you as well. Make sure your responsibilities are not pouring over into your life so there is no time left for you. We also in term one began to discuss strategies for teaching mixed-ability classes, learning styles, etc. By the end of term one, they are ready to realize that all their pupils are not the same and it is heartening to see them come to this awareness.

The Advice and Guidance co-ordinators in more than half of the visited schools had three or more years of experience in this role and several had kept this role for more than seven years. Not surprisingly, these long-term co-ordinators had developed the most materials for use in their school-wide, beginning-teacher meetings. They also had the best sense of which department heads were or were not providing enough support to their beginning teachers and subtly or even overtly compensated for the latter. One such department head remarked, "I mostly leave all the generic teaching issues to [her school's AG co-ordinator] and just focus on whether they [the beginning teachers] have any questions about teaching science".

Other in-school support providers

The induction roles played by other science teachers, staff in other departments and science laboratory technicians also can be important. The support provided by technicians was described previously. The most common way that other science teachers help a beginning teacher is through informal means such as conversations at interval or lunch time. All secondary schools have a 15–20-minute interval in the morning, when the entire school staff comes to the staff room for coffee and refreshments while the pupils have a recess. In our school visits, it appeared that almost all the teachers showed up for these collective breaks. As a result, beginning teachers have a brief chance to discuss anything on their mind with virtually any other teacher in the school. Beginning teachers stated that they often obtained quick advice from someone during interval, as illustrated by this first-year teacher's remark: "I get something done during interval just about every day. It's easier to talk face-to-face than leaving a note in someone's mailbox and trying to connect later". A similar phenomenon occurs at lunch time, although less so because attendance is lower (half to three-quarters). Sarah's story illustrates the kinds of discussions that can arise at such times.

Help from colleagues in other subjects is also informal but is more limited. Typically, their support also would occur during interval and lunch. However, one other way they can provide assistance is by letting novice science teachers observe their classes; Advice and Guidance co-ordinators in some schools urge beginners to observe classes other than science ones. The above roles are not considered part of the formal AG program of the school, although national guidelines exhort every experienced teacher and all school staff to advise and assist beginning teachers as needed.

Support outside the school

A few sources of support exist beyond the school:

- the regional Advisory Service holds workshops and assists schools;
- some teacher preparation programs hold workshops for graduates;
- a few colleges/universities also run courses for any beginning teacher.

The National Ministry of Education partially funds several regional Advisory Service offices which, among other things, are responsible for offering induction services. In the greater Auckland service area, advisors invite principals to send their first-year teachers to a day-long workshop once or twice during the school year. The regional science advisor holds a workshop specifically for any secondary science teacher in the region. In the greater Wellington service area, advisors traveled to schools that hosted four after-hours sessions during the year for secondary beginning teachers of any subject at any school in the area.

While the overt agendas of these workshops or sessions include learning some pedagogical strategies for teaching science and exchanging ideas for science practicals, the most important intent is for beginners to provide support for each other. Also, the workshop organizers regularly bring in second- and third-year teachers who talk about ways they got through their first year. Schools also have the option of requesting induction support for an individual teacher from the Advisory Service. This help is particularly important for rural secondary schools, where a science teacher may well comprise the entire science department and sorely need outside advice.

Almost every beginner reported exploring others' experiences in relation to their own at Advisory Service events to be invaluable, particularly learning what kinds of induction support teachers in other schools were receiving. It was frequently a profound psychological relief to discover that what they were going through (e.g. feeling inadequate) was common or even universal. Thus, like the in-school meetings with Advice and Guidance co-ordinators, these Advisory Service events are a kind of facilitated peer support within New Zealand's teacher induction provision.

Both the Auckland and Wellington area advisors had to work hard to recruit attendees, starting with having to survey area principals to identify their beginning teachers. Also, with the decentralization of education funding over the last decade, the Advisory Service typically has to charge schools for a portion of their services' costs. Many schools do not send their novices to these sessions and advisors can only help individual teachers sparingly.

Some colleges and universities offer workshops and courses specifically for beginning teachers. Certain teacher preparation programs are starting to run one-day workshops for their own graduates who are teaching in the area. Some institutions have also for some time offered courses for any beginning teachers. Teachers convene one evening per week during a term and cover topics similar to those addressed in the Advice and Guidance meetings at schools, such as classroom management and dealing with stress. Only two of the fifteen schools visited had sent beginning teachers to these courses.

Varied induction activities

Figure 6 below describes the extensive repertoire of induction activities that support providers might use. It also notes how prevalent activities were among the schools we visited and how frequently they occurred within a given school. Activities are grouped by their relative commonality among the fifteen visited schools as follows:

- 'universal' activities occurred in thirteen or more schools;
- 'common' activities occurred in eight to twelve schools;
- 'less common' activities were found in two to seven schools.

Figure 6 also serves as a summary of some activities that have already been discussed. Two key induction activities are elaborated below – those of formal and informal observations, and facilitated peer-support meetings. Finally, we discuss how beginners receive help with homeroom duties. This support activity was not strongly identified as part of the school's Advice and Guidance program. Nevertheless, it surfaced during interviews as a secondary yet nonetheless important type of support.

Induction Activity	Prevalance	Examples	Frequency
being observed*	universal	teaching observed by Department Head teaching observed by AG Co-ordinator, Principal, buddy teacher or other science teacher	2–8 times during year 0–2 times during year
facilitated peer support meetings*	universal	meet during school if free periods permit, or meet during lunch or after school	weekly to monthly
informal support*	universal	conversations with staff during interval* conversations with staff during lunch*	daily 1–2 times per week
school orientation and handbook	universal	visit school at end of prior school year one-day orientation before school begins handbook of school policies, resources, faculty	one-time activities
scheduled meetings with HOD*	common	planning or debriefing observation of teaching* setting goals and discussing progress address PRT challenges, problems planning science units or lessons discussing formal teaching appraisal recommending off-site science workshops and courses	alternate weeks to monthly
scheduled meetings with AG Co-ordinator	common	monitoring personal stress and welfare monitoring provision and use of release time address PRT challenges and problems identifying needs and corresponding resouces arranging participation in PRT workshops/courses recommending off-site courses on non-science issues	alternate weeks to quarterly

[1]Universal = Occurs at >90% of schools. Common = Occurs at 50–90% of schools.
*Indicates activities illustrated in Sarah's story.

Induction Activity	Prevalance	Examples	Frequency
observing other teachers	less common	observing Department Head, other science teachers observing science teacher at another school observing teachers of other subjects informal observations of other teachers	1–2 times per year, total weekly to monthly
assistance from buddy teacher*	less common	where to find things in the school whom to speak with for particular problems how to get things done unofficially in the school how to counsel pupils in homeroom ideas for classroom management*	alternate weeks to monthly
advice from science lab technician	less common	how to set up, operate science apparatus how pupils can effectively use apparatus/materials caution on common or cricial science safety issues recommend science activities for unit topics	monthly to quarterly
assistance from other teachers	less common	from science teachers about their science specialty from other subject teachers about pupils, cohorts	monthly to quarterly
off-site workshops and courses	less common	regional 1-day workshops* regional after-school meetings 1-day workshop by teacher preparation institutions courses at colleges/universities regional and national science teacher conferences courses by Teachers Refresher Course Committee	1–2 times per year quarterly 0–1 time per year 1 evening/week for 1 term 1 time per year 1 time per year

[2]Less common = Occurs at 10–50% of schools.

Figure 6:   Induction activities for beginning teachers

175

Formal and informal observations

Observation of teaching is a key activity of schools' induction programs and comes in several varieties:

- formal observation of novice's teaching by their department head or AG co-ordinator;
- informal observation of novice's teaching by their department head, AG co-ordinator, buddy teacher or other science staff member;
- novice's formal observation of their head of department, other science teachers, buddy teachers, teachers of other subjects or teachers at other schools;
- novice's informal observation of teachers in their own school.

In many schools, principals also observed first-year teachers once, but as part of appraising their performance rather than providing Advice and Guidance support. We use 'formal' to refer to lengthy (entire class period or significant part of one), scheduled and documented observations, and 'informal' for *ad hoc* or loosely scheduled, shorter (even for as little as a few minutes) and undocumented observations. 'Documented' refers to whether a completed observation form or other written notes are placed in the teacher's personnel file.

The universal type of observation among our visited schools was the head of department's observation of the beginner's teaching. This takes place two to eight times per year, with four to six observations being a more common frequency. Every teacher in the school is observed about twice per year for formal appraisal of their performance, but national Advice and Guidance guidelines recommend additional observations of first-year teachers to support their development. Advice and Guidance co-ordinators also may observe teachers, in addition to the observations conducted by department heads.

A brief survey we administered to more than thirty beginning teachers from twenty-five schools during three regional workshops for novices indicated a similar frequency of observation: all but four novices responded that they had already been observed from one to four times by their tenth week of teaching. These novices generally found such observations helpful, although the nature and amount of the department heads' feedback was diverse – from mostly oral comments about a few points to a few pages of notes about many things. All but two of these novice teachers reported that heads of department or Advice and Guidance co-ordinators had provided both written and oral feedback about what they had observed.

We found that beginning teachers, including Sarah, were generally comfortable with being observed, even though their department head and their administrator serving as the school's Advice and Guidance co-ordinator play dual roles of both supporting development and officially appraising performance. Also, again as with Sarah, most heads of department negotiated with their beginning teachers over selecting a class to observe and the aspects of teaching to be the foci of the observation. From the survey described above, three-quarters of these novices indicated that they had had a role in selecting the class to be observed and half reported that they also had an opportunity to influence the focus of their support provider's observations beforehand.

Although nationally recommended as part of an Advice and Guidance program, only a minority of the visited schools ensured that novices observed other teachers. Typically, the AG co-ordinator urged novices to do this or arranged it for them, as did Sarah's AG co-ordinator, Mr. Hastings. Even among such co-ordinators who gave attention to this induction strategy, some did not know whether or not the beginning teachers had, in fact, arranged and completed observations. A few co-ordinators and beginning teachers volunteered that they felt it was particularly useful to observe teachers in other subjects as well as other science teachers. This observation strategy permitted novices to focus on science-specific aspects of teaching when observing a science colleague and classroom management or other general teaching strategies when observing teachers in other subjects. In our survey of beginning teachers during their tenth week of teaching, just over half had observed another science teacher once or twice and two-fifths had observed teachers in other subjects once or twice. Only a quarter had observed teachers in another school at that point in the school year. Regional science advisors reported that observing science teachers in other schools is more common and more important for novices in smaller, typically rural, schools, where they may be the only science teacher on staff.

In over half of the visited schools, informal observations were significant and important induction activities. Sarah found it very helpful when her buddy teacher briefly observed her classroom management on a couple of occasions. The following comments by beginning teachers and a head of department at four different schools illustrate the commonness of informal observation and the perceived usefulness of it:

> At first I hated being observed, but now I don't even notice it. Teachers come in and out of your class and I don't even notice that there's another teacher there because I've been observed so much. Also, I go into her [the HOD's] third-form class all the time, about once a week. (A first-year science teacher)

> I have made a very conscious effort to drop in frequently for quick observations. I personally think you can get an enormous amount of

information from those kinds of visits, including the climate of the class and what that indicates about the teachers' management. It's important to do this often, because you otherwise won't be able to tell whether you've happened upon a particularly good, bad or just average day. It also desensitizes them to your presence, which lets you know more about their actual practice. (*A science department head*)

I hang around the back of her class more than she realizes and get a lot out of that. I probably drop by some teacher's class twice per week. (*A second-year science teacher*)

I'll hear that a teacher is doing some science activity that I want to see before I have to do it. They're happy to have me come watch. I bet I do this about once a month. (*A first-year science teacher*)

The acceptance of the informal observation described above stems largely from a general staff culture of being supportive of beginning teachers. The frequency of informal observation can be partly explained by the prevalence of practical science instruction. Although many materials and much of the apparatus are located in the science department's resource rooms, frequently these are distributed among the school's science-equipped classrooms at any given time. With practicals being taught almost daily, a science teacher may often have to enter another teacher's classroom to get something. During interviews with both beginning and experienced teachers, it surfaced that such occasions for entering others' rooms often led naturally to longer pauses in order to observe teaching informally.

Facilitated peer support meetings

In every school we visited that had more than one beginning teacher (thirteen such schools), the Advice and Guidance co-ordinators convened all their beginning teachers every two weeks during most of the year. Figure 7 below provides an outline of what one Advice and Guidance co-ordinator

Term 1	Term 2	Term 3	Term 4
first lesson/day/week	history of the school	teaching grade 8/9 pupils	case studies in pupil
school instructional	school structure	role of Board of Trustees	behavior
resources	expectations for pupil	arranging substitute	professional language
staff support network	behavior	teachers	relationships with pupils
homeroom duties	roles of Department	school-wide exams	year in review
classroom management	Heads	special education	looking ahead
classroom discipline	roles of Guidance	cultural differences	school finance
detention/discipline	Counselors	sports organizations	
system	roles of principal	teaching controversial	
pupil progress reports	outdoor education	issues	
parent/teacher interviews	teaching in Co-Ed school		

Figure 7: Sample schedule of topics for facilitated peer-support meetings

discussed during these bi-weekly meetings. The topics listed are fully representative of the topics we saw in similar documents at the visited schools and heard about in Advice and Guidance co-ordinator interviews. However, the scheduling of particular topics varied widely. While most Advice and Guidance co-ordinators emphasized classroom management topics, writing pupil reports and communicating with parents in Term 1, their opinion of when it was best to discuss other topics differed.

Many co-ordinators seek to strike a balance between letting the novices' week-by-week needs dictate the order of topics and their own beliefs about the most suitable timing for introducing topics. Co-ordinators emphasized that, in addition to bringing information to novices, they spent a lot of time (or even most of it) in many of the sessions addressing whatever practical, emotional or other needs the beginners brought up.

This co-ordinator's description of meetings illustrates how she determined the topic of her meetings:

> At the first PRT [provisionally registered teacher] meeting, they brainstormed some topics that they would like to address during the year. I also came prepared with about ten topics and asked them whether these seemed useful. With each group, the lists or emphases are different.

Another co-ordinator's comments describe both his meeting topics and how often he schedules meetings over the course of the school year:

> In their first week, I met with them every day to see how it's going. I meet with them once per week during the rest of the first term. I ask what's going well, and what they need help with. It's always classroom management. It's always relationships with pupils, how to mark pupil work. Prior to first events, I try to prepare them, for example, prior to first parent reports. I photocopy examples and we go through them. Prior to the first parent evening, I role-play with them. I ask, how are you going to deal with this one? As the year progresses, I tend to see them less, which mostly is O.K. because they are developing. Plus, I have an open door and I do get takers.

Advice and Guidance co-ordinators and beginning teachers generally viewed this facilitated support as quite important. One co-ordinator related: "I've always believed that peer support is the most crucial thing. So, basically, I often just get them started and they get on with it, helping each other." Similarly, a first-year teacher in a different school commented: "Those meetings were very, very important for me. Mr. [her co-ordinator] always had the information we needed and I really needed to talk with the other teachers about what I was going through. Someone usually had a terrific idea that helped." However, not all beginning teachers gave glowing reviews of this part of the induction program: "I felt the PRT meetings weren't useful after the first six months. I had grown beyond this."

Help with being a form teacher

> The biggest surprise of actual teaching was the amount of work involved in being a form teacher. There wasn't a clue about this in teacher preparation, even in the practice teaching.

These retrospective comments by a second-year teacher illustrate that being a form teacher (homeroom duties) constitutes a substantial new effort for beginning teachers. Teachers and administrators often referred to this work as a focal site for carrying out 'pastoral' responsibilities related to the pupils' welfare. However, a lot of pragmatic business occurs here each day – attendance, announcements, disciplinary actions, etc. Whenever any of the school's teachers have difficulty with a pupil's behavior during their classes and want outside intervention, the first procedural step for minor infractions is to ask the form teacher to address the pupil's problem. The form teacher then has to find time within the form period or other moments of the school day to counsel the pupil.

Because teacher preparation programs typically cannot enable students to understand the reality of this upcoming responsibility, Advice and Guidance programs need to ease beginning teachers into this aspect of the job, or at least give them steady advice on how to be effective. One Advice and Guidance co-ordinator tells her charges, "Especially watch your involvement as a form teacher". She describes her school's policy this way: "The administration takes care to give pretty nice form classes to year one teachers. We don't throw them in the deep end."

Schools supported novices in quite different ways: avoiding assignment of any form classes to beginning teachers; assigning whatever form classes are perceived to comprise 'easier' pupils to handle; enlisting Advice and Guidance co-ordinators or heads of department to help with the home room – the last being the most common support method. Schools used varied approaches to this latter support method as well: the department head or Advice and Guidance co-ordinator might jointly conduct the form period with the beginning teacher for the first few weeks, gradually phasing the novice into full responsibility for it. Other support providers observed or 'shadowed' the beginning teacher as they conducted form period. Still other support providers just made a point of being sure to discuss how form periods were going when they met with novices on other occasions, such as during the facilitated peer support meetings or during regular one-on-one meetings with them.

The role of professional development at large

Although first-year teachers are already experiencing substantial professional development through the induction program, they also have requirements and opportunities to participate in the professional development available to all teachers in the school. The only required participation is in school-wide or departmental meetings. Typically, most are administrative, but some are learning sessions: school or departmental staff meetings occur from as frequently as alternate weeks to as rarely as every other month.

Discretionary professional development opportunities are often more substantive. They include day-long courses offered throughout the year or week-long courses provided between terms, as well as regional or national science conferences. Colleges, universities and the regional Advisory Service offer the one-day courses. A national, teacher-run Teacher Refresher Course Committee offers week-long courses between school terms. National science teacher conferences occur only every other year, while regional science conferences occur most years. A couple of department heads all but required beginning teachers to join relevant science teacher associations. However, most science department heads placed little emphasis on this.

The national Ministry of Education provides every school with earmarked professional development funds that average out to four days of substitute (relief) teachers for every teacher in the school. However, these funds also have to cover transportation, registration and other costs as well. For remote rural schools, this money is severely limited due to the extra cost of transport (by car). As a result, schools usually provide fewer than four days per teacher in order to cover other costs and most schools require teachers to make an out-of-pocket contribution to such costs. Most departmental heads and Advice and Guidance co-ordinators clearly informed novices that funds were available for substitute teachers. In some schools we visited, support providers emphasized to novices that they are entitled to the same share of professional development funds as every other teacher in the school, urging novices to take advantage of them.

As with all teachers, beginning teachers can learn about out-of-school professional development opportunities by scanning announcements that administrators post in the staff room, advertisements in the education newspapers found in the staff room or through the national *Gazette*. However, department heads and Advice and Guidance co-ordinators often directly alert novices to courses.

About one-third of the beginning teachers we talked with took a one-day, off-site course at least once during their first year. For many of these teachers, this was in addition to participating in off-site workshops expressly for beginning teachers. A few first-year teachers went to two courses. Only a few novices mentioned going to science conferences or taking a course between terms. However, a national science education specialist remarked, "I've been amazed recently at the numbers of first- and second-year teachers at the science conferences. It's still not many, but, historically, you saw very few there. I don't know what's causing the change."

One department head brought to light the implicit learning opportunity below, which she transformed into an induction strategy. Because this interview occurred on our last day in New Zealand and this induction strategy had never surfaced previously, we suspect it is uncommon but were unable to find out how frequently it occurred among other schools.

> In my department, all teachers assigned to a junior, integrated science course get together now and then to plan the course. When there are beginning teachers, I make sure that all the junior science teachers help them learn how to teach these classes, by meeting more often than they would normally, and by making sure the beginning teacher never gets assigned to be the leader for any unit in the course.

Reduced support for second-year teachers

While induction policies and programs for beginning teachers span the first two years, they emphasize support of first-year teachers. In practice, this means that most kinds of support are reduced or eliminated for second-year teachers. The varied frequency or amount of support indicated in Figure 8 below consists of averages based on our visits to fifteen schools cited as having exemplary support programs. Understandably, all second-year teachers related that they especially missed the first-year's reduced teaching load and the resulting free periods. A common remark was that of

Component of Support Program	First Year	Second Year
Free periods	4-6 frees	2 frees
Meetings with supervisor	weekly	monthly
Being observed	2-8 times	2-4 times
Observing others	1-3 times	-
Informal observations	monthly	every 2 months
Interacting with buddy	every 2 weeks	every 2 months
Group meetings	every 2 weeks	monthly
New teacher workshop	1	-
Other workshops/courses	1	1

Figure 8:   Differences in support between first- and second-year teachers

wishing they had done more observation of other teachers' classes in the first year when their release time would have made it easier to schedule.

Almost all second-year teachers felt it was appropriate that programs reduce their participation in the facilitated peer-support meetings. Some did not feel the benefits were strong enough to warrant any further participation in them, but did not mind taking part on a reduced frequency if only to share their prior experiences with new first-year teachers. One school required second-year teachers to continue participating along with the first-year teachers.

Less-extensive induction programs

It would be inaccurate to conclude from this chapter that every beginning teacher in New Zealand experiences a wonderful system of support. Much of the chapter is based on data from schools recommended to us by knowledgeable insiders as having the strongest induction practices. We wanted to learn about the perceived 'best' possibilities of teacher induction in a country where policies and money provide a good context. However, we wanted not only to understand such practices in New Zealand, but also to have better sense of the entire spectrum of induction programs in the nation. Toward that end, we additionally observed and interviewed beginning teachers at regional meetings.

Even in the schools with purpoted exemplary Advice and Guidance programs, we found instances where the implementation of the program described by beginning teachers was less than that described by the schools' support co-ordinators. For example, during interviews with beginning teachers at a few schools, it became apparent that they interacted with their supervisors and co-ordinators less frequently than had been described by the latter. [18]

Support programs among the nation's schools at large are considerably less extensive, for example: less release time, fewer observations, fewer group meetings with the co-ordinators, fewer individual meetings with the supervisor. To illustrate the extreme low-end of the implementation range, here are a couple of challenging examples. One beginning teacher in her second term reported that she had never yet had had an individual meeting with her assigned mentor, except for an initial orientation session. Another beginning teacher in term two said that he appreciated regularly using all his free periods to relax and catch up on marking pupil work, i.e. no formal induction program activities had thus far in the year been afforded this teacher during his free periods. While national recommendations encourage these uses of release time as some among a range of possibilities, the intent is for schools to provide an overall system of support and development during at least part of the release time.

5. Enabling Factors Supporting Induction within the Culture of the Educational System

What are some central aspects of the New Zealand educational system that make it possible for beginning teacher support programs to be effective?

A universal commitment to beginning teacher support

There is a pervasive culture or belief throughout the educational system in New Zealand that beginning teachers should be supported. Participants at all levels of the system assume that beginning teachers have particular needs and, therefore, the system must pay explicit attention to addressing them. Many beginning teachers state that they feel free to approach almost anyone in their department for advice: for example, they feel they can ask other teachers to drop in to see how they teach some specific topic/activity. This strong culture of support makes it easier to implement beginning teacher support programs and activities.

"I believe teachers would walk out if the government tried to drop the Advice and Guidance program" (a second-year teacher). Such sentiments reflect the striking level of importance attached to the beginning teacher support program, especially in light of the major changes the current national government is demanding of teachers. While many teachers complain about these other changes and indicate they ultimately may leave teaching because of them, they cannot imagine that even an activist government would consider eliminating or even reducing the Advice and Guidance program to save money. They view the program and its effectiveness as a given. We heard many unsolicited comments (some impassioned) about the importance of meeting beginning teachers' needs.

Teachers and school-level administrators also were willing to invest in the effort to support beginning teachers, even though they fully realized the considerable risk that the beginning teacher will move on to another school after their first or second year, or even during one of them. This was illustrated by an Advice and Guidance co-ordinator who remarked:

> We are obliged to support a provisionally registered teacher for even just 12 weeks, and document that support, because provisionally registered teachers must be able to document their Advice and Guidance programs over the entire first two years when they apply for a permanent certificate.

The Director of the Teacher Registration Board commented:

> A positive view of professional practice would be that, although beginning teachers may move on to another school, you still would provide them with really good professional development and

support because they'll take these skills with them to wherever they teach. You have made a contribution to the profession as a whole.

Many support providers viewed their assistance of the individual as a commitment to the teaching profession and the entire country's need for strong and successful teachers and teaching. National officials also commented that they took a dim view of the school administrator who fails to support beginning teachers, because they are failing to maintain and advance the professionalism of teaching in New Zealand. In other words, some interviewees expressed the view that supporting beginning teachers is an important part of the definition of being an education professional.

Attention to initial teaching conditions

The prevailing orientation is therefore to put a premium on the needs of beginning teachers. Administrators and department heads arrange beginning teachers' loads to ensure the most appropriate teaching assignments that are possible within the particular school's circumstances. Department heads often noted that they would avoid assigning the demanding, grade twelve courses to first-year teachers. These are seen as very fast-paced courses that would put too much of a burden on the beginning teacher. One second-year science teacher related this experience:

> Last year, they had the only other chemistry teacher teach a single class of thirty-five pupils for [grade twelve] chemistry, but now we both are teaching a grade twelve class with fifteen pupils each. They didn't want to burden me in year one with the extra work of learning how to teach the grade twelve course. Although the pupils are a little easier, the exams and pace of the course make it pretty full on.

At the other end of the spectrum, department heads claimed they would not assign beginning teachers to classes comprised heavily of low-ability or otherwise challenging pupils. Several department heads noted that experienced teachers are best able to help pupils who have the most challenging learning needs and therefore warrant the opportunity of having the best (more experienced) teachers. Consistent with this, a number of department heads said they personally took the most difficult classes. Staff at regional Advisory Service offices, who work day to day with the varied schools in their area, strongly expressed that the general New Zealand culture is to give very thoughtful attention to a beginning teacher's assignment. Experienced teachers are expected to take some of all kinds of pupils, not just the best pupils.

Here is an influential outcome of attention to a seemingly minor national recommendation of the Advice and Guidance program – locating the beginning teacher in a classroom near the supervising or buddy teacher.

It was indeed common to find that beginning teachers' classrooms were next door to their supporting colleagues. In many schools, this meant that a more experienced teacher had to relocate classrooms so that the incoming novice could be next to or nearby the head of department's classroom. This proximity fostered natural interactions that might not have otherwise taken place: for instance, dropping in on each other's class, overhearing something in each others' class and talking about it later, as well as getting or offering little pieces of advice between classes.

We also found a few striking examples of schools making a major effort to give novices an appropriate room. For example, one science staff in a crowded school, where most teachers had to rotate among classrooms rather than have their own, voted to give the beginning science teacher a dedicated classroom even though it meant an experienced teacher would have to abandon it and move around classrooms each day. The beginning teacher explained: "They didn't think it was fair for me to have to run around the school all day on top of coping with everything else in my first year".

6. A Summary of New Zealand's Main Induction Features

We highlight below nine numbered points that we believe are important for an accurate understanding of teacher induction in New Zealand and discuss some lessons that this study can offer for extending or clarifying knowledge about teacher induction internationally.

(1) A tumultuous and pressured employment environment heightens the need for support.

Just learning to teach is a daunting experience for a novice anywhere in the world. But in New Zealand, a new teacher's working life also is harried because of on-going, major changes to the educational system that have daily impact on a teachers' job. Beginning in 1989 with the severe upheaval from the near instant elimination of all intermediary levels of the educational system, educators and administrators have faced a series of significant although less severe structural changes in schools and teaching. [19]

Here are some examples of major changes that teachers are facing: schools getting into the business of competing for the best pupils and staff; the introduction of national curriculum standards for science; intensive professional development to revise school science courses so they will better reflect these standards; changes in the nature and scoring of several major external examinations; the implementation of a performance management system for determining annual salary increases that is more labor intensive and specific than the former annual appraisal by administrators.

Also, an often-adversarial relationship between the Ministry of Education and the strong Post-Primary Teachers' Association has at times created a negative emotional climate for these changes.

The following comments by a second-year science teacher indicate that the above factors can quickly affect novices' feelings about the profession:

> I love teaching. I'll be a teacher for five years but I don't know about longer. I don't know if I can keep my job of teaching with the pressures on teachers in New Zealand. The day I wake up and don't enjoy it is the day I'll do something else. I think teaching is in my blood and I'm good at it, so I'll try to stay in education somehow. But I honestly think New Zealand is killing off its teachers and it seems to get worse and worse.

These sentiments echo a TRB report that found only 22 percent of second-year teachers thought they would still be teaching in ten years time.

> [The beginning teachers] enjoy teaching, yet feel under extreme pressure of overwork, excessive paperwork and administrative demands, and feel greatly underpaid and undervalued. These are not, on the whole, restless people who are leaving the profession because they are bored or want a change [...] They reflect rather a great sadness that they were finding it impossible to gain satisfaction from their chosen career, either in terms of professionalism or in terms of living a balanced life. (Mansell, 1996, p. 22)

This past decade of change also affects supporters of beginning teachers. They are fatigued, less clear about which things to emphasize with beginning teachers or what to say about them and are more challenged to find the time and circumstances to carry out support activities.

(2) *Science departments strongly determine the curricular burden on beginning teachers.*

Every beginning science teacher in the world must for the first time decide exactly what science topics to teach every day and how to teach them. In New Zealand, the national science framework only lays out generally what should be taught. There is no tradition of using textbooks as the *de facto* determiner of day-to-day curriculum decisions. In schools with strong science departments, department heads and staff have spent time wrestling with the translation of the national science framework to develop the specific contents of science courses, compiling extensive sets of curricular resources for the integrated science units taught in the middle grades. The science department at Sarah's school has done this, so her burden in deciding which topics to teach for grades eight and nine and how to teach them is relatively light. As she commented, "With the units already being prepared here, it saves a lot of time on planning".

Notice that we have used the term 'strong' departments rather than 'large' ones. We visited large schools with large science departments where much less curricular specification was laid out. These large schools usually had lots of science curriculum resources, but it was left to individual teachers to decide what to teach, a particular challenge for beginning teachers. Sarah noted, "I've talked to people at other schools, like my friend Glenda, and they pretty much are on their own for lesson planning".

We did not visit smaller secondary schools, but, as noted earlier, it is widely known that beginning teachers can face a serious curricular burden there, since few if any other science teachers exist to confer with and advise.

(3) Teachers face content challenges teaching middle-grades science.

Both teacher preparation and induction programs need to address misalignments between college science and secondary school science. Teachers teaching science in the middle grades have strong science backgrounds in a specialty. Lower secondary teachers and upper secondary teachers are one and the same and their teacher preparation programs require a degree in science or considerable tertiary science coursework. Before or during teacher preparation, prospective teachers acquire strong science backgrounds in a particular scientific field – typically biology, chemistry or physics – that are useful for teaching senior school science specialties.

However, science teachers do not have a sufficiently broad science background specific to lower secondary science. The science content of teacher preparation is misaligned with the school science curriculum in the middle grades. The science course for grades eight and nine is integrated science, drawing upon life, earth, physical and space sciences. In teaching integrated science for the first time, beginning science teachers must scramble to learn topics they may not have encountered since their own years in secondary school, as illustrated by these comments from a science department head, who is a biology teacher:

> The content of junior [lower secondary] science can cause difficulties for the beginning teacher. To address this, the department has extensive lesson plans prepared, practicals ready, handouts provided, etc. However, you still simply have to learn it and teach it. I'm developing the science course to extend general science to grade 10 for the first time at our school. My chemistry stopped in college, so I'm having to ask questions, read, do what teachers have to do to learn the science for general science.

(4) Screening prospective teachers permits induction programs to be supportive.

Everyone seeking to teach must complete a teacher preparation program to obtain the highest salary scale; this applies even to former science technicians from industry (like Sarah) or even Ph.D. scientists. Therefore, induction programs do not carry the burden of weighing the suitability of people who are pursuing teaching as an alternative career and addressing their special needs.

Further, not everyone seeking admission to a teacher preparation program gains entry; these programs screen these applications for suitability to teaching. Teacher preparation programs include substantial practice teaching and additionally screen out those who have serious difficulties during their practice teaching placements.

The result is that schools mostly assume that beginning teachers are prepared and suited for teaching and can focus their induction efforts on developing this potential. Beginning teachers still fail and are denied permanent registration, but very rarely. Therefore, the 'provisionally' registered teachers are provisional more in the sense of going through a temporary, distinct phase of being a novice rather than of being tenuously employed and likely subject to dismissal.

In fact, standard practice and the negotiated national teacher contract regards provisionally registered teachers as permanent hires, subject to confirmation. From the novices' perspective, having relatively high employment security makes them more likely to perceive the actions of department heads and administrators as support rather than as a threat to their future and consequently prompts beginners to be more open in expressing their need for assistance.

(5) School control of induction results in programs that vary widely in terms of level of effort.

In creating their individual Advice and Guidance programs, schools have latitude to use varied combinations of people and activities for providing support. But this unmonitored flexibility also means that there are schools where the induction 'program' can be limited just to the fact of the release time, i.e. where teachers receive their reduced teaching load but no support program is created for their development during this time. As an administrator in a supportive school noted:

> As I understand it, some schools ignore the Advice and Guidance program – beginning teachers are basically on their own.

(6) Understanding teacher induction requires looking beyond the ostensible program.

If we had confined our study of New Zealand teacher induction to its formal components, we would have missed the following:

- science department laboratory technicians contribute to the implementation of hands-on methods in science practicals as standard instructional practice and enable beginning science teachers to accomplish them;
- the influence of initial teaching conditions: for example, administrators and department heads typically try to avoid assigning the most demanding courses and pupils to beginners.

Additionally, we would not have encountered the universal but informal support provided by staff during morning interval and lunch time. So, when seeking to understand the experience of beginning teachers and the reasons for and nature and effectiveness of programs to support them, it is essential to investigate beyond the formal induction program itself.

(7) Science teachers may have greater need for support than other secondary teachers.

Where science teachers are truly expected to help pupils do science rather than solely come to know it, they need support in initiating this kind of instruction. To repeat earlier cited remarks made by an administrator:

> The universal experience of beginning teachers of needing more time is compounded for beginning science teachers. They have to become familiar with new materials, equipment, facilities, etc., needed for the practicals.

In New Zealand, the existence of laboratory technicians makes it easier for a beginning teacher to provide hands-on learning experiences from the outset. Also, strong science departments having well-specified curricula, including procedures and apparatus for practicals, render novices better able and more likely to provide active learning experiences. So, in New Zealand, things outside the formal induction program enable novices to use hands-on teaching methods readily.

But what about countries where schools do not have laboratory technicians or strong department staff assistance with hands-on instructional experiences? Perhaps induction programs that direct specific assistance to beginning science teachers in teaching active science lessons will increase the likelihood that they will adopt these instructional methods and be more effective in carrying them out.

(8) Requiring teacher induction and providing resources can generate substantial effort.

By policy, New Zealand requires teacher induction and expects it in practice. National policy requires schools to develop an Advice and Guidance program for their beginning teachers. Even teachers with extensive prior experience teaching in other countries must participate in it. National policies have been in place for twenty-five years and are accreting into a stronger induction system over time. Teacher preparation programs and the Post-Primary Teachers' Association both impress upon prospective secondary teachers that, when they get hired, they have a right to 20 percent release time in the first year as well as to an accompanying induction program during that time.

Further, teacher induction is a funded mandate. Money pays for time, i.e. the Ministry earmarks funds to cover 20 percent paid release time for every beginning teacher in the country, which is paid directly each year to those schools with a first-year teacher. The Ministry also funds limited regional resources for professional development services to beginning teachers. What does this achieve? Beginning teachers in every school we visited were receiving their release time and 90 percent of beginning teachers in a national survey viewed their induction program either as good or very good.

While most novices receive the benefits of a reduced teaching load, a lack of external monitoring allows some schools to fail to provide a support program for helping novices use the release for their initial professional development. However, in schools that take this mandate seriously, we saw a rich variety of substantial programs for supporting and developing beginning teachers.

(9) Facilitated peer support meets particular needs.

Among the many types of support activities we encountered, we were struck by the importance of facilitated peer support. We use this term for the frequent meetings when administrators convened all the beginning teachers in the school or the special day(s) when the regional Advisory Service convened beginning teachers from many schools. The field of teacher induction often places an emphasis on providing support through experienced teachers who use mentoring or other induction activities. However, the facilitated peer support activities addressed an important need that those other induction strategies are less able to fulfill – providing opportunities for beginners to express more candidly their need and experience. The regional meetings where teachers came from different schools provided even more safety for full disclosure than the school-based meetings. The exchanges of induction experiences also diversified the participants' expectations of the kinds of support they might request or expect from other support providers. Further, meeting with peers from other subject areas broadened novices' perspectives about several aspects of teaching.

In conclusion

After completing this study, it now seems obvious that an effective way of addressing the very wide-ranging needs of beginning teachers is to employ a variety of support providers and activities. Induction programs should attempt to meet novices' diverse needs – emotional, employee, practical, psychological, curriculum specification, knowledge and skills in both general and subject-specific pedagogy, and more. Programs often identify and recruit mentors who can tackle these many needs, but no single individual can have the requisite personal traits, skills, experience and knowledge to address them all. A common accommodation is to recruit someone who is available and has as close a fit as possible to the beginners' needs. However, this New Zealand study suggests that an alternative approach is a program that enlists several complementary sources of support that use a variety of induction activities. Mentors, induction program co-ordinators, other science staff and buddy teachers employ facilitating peer meetings, individual consultation, observation of novice and expert teaching, and more. Such activity can more readily provide comprehensive teacher induction.

Acknowledgements

So many New Zealanders went out of their way to help us. We are grateful that many people let us know them, as well as their work; for example, faculty at Wellington College of Education led us through a traditional Maori welcome ceremony. We have come to believe that many educators assisted us, not just because New Zealanders are generous by nature, but also because they take teacher induction seriously, are proud of it and have a professional interest in making sure we understood it fully and accurately.

Thanks go to Lydia Austin, a senior science educator at Auckland University, for arranging much of the itinerary of our first data collection, scheduling appointments with faculty at two other teacher preparation institutions as well as her own. We especially thank these faculty for extending so much time to us: Carolyn Barr and David Salter at Auckland University; Gillian Ward and Mavis Haigh at Auckland College of Education; Barbara Hollard at Wellington College of Education. Lydia and her physicist husband Geoff also hosted us and acquainted us with historical perspectives of and recent trends and current issues in the overall New Zealand educational system.

Carol Young and Barbara Hollard, science and health education specialists at professional development centers for the Auckland and Wellington regions, respectively, scheduled visits, observations and interviews for us at fifteen schools widely regarded as having excellent induction programs. They also invited us to observe their new science teacher workshops where we could talk with beginning teachers from schools having a wider range of induction programs. Mary Munro of the Wellington center spent a full day talking with us at length during which we also were able to observe her beginning teacher meeting. At the Teacher Registration Board, director John Langley and senior researcher Ruth Mansell gave us valuable direct knowledge of national induction policies and their implementation. Almost a dozen staff at the national Ministry of Education carefully explained the national science curriculum and initiatives to implement it. Rob Willits and colleagues at the Post-Primary Teachers Association explained the union's role in relation to new teachers and shared Post-Primary Teachers' Association data on teacher retention with us.

Given the daily pressures in schools, the dozens of teachers and administrators of the schools we visited probably had to make the greatest sacrifice in arranging time for talking with us and displayed their generosity in agreeing to us observing them. We dearly wish we could thank them specifically, but we promised confidentiality during all of our data collection. Not surprisingly, we close with an emphatic round of thanks to all of the beginning teachers we met. They, more than anyone, had to squeeze time from a seemingly overwhelming schedule to speak with us. We hope they will keep teaching, learning about teaching, and keep their enthusiasm for both. We are glad they have induction programs that makes all this more likely.

Chapter 5

Being and Becoming a Mathematics Teacher: Ambiguities in Teacher *Formation* in France

David Pimm,
with Daniel Chazan and Lynn Paine

For a cultural outsider to shadow a French secondary mathematics teacher for a week during the first year of teaching is perhaps repeatedly to be surprised. The work required is varied and not even predominantly based in a single institution, a school. Indeed, at first sight, it may seem an error even to consider *stagiaires* (as all first-year teachers are commonly known: broadly, 'probationers' or even 'inductees') as beginning teachers at all.

Nevertheless, for reasons which will soon become clearer, we think it important to appreciate the core ways in which this year spent as a secondary *stagiaire* teacher is indeed the first year of teaching. Our reasons include that key benchmark of having full, sole responsibility for teaching a class throughout the entire school year, as well as the more pragmatic reality of earning a full teacher's salary and a year's seniority for this year, just like any other teacher in the national system.

However, first-year secondary school teachers in France only teach one-third of the normal contact hours taught by secondary teachers throughout the educational system. Yet, because these *stagiaires* are fully-paid teachers, they represent a significant financial cost to the government – public school teachers being state employees in France. [1] In consequence, it can be informative to see aspects of the *stagiaire's* work during this initial year as centrally related to issues of entering the profession of secondary school teaching, with its linked set of questions: the whos, whats, whens, wheres, whys and hows of induction.

There are also more subtle versions of these questions lying behind the apparently innocuous and seemingly transparent label of 'first-year mathematics teacher' (which provides one of a number of reasons why we have retained the French term *stagiaire* throughout this chapter). A key question that the French 'case' raises is when – rather than who or what – is a new teacher? And into what is a novice mathematics teacher being inducted during this first, post-recruitment year?

E. Britton et al. (eds.), Comprehensive Teacher Induction, 194–260.
© 2003 *Kluwer Academic Publishers. Printed in the Netherlands.*

Much of this chapter underlines the profoundly disciplinary nature of secondary school teaching in France and the rootedness in the academic discipline of almost all first-year teacher tasks. A new mathematics teacher is unquestionably being inducted into a fundamentally *mathematical* teaching culture. The French system's responses to the first five questions about induction all reflect this subject-focused view. Later in this chapter, we explore the sixth question listed above, namely *how* induction is enabled to be carried out. In order to understand 'how', we are inevitably drawn to the ways in which, despite the presence of certain fixed hierarchies, important boundaries are permeable (both between institutions and between the functions carried out by those involved) and transitions across boundaries are repeatedly required of secondary *stagiaire* teachers themselves during this year.

We have used the word 'system' advisedly in the previous paragraphs. In a way that differs from each of the cases discussed so far in this book, France has a significantly *national* system of education, including a uniform approach to what we are viewing as new teacher induction, though the latter has only been in place for a decade and represents an important disjuncture in a culture whose approach to many aspects of education both reflects and values tradition, continuity and consistency. But, as will also become clearer, the fact of there being only one induction system does not by any means lead to a single or uniform practice. The nationally specified system is enacted in quite different ways in different places – and at times differently across different subject areas within the same place.

The structure of this chapter has initially been shaped to provide information about various facets of the teacher education system and to offer discussion of the different beginning teacher tasks assigned to a secondary *stagiaire* by the state, before broadening out to explore particular features or themes that struck us as especially interesting. Most of these tasks are briefly instantiated in the opening vignette below, where the reader will meet Monique, who was a first-year secondary mathematics teacher during 1999–2000.

We have chosen the week rather than the day as the initial unit for discussion here, because there is considerable variation in *stagiaire* activity within any given week, while there is a far greater regularity from week to week in terms of the range of tasks required. There is also some variation from month to month, particularly at the very beginning and toward the end of the school year, with every task only being undertaken at the same time roughly in the period between November and March. At the beginning of the school year, class teaching is preoccupying; towards the end of the school year, the written submission and oral presentation of the 'professional memoir' *(le mémoire professionel)* to an examination panel (and the impending permanent certification decision to which it contributes) is of more pressing concern.

1. 'One Foot in the Classroom': a Week in the Life of a *Stagiaire* Teacher

Monique is 23 and teaches mathematics for an hour four days of the week (each class 'hour' actually being fifty-five minutes long) to her eighth-grade class in a *collège*, a lower secondary school. [2] This is their entire mathematics for the week, apart from an additional hour's supervised remedial work (*heure de soutien*) that by now in the school year (late fall) only some of the class attend. Besides teaching them for the whole year, Monique assigns and marks their homework, provides them with individual help outside of class, meets with their parents at parents' evenings and is responsible for providing their final grades. She is acknowledged as a teacher by all, including her class and their parents, as well as the other teachers in the school, who refer to her variously as their 'young colleague', their 'new colleague' or, mostly to others, as 'the *stagiaire* teacher' or simply 'the *stagiaire*'.

Monique is a teacher because the previous spring she successfully passed the CAPES in mathematics, a challenging and highly competitive national secondary teacher recruitment examination. Monique *is* a teacher, but she teaches considerably fewer classes than her colleagues do because she is a *stagiaire* teacher. Normally, permanently certified mathematics teachers teach four or five classes to comprise the contractual eighteen contact 'hours' of teaching a week. [3] In France, to be a full-time first-year teacher does not mean teaching full-time.

As with all secondary school *stagiaires*, Monique has been provided with a 'pedagogic advisor' (*conseiller pédagogique*) for this first year of practice, who was appointed by a regional pedagogic Inspector for mathematics (also known by the initialism IPR). In Monique's case, this mentor is a considerably older mathematics colleague in the same school, who teaches, among others, a class at this grade level.

> My advisor comes regularly to see me, for roughly an hour every two weeks and I see her class once every two weeks – we usually alternate – and we talk about it for an hour afterwards. And when I need advice about something, I go to find her or call her up. On the other hand, she doesn't say to me of her own accord, 'You should be doing this, this, this and this'. She really leaves me to my own devices. But if I feel lost, I can ask for her advice. I've got the impression that, depending on the advisor, some are pretty directive and others are more relaxed. But when I have a problem, I have no hesitation in speaking about it, there's no difficulty with this.

This week, Monique has been observing her pedagogic advisor teaching an eighth-grade class and comments:

As for me in her class, I know I'm to be at the back. And currently, I'm watching how she speaks to them. For instance, I'm having some trouble with how I spread my comments around the various pupils. I'm trying to look at this, but I frequently get distracted by the content of what she's saying. So I often end up not really looking at the thing I came in planning to observe.

On Mondays, Monique drives forty-five miles from where she is living and teaching to her IUFM, an institution specifically concerned with teacher education and development which was created nationwide just ten years ago in 1991. (IUFM stands for 'University Institute for the *Formation* of Teachers' – many abbreviations and initialisms are employed in France, especially in education – see the *Glossary of Terms* on p. 383.)

This Monday afternoon, she is taking part in one of a series of short courses on general education topics, where she works alongside secondary *stagiaires* from a range of different subject backgrounds. The theme of this afternoon's class is an aspect of classroom management focused on the asking of questions and ways of working with pupil responses, as well as exploring a variety of available in-class sanctions. [4] She stays overnight with a fellow mathematics *stagiaire* who has the good fortune to be teaching at a school in the city where the IUFM is located, although the costs of all *stagiaire* accommodation while attending the IUFM, as well as travel expenses, are reimbursed by the Institute.

On this Tuesday, as each week, Monique spends the whole day at the IUFM again, where the entire mathematics group of some thirty *stagiaires* for the area meets together. At the beginning of the day, they spend a little time catching up and exchanging tales of their teaching since they met last week. But the core morning task is directed by their *formateur*, a mathematics teacher educator employed part-time at the IUFM who, in addition, is herself still a part-time *collège* mathematics teacher. The *stagiaires* are to develop and negotiate a grading scheme for a lengthy and mathematically challenging eleventh-grade, two- and three-dimensional geometry assignment. (This task first entails their solving the problems themselves in groups.)

They then correct and grade an entire class set of homework papers. Their composite analysis of pupil errors is detailed, sophisticated and systematic, and there is much discussion of possible reasons for the mistakes that were made and related teaching issues. Detailed correction and accurate marking of pupil homework is a significant part of French secondary mathematics teaching. Some *stagiaires* make mention of relevant mathematics education research readings they have come across while working on their professional memoirs, the latter being a significant and innovative feature of the first year of teaching.

197

The afternoon is spent in different groups working on developing their professional memoirs, a major year-long project usually casting an analytic look at some aspect of their own emerging practice. Monique and her fellow mathematics *stagiaires* look at and discuss six articles taken from a national journal called *Petit x* ('Little *x*'), which focuses on issues in the teaching of lower secondary school mathematics. This refereed journal publishes accounts of mathematics education explorations with an academic and research orientation and is of particular interest and relevance to *stagiaires* and their IUFM *formateurs*.

Once Monique has identified a clear topic, she will be assigned an individual memoir tutor. She comments on her current state of thinking about her memoir:

> They asked us to find a topic right away, which is not easy when you have one foot in the classroom with its own difficulties that arise. We have to come up with other sorts of problems, ones a little further away from the immediacy of the day-to-day stuff. It's hard to find the time to have preferences.

> We've had one or two sessions before [like this one, at the IUFM], where we took a look at memoirs from previous years, and we saw examples of their features, working hypotheses, what took place, all that. Which was interesting, but right away we had to come up with our own topic.

> At the outset, I was going to work on conjectures, how to have pupils appreciate the difference between conjectures and proofs. Then I saw that this was rather vague and I didn't see how I could implement it at all. As a result of listening to others talk about their ideas – we were in a workshop group of about ten – I finally decided that I'll deal with the notion of converse, how pupils tend to confuse theorems and their converses. But it's still the same thing; I don't yet know how I'll work on it.

After this day and a half spent working at the IUFM, Monique drives back to her own flat that evening to prepare her next day's morning class [5] which is on geometric transformations. After this, her afternoon is free to work: virtually no French educational institution is normally in session on any Wednesday afternoon.

Thursday morning, as well as teaching her class, Monique works for an hour with some of her pupils who are having difficulty with mathematics, as well as thinking over the ideas and discussions of the IUFM days. This Thursday afternoon she spends as a participant–observer in a nearby senior secondary school (a *lycée*, comprising grades ten to twelve), in order to gain some experience of another level and type of secondary school that she might be appointed to teach in next year when she hopes and expects to become permanently certified. She is present for two lessons, spending some of the time during the first one observing the teaching of this general grade ten class (normally the last year of compulsory schooling). Some of the time she circulates, helping individual pupils work on their statistics tasks involving standard deviation, variance and the use of hand-held calculators. The introduction of considerably more statistics into grade-ten mathematics is part of a recent *lycée* curriculum reform.

For the second lesson, she works with the same teacher in a 'module', that is a class period timetabled with just half the class present, in order to provide some more specific tutoring on technical mathematical exercises. This is a common mathematics structure for grade ten in the *lycée*, with three fifty-minute, whole-class periods for the *cours* (the main academic content as broadly specified in the national curriculum) and two 'modules' (one for each half-class). Some of Monique's fellow mathematics *stagiaires* are teaching such a class.

Here, it is an all-female class, whose members are intending to become health professionals, and they are working on transforming and graphing functions. In between these two classes, Monique talks with this teacher, her other assigned pedagogic advisor, about his lesson plans and aspects of what she has seen and experienced during the course of the afternoon. They have only just met, so she is a little diffident about saying what she thinks. As their time together progresses, she will likely teach more and mark pupil work from these classes as well.

This second half of the week is somewhat quieter, in the sense that Monique can concentrate mostly on her lesson preparation and marking at home, only going into the school to teach her lessons and to observe/discuss with her pedagogic advisor – and also to meet a couple of friends she has made on the staff for lunch. (In France, secondary teachers are only present on site to teach their lessons, to meet with pupils or to attend meetings or to see to other administrative duties, rather than be there throughout the entire school day. They have no office space, not even a place to leave personal things; teachers can claim tax relief on a room maintained as a home office where they live, a civic recognition of this fact.) In a few weeks' time, Monique will attend a 'class advisory meeting' (*conseil de classe*), where all members of the school's staff who teach a particular group of pupils get together once a term, in order to discuss each individual pupil's overall progress. [6] She needs to prepare for this meeting carefully.

During this week, Monique has:

- prepared four lessons, taught them in her lower secondary school and marked her pupils' homework;

- tutored a smaller group of her pupils in mathematics;
- observed her pedagogic advisor teach and discussed features of the lesson with her;
- observed, participated in and discussed two lessons taught by a second teacher for an afternoon in a different school (upper secondary) in the same town;
- worked on aspects of teaching (both general and subject-specific) for a day and a half in a third institution – the IUFM – in a different city, in both varied and subject-specialised groups of first-year teachers like herself;
- continued to think about and started more detailed preparatory work on her professional memoir.

These are all tasks that, next week, she – and many thousands of other first-year secondary teachers in France – will carry out once more. It broadly outlines the range of what the national programme for new secondary teachers requires.

2. A Brief Interlude on Two Key Terms

What is this thing, a *stagiaire* or *stagiaire* teacher, that Monique has become simply by courtesy of passing an examination? And what is this *formation* she is undergoing, directed by *formateurs*? These terms are employed in this chapter as markers of difference. French is not just a different language from English, it is both a carrier and a shaper of a different culture, one that is expressed by and to some extent reflected in that language. (Recall the Bourdoncle quotation to this effect on p. 14 of Chapter 1.)

There are two key French terms (and related words) that we need to discuss. The fact of their having no adequate direct equivalents in English, despite their centrality to teacher preparation in France, reflects a somewhat distinct orientation to the process of what we call (and think of as) 'teacher education' or, historically, 'teacher training'.

It is for this reason that we have decided not to try to translate them, preferring to leave them as italicized and thereby slightly opaque terms for anglophone readers. Marking them out in this way also allows a discussion of the non-trivial dialogue between the more permeable and less-fixed French distinction between the categories of 'initial' and 'continuing' *formation* and the decidedly non-equivalent North American dichotomy of 'pre-service' and 'in-service' education. [7] One significant instance of 'ambiguity' signalled by our chapter title occurs in relation to this collision of categories. We return to an explicit discussion of this point at the end of this chapter. These two sets of words are as follows. First, there is the process labelled by the noun *la formation*, the associated transitive verb *former* and the person who carries it out, a *formateur*. The second set is the noun *le stage* and the person who undertakes one, a *stagiaire*, and sometimes the one who supervises the *stage* on site (here, in the school), a *maître de stage*.

The word *formation* is usually translated into English as either 'education' or 'training', but is actually not the same as either. It has connections to 'making' or 'shaping' something or someone, but also has a specific usage in relation to entry into a profession: *formation* is what someone undergoes to become a member of that profession. [8] Reading *formation* as the English word 'formation' is not so widely adrift, but there is still the general question of what it means for someone to 'form' someone else. However, the process does not stop when one enters the profession: one can undergo *formation* at any point in a career's time-line. Grammatically, *formateur* is also an adjective as well as a person, meaning 'formative', as in a 'formative experience'. So, etymologically at least, a human *formateur* is one who is to provide formative experiences.

As for the term *le stage*, it connects historically to a notion of master/apprentice work, where the apprentice is working for the master (hence the term *maître de stage*) under his or her direct supervision and guidance. A *stage* is thus one type of *formation*. A *collège*-level French dictionary definition of *stage* runs as follows:

> a period of *formation* where one learns something.

In other words, a *stage* is an indefinite but clearly time-demarcated term related to undergoing some intended educational experience. This notion is very well suited to the framing of teacher induction as a particular phase in the life of a teacher, one with clear boundaries. But a *stage* also relates to the practice of the relevant profession *in situ*, of being – as the French say – on the ground *(sur le terrain)*.

As for the word *le stagiaire*, the variety of specifications across French–English dictionaries signals the instability of its translation. In one, it is rendered as 'trainee', in another 'probationer'. To be a *stagiaire* is to be at the same time 'on the ground' and in *formation*. Right across the French civil service, to become a *stagiaire* in whatever chosen profession requires the passing of a competitive examination. You are a new recruit in the first year of professional practice, prior to receiving confirmation of tenure.

In fact, however, any participant in a *stage*, irrespective of the extent of their professional experience and status, is called a *stagiaire*: for instance, an experienced teacher undertaking what we would call in-service education. Nevertheless, in the context of this chapter, *stagiaire* will refer specifically and exclusively to a first-year secondary teacher (hence, someone prior to permanent certification but who has been successfully recruited as a teacher).

Stages are also clearly temporary. For teachers, after undertaking this now-obligatory initial *formation* in order to receive tenure as a teacher from the state, participation in any subsequent *stage* as part of their continuing *formation* is usually optional (the one exception is that Inspectors can direct teachers to take specific courses). None further are generally mandated by the state in the life of a teacher, although they are certainly made available under the auspices of the IUFMs and, in mathematics, with the considerable assistance of the teachers associated with the Research Institutes on the Teaching of Mathematics (the IREMs – see section 6). One *formateur*, commenting on the temporary nature of the general meaning of *stage*, said she advises her *stagiaires* to refer to themselves as 'teachers in their first year of teaching' rather than *stagiaires* to their classes, so as to avoid confusion or concern in parents' minds about how long they will be with this class.

It is striking to us that, in France, *formation* of teachers is not called 'teacher education': rather, a closer translation would be that of teacher *shaping*, referring to a very deliberate process, one that is not teaching specific but relates to many professions. There are doctors and engineers and nurses who are likewise 'shaped' for their civil-service professions – and they too participate in *stages*, situated practica of various sorts (akin to legal 'articling' or 'clerking'), related to their intended profession.

Also, as we shall discuss later, each of these novice, untenured *stagiaire* professionals undertakes a professional memoir prior to receiving tenure within the state system. (The fact of this term transcending teaching is somewhat similar in effect to the Swiss-German term *Berufseinführung*, which is also used across various professions – see Chapter 3: partly comparable phase-specific rather than profession-specific terms in English include those of 'intern/internship' and 'apprentice/apprenticeship'.)

In France, teachers are not said to be 'educated' or 'taught' about their profession, nor are they specifically said to 'learn' (about teaching, at least) – all words which are more commonly used in relation to school, pupils and their teachers. For whatever cultural and historical reasons, linguistically at least, teachers are normally *shaped* or *formed* rather than *educated* or *taught*.

Finally, although we have no opportunity to pursue it here, some in certain purist academic circles would claim there to be no 'knowledge of teaching' (what we would term 'professional knowledge') in the same way that there is, for example, 'knowledge of mathematics'. Culturally, the term *savoir* (knowledge) has a very high status, with mathematical knowledge the most highly regarded of all. As one *formateur* in charge of general *formation* for an IUFM phrased it:

> It [this tension] involves the problem of knowledge and knowing in relation
> to *formation*. For some, there is no *savoir*, only *compétence* [know-how].

Part of the undergirding logic of the French secondary teacher-recruitment system (and despite a strong intellectual challenge from certain quarters within education) is a persistent belief that succeeding at a nationally competitive content examination – the CAPES or the *Agrégation* (see later) – demonstrates acquisition, indeed mastery, of the knowledge that counts. And publicly demonstrated mastery of such knowledge is still the prime qualification to be a secondary school teacher in France.

3. Some Observations about the System of National Education in France

In France, if it exists, it exists nationally.
(a national-level Inspector General for Mathematics)

As our earlier description of Monique's experience suggests, the structure of her and other *stagiaires'* work week(s) is in substantial part determined by a national system of teacher induction which shapes secondary teachers as they enter a comparably national educational system. So in order to appreciate some of these systemic effects better, we turn toward providing a brief account of certain general features of the wider educational system in France.

In particular, we focus on the geographically distributed nature of educational responsibility delegated from the national Ministry of Education to its regional Academies, the role of the Inspectorate and the reward system of teaching envisaged as a stable, life-time profession, and the nature of the two types of secondary school (the *collège* and the *lycée*), before finally turning to the newly-constituted teacher *formation* Institutes (the IUFMs).

The Ministry of Education and its Academies

In France, national government institutions play an appreciable role in much of civic life. In consequence, the structure of institutions concerned with teachers, as well as the nature of the shifting relationships among their personnel and between the institutions themselves comprise a significant part of being and becoming a new mathematics teacher there. Readers unfamiliar with the French system might initially fail to notice some of its striking features and effects. In particular, we have remarked on the ways these factors challenge certain ways of thinking about relationships among teacher preparation and induction (not least their presumed separation) that may be taken for granted in many anglophone countries.

All teachers working in the state educational system are civil servants, whose pay and working conditions (including class contact hours) are centrally determined for the country as a whole – and permanent teacher certification, granted by the Ministry of Education, is a national qualification. Just under one in every six members of the working population in France is a civil servant *(fonctionnaire)*, including members of other professions such as engineers, doctors and nurses: six percent of the total working population works in education.

The French education system is a national system, in the sense that there is a centralized Ministry of Education in Paris which broadly controls, legislates and issues edicts (in the weekly *Official Bulletin of National Education,* the BOEN) concerning what shall be the case for the entire country, whether in respect of the national curriculum, school organisation and emerging priorities, teacher working conditions or aspects of teacher *formation*, whether initial or continuing.

However, despite historical precedent and in keeping with a general state move toward greater decentralization that has been in effect since the early 1980s (and in secondary education in particular since 1985 – see Hatzfield, 1996), there is considerable variation across France within parts of this national framework, which at first sight might not be expected. This variation is more than tolerated, it is actually seen as a strength of the system. It is able to arise partly from the generality of specification at the highest level and partly from the relatively sparse nature of many such edicts.

For instance, the actual law creating the IUFMs (part of a huge reform of education in general, following serious school disruption and widespread strikes in 1989) simply specified almost within one line that institutions called *University Institutes for the Formation of Teachers* would be created, and a commission (the Bancel commission, named after its chair) was then established to specify what they would do and how they would function.

An IUFM-based mathematics *formateur*, reflecting on the system as a whole, observed how, despite being a national, centralised system, it nevertheless manages to incorporate considerable freedom. She offered as an example the requirement of the production of a professional memoir by first-year teachers.

> In France, the *formation* of teachers is up to the Minister of Education. Therefore there are national, institutional texts. According to these texts, a professional memoir is compulsory. You can find the ministerial circular itself. What is important to understand, however, is that each IUFM is free to adapt the *formation* it wishes while staying within these broad outlines. There must be a professional memoir everywhere. But each IUFM implements the professional memoir it wants.

In terms of the national structure of education, there are 25 geographically-organized Academies in mainland France, with each Academy being the regional outpost of the national Ministry of Education, responsible for the organization and functioning of education in its own geographic area. [9] Each Academy is headed by a Rector, who is the direct representative of the Minister of Education in the Academy. This is a key political appointment made by the president of the French Republic. The *Rectorat* is the name of both the administrative body of the Academy and the physical place where it is housed.

Each Academy's mandate includes control over and inspection of all state elementary and secondary scholastic establishments and their staffing, including near-universal, pre-school education (90% attendance) from age three. This is in addition to ensuring adherence to the national curriculum, all initial and continuing teacher *formation* via the IUFM and maintaining close links with the universities within each Academy (though they are funded and controlled separately). [10]

Every Academy proves to be one site for potentially varied interpretation and implementation of national directives according to more local conditions and traditions. The partial devolution of educational responsibility to the Academy level of decision-making is an increasing trend. One instance of this involves newly-certified teachers now being appointed by the Ministry of Education to the Academy rather than directly to individual schools, as used to be the case. As one Academy mathematics Inspector commented:

> You are aware that we live in a very centralised system. There is Paris and then the rest of France. [...] Paris says so-and-so will go to this Academy and so-and-so will go to that Academy. And since last year [1999], that is all that is said. Once they arrive in the Academy, there is then an internal movement where one says this one who has just arrived in the Academy, he will go to this *lycée* or to that *collège*.

After her *stagiaire* year, Monique will certainly have to move to a different school. She will, most likely, be required to move to an Academy in the north of France, where a considerable majority of all new secondary teachers are currently deployed for their first permanent positions. [11] While Monique and her new colleagues can request the level of secondary school (*collège* or *lycée*) they would like to teach in next year, most *stagiaires* do not, as it would constrain their possibilities even more in terms of where they might be sent.

All of the above speaks to a national, centralised education system, though one increasingly willing to delegate aspects of its authority and control to its geographically-distributed Academies. Without any detectable sense of irony, one *formateur* we spoke with observed of her professional life: "I have been working in national education for the past thirty years".

Her working life to date had included extensive secondary school mathematics teaching, as well as offering continuing education courses to practising teachers via an IREM and working with first-year mathematics teachers, both as a school-based pedagogic advisor and as an associate *formateur* (a temporary but potentially renewable appointment) within an IUFM. The perceived continuity implied by her remark speaks to the theme of fluid transitions and permeable boundaries across various institutional settings that will be discussed later in section 7.

The centralised nature of education in France is not just as a backdrop for Monique and all new teachers. In fact, it serves to shape the nature of their *formation*: for they are being shaped, not to become teachers serving a particular community or to accommodate primarily to the local needs of an individual school, but to be members of a national teaching force, a generalised profession able and willing to serve the entire country. Although *formation* is determined within the Academy as well as at the national level, there is no strong sense in which even the Academy is simply 'training' its own teachers. They are being 'educated' to become part of the national teaching force and, as such, they may well teach in a number of different geographic areas in the country during their career.

The Inspectorate

One way this national system is maintained is through a mechanism that gives a great deal of control to a relatively small number of Academy-based subject specialists. Who these people are (as well as their qualifications – many are former mathematics teachers) signals much about what is considered important in France. We turn now to the Inspectorate, who embody this responsibility, namely the valuing of subject-matter knowledge and a commitment to maintaining a national system of subject-matter specialist schoolteachers.

Even though Monique and many of her fellow mathematics *stagiaires* will not necessarily interact directly with any members of the Academy Inspectorate during their first year of teaching, IPRs nonetheless influence her *stagiaire* experience in important ways. We have taken the time to discuss in some detail the roles and duties of the Academy subject Inspectors here, because even following the creation of the IUFM system which assumed much of their former role in relation to and responsibility for *stagiaires*, IPRs are still powerful and influential figures in the induction of new teachers, as we document toward the end of this sub-section.

The Inspectorate of the Ministry of Education is a complex body which operates at both national (where they are known as IGs, general inspectors, about which we say little here) and Academy levels. Each secondary school subject has one or (usually) more *Rectorat*-based Regional Pedagogic Inspectors (IPR) in each Academy, who play a key role in many aspects of the education and evaluation of all secondary teachers of this subject, as well as monitoring public school provision in relation to the curriculum and its teaching.

The IPRs are responsible to the Rector of the Academy and act and speak with his or her authority: it is the Rector who formally instructs them to visit classes and inspect teaching in general (though the IPRs themselves select which teachers and schools to inspect), and it is the Rector to whom they report on what they find. For a schematic representation of the main lines of responsibility within the educational system, see Figure 1.

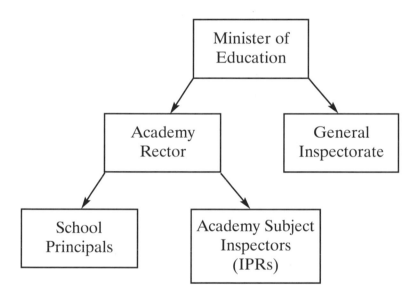

Figure 1:   Broad delegation of authority within the French educational system

Note that school principals are not in direct relation to IPRs in this hierarchy, nor do the IPRs report to the General Inspectorate directly, even those within the same subject area. [12] For the purposes of this chapter, we are only considering the Academy mathematics Inspectors, because they are the ones who affect the *formation* of new secondary school mathematics teachers most directly.

Teachers are paid more each year based on seniority, moving up the long salary scale incrementally. An inspection by an IPR, and the evaluative report that is filed, is almost the only way *any* teacher in the system can obtain greater salary advancement than this, which is one of the primary rewards of the French educational system. These reports influence the *rate* at which teachers receive pay increments within a nationally-determined pay scales. [13] Each IPR carries out up to a hundred teacher inspections each year.

Another role in general teacher education that the IPRs play is to determine the subject-specific in-service courses (*la formation continue*) to be offered to all of its teachers by the Academy for the coming year. The IPRs consult with teachers and school principals, as well as drawing on observations arising from their visits to classes and from seeing what the main national educational trends are, in addition to policy directives and initiatives from the national Ministry. They subsequently draw up a continuing *formation* plan for the year for the whole Academy. Once approved by the Rector, this list is then passed to the IUFMs to organise and implement (though this is a very recent change in institutional responsibility which has transpired only since 1998).

As was mentioned above, the subject IPRs have a particular responsibility for new teacher *formation*, though a dramatically reduced one compared with a decade ago (which was initially a source of friction and dissension between some inspectors and the nascent IUFMs, we were told). The IPRs' current involvement with first-year secondary teachers starts with them deciding in which schools the *stagiaires* will be placed and identifying a suitable pedagogic advisor for each one. This planning work is started as early as the October of the year prior to the *stagiaire's* arrival (and therefore long before the recruitment examinations have been taken). In consequence, at this point the number of *stagiaires* allocated to the IUFM in each subject area simply forms a component of the Inspectors' staffing plan for the Academy as a whole and the placement cannot be influenced by any individual characteristics of the *stagiaire*, as these cannot be known.

As qualified teachers recruited to the national teaching force, *stagiaires* form part of the IPRs' staffing capability available to cover gaps in teaching provision. But, nonetheless, there must be suitable classes available for them to teach. Those vacancies for the coming year which are not filled by *stagiaires* must be filled by a combination of temporary teachers (known as *vacataires*, who may teach a maximum of 200 hours a year), uncertified teachers and 'replacement teachers'. This last category comprises certified teachers who opt for this status (they perform 'substitute teaching' functions rather than have a specific post in a single school) and are first appointed to an Academy as a whole in this capacity, and subsequently by the Academy to cover a specific geographic zone within it. [14]

At the other end of the *stagiaire* year, it is also the Academy subject Inspectors who officially determine whether or not *stagiaire* teachers become permanently tenured within the system at the end of their first year of teaching. This is the move from *stagiaire* teacher to *certified* teacher, which brings a permanent entitlement to teach in the national public education system. Bearing the discussion of replacement teachers above in mind, who are an exception, a *certified* teacher is the recipient of one of the country's numbered education positions in a specific school.

IPRs do not automatically inspect every *stagiaire* teacher themselves, but if there is concern expressed either from an IUFM *formateur* or the pedagogic advisor, they will make an inspection. Additionally, every *agrégé stagiaire* (someone who has passed the higher-level *Agrégation* recruiting exam rather than the CAPES – see section 4) is inspected. A number of other individuals contribute information and opinions toward the certification decision: for instance, the school-based pedagogic advisor, the school principal where the *stagiaire* has actually taught all year, the IUFM teacher *formateurs*, the jury who hears the oral submission of the professional memoir (comprised mostly of the foregoing). But the final decision rests completely and fundamentally with the Academy subject Inspectors.

We wish to stress that this crucial decision regarding who is permanently confirmed in the national teaching force is taken by a subject-matter specialist – in our case, a mathematics specialist – rather than by a possibly generalist administrator (e.g. a school principal or an Academy bureaucrat). Such is the regard for disciplinary knowledge in its secondary teachers that France entrusts the final decision as to who is to become a mathematics teacher to one of their own.

The institutions of secondary schooling (the *collège* and the *lycée*)

School education in France has two main structural phases: 'elementary' (the pre-primary and primary 'first degree', up to grade five inclusive) and 'secondary' education (the 'second degree', grades six to twelve). There are two basic types of secondary school, structured by pupil age: the *collège* (also referred to as the first 'cycle' of secondary education) and the *lycée* (the second 'cycle' of secondary education). The lower secondary school (the *collège*) covers grades six to nine; every subject at each grade level is intended to be taught by a subject specialist teacher. [15] This means that, in France, *all* lower secondary pupils from grade six onwards are customarily taught mathematics by a teacher who has an extremely strong academic preparation in that subject.

One requirement of a national reform initiated in 1975 was that all pupils should attend unstreamed *collèges*: that is, there should be no grouping by ability, a decision that has exerted considerable influence on the shape of French secondary education over the past twenty-five years. This egalitarian, comprehensive principle has recently been reaffirmed at the national level, despite pressures to select among and stream pupils within the *collèges*. Nevertheless, economic and other forces do obviously still shape the geographic catchment area intake of different *collèges* (as they have always done). One of the main forces for both the on-going national curriculum reform and the developments in teacher *formation* of the past decade in the *collège* has been the changing population of pupils, both in terms of their geographic and cultural origins and backgrounds.

The upper secondary *lycée* usually covers grades ten to twelve, though historically *lycées* referred to full grade-range secondary institutions (many originally military in nature). [16] Most importantly from our point of view, there is no distinction in the training of subject specialist teachers who will teach mathematics in *collèges* and in *lycées*.

Secondary education is compulsory until reaching age sixteen (home schooling apart, which is rare is France). Hence, technically, pupils accordingly can leave either at the end of *collège* or grade ten. During the 1980s, however, at a time of growing teacher applicant shortages which in part subsequently led to the creation of the IUFMs, a national education goal was announced of having 80 percent of the age cohort taking the *baccalauréat* – the national, academic, high-status school-leaving examination taken at the end of grade twelve, that determines access to higher education. At the end of 1998, a figure of roughly 70 percent had been achieved. However, it was brought about by the creation of a significant number of further routes for *baccalauréat* study and predictably brought with it critics' charges of the 'watering down' of this qualification.

The place and role of the IUFMs

Monique may not realise this, but her experience as a secondary *stagiaire* teacher is quite different from that of a first-year teacher only a decade previously. Even though the Inspectorate is a legacy of the Napoleonic era, the institution more directly involved in Monique's weekly shaping is a product of very recent political will (and, as such, is vulnerable to shifts in that will). The earlier mechanism for inducting newly-recruited secondary teachers into the profession heavily involved the Academy Inspectorate.

Prior to the creation of the IUFMs, the CAPES examination (which, along with the Academy structure and the Inspectorate, has a very long history) was used as now to select and recruit new teachers at the secondary level. However, for the first year of teaching, these novice teachers were placed by the Inspectors in a succession of teacher practica in someone else's class in different schools (*stages de pratique accompagnée*, which are discussed further in section 5) for a month or two at a time. This school-based work comprised one-third of a certified teacher's normal load, just as the current situation does. For the remainder of their work time, they attended courses under the responsibility of an Academy subject Inspector. Thus, the one-third of normal teaching load for a newly-recruited first-year teacher has a much longer history than the IUFMs. But the setting, nature and responsibilities of that teaching have significantly changed, as have the other tasks a new teacher is expected to undertake, as well as the number and nature of those individuals involved in this *formation*. Much of this work is now directed by *formateurs* associated with the IUFMs.

Consequently, we now take an initial look at this new institution, the *University Institute for the Formation of Teachers* (IUFM), created to undertake the revised method and means of new teacher *formation* that Monique experienced. In October, 1990, the first three experimental IUFMs were set up and, in 1991, the creation of one IUFM per Academy followed. [17] The main intent of this new institution was to increase both the intellectual status of teacher education – especially at the elementary level – and the professionalisation of teachers – especially at the secondary level. Bernard Cornu, who was the Director of the Grenoble IUFM at the time of this interview and one of the chief architects of the entire IUFM system nationally, expressed it (in English) as follows:

> The political decision was taken before they knew exactly what they wanted to do. This is in the orientation law, which in July 1989 asserted. "There will be created in each Academy an IUFM. [...] They are to be public establishments of higher education [...] They carry on initial *formation* for teachers. They participate in continuing *formation* and educational research." And that's it.

> So the Bancel Commission needs to be seen in the spirit of the educational system at the time. The orientation law for education proposed a huge series of measures. At this time, we started speaking about the pupil, the learner, as the centre of the system. There was also a lot of reflection about teachers' education. There was a feeling that [secondary] teachers in our country had a very high level in their subject, in their discipline, but got almost no training in the professional component. [...]

> So there was a will for improving the professional training of secondary teachers and establishing strong links between universities and primary teachers' training. The other point at that time was that universities were considered as having failed in teacher education. They were not interested in that. Some people, some professors in universities, were interested, but globally speaking the universities showed no interest in teacher education. [...] Another point to take into account is that ten years ago we had a very serious lack of teachers. We had very few students willing to become

teachers and this was really a problem for us. So the first motto of the IUFMs was *"Recruter plus, former mieux"* – recruit more, train better.

The number of students increased a lot. Now, in the IUFMs in France, it's almost 90,000 students all together. We now have a lot of students really wanting to become teachers and knowing why, which is very new. Previously most of them were students, going to university, studying at university, and at the end [after passing the recruiting examination] they say, "Okay, well, I'm a teacher". Because it was the natural way. Bancel [an Academy rector who headed the commission bearing his name] often said when you ask people in the street, "Do you know how to become an engineer?", they would say, "Yes, I go to a school for engineers"; "Do you know how to become a doctor?" "No problem. You go to a medicine faculty." And then, "Do you know how to become a teacher?", "No, I don't know." People didn't know that kind of thing. Now there is clearly a path to the teaching profession. This is the IUFMs.

The IUFMs are, in some sense, the professional 'training' arm of the Ministry of Education at the Academy level: for intending teachers preparing for the recruitment examinations, for *stagiaire* teachers' initial *formation* and for permanently-certified teachers' on-going development. So, in terms of Figure 2 in Chapter 1 (p. 4), the IUFMs now operate at all three levels indicated there. (This is even though the in-service role has only been fully taken on in the last few years; the shift is signalled in the move between the original Ministry term 'participate in' that Cornu used and sole responsibility for ensuring its provision, as is now the case.)

The IUFMs thus comprise part of the answer to the question of the 'where' of French induction and their 'employees' connect to the question of 'who' undertakes induction. There are certainly significant links between the IUFM and some or all of the universities geographically located within any given Academy (at least one such institutional link is mandatory). Much of the work of preparing post-degree students for the recruitment examinations is often ceded to relevant university academic departments and, reciprocally, some of the current IUFM staff may be working on temporary secondment from these departments. Many staff are, however, directly employed by the IUFM, either on temporary or permanent, part-time or full-time contracts.

The non-university-based staff appointed to an IUFM basically fall into two categories: those who have a contractual teaching assignment as 'associated teachers', usually secondary school teachers (seconded either full- or part-time, but always temporarily) and *enseignant–chercheurs*, permanent, university-level faculty whose primary appointment is at the IUFM. We return to the question of who are the *formateurs* in section 7.

Finally, each IUFM has one main 'seat' (often in the same city as the Academy *Rectorat*) and other 'centres' and satellites, at least one per geographic *département* (see note [9]), sometimes two. In terms of the physical plant, many of these Institutes have been housed in the buildings of the former Normal Schools, where elementary teachers used to be trained completely separately from the university system. One intent of the creation of the IUFMs was to have a single tertiary-level institution engaged in educating both elementary and secondary teachers, despite dramatically differing philosophies historically lying behind these enterprises in France. The next two sections describe and discuss in detail the work carried out at and by the IUFM, focused first on pre-recruitment students and then on secondary *stagiaire* teachers.

4. How to Become a Mathematics Teacher

What did Monique and others like her have to do to become a mathematics *stagiaire* teacher? And, more generally, what determines who becomes one? Figure 2 depicts the most common route and its detail is discussed below.

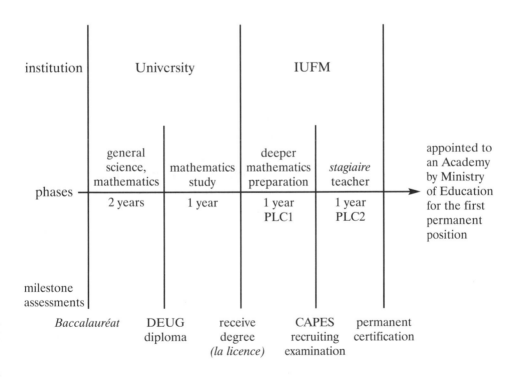

Figure 2: *A summary of the usual CAPES route to becoming a secondary mathematics teacher*

Future secondary mathematics teachers typically study for four years in tertiary-level institutions after they have completed their school-leaving *baccalauréat*, success in which examination guarantees access to university education. The first three of these four post-*baccalauréat* years are normally spent at university, taking courses which to an outsider's eye are not in the least specific to intending teachers. (To the insider, however, these courses in mathematics and science are precisely educating them to be the mathematicians they have to be in order to be selected as a mathematics teacher in France in the first place, though not necessarily preparing them for the actual job.)

The customarily required background for most future secondary mathematics teachers is to follow the general science path for the first two years at university (with a common curriculum across all universities in France) and to pass the DEUG, a university diploma, covering courses in mathematics, computing, and physics or chemistry, with examinations at the end of the second university year. Students then go on to a third university-based year, specializing solely in mathematics, in order to graduate with a university Bachelor's degree (known as the *licence*) in mathematics.

Intending secondary mathematics teachers then have to succeed at a highly competitive, subject-specific, national recruiting examination in order to be accepted into the national public teaching force. The most commonly taken one is the mathematics CAPES (details of which are given below). To become a state teacher in France, one must be an E.U. (formerly, French) citizen on the day the recruiting exam is taken (something which reflects the school's perceived role in educating future French citizens). Candidates are ranked nationally within each subject and the number of passes is based on the anticipated number of teacher vacancies a year hence.

The fourth year, then, is spent specifically preparing to take the CAPES teacher recruiting examination, normally as a student affiliated with an IUFM. Within the IUFM where these post-degree students belong administratively, they are frequently referred to as PLC1s (teachers of *lycées* and *collèges* year 1), a naming which suggests they are in the first year of their teacher *formation*. They are, however, not yet teachers. Secondary *stagiaire* teachers, those who have passed a recruiting examination, are also referred to as PLC2s *inside* the IUFMs. However, as will be discussed in more detail in section 7 of this chapter, the apparent continuity of experience and framing tacitly implied by this simple nomenclature belies the actual complexity of status, transition and perception that individuals experience during these two key years prior to full certification. For now, however, we shall simply take it at face value, even though institutional naming is seldom random or not thought through.

The intent of this year's work as a PLC1 is first and foremost to deepen the command and understanding already gained of mathematics taught in the first two years of university, in preparation for the written part of the CAPES examination. It is also to provide some preparation for the two subsequent oral examinations. (In some Academies, this latter preparation includes a short observation period in secondary schools of at least a week's duration, sometimes two or three, though the time in school can be variously distributed over the year or concentrated as a single block between the written and the oral examinations.)

While PLC1s can be seen as *prospective* teacher candidates, the considerable majority of them (seven out of every eight in mathematics in 1999) will *not* become *stagiaire* teachers the following year (to us a striking state of affairs), as they will not succeed in passing this recruiting examination. While they have the right to retake the CAPES examination as many times as they wish, they can only be a PLC1 student affiliated with an IUFM twice.

Although these students officially 'belong' to the IUFM, many of the courses intended to prepare PLC1 students for the CAPES examination are commonly taught in nearby university mathematics departments by their faculty rather than at the IUFM itself. Most of these university mathematics professors have little or no link with school teaching or education in general. Commonly, preparation for the written part and the first oral examination is carried out in a nearby university mathematics department, while preparation for the second oral examination is conducted at the IUFM by mathematics *formateurs* (see below for more detail).

A relatively small but significant minority of future secondary mathematics teachers spends a fourth year entirely at university (the year following completion of their *licence* in mathematics) studying for a master's degree in mathematics. They then, in the subsequent year, prepare to take a higher-level, national competitive teacher recruitment examination called the *Agrégation*, which is entirely mathematical in nature, again predominantly written, but including a highly competitive oral part. It used to be felt that every *lycée* mathematics teacher should be *agrégé*, but this is certainly not the case at present. By no means do all or even most *agrégés* go on to be a teacher in secondary school: a considerable number go on to teach in the tertiary sector (e.g. in *classes préparatoires*, not discussed in this chapter).

Individuals wishing to sit for the CAPES need not be enrolled at an IUFM as a PLC1 student. They can prepare themselves as 'free' candidates (*candidats libres*) – an explicit reference to the canon of liberty and openness in government functionary positions in a meritocracy. About ten percent of all candidates taking the CAPES examination in mathematics each year follow this route.

215

The other possible route into secondary teaching is by means of what is literally termed an 'internal CAPES', a slightly different certification examination available both to unqualified teachers who have already been working in the system for five years – who were mostly taken on during times of teacher shortage – and to other civil servants who are 'internal' to the government service (who have consequently successfully passed some state recruiting examination).

The form of the CAPES

The written part of the CAPES comprises two five-hour written papers, is purely mathematical and covers the entire mathematics curriculum from the *collège* right up to the end of the DEUG. But it is examined at a deeper level than at the university. Those successful at this written exam (roughly double the number who eventually pass) then prepare for the oral part of the CAPES examination which is based mainly on the *lycée* mathematics curriculum, and is still primarily mathematically-based. After taking and passing the written part of the CAPES (which is offered only once in March each year and can be taken in each Academy), a teacher candidate goes to Paris in July of the same year for the oral examinations taken in front of a small panel known as a 'jury'.

Oral 1 requires the selection of an envelope that contains two mathematics topics, followed by the candidate preparing to teach a twenty-five minute 'lesson' on one of them. The mathematical level is to be high (at least *lycée* and possibly from the first two years of university). There are two hours to prepare, with no access to any external resources, before the candidate gives a lecture in front of the three examiners comprising the jury (themselves *lycée* mathematics teachers, university mathematicians and mathematics Inspectors), who are not allowed to talk during this time. As one *stagiaire* wryly observed, "It is primarily a conversation between you and the blackboard".

Then the jury members ask questions for twenty minutes. The topics come from a list of about ninety (in number theory, algebra, statistics, probability and analysis) published at the beginning of the academic year. In one Academy, PLC1 students had been prepared for this part of the oral exam by a course for roughly three hours per week throughout the year.

Oral 2 is somewhat more practical and slightly more school-focused, on a topic in a different main area of mathematics from the one chosen for oral 1. The jury offers two specific mathematical topics and the candidate selects one of them and is to create a exercise set of three to five questions ranked by level of difficulty that explores and encompasses the mathematical topic right across the *collège* and *lycée* levels. Again, there are two hours to prepare, but this time access to a set of textbooks for the *collège* and *lycée* is provided. One *stagiaire* commented about her previous year's experience with the CAPES second oral examination:

> There are twenty minutes to explain why you have chosen these examples, your choice of level for them and to show how you understand the topic. Then in the next twenty-five minutes, the examiners get to question you and ask you to solve one or two of them.

All those who pass the CAPES (currently, the pass rate is about 10–15 percent of applicants) now have to go for an IUFM-based year (usually their second) as a *stagiaire* teacher. This may involve a change of geographic location, because they are now functionaires who can be moved according to the wish of the Ministry of Education for its own purposes. Most significantly in this regard, there are more than six thousand students studying for the mathematics CAPES in the greater Paris area (that is some four-fifths of the candidates nationally). PLC1s are students and hence can register where they want. Yet literally only a handful of *stagiaires* are located at the Paris IUFM, as there are virtually no teaching vacancies within central Paris itself. However, there is a considerable number of *stagiaires* at the two adjacent Academies of Versailles and Créteil, and it is to these two Academies that most newly-certified mathematics teachers are appointed.

Succeeding at the annual CAPES national competition, as Monique did, means you have been recruited as a secondary teacher in France, even though you have not yet been confirmed as a permanent member of the public teaching force, with all the rights and responsibilities that this civil-service position entails. All indications are that success in the CAPES is an attestation of considerable mathematical ability and that this is what is still prized by many within the system.

Compulsory *formation* is what the state now requires, in order to 'shape' a *stagiaire* for permanent certification. For this PLC2 year, *stagiaires* are paid a full teacher's salary, they can join the teacher's union, they have the right to strike as any civil servant has, and in almost every setting they are acknowledged as teachers (subject to confirmation of permanent tenure which empirically is usually granted to those who complete the *stagiaire* year).

Receiving permanent certification in the educational system at the end of the *stagiaire* year (or after a second, repeat year if necessary – in one Academy, this figure ran at about 10 percent annually for mathematics) guarantees a teacher the possibility of a job for life and a government pension at the end of it. The attractiveness of this, especially during times of doubt about the economy or uncertain employment in other areas, contributes to a considerable stability in the teaching force, a sizeable majority of whom are career teachers.

If certified teachers stop teaching for a while, apart from being granted prior approval for paid or (more commonly) unpaid leave by the Academy under various circumstances (e.g. for maternity or family reasons), they lose their status as tenured, nationally-certified teachers and have to retake and pass the CAPES examination once again in order to regain it. Such unpaid leaves from an Academy, even for quite lengthy periods, are often granted, but they are dependent on administrative willingness. In addition, the challenge (and variation in both number of candidates and pass standards from year to year) of this recruiting examination also encourages teachers to continue teaching. While at certain periods the size of the pool of high-quality potential new recruits to the profession may not have been as large as desired (for instance, at the end of the 1980s, just prior to the creation of the IUFMs), teacher retention within the system in France does not seem to be a major preoccupation of the Ministry at all.

As noted, once candidates have passed both parts of the CAPES, they have been recruited as new secondary teachers and, as a civil servant, are administratively allocated to a particular Academy's IUFM. The simple fact is that the required competence to be displayed in a performance in order to become a secondary mathematics teacher is almost entirely that of being able to do mathematics at an extremely high academic level. There is a strong rehearsal aspect to the PLC1 year preparation. PLC1 students have studied and practiced for this mathematical performance for the previous seven months in the case of the written component and for as much as ten months in the case of the oral ones.

The extent of the connection (or lack of it) between this performance and what is required of a secondary mathematics teacher has been the source of much contention and criticism from certain educational quarters. Nevertheless, attempts to reform the CAPES in even relatively minor ways have been met with fierce, indeed on occasion vitriolic, condemnation and entrenched resistance: the latter's continued assertion is that it is *savoir* alone that counts, pedagogy (sometimes denigrated as 'mere' *compétence*) rarely gets a look in. However, as will become more evident later, this is not always a simple binary opposition (see note [24]).

5. Settings and Occasions for *Stagiaire* Learning

The CAPES (or *Agrégation*) recruiting examination creates a very sharp entry point to becoming a *stagiaire* teacher, as the successful candidates only hear in early- to mid-August which Academy they will work in and perhaps only a few days before the school year begins in early September which school they will primarily be associated with. They need to find lodging and become orientated to place, school and IUFM in very short order.

The next question we turn to is what do *stagiaires* do and what are the things they are to learn during this year? As our initial description of Monique's experience suggests, first-year teachers are directed to undertake a wide variety of tasks. In this section, we describe and illustrate these in more detail and yet with some greater generality, though bearing in mind the freedom and variation that exists between Academies. We also attend to the specification of certain contexts, freedoms and constraints within which these tasks are to be carried out, as well as provide some sense about where these directives come from and who is involved in their origination and development. In terms of the induction questions listed at the end of the chapter introduction, this section looks primarily at the wheres and the hows of induction.

This section's intent, therefore, is to integrate the information contained in the previous two sections (about the system of national education in France and the recruiting examination routes into teaching) with our understanding that *stagiaires* like Monique (who are engaged in undertaking all these different tasks) reflect the system's perception of what a first-year secondary teacher should be engaging with. As well, the system broadly legislates whom the *stagiaire* is to encounter along the way. What a new secondary mathematics teacher becomes inducted into is shaped by structured encounters with various sets of individuals and the related institutions that specify their roles. We thus try to explore how the way a *stagiaire* week is set up creates opportunities for types of *formation* that the system values.

The system envisages a tri-partite division of *stagiaires'* work-time. Broadly, a third of their working week is to be spent undertaking a school-based *stage* (for the entire school year). This *stage* is evaluated and reports on it contribute to the permanent certification decision on each *stagiaire*. Another third of their time is to be spent working at the IUFM, taking a variety of compulsory and optional generalist courses (for half a day each week) and working in a disciplinary grouping (for a whole day each week). These courses are assessed and also contribute towards the certification decision. There is also a second, shorter *stage* for thirty class hours in another school, often arranged as ten to fifteen morning or afternoon sessions. Lastly, roughly a third of the time, unevenly spread throughout the year, is to be spent preparing the professional memoir submission, which is also evaluated. Each of these settings offers structured, shaped possibilities for new teacher learning.

Figure 3 shows an outline of a 'typical' *stagiaire* week, one which is undoubtedly false for any given mathematics *stagiaire* in any given week. But it provides a good 'average' for the middle part of the school year (and was generated by and agreed to as such by a group of more than twenty-five such *stagiaires* in one Academy). The legally-enforced European work-week at the time of the study was 39 hours (recently reduced to 35) and France's contracted teaching expectations for certified teachers somewhat respect this, in that a paid hour outside class (for preparation and marking) is included for every hour spent in class.

Setting	Role	Hours/week
stage en responsabilité	teach one mathematics class	6
	prepare classes and mark work	12
	meet with pedagogic advisor	1
	administrative work (parent-teacher meetings, dealing with marks, *conseil de classe*)	1
stage de pratique accompagnée	observe and teach	4
	prepare and mark	5
	meet with teacher	1
IUFM	subject-specific courses (1 day)	6
	general courses (1/2 day)	3
	work on professional memoir	2

Figure 3: An average stagiaire week (from November to March)

This table indicates the plurality of places where a *stagiaire* is legitimately instructed to attend. It is worth noticing that *stagiaires* need to move around a good deal in order to meet these expectations, to gain what it is presumed they need. France, in this regard, proved more varied than any other site we studied. It can be quite instructive to compare this with a general week in the life of a first-year secondary mathematics teacher elsewhere, in terms of the diversity of both the settings and the opportunities to learn more about mathematics teaching.

The remainder of this section is structured by the settings where these opportunities take place. We also feel it worth attending specifically to the interrelations among the personnel involved with the *stagiaire* teacher, in order to gain a better sense of whose hands are involved in this shaping and whether induction occurs primarily courtesy of those already within the school teaching profession or by others situated in a different relation toward it.

Setting 1: Work in schools

There are two separate, school-based commitments, *stages*, fairly distinct in terms of both scale and nature. *Stagiaires* have a notional one-third of their time allocated to the *stage en responsabilité*, though the above table suggests it requires more.

The stage en responsabilité (the 'responsible individual' stage)

The mathematics *stagiaire* starts work at the very beginning of the school year with a legislated teaching load of between four and six contact hours per week in a school, with a class allocated by the principal of the school to which the *stagiaire* has been assigned by an Academy IPR. Because the compulsory mathematics class time at both the *collège* and *lycée* levels falls within this range mandated for all first-year secondary teachers, *stagiaires* in mathematics find themselves teaching one class throughout the year, with the likely addition of some support time for pupils in difficulty.

In a *collège*, this placement is recommended to be a seventh- or eighth-grade class, neither of which is a significant transition year – either arrival from elementary school or the year in which the *collège*-end *brevet* national examination is taken. In a *lycée*, it should be a grade ten class – which is both the last year of compulsory schooling and away from those preparing for the very high-stakes *baccalauréat* examination during grades eleven and (especially) twelve. Despite this strong recommendation, exceptions apparently abound more commonly at the *collège*. [18] While the particular school and pedagogic advisor placement is carried out by a mathematics Inspector, the actual class assignment is the responsibility of each school principal, some of whom may not have been fully aware of the *stagiaire* placement guidelines. Also, other pragmatic considerations may have come into play in some of these placements.

Without question, this is the *stagiaire's* class: he or she is responsible (again the name of the *stage* is significant) for the mathematics teaching in its entirety. Apart from an initial IUFM orientation day, usually just before the school term starts (which one *stagiaire* described as 'where they gave us a bunch of advice so we didn't make complete fools of ourselves'), in some Academies their work at the IUFM may not start up in full force immediately after the return to school at the beginning of September. This is in order that they can concentrate their time and effort on starting teaching their class and familiarising themselves with their school and suroundings during the first few weeks.

For many of the *stagiaires* we spoke with, this is what they see themselves focused on most clearly at the outset; this is them most evidently 'being' the new mathematics teacher they have just succeeded in becoming. We discuss certain aspects of observed *stagiaire* mathematics lessons in the next section.

The pedagogic advisor (conseiller pédagogique). As with Monique, every new mathematics *stagiaire* is assigned a pedagogic advisor by the Academy mathematics Inspectorate: the pedagogic advisor is a mathematics teacher almost always in the same school as the *stagiaire* and frequently teaching one class at the same grade level. The pedagogic advisor is also appointed as an 'associate *formateur*' at the IUFM for this school year.

We were told a number of times that it is generally considered an honour to be asked to be a pedagogic advisor, providing a certain recognition by the system (embodied in the person of the mathematics Inspector), despite it only attracting a relatively small amount of additional money (some 4000FF for the year, roughly US $750). Some pedagogic advisors with whom we spoke expressed a wished-for preference of receiving a small amount of release time instead. To be invited to serve in this capacity certainly indicates acknowledgement by the mathematics Inspector.

The core aspects of the role of pedagogic advisor are nationally specified in a Ministry of Education circular (BOEN, 1992; *emphasis in original*). He or she:

- **welcomes** and assists in integrating the *stagiaire* into the pedagogic team of the class and the subject. [...]
- **ensures the *stagiaire* is accompanied** in his [or her] taking responsibility for the class, by means of: advice, exchange, appraisal of mutual class visits. [...]
- **assists in analysing practice** by establishing conditions which will allow the *stagiaire* to make explicit and justify steps taken and related choices. [...]
- **keeps an eye on the quality of the [professional] dialogue**, invites questions, encourages initiatives and leads the *stagiaire* more and more into working with the team. [...] is in contact with the [IUFM] *formateur* responsible for supervising the *stage* and advises the *formateur* without delay if he [/she] feels the situation is of concern, particularly during the visits by the *formateur*.
- **as a *formateur* associated with the IUFM,** he [/she] is invited to take part in an initial half-day at the beginning of the year, in order to be informed about the organization of the year and the *formation* arrangements of the IUFM. By being informed about the content of the *formation*, he [/she] can help the *stagiaire* better connect this *formation* with everyday life in school.
- **participates in the evaluation of the *stagiaire*,** by preparing an evaluation report of the *stage en responsabilité*.

On the one hand, this can be seen as quite a detailed spelling out of the intended *role* of a pedagogic advisor, irrespective of circumstance, geography or subject. On the other, there is no detail as to *how* these goals are to be achieved, nor is there any mechanism for ensuring these functions are carried out. Right in the specification of the role is the two-fold task of support and evaluation which can provoke conflicting responses. Most *stagiaires* with whom we spoke had praise for the work their pedagogic advisor had undertaken with them, but also occasional disagreement. Among the many positive experiences reported to us by *stagiaires* was valuing the *reciprocity* of visiting classes (as envisaged in the national framework document), rather than simply the pedagogic advisor having the right to enter the *stagiaire's* classroom. Nevertheless, it still pointed up for us the norm in relation to novices being the ones observed in their practice, while a mark of being a more experienced or established teacher is a right to privacy. Teaching as an individual, private act is a strong part of French teaching culture.

Some detailed examples we heard included instances of how their experience with their pedagogic advisor had differed markedly from the desired institutional 'norm' that this above specification envisages. One extreme instance was where, according to the *stagiaire*, the pedagogic advisor did not come for the first two weeks:

> to give me some time, but I'd already had time for some stupidities – over-formal notation, too difficult homework. After a month during which there was a lack of dialogue and explanation of her criticisms (for instance, that I didn't listen enough to the pupils' wrong responses, though the pupils didn't seem to be having problems), she did not come again and I carried on alone. Apparently, she wanted me to follow her example, but I found her *cours* poorly constructed (few explanations, many exercises).

Clearly, particular relationships cannot simply be legislated for. Whatever transpired, the *stagiaire's* liaison with the pedagogic advisor was repeatedly commented upon (whether positively or negatively) as a key one in relation to their year as *stagiaires*.

Here is one *stagiaire* in her mid-twenties talking about how she functioned with her pedagogic advisor, whom she judges to be between forty-five and fifty years old. The *collège* is relatively small, with about five hundred pupils and thirty-seven teachers; she is the only mathematics *stagiaire* there, but there are others in other subjects in the same school:

> I teach grade eight in a *collège*, where I am in charge of a single class, four hours a week. When she [the pedagogic advisor] is in my class, she goes to the back and tries to make herself invisible. Usually she takes notes on what I am doing, small points of detail. And at the end of the lesson, neither of us has a class, so we talk for an hour about the lesson, about what she thinks I can improve, things like that.

> She tends more to tell me about things that didn't go well than those that did. And of course there are bits of advice I don't want to hear. For instance, the first time she came to see me, I spent a little bit of time with two pupils who were having major problems,

doing [geometric] constructions with them. And she told me that, during the time that I spent with these pupils, the rest of the class drifted and that I should have let those two drop by the wayside, as I didn't have time to concern myself with them to the detriment of everyone else. That stayed with me.

In the end, I didn't want to accept that point of view. So when my IUFM *formateur* came to see me, he put it a little differently. He told me I should be a little more dynamic, that I should provide them with something to be getting on with, things to do for those who work quickly, in order to free up some time for me to get caught up with the weakest pupils. But not to drop them completely like that.

The IUFM *formateur* comes twice during the year, this was the first time – those in different subjects get their first visit earlier or later. In mathematics, they come very early because they think there are small things they can help us to put right straight away, before things completely deteriorate. And if that visit doesn't go well, they can come a third time, instead of twice. So they say to us that the first time they come, they come as a *formateur* and they are not really seeking to evaluate us, even if they are also doing that. It's quite ambiguous, wouldn't you say?

There are a number of features of note in this excerpt. One is the strength of self that comes through (the mentor's comment is simply framed as a 'point of view'), while another is the fact of having a second place to go for advice and a third is the explicit identification of the role ambiguity of support *and* evaluation, though interestingly it was remarked upon here in relation to the IUFM *formateur* rather than the pedagogic advisor.

The fact that the following sentence is italicised in the handbook produced in one Academy for mathematics *stagiaires* and pedagogic advisors suggests it is a contested or at least contentious issue:

> *These visits (by the IUFM formateurs) are in no case inspections, neither from the point of view of the regulations nor from the point of view of the role they play in the formation plan (the linking of theory and practice).* In relation to evaluation, their role is to allow a certain homogeneity of appreciation, a view of the whole and an external look.

We return to this issue later in the chapter.

Evaluating the stagiaire's stage en responsabilité. Who writes a report on a *stagiaire's stage en responsabilité*? There are potentially as many as four reports on the *stagiaire's* teaching progress in this school during this first year that form part of the certification file. Two must be written by the school-based pedagogic advisor and by an IUFM *formateur*, and a third may be prepared by an Academy mathematics Inspector, if such an inspection is made because of a certification concern. Lastly, the school principal must prepare a report on each *stagiaire* at the end of the school year, which also forms part of the certification file judged at the end of the *stagiaire* year.

The principal also contributes an administrative mark, curiously the only element from this entire first year of teaching which stays on this teacher's permanent teaching record maintained at the Ministry of Education. We say 'curiously', for principals may have had little direct experience of the *stagiaire's* teaching. They also have a vested interest in the *stagiaire* contributing broadly to the life of their school (hence such a report might complain that the *stagiaire* was not as visible as he or she might have been), whereas this is only one of a number of places where the *stagiaire* has a responsibility to be.

The extended interview excerpt given in the previous sub-section also raises a number of points related to the interaction of these settings for learning. Although the pedagogic advisor is there in the school, intended to be close at hand on a regular basis, an IUFM *formateur* in a different relationship to the *stagiaire*, one usually developed in a different institutional setting, normally arrives in the school twice during the year. For some *stagiaires*, it is the IUFM *formateur* who is the more known, trusted and familiar point of reference; for others, it is undoubtedly the pedagogic advisor.

One *stagiaire* commented as follows on the split role of his pedagogic advisor *vis-à-vis* support and assessment:

> But it's true that I don't have a great many questions to ask him either. I don't know why – since it's a bit strange, you know, to say that he is there to help us and then he comes to evaluate us as well and to produce a report at the end of the year that will determine if we are accepted.

The IUFM information document provided to every mathematics *stagiaire* and pedagogic advisor in one Academy we visited includes these words:

> The pedagogic advisor's function is one of assistance and advice [...] their participation in the final evaluation should not impede effectiveness; rather it should serve to reassure the *stagiaire* due to the presence at the heart of the evaluation committee of someone who knows him or her well and who is not basing an appreciation on incomplete elements of observation.

The potential ambiguity between support and evaluation when these functions figure on the same individual is a very general issue in induction and was referred to in Chapter 1, as well as in other case chapters. We return to it in section 7 of this chapter, when looking at some ambiguities in the status of a secondary *stagiaire* teacher.

Additionally, the IUFM *formateur* may have a prior relationship with the pedagogic advisor. For example, since 1998, the IUFMs have been given complete responsibility for organizing and arranging all of the continuing *formation* provision for each Academy. So the IUFM *formateurs* may increasingly have worked with the pedagogic advisors as teachers in their own right (e.g. as leader of and participant respectively in a continuing *formation stage* or as co-workers on some project at an IREM).

When an IUFM *formateur* visits a *stagiaire*, what are some issues around this crossing of institutional boundaries? Here is one *formateur's* view, who had herself formerly been a pedagogic advisor in a *collège*.

> First of all, it obviously depends on the school and the particular pedagogic advisor. In other words, there are pedagogic advisors with whom I discuss things as one equal to another and there are others who take me for the Inspector coming to call. And I even want to say it is almost the whole school who thinks of the IUFM *formateur* as an Inspector. Recently, a teacher in a school whom I didn't know said that to my face, "Ah, you come from the IUFM, you are an Inspector". [...]
>
> I have the impression that certain pedagogic advisors somewhat – 'protect' is the word I'll use – their *stagiaire*. When I make a visit, sometimes the pedagogic advisor is there and sometimes not, it depends. I say to the *stagiaire*, you decide, it's up to you. In other words, if your pedagogic advisor wants to attend your class and you don't want them to come when we visit, say so. And after the class, there is a discussion with the *stagiaire*, and the pedagogic advisor is present or not according to the wish of the *stagiaire*. [...]
>
> Sometimes the pedagogic advisor sits off to one side, not taking part, and sometimes they do take part, a three-way discussion, which is interesting. But sometimes if they are sitting back, and I say something to the *stagiaire*, the pedagogic advisor always seeks to explain it away, "Well, after all, OK, it's not serious, but you should understand ...", they come right forward to protect.

This excerpt raises many interesting questions about territoriality and perception in the relationships at work among individuals and between the institutional affiliations concerned.

The stage de pratique accompagnée (the 'accompanied practice' stage)

For thirty class contact hours during the first year (it used to be forty-two), usually between November and March, *stagiaires* participate in a second school-based *stage*. They spend the equivalent of half-a-day or more each week mainly in the classroom of a teacher, one who teaches at the other secondary level from the one they are already teaching at. (So this *stage* would be in a *lycée* if the *stagiaire* were teaching at a *collège*, and vice versa.) This *stage* is more like a conventional North American pre-service practicum experience, in that the *stagiaire* is in another teacher's classroom who is customarily present and the *stagiaire* is made use of as the regular classroom teacher sees fit. Nevertheless, the IUFM encourages all sorts of *stagiaire* activity in this setting, including independent preparation and class teaching, setting and marking homework, as well as working alongside the teacher in class. [19]

Many of the *stagiaires* we spoke with commented on how they enjoyed the experience of being in a different school and a variety of classes with another teacher, but did not like reverting to more of a student status of not being the teacher with their own pupils and, hence, not being the one in control. This provides a further instance of a need for somewhat fluid boundaries within the thinking of the *stagiaires*, in terms of their own sense of self and their developing professional autonomy. This discomfort also, for us, served to underscore the at-times fragile nature of this sense of *stagiaires* as teachers in their own minds.

Setting 2: The work at the IUFM

Here, we concentrate on the range of experiences available to *stagiaires* when they are at the IUFM for a day and a half every week throughout the school year. The scheduling and nature of the *stagiaires'* own teaching is such that their work at the IUFM is not interrupting their work week: it comprises an integral part of that work week. Their main class teaching is work for which they are fully responsible: it is what we would see as part-time teaching, but it is unquestionably complete in itself. This IUFM-based work is to support that school teaching, but also to go beyond it, looking ahead to subsequent years where the demands will be different and greater, as well as to provide a theoretical 'education' alongside and in close dialogue with this emerging practice.

The disciplinary day at the IUFM

Recall Monique sitting with her group working on and then marking a long, challenging geometry assignment. For an entire day a week, groups of between twenty and forty mathematics *stagiaires* work together with IUFM-based *formateurs* on issues of teaching mathematics, of curriculum and task analysis, of pupil errors and misconceptions and how to think about and frame their work in an academic manner.

In one Academy, an hour of each disciplinary day was spent in discussion and debates of topics generated by *stagiaires* in their day-to-day teaching practice, but were used as springboards into making links and bringing theorised notions to bear on them to assist and clarify. This Academy's offering for the disciplinary day over the year was in four parts:

- *lycée* and *collège* curricula and ways of working in these settings;
- workshop on didactic practices;
- communication and information technology and the teaching of mathematics;
- objects and methods of research in *didactique des mathématiques* (see section 6 for more detail).

Parts of some days were spent explicitly on supporting group work on the professional memoir, introducing the *stagiaires* to a specific literature including certain theoretical notions and research methods to some degree from an academic discipline known as *didactique des mathématiques*.

The disciplinary day is where a sense of a cohort and group identity get built up during the *stagiaire* year. Once again, it is with same-subject teachers working together on their joint area of specialisation.

> I am interested in what you say about [induction practices in] other countries, because in France we think it is something that is very poorly done, welcoming someone into a new profession. It is left completely to chance. Except, well, the fact of being a PLC2, which is this notion of contingent progress. And one of last year's *stagiaires*, when the construction of a web site was proposed, said, "It would be good to stay in touch with the tribe". And all of them said that, so you can see it is a very strong thing. And afterwards [following permanent certification], when you are in school, it really depends. Those schools in difficult areas, but which function, schools in which the group of [mathematics] teachers has a strong sense of solidarity, they work together a lot. And in those places that don't work, the teachers don't ever see each other. But you see that is not at all organized by the system, it's left completely to chance for now. (An IUFM mathematics *formateur*)

The notion of 'tribe' is an important one. Various things support the integrity of a tribe: shared experience, shared practices, shared tools and shared language among them. All of these are engendered during the discplinary day at the IUFM.

The non-disciplinary half-day at the IUFM

Stagiaires spend the generalist half-day in a range of short courses and workshops usually of a few weeks' duration, some of which are compulsory and some optional, chosen from a range. Examples of compulsory courses in one Academy included: classroom management, and the use of audio-visual and information technology.

Exemplar titles of optional courses in the same Academy included: cultural diversity (welcoming immigrant, non-French-speaking pupils and temporary visitors); the pupil: actor in the social organisation of the class; adolescence and violence; helping pupils in difficulty and working with difficult pupils; struggling against demotivation and its consequences for classroom management; analysis of professional practice; education for health; the education of mentally-handicapped adolescents; inside and outside school: possible partnerships; the job which is waiting for me; outside of disciplinary pedagogy: how to 'optimise' your functioning, individual and collective, in the school.

Those teaching these courses and workshops include: IUFM *formateurs* from a range of departments, university faculty (e.g. sociologists), nurses, CPEs (see note [4]), assistant social workers, *collège* vice-principals, school principals, and representatives of various outside groups and associations. Interestingly, some of the indicated audiences for these classes cut across the elementary/secondary levels and some involve *stagiaire* CPEs as well. Most classes are held at the IUFM, while a few are school-based, and are usually run in groups of fifteen to twenty *stagiaires*. Chosen topics include those which, in many other countries, are dealt with during pre-service preparation. However, the way they are able to be engaged with here allows pertinent issues to be explored in the midst of the group of *stagiaires'* own teaching in multiple schools.

This is also the only time, for half a day in a very full and varied week, that first-year teachers have the opportunity to think and discuss across subject-matter lines with teacher colleagues who are not mathematicians (and sometimes with CPEs who are not even subject-matter teachers). It is also the one occasion in the week where both the school and the pupil can be perceived and explored as coherent entities. (One task for a compulsory course in one Academy was to follow a pupil from the *stagiaire's* class through an entire school day.)

The person in charge of the non-disciplinary *formation* at an IUFM we visited observed how *stagiaires* frequently criticise and complain about these sessions by around the middle of the PLC2 year. She used an image (which she attributed to Claudine Blanchard-Laville) of a river where on one bank the identity is that of 'student' and on the opposite bank that of 'teacher'. The task facing the *stagiaire* during the PLC2 year, then, involves crossing this river from one bank to the other.

> In October, they are near the bank they must leave behind. Initially, they are not too angry with the general *formation*. But when they find themselves right in the middle of this river, it seems like they can neither go forward nor back. That's when the anguish comes and they criticise us greatly.

> There is no response possible, but they think we are not responding to their questions and complaints. A common one is that here [at the IUFM] they treat us like pupils [*élèves*], but there [in school] we are treated like teachers. They have succeeded in passing the recruiting competition, the CAPES is at the apex, they believe they are as good mathematically as they will ever be, they have a class, and they are very shaken by about March as they have tried to project onto themselves the role of teacher. And for them to be prepared means not to suffer: they are suffering, therefore they are not or have not been sufficiently well prepared. This internal debate is very characteristic of new teachers.

> Our challenge here at the IUFM is to find a way to be with them, to accompany them so they can pass from one bank of the river to the other.

To the extent that it is successful, this transition in France unfolds over the *stagiaire* year, a year characterised in part by this ambiguity about status.

Setting 3: Working to connect these two settings (the professional memoir)

In the opening vignette, Monique described some of her initial thoughts about and preparation for what will become her professional memoir, a written text that is to be submitted in the late spring and subsequently defended orally before a small jury. The memoir is to report on some detailed exploratory work, often carried out either individually or in a *stagiaire* pair, relating to some aspect of practice or a mathematical issue, one that has usually arisen in the course of teaching.

The memoir was intended as a significant opportunity for teachers to work on their own professionalisation, to stand slightly back from their first class teaching and to explore it. It is thus an important setting for the integration of 'theory' and 'practice'. (The reflexive verb *se former* carries this sense of *stagiaires* working on their own induction, as actors with force in this process in their own right.)

Neither the *stagiaire's* predecessors if they became certified more than a decade ago nor their pedagogic advisors will have written such a memoir. Over time, however, as more teachers selected as pedagogic advisors are themselves IUFM-trained, this differentiation will eventually cease (in another thirty years, maximum) and common experience will once again likely hold between novice and more experienced teacher. But at present, it is a disjuncture in the system.

The professional memoir requirement for new teachers appeared concurrently with the establishment of the IUFMs. Below is its first official national specification.

It [the professional memoir] rests on the analysis of professional practice, especially that encountered during the *stage en responsabi-lité*, and should allow verification of the *stagiaire* teacher's ability to:

- identify a problem or question to do with this practice;
- analyse this problem and suggest lines of reflection or action, with reference to existing work in the area.

It should neither comprise a simple recounting of individual work without analysis or critical reflection, nor be solely a theoretical or historical piece outside of the experience of the *stagiaire* teacher.

This memoir, prepared either individually or collectively, should not exceed 30 pages (excluding appendices).

The oral submission should be individual and allow verification of the *stagiaire's* involvement in the work and to assess his or her capacity for argument. (BOEN #27, 11/7/91)

Recall this memoir is, in part, used as a mark of professionalism and increased professionalisation of teaching. But it is also envisaged as a way to connect theory and practice and, perhaps, to soften the disjuncture sometimes felt between IUFM-based and school-based tasks. Another mark of being 'not quite a teacher', then, besides being observed in their teaching, is the fact that *stagiaires* must work on *formation* and the memoir at the IUFM. Once they become certified teachers, they never have to write another memoir, nor is this something they see certified colleagues engaged in.

Claude Comiti, a mathematics didactician and someone closely involved with the original creation of the memoir element of the IUFM specifications [20], commented:

The memoir is very important in many professional *formations* in France, in particular in that of social workers. In their *formation*, they have a professional memoir, as do youth workers and ministry of justice workers. If you like, in the *formation* of any professional, this memoir is a means of creating a space of interaction between the theoretical notions they have had in their *formation* and the terrain in which they have to work. The professional aspect is really very important.

And what must also be avoided is the transformation of this idea into a report on their *stage*. That's not the intent [...] and the memoir supervisor must shape a memoir in which the *stagiaire* is required to transform his [/her] first enquiries into real questions which the memoir should try to answer. And in other cases, there are memoirs that are solely narratives: a little better than simply 'what I did', but still narratives or syllabi or lesson plans.

At thirty pages, these memoirs are not that long, but preparing one is a significant task. There is more than one national professional journal which sometimes takes such material. One key instance is the national lower secondary school journal *Petit x* (published by the Grenoble IREM), which is increasingly intended primarily for *collège* mathematics teachers and IUFM-based initial and continuing *formation*. [21] Here is a list of some mathematics memoir titles, taken from Artigue *et al.* (1998), a book discussed in the next paragraph.

> The figure in geometry;
> Leading pupils in grade six and seven to distinguish an object from its representation in Cavalierian perspective: reasons for hope;
> Can one educate geometric perception in three dimensions?
> Angles, a new notion: which instrument to choose?
> Proof: centre of interest;
> Graphing? Technical drawing? An assistance or a further difficulty?
> Linear maps in eighth grade;
> Obstacles linked to the learning of cosine;
> How to introduce the notion of absolute value in tenth grade?
> Can one learn to reason? Tenth grade and an ES grade 11 class;
> Toward a formative way of correcting students.

The memoir was the most contested part of the initial IUFM requirements. Early concerns about the memoir as part of initial *formation* are noted by Michèle Artigue and her colleagues in the introduction to a collection of 'the best' professional memoirs from their Academy, entitled *Between Theory and Practice: the IUFM Professional Memoir in Mathematics*. They indicate a potential ambiguity of purpose:

> Was it right to see the memoir as an initiation into research or should the 'analysis of practice' dimension be emphasised? (pp. 9-10)

These authors go on to claim that, eight years later, whatever else the memoir has become, it is now seen more and more as a device for the initial *formation* of teachers.

> Today, it [the professional memoir] seems to we *formateurs* as an essential component in articulating theory and practice that we are trying to bring to life in the second-year IUFM professional *formation*. It is an essential component because it occurs at a point when the *stagiaire* teacher, in the daily complexity he [/she] is managing, is going to cut into a reduced but coherent domain, taking the time for a deeper study which does not allow simply handling daily demands, while also taking into account that others before him [/her] have posed themselves similar questions and that his [/her] own work contributes to moving collective reflection forward. (p. 10)

Concerning the relation of the memoir to research, Bernard Cornu observed:

> The memoir was not considered as research activity. But it's the only opportunity for a future teacher, to use Claude Comiti's phrase, to work in the *spirit* of research and to use *tools from* research.

As we saw, at the national level there are not very many instructions specifying a memoir; one way or another, it should make reference to a practice. But once the problem has been identified, it is up to the IUFM *formateurs* in particular Academies to interpret what that means in actuality.

For instance, as one *formateur* observed, if a *stagiaire* decides to analyse a textbook seeking to show something or other, is that considered to have a practice element in it? The speaker thought so, but saw the problem as not exactly that of knowing when to tell about something that happened in a class. The problem was in knowing whether the type of question the *stagiaire* is posing is of interest for the profession. And for the profession it is perhaps of interest to know, for instance, whether the sort of exercises usually given about this topic eventually result in the pupils having a false conception about it. "It is not a class-based experiment, but it is also of interest."

Another *formateur* who works with *stagiaires* on the memoir in a different Academy commented:

> We present it [the professional memoir] as a period of time, as a temporary break from teaching practice. In order to see the habitual moves of the teaching profession by means of taking a step back, you need to take the time to think. It's a period when they are going to think about a teaching problem that concerns them as beginning teachers.
>
> And we encourage them to discuss it with their pedagogic advisor, as it is in this respect that we think it connects with their *stage en responsabilité,* because the majority choose to carry out their observations and experimentation in the class for which they are responsible. It is not compulsory to do this at all, because if they ask they can work in pairs. But this is unusual [in this Academy].

This *formateur* runs five collective sessions of three hours each with a dozen *stagiaires*, after which she works individually with them on their memoirs. Part of the shared time involves working from a base set of readings, mostly other memoirs or articles from *Petit x* (about which she comments, "It's becoming more and more a journal of *formation*").

At one IUFM we visited, in mathematics there is a separate, IUFM-appointed director for the memoir – again, usually someone school-based – instead of the pedagogic advisor for the *stage en responsabilité* who is

233

commonly also appointed the memoir director in most Academies. Because the memoir is the responsibility of the IUFM, the freedom is there to appoint another advisor. A mathematics *formateur* from this IUFM explained her reasons for this variation from the norm:

> We think the more *stagiaires* can have contact with different teachers, the better it is. They are already very influenced by their pedagogic advisor and we think they should be in touch with the maximum – not thousands, but this would be three. If you don't count the other IUFM *formateurs*, there is the director of the memoir, the [IUFM] person who supervises the *stages* and the pedagogic advisor. [...] In addition, we often use those who were themselves PLC2s as memoir directors, and who are therefore newish teachers who couldn't be used as pedagogic advisors or *maîtres de stage*. We like it, but it is not systematically done.

Once again, this emphasizes the relative newness of the IUFM-based *formation* for secondary mathematics teachers, and also how most practicing teachers were not themselves 'formed' in this way. This is one small way of allowing relatively new teachers to be seen as having sufficient experience of a particular kind to be able to contribute to the *formation* process of the mathematics 'tribe'.

One growing and now-considerable resource in each IUFM is the previous years' memoirs to which *stagiaires* frequently turn. And this is one reason why texts arising from individual practice have started to appear. The Artigue *et al.* (1998) book mentioned above is one. Another, a booklet on memoirs for tutors (Nadot, 2000) from the Versailles IUFM, begins with the interesting concern:

> In conjunction with the courses and the *stages*, the memoir constitutes one of the settings for the *formation* of teachers. It would be regrettable if it were considered as a test to evaluate 'abilities already in place', rather than as a means to develop new professional know-hows [*compétences*] in those who have just been recruited. (p. 7)

In conjunction with IUFM web sites, the public aspect and product of individual IUFM practices is now becoming more widely available to all. (For more on the professional memoir, see Appendix C.)

Looking back

Monique and other mathematics *stagiaires* experience various aspects of working in all of these settings – and all of them within a single week. Here, we summarise this section by pointing out some common features despite this diversity and end with a look toward to the future.

Firstly, these compulsory opportunities for *stagiaire* learning are varied. First-year teaching and learning about teaching in France take place in a number of settings and require quite different things of *stagiaire* teachers, most especially flexibility, as both their status and sense of their own emerging teacher identity has to be in considerable flux as they move between institutional settings that frame them differently.

Secondly, these experiences bring them into contact with a consider-able number of different people in varied roles: the IUFM *formateurs*; the pedagogic advisors; the school staff in two schools including their administrators, as well as teachers both in mathematics and other subjects; the memoir tutor; different groups of pupils; parents; possibly one of the Academy Inspectors – the list is very long. These individuals have a complex set of relationships with each other, as well as many belonging to a variety of institutions which frame their encounters with the *stagiaire* (see Figure 4).

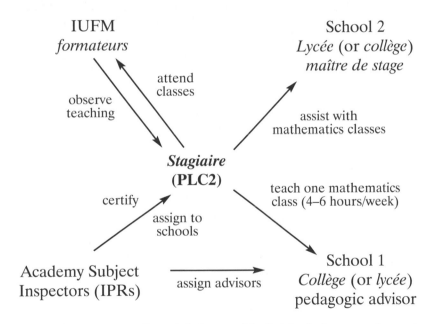

Figure 4:   The various influential sites and individuals for a mathematics stagiaire

Thirdly, with the exception of the regular, non-subject-specific half-day of IUFM *formation* each week, virtually every single other encounter the *stagiaire* has is sharply focused on and invested in mathematics and its specific teaching. So their PLC1 year leading up to the recruitment competition is almost entirely spent working at mathematics and their second year is almost entirely spent thinking about and working with mathematical education theory and practice. It is also mathematics that is the defining feature of the 'tribe' of mathematics *stagiaires* that an IUFM shapes and initiates. We end this section with a short look toward the future. Ten years after the inception of the IUFM system with its tasks and settings for new teachers, a report was requested by and produced for the Ministry of Education (presented in 2001), recommending improvements to the IUFM system. This report made a number of recommedations concerning extending the period of *formation* beyond the *stagiaire* year.

Here, Bernard Cornu, one of the two authors of this report, comments on the perceptions of and certain tensions among various institutions involved in new teacher *formation*, in relation to potential developments involving an additional year of *formation*. Some of the issues raised involve questions of demarcation of boundaries and institutional 'ownership', responsibility and control.

> The year before the [recruiting] competition, which is mainly focused on the subject, the universities would like to take it inside the university. So many universities, they will say, "We are in favour of two years at the IUFM, but the two years after the competition. And the first year will just be put in the university. Because it's on the subject."

> We have to keep the first year and try to professionalize it a little bit and keep the third year and provide a global process for teacher *formation*. This also is a very complicated debate with the universities.

> I think everybody agrees with the fact that the PLC2 year is not enough for a strong professional training, clearly. If we want to enlarge it, if we go to the first year, the university says, "No, this is for the subject". And if we go to the third year, the Academy says, "Oh, they are ours. They are not yours."

> [Interviewer: And during the PLC2, you see them as yours. There isn't the same debate with the Academy during PLC2?] Yes, there is. But it's more clear, because administratively they are ours. They are registered in the Institute [IUFM], they are paid, they get a salary in the second year. We write all the documents for that, pay them, and so on.

> So clearly we are the employer, yes. And they owe part of their duty to schools. They must teach one third of the normal duty [of a teacher], and so for this third, of course, the Academy says, "They are ours".

We return to discuss these interesting and significant issues in section 7. But first, in the next section, we examine certain features specific to *mathematics* teaching in France which contribute to the mathematics *stagiaire's* disciplinary induction to the teaching profession.

6. Some Specific Elements of the Mathematics Teaching Terrain

One of the key questions we kept returning to in our study was whether there was anything specific about the induction of *mathematics* (or *science*) teachers in the various sites we were looking at, or whether whatever forms of induction were available were general, at least with regard to the subject matter being taught. One theme that this chapter explores is how what a new mathematics teacher is inducted into is the intensely disciplinary nature of secondary school teaching in France. What a novice is being inducted into is being a secondary *mathematics* teacher and not simply being a secondary teacher.

Mathematics has a particular status and role in French education and culture, one that makes it unlike any other school subject taught. Mathematics is still frequently held up as the paradigm of knowledge (*le savoir*) and valued for its training of the mind and its strong links with reason. Yes, it is to be studied compulsorily throughout the *collège*, but so are French, Science, Technology and many other subjects (there are very few options available, none in grade 6). Yes, mathematics is the second major school subject: apart with French, which has more, mathematics has the highest number of hours per week devoted to it, though that position is currently under challenge.

In March 2000, a multiple-signature public letter to the national newspaper of record *Le Monde* appeared, protesting the proposal to reduce the number of hours dedicated to mathematics in the secondary school. Its final sentence declares:

> The teaching of mathematics in secondary school should occupy the place that its importance deserves in the scientific and cultural development of our country. (André *et al.*, 2000, p. 8)

As with other subjects, there is a nationally-specified mathematics syllabus for the *collège* produced by the section of the Ministry of Education concerned with school education (CNDP, 1999). At only 100 pages, covering four years of schooling, it is not a huge document. It contains extracts from official documents specifying compulsory and optional school subjects, and the number of hours per week to be taught at each grade level (four in grades 6 and 9, between three and a half and four and a half in grades 7 and 8 for mathematics).

Interestingly, the language of the document is one of the *formation* for the pupil rather than the teaching. Mathematics is framed in terms of three broad goals in this document: as a discipline of general *formation* (related to the capacity for experimentation and reasoning, and to that of imagination and critical analysis), as a provider of applicable tools and methods (which nevertheless possess their own autonomy) and as a means of expression (in particular, linked to the practice of making arguments). It is in the first category that we read, "They [mathematics] contribute[s] in this way to the *formation* of the future citizen" (p. 15).

Following a couple of general orienting pages, each grade level's syllabus is presented in tabular form with three columns: content, required *compétences* (here all specifying verbs are in the infinitive, such as, for grade 7, 'to write an expression corresponding to a given sequence of operations' or 'to construct the circumscribed circle of a triangle') and a brief commentary (including, on occasion, very cursory examples). The mathematical areas are organised into three categories, always presented in the same order: geometric work, computational work, organisation and handling of data and functions.

The accompaniment for each grade level comprises some half-dozen to a dozen pages, providing a mathematical overview and discussion of certain areas or conceptual difficulties and approaches. However, there is almost no explicit pedagogical discussion in this document (though various trace presences of tacit assumptions about school pedagogy is another matter).

This document is what every *stagiaire* and certified mathematics teacher needs to refer to when preparing their mathematics course (*le cours*) for each class at whichever *collège* grade level. A primary and central task for all *collège* teachers is to take this relatively sparse document and turn each grade-level specification into structured sequences of lessons, known as 'chapters'. It is to this notion of *cours* that we now turn. A sizeable proportion of the disciplinary day activity at the IUFM has connections to exploring, theorising and illustrating ways of engaging with this core teacher task.

The *cours*

A key notion for the beginning mathematics teacher is that of '*le cours*', the formal, mathematical content to be organised and taught. They have experienced it themselves as pupils in school. They observe it being enacted in their pedagogic advisor's classroom and in their visits to a school in the other 'cycle'. They hear teachers in the staff room talking about their *cours*. It is in large measure what their primary teacher task is perceived to be. But in all of our twenty some *stagiaire* interviews, it was not referred to as 'the' *cours* but as 'my' *cours*. The sense of personal investment in the design and presentation of this course seemed very strong.

A common remark made to us was how, despite there being a nationally specified syllabus/curriculum for mathematics, 'everyone teaches their own *cours*'. A few commented that this was actually illusory, that there was a great similarity across mathematics lessons one to another, but felt it can nevertheless be an important illusion. A second-year teacher, whose first permanent posting (as very many are) was to a challenging setting in an outer Paris suburb [22], observed that, if the setting and pupils one is teaching do not offer very much initially, investing oneself into the writing and construction of 'my *cours*' is one place where a beginning teacher can get some pleasure, some sense of professional satisfaction.

In the ten *stagiaire* lessons we observed and videotaped, there was a visible sense of ritual around the presenting of *cours* material. It was specifically identified as such by the *stagiaire* teacher (as it was in the six other lessons we observed by certified teachers) and marked off in a number of different ways. The pupils took out a particular book and their coloured pens and a ruler. A form of dictation took place via the blackboard. Pupils were to make their own neat copies in their notebooks. The attention to the form, e.g. the numerical structuring and accurate labelling of the type of statements presented (definition, proposition, remark, ...), was high, while the focus was undoubtedly on the content. While the teacher dictated, the pupils were often still asking questions and were themselves mostly caught up in this task. [23] And the teacher was not solely dictating, vocalizing what was to be written as he or she wrote it on the blackboard: there was a meta-commentary going on (talk about the writing) while the privileged written text was being transferred.

This was a form that *stagiaires* would certainly have met when themselves school pupils and also likely seen contemporaneously in the classes of their pedagogic advisor and *maître de stage*. There was also a strong emphasis on oral fluency in pupils in the mathematics register (Pimm, 1987), as well as a marked attention to precision in the use of technical terminology (arguably related to the third goal in the national syllabus, mathematics as a means of expression). Pupils were frequently called upon to read aloud from the textbook or their *cours* notebooks to the class (either problem statements or general propositions), as well as to read aloud what was written on the board.

One sequence we noticed was the use of a 'preparatory task', followed by some theoretical presentation and work on notions in the *cours* itself, followed by pupil-worked exercises, though all three of these tasks did not take place in any single lesson: based only on this small group of lessons, we are tempted to surmise that 'the lesson' by itself was not the main unit of curriculum planning. This was confirmed by various insiders as being a current *collège* norm and, to a lesser extent, a *lycée* one as well.

The preparatory task was always in the form of particular situations which, in principle, could be profitably generalized. Such mathematical tasks are widely available in various textbooks (not always good ones), in IREM documents, in the lower secondary professional journal *Petit x* and on the Internet. This aspect of choice among and design of these initiating tasks was worked at heavily at the IUFMs we visited during the disciplinary sessions. At the IUFM, *stagiaires* learn how to select and amend mathematical tasks; in other words, they find out how to look at the connection between the mathematical meaning and the construction of a classroom task.

As one *formateur* educated in *didactique des mathématiques* commented:

> For me, at a theoretical level, it is closely tied to Brousseau's [1997] 'theory of situations', even if I choose not to teach a course on the theory of situations!

One contested area, which is being worked out differently in different IUFMs is the extent to which, in order to pursue their profession, *stagiaires* need to be taught explicit elements of or even courses in *didactique des mathématiques,* seen either as a resource for their daily work in class or for their work on the professional memoir. (We discuss this further in the next sub-section.) This subject-specific discipline provides a third apex to the sometimes binary split between 'discipline' and 'pedagogy' (see note [24]).

Subsequently, we came across an article in the Spring 2001 issue of the journal *Petit x* which both echoed this observation and problematised its omnipresence as a pedagogic 'norm'. Entitled 'Activities: a theme in need of reworking', the article's abstract reads as follows:

> Do 'activities', fashionable in textbooks, really allow mathematical learning? What do new [literally 'young'; here meaning with less than five years' experience] teachers think about this? What is the minimum amount of *didactique* that should be introduced in *formation* in order to emphasise the viewpoint of the conditions necessary for pupil acquisition of knowledge when selecting or rejecting tasks found in the textbooks? (Rousset-Bert, 2001, p. 61)

The topic of this article thus links a core framing of certain notions in *didactique* to the ability of a new mathematics teacher to act wisely when faced with the challenge of selecting tasks from school textbooks (or other sources), as well as questioning a fashionable shift in a specific classroom practice. This discussion raises a particular form of a more general question explored in Chapter 7 of this book, which is concerned with asking what is the 'curriculum of induction', who holds this knowledge and where does it reside.

Unquestionably, in France, there is a technical language and approach for looking at issues arising from mathematical teaching situations and the design of classroom tasks which inform many of the mathematics faculty (the *enseignant–chercheurs*) who hold permanent, university-level academic posts in the IUFMs. And to a greater or lesser extent, more or less explicitly, this way of thinking is being passed on to some mathematics *stagiaires* as part of their *formation*.

One thing in particular that stood out from the post-lesson interviews we participated in following lesson observations was the frequent clarity of focus and sophisticated purpose behind the systematic design of the mathematics tasks, even ones that were subject to subsequent criticism. The general level of many discussions between *stagiaire* and *formateur* was significantly more sophisticated than comparable discussions with first-year, lower-secondary mathematics teachers in our experience. It also points up how difficult it may be for some *stagiaires* having their pedagogic advisor as their professional memoir supervisor, someone who is perhaps not comfortable with or even privy to a didactic orientation. However, nor by any means are all *formateurs* even within a single IUFM mathematics department steeped in the traditions and formulations of *didactique des mathématiques* as the only form of academically-codified knowledge about the classroom teaching of mathematics.

What is particularly interesting, however, is the ways in which established schoolteachers nonetheless play a significant role in the bringing in of the new, across a disjuncture of how they themselves became teachers. The considerable majority, then and now, share the CAPES examination as their route into teaching. But the majority of teachers currently teaching in the secondary system have had no experience of the IUFMs (either as student or *stagiaire* teacher) and potentially little contact with them, as enrollment in continuing *formation* courses is not that great.

However, it is not simply the first-year teachers being inducted into (literally being 'led into') the old without the old also having to accommodate to the new. In some areas (such as knowledge and use of new technology, a contested and resisted requirement of all mathematics teachers by the most recent reform of the national curriculum), such novice teachers are in the vanguard, even the *avant-garde* of practice inside the *collège* (and *lycée*). *Stagiaires* also bring with them, to a greater or lesser extent, a new and different sort of pedagogic content knowledge, together with a particular language for talking about tasks and didactic situations.

The pedagogic advisor was present during six out of the ten post-lesson *formateur* discussions with the *stagiaires* that we attended. These pedagogic advisors had been present in the same classroom (and had been there regularly), but had not necessarily participated in the same pedagogic event. It would be easy to overstate this. Nevertheless, our sense was, in these instances at least, that it was the *stagiaire* who negotiated meanings and experiences between, on occasions, two separate though not distinct cultures. It was the *stagiaire* who had a prolonged working relationship with both of those present in the room (these took place at the time of the second IUFM *formateur* visit in March). It was the *stagiaire* who was involved in integrating these ways of talking and viewing a classroom.

The IREMs

One significant mathematics-specific singularity in France is the national network of IREMs – *Instituts de Recherche sur l'Enseignement des Mathématiques* (Research Institutes on the Teaching of Mathematics) – located in an individual university mathematics department, one in every mainland Academy. These have existed for over thirty years, the first ones being established in 1969 by the Ministry of Education following pressure from the national, public institution mathematics teaching association APMEP, in order to support the rapid 'retraining' of many secondary mathematics teachers struggling to teach 'new' mathematics syllabi introduced progressively during the period 1969–1972.

In addition to the part-time allocation of certain university-based mathematicians to the IREMs, schoolteachers were seconded from *collèges* and *lycées*, both to teach and take courses. The IREMs did not (and do not) accredit these courses, which on the one hand meant they did not form part of the institutional structure, but on the other meant that there was considerable freedom for the teachers and participants to shape them to their own ends. This relative institutional freedom continues to be much valued and cherished.

Fairly soon, the work of the IREMs far out-reached their original mandate and work began to move toward broader mathematical educational issues and concerns (a double mission of teacher education and exploratory investigation) in the teaching of mathematics at both the elementary and secondary levels.

> A very important part of IREM activity was soon devoted to pedagogical innovation (particularly 'active experimental research', which united pedagogical theory and classroom experimentation). Criticism of syllabuses and textbooks, the study of new techniques (especially in the audio-visual and computing fields) and generally the questioning of standard practices and institutions. (IREM, 1984, pp. 5-6)

The IREMs, in keeping with this chapter's theme of variation within a uniform structure, vary considerably in structure, focus and approach to their work – they function independently of one another. Each is consequently a product of its individual and institutional history in terms of how it has developed, what topics and level different groups have worked at (the history of mathematics here, work with new technology there, a focus on the teaching of algebra in a third place, a stressing or de-emphasizing of *didactique des mathématiques,* and so on). Nevertheless, there are cross-IREM gatherings and co-ordination meetings in order not to duplicate effort, as well as inter-IREM commissions which work on common issues and concerns. It makes sense to speak of an IREM network. The IREMs were and continue to be key places for continuing *formation* for mathematics teachers in France, as well as publishers of an extensive, innovative and broad range of pedagogic material in mathematics.

But they are a singularity, in that there are no IRE's for any other school subject (apart from history/geography in some places, but to lesser effect). There are current proposals being discussed that the IREMs be moved to become part of the IUFM structure and there are some good institutional reasons to support such a rationalisation. There is considerable resistance to this proposal, however, from those who worry that the IREMs (and the considerable intellectual and personnel resources they embody) will disappear once incorporated into the IUFM, precisely because the system still does not welcome such glaring singularities.

Didactique des mathématiques

At various places in this chapter mention has been made of a highly theorised research approach to issues in mathematics education in France known as *didactique des mathématiques.* This field came into being roughly at the time of major reforms in mathematics curricula around 1970. Guy Brousseau, one of the founders of the field, specified its boundary as "the study of phenomena bound to teaching in [its] specificity for the subject matter taught" (cited in Balacheff, 1988, p. 75).

Since 1980, there has existed an international journal *Recherches en Didactique des Mathématiques* and an increasing number of research articles and books have appeared extending this field over the past twenty years. There is no space in this chapter even remotely to touch on this field. Interested anglophone readers would do well to look at Brousseau (1997), particularly Chapter 6, as well as the Kieran (1998) and the Herbst and Kilpatrick (1999) reviews of this major work. In addition, Margolinas (2000), Artigue and Perrin-Glorian (1991), Balacheff (1990) and Laborde (1989) all provide helpful perspectives for English readers. Finally, there is a broad attempt in English to delineate the general, cross-disciplinary history of this French set of approaches to studying issues of teaching and learning in an article entitled 'French *didactiques*' (Caillot, 2002).

Didactique des mathématiques is unquestionably a significant feature of both the intellectual and educational landscape of mathematics education in France, though it is by no means an uncontested one, even within IUFM-based mathematics *formateurs*. For the purposes of this chapter, what is important is to appreciate that there is a strong contender for mathematics-specific didactic knowledge (*savoir*, not *compétence*) for novices to address in a 'curriculum of induction'. It resides institutionally to varying degree within mathematics departments in IUFMs, within IREMs and within a few individuals working primarily within university mathematics departments. It is embodied in various journals and publications (including *Recherches en Didactique des Mathématiques* and *Petit x*, but also in *Repères*, the inter-IREM journal). [24]

The new 'curriculum of learning to teach' that the IUFM system represents does not legislate *didactiques*. There is no common national induction syllabus, the way there is for academic subjects in schools. But the substantial presence of various French *didactiques* is felt in various ways and places throughout the *formation* system.

7. Looking More Generally

Up to this point, we have chosen to look closely within each component of the novice's induction experience, either within particular sites for *stagiaire* learning or, in the previous section, at mathematics-specific features of the terrain. In this penultimate section, our goal is to look across the whole and try to discuss salient themes. For us, four things stand out in particular which we would like to discuss further here:

- how the centralised and national nature of France's education system shapes its systemic approach to induction within this frame;
- how this encompassing system is relatively stable, yet remains somewhat dynamic/fluid;
- the way in which shared units and continua of time come into play to assist the system's functioning;
- how ambiguous/changing boundaries arise and are drawn upon in relation to the system's functioning.

The remainder of this section is organised around these points.

Centralised and systemic: 'In France, if it exists, it exists nationally'

A question we have only started to explore here has to do with the 'systemic' nature of what occurs both to produce and to reproduce those who will teach in the secondary school system. Ten years ago, a change brought about a substantial disjuncture in the system by which secondary teachers are 'formed', even if the recruiting examination mechanism by which they are initially selected has changed little over two centuries (and has proven very resistant to attempts to modify it even slightly).

As we look across the educational system, at the *formation* of new teachers as well as the organisation and focus of mathematics classroom teaching, we see a profoundly national system. Its ability to be national rests on its organisation as a system and there are many mechanisms which underscore both these systemic and centralised aspects. For instance, with respect to the school system into which *stagiaires* are being 'inducted', there is an institutional differentiation in terms of *collège* or *lycée*. (There is also often a geographic and cultural shift regarding pupil socio-economic status and other differences between the places where many novice teachers grew up and the location of their first few years of full-time work as a certified teacher, but it is less clear that this mass importing of newly-certified teachers into a few northern Academies will prove to be an enduring phenomenon.) However, apart from ensuring that *stagiaires* experience some time in both types of school (and this can still be in only one type of *lycée*), albeit by means of quite different *stages*, the system does not differentiate the *formation* of new secondary mathematics teachers in terms of their possible destination.

In addition, the one significant differentiation in *formation* – namely whether or not a professional memoir is compulsory – is determined not in terms of future destination but rather by examinations have already been passed (namely the CAPES or *Agrégation* recruiting competitions) in order to become a secondary *stagiaire* teacher in the first place. What is clear is that there is a far greater uniformity than difference perceived by the system between the two types of secondary school, at least regarding the presumed needs of those who teach there. And that similarity expresses itself strongly as a common disciplinary culture – in terms of our interest here, that of mathematics and its teaching.

The national-level mathematics inspector's comment 'In France, if it exists, it exists nationally' still has considerable force. The IUFM system is also a system and, in almost every respect, it is both national and subject-independent, though at its heart much of its work at the secondary level is discipline-focused. The pronouncements issued via the national Ministry of Education's Official Bulletin set the broad parameters for the system as a whole. But this nationally-set framing layer of specifications is relatively thin. There is a good deal of variation observable across the system (both within and across school subjects), a fact which did not seem to be viewed as problematic by those whom we interviewed, even within the General Inspectorate. The consensus was that the system could both contain and benefit from it.

For instance, one such broad specification is that all *stagiaires* (unless they are *agrégé*) must present a professional memoir (irrespective of subject matter) and there will be so many hours instruction made available for it. Some mathematics *agrégés* nevertheless do decide to present one in certain Academies. But how those hours are spent (in workshops on a range of subjects, in paired tutorials, in individual consultation with one's memoir tutor, …) varies considerably from Academy to Academy within a single subject. There is systemic license for variation accorded to the next level in the system. So parts of what the first year of teaching looks like for individual mathematics *stagiaires* depends considerably and non-trivially on the particular IUFM and specific Academy where they receive their *formation*. Nevertheless, they are being trained as a cadre of mathematics teachers for national education.

There are some subject-specific particularities or singularities in the system as well, though there was also some unease expressed in certain administrative quarters, at least because of one of them. The IREMs are particular to mathematics – there is not the same institutional home and funding for pedagogic work on physics or even French language education, for instance – and the IREMs still play a key role in the *mathematics* continuing education structure of the nation. But although they are specific to mathematics, something that attests to the singular importance this subject plays in the country's education system, they still exist *nationally*.

One core challenge to the continuation of any system is variation and how it is perceived and contended with. To what extent is the system a conserving one that pulls the new toward the centre, the norm or the legislated? To what extent does the system allow itself to be pulled (perturbed in one sense without becoming perturbed in another) by those new members who renew the living system just like replacement cells in a human body?

These questions are clearly general. France provides simply one instance of the forces involved being played out in a particular historical and cultural *milieu*. David Antin (1987), although writing about literary genres and new instances of them, could equally well have been writing about educational systems and tolerance of variation within them when he observed:

> Seen from this viewpoint, the viability of a genre like the viability of a family is based on survival, and the indispensable property of a surviving family is a continuing ability to take in new members who bring fresh genetic material into the old reservoir.

> So the viability of a genre may depend fairly heavily on an avant-garde activity that has often been seen as threatening its very existence, but is more accurately seen as opening its present to its past and to its future. (p. 479)

Stability in the presence of constant change

Antin's comments seem quite resonant to us. Induction can be seen to be about the means offered, sanctioned, tolerated, as well as those that happen unnoticed by which the system takes in new members. *Formation*, that key French term, namely the shaping that occurs (including self-shaping) as a novice recruit becomes more of a teacher, is compulsorily in the hands of this system. The induction system in France has reformed itself from within. What roles do the old guard play in the shaping of the new, via their roles as colleagues, as pedagogic advisors, as IUFM *formateurs*? Is the *avant-garde*, here, best seen as some of those who work within the IUFMs themselves?

There is a French tradition of experimentation with the new in certain settings for a year, learning from and revising in the light of experience, before a global decision is made about how to impose the new nationally by means of systematic specification. This can be seen with curriculum revision; it can be seen with the creation of the first three trial IUFMs prior to complete national implementation. It can also be seen with the very notion of the *stagiaire* teacher period being a year in length (a full school cycle). A year is thus a common unit of time that is used to make decisions about both institutions and people in education.

It is almost as if there is a systemic response attempting to avoid precisely the feature Gramsci identified in another context:

> The crisis consists precisely in the fact that the old is dying and the new cannot be born; in the interregnum a great many varieties of morbid symptoms appear. (cited in Pimm and Love, 1988, p. ix)

Consequently, there is a great deal of regular tinkering with the French education system – arguably, to some extent, to try to avoid such crises. The curriculum in particular is always undergoing minor 'reform', punctuated by more major upheavals roughly every decade. But there are not that many genuine crises in the sense of major discontinuities (though the problems arising from the new mathematics curricular reform of the late 1960s which led to the establishment of the IREMs could be seen as one instance). Interestingly, the 2001 Cornu-Brilhaut report on IUFM reform sent to the Minister of Education proposed minor reforms to the CAPES recruiting examination system, which initially proved far more contentious, for instance, than their suggestions about an extended 'PLC3' year – see below.

The educational system in France still bears the fingerprint of Napoleon, yet it also has the forward orientation of the twenty-first century. Ten years ago, in France, a new system was created, which in a significant sense could be seen to outsiders as a national, geographically-distributed induction system for new teachers. Unsurprisingly, this new institution initially created considerable turbulence in the system, not least in terms of its interface with the existing educational system.

Long-held views always influence even those things that have been created to change them and, to date, the IUFMs and their work have been no exception. The longevity and stability of the teaching force in France and its considerable involvement in new teacher *formation* means that, in some sense, tradition is dominant, despite some moves to perturb this hold. IUFMs are situated in major cities whose centres often contain the most sought-after schools. The general tendency arising from a system regulated by seniority and accumulation of 'points' is for the teachers in such schools to be older. A number of the *stagiaires* we interviewed spoke of a distance between them and their pedagogic advisor in terms of not wanting to teach like them, as well as some recognising that the schools in which they will be teaching in the subsequent year would likely be significantly different.

There has to be tension in a situation of both tremendous stability and significant change. Each week, *stagiaires* live this tension as they go between different institutions that reflect different commitments to them, both of which have the power to shape their images of themselves. These places also influence their growing sense of who and how they *should* be, as well contributing to shaping their place and role in the wider educational system.

Time

As we learned more about the system in France, it became clearer how part of the functioning of the system depended on certain aspects of time. In this sub-section, we briefly explore two themes.

The common unit of the pedagogic hour

The Ministry of Education (through the Academy structure) is the 'employer' of both teachers in schools and the IUFM staff, and contracted 'hours' of service are a common unit that permeates the system. Fluidity of allocation of teachers' contracted time across institutional boundaries is hence greatly enhanced, as well as being adjustable year by year (though this also can lead to unhelpful uncertainty, both for the individual teacher/*formateur* and the IUFM). It preserves tenure and seniority within a single system and provides a certain force to the claim of its employees working for national education, wherever in the system they work.

It also allows teachers flexibility to choose or to be invited to do things other than simply teach with their contracted hours (for instance, to be seconded for so many hours a week to work in conjunction with an IREM, either on a project or to run in-service courses for other teachers). The flexibility of identification (schoolteacher/*formateur*) that is permitted by a national Ministry of Education with a uniform 'currency' of allocated hours supports the bridging of theory and practice in certain ways. The question of an appropriate *formation* for IUFM *formateurs* is also under discussion.

The pre-requisite of time for induction

The variety and depth of experience available to a first-year teacher in France is clearly predicated on there being recompensed time available within the system. *Stagiaire* teachers are paid as full-time teachers, a fact which non-trivially contributes to the reality of this being how they are seen throughout the system. The value and status accorded to the successful passing of exams and gaining of diplomas in France also contributes significantly to this perception: a tenured secondary teacher is one who has been certified to know.

The system determines those experiences deemed formative for all *stagiaires* to have and invests in them (and here again, the fact that it is a unified and national system is significant, because it means the system is most often investing in itself at the same time). But the state does not need to specify things in detail: it trusts to some considerable extent. It allows variation within itself, provided the broad framework is respected. In this way, some of the rigidities of a large centralised system are ameliorated.

What to us from the outside look like induction tasks, in France are viewed simply part of initial teacher *formation*, part of what the state system has decided are the appropriate tasks for a first-year teacher prior to permanent certification. Induction, in this sense, is part of being a new teacher and not something external or additional to being a teacher in the first year of service. But also other teachers in the system have time to work with new teachers as well, to visit their classes and to have them in theirs and to discuss their observations immediately afterwards. This is enabled by a nationally-contracted norm of eighteen contact hours for certified *collège* and *lycée* teachers (fifteen if they are *agrégé*).

Supported time to do other things than simply be in front of a class teaching seems to us to be almost a necessary prerequisite for successful induction, because while classroom experience may well be a necessary contributor to certain sorts of teacher learning, it is not and never will be sufficient by itself. In France, systematic steps are taken in order to allow new teachers to engage in such practice. But also matters are arranged so they have time, support and access to a range of intellectual tools in order to go to work on that early experience, to help mould it into a reflective practice that can serve novices better than simple experience alone.

Fluid and ambiguous boundaries

It is in the nature of turbulence that it occurs at boundary surfaces. Again, one feature of the French system that arguably seems to assist its functioning relates to the fluidity of certain boundaries. However, the experience of novices faced with certain fluid boundaries may prove to be one of unsettling ambiguity.

To our outsider eyes, there are boundary issues everywhere in France: many of these are connected to our early questions of the what and the who (the providers, the recipients) of induction, as well as the perhaps less-familiar one of asking *when* is a new teacher. This sub-section is therefore divided into a discussion of four main themes in relation to the question of fluid and ambiguous boundaries:

- the nature of the relevant knowledge (what is to be learned);
- the providers of initial *formation* (the institutional complexity and who gets to be a *formateur*);
- the recipients of initial *formation;*
- the distinction between initial and continuing *formation*.

The nature and location of the knowledge deemed relevant to stagiaires

Within the former, supplanted system of secondary teacher *formation*, the 'curriculum' that was 'taught' was directly controlled and monitored by the Inspectorate: they either ran or chose who would run the courses for new teachers and determined the 'curriculum'. They additionally chose the sites for new teacher practica and the teachers in whose classes the novices would learn about teaching. The subject-matter IPRs were significant figures throughout the induction system and were in a position to impose considerable uniformity, and a supervised apprenticeship model ruled.

With the new IUFM setting, other voices are now heard and sanctioned, other 'knowledge' is made available to novices. And that knowledge is now framed within a 'university Institute' setting. While the boundaries of that knowledge continue to be debated within the IUFM structure – for instance, the relative importance and approach to disciplinary and professional knowledge (and as a perturbing third element within that mix the degree of explicit or implicit involvement with subject-matter *didactique* – see note [24]) – a different group now decides about content and the location of many of these borders, even though the state power of acceptance or rejection of new members still firmly resides with the IPRs.

As Bernard Cornu observed:

> Some people say the IUFMs are against knowledge, against the disciplines, and they just think about pedagogy, didactics, general

discourse, and so on. Clearly it's a debate, so we have to enter this debate. We have to show that, in fact, we do think that knowledge is the first competence of a teacher. But this is not enough, because we think that there is no possibility for a general discourse about teaching, about learning, about pedagogy, if it is not linked with a content, of course. But in France we have this debate, knowledge versus pedagogy which is very hard for the moment. [...]

It's a French opposition. If you speak about pedagogy, it means that you are against knowledge, necessarily. And if you are in favour of knowledge, certainly you are against pedagogy. So we have to show that there is, not a 'third way', but a right way. This is one of the major problems we have.

Whatever else, *stagiaires* need to walk and repeatedly cross the border between theory and practice, to integrate their extensive academic and growing professional and didactic knowledge, as they themselves pass from one side of various 'rivers' to the other on a weekly basis.

As a final small instance of fluidity in the face of sometimes sharply-drawn boundaries, one only has to look at the journal *Petit x* itself. It is neither predominantly an academic research journal, nor is it what is customarily called a professional journal (e.g. the U.S. NCTM *Middle School Mathematics* or the U.K. *Mathematics Teaching*). *Petit x* articles are academically reviewed; it publishes pieces that have a research orientation while concerning itself with issues of practice, and its authors are frequently both teaching in schools and working in higher education (whether at an IREM or at an IUFM). And it is with a similar intent that the professional memoir comprises an important tool in initiating novice teachers into examining school teaching 'in the spirit of research'.

The providers of initial formation

There are some issues of status, hierarchy and relationship among the various individuals involved in the *formation* of a *stagiaire* teacher. We focus here on a feature of the system, one which relates both to the 'who' and to the 'how' questions of induction from the introductory discussion: who is involved in providing induction and how is this system possible?

Roughly 80 percent of those who work in the IUFMs are secondary school teachers: of these, a considerable number temporarily work both in secondary education and post-secondary teacher *formation* at the same time. (The rest are seconded to the IUFM full-time, while maintaining their permanent school-teaching position in the long run.) In consequence, it is possible to find current practitioners engaged part-time in new teacher *formation* without their having to leave the classroom, something which can prove a difficult and usually one-way decision for practicing teachers in other countries. This possibility also ensures greater contact with current practice and school conditions.

The remaining 20 percent are tenured *'enseignant–chercheurs'*, either 'associate professors' *(maîtres de conférence)* or 'professors' *(professeurs)*. They teach precisely half the annual number of contact hours (192) that an associate *formateur* recruited from secondary education does (384). This is because half of the allocated time for such positions is intended for research, just as with any university position, and it is on the basis of this research that such academics are evaluated.

Bernard Cornu described two changes he proposed in the reform report to the Ministry of Education.

> We want to increase the number of university staff, that is profes-
> sors and lecturers [*maîtres de conférence*]. Because, for the moment,
> it's around twenty percent, less than twenty percent perhaps. And
> about eighty percent are secondary teachers. We want to find a
> good balance between permanent staff and associate *formateurs*.
> We would like to increase the part of associate *formateurs*, but
> mostly by giving them a more precise status. For the moment, they
> are in a strange position. They are named for one year. They never
> know if it will continue the year after. Most of the time it continues,
> of course, but there is no real contract with them. It's a problem for
> their promotion and there are some difficulties financially too.
>
> So we want to establish a more precise status for these kinds of
> people, saying, generally speaking, that they must keep a link with
> the classes. And there are two ways for that. Either they are partial
> time in the Institute [the IUFM], or they are at the Institute for a
> given period and after that they go back into schools.

The recipients of initial formation

We have earlier alluded to some shifts across boundaries required of *stagiaires*. For some part of the week, *stagiaires* are seen pretty much as teachers; at other times, they are more prone to reverting to their previous status as students, though they are not referred to as such. This is one use of the *stagiaire* label, though more often within the IUFM context, *stagiaires* are referred to as PLC2s, emphasising also where they have mostly come from (PLC1), as well as marking the fact that the P is for *professeur* (teacher) in the designation.

One teacher educator (who had herself been a pedagogic advisor when she was still working in the schools) commented on this fluid or ambiguous status of the *stagiaires*.

> Yes, even they [the *stagiaires*] say so [that it is ambiguous]. For instance, the other day in a session we talked about the visits we had carried out, since we, as IUFM *formateurs*, also go to see them in their schools. So I went to see these nine *stagiaires*. I was there for an hour in their class and afterwards we talked about the class. And they said to me, "We were really stressed by your coming", and I said, "But when your pedagogic advisor comes to see you, are you also stressed?" They told me, "No, it's not the same, because they are colleagues, we work in the same school. And we prepare and discuss together often, we prepare things together on an equal footing. We do the same things."

> So there you are. They tell me they are less stressed if it's their pedagogic advisor who comes into their class than if it's me. Therefore, when they come here [to the IUFM], it means that, at bottom, they feel themselves to be more like students. But it also means that in their schools they feel themselves to be teachers. You can also see it that way.

But not all the boundary crossings are across institutional lines (or involve their representatives, as in the instance above). One *formateur* commented about whether a *stagiaire* is seen as a full teacher:

> But I've often heard pedagogic advisors, when we get together, say for instance, "That's all very well, but what do we say about the fact that we are going into the *stagiaire's* class? It alters the status of the *stagiaire*." It points up that this first-year teacher is someone whom someone else comes to see, while no one comes to see the other teachers.

One aspect this quotation underlines is how being observed (whether you wish it or not) is somehow characteristic of not being a fully-accredited teacher, at least in a pedagogic culture where teaching is framed as an individual, autonomous activity that takes place behind closed doors. To have the power to control access to your teaching and your classroom (other than visits made by the Academy Inspector and, under certain circumstances, by the school principal) marks a fully-fledged teacher.

Initial and continuing formation: when is a new teacher?

One of the interesting things about the French situation to us as outsiders is how a number of apparently obvious and unproblematic anglophone educational distinctions (and related terminology) do not fit with the actuality found in France. In this regard, it is worth recalling Hugh Kenner's (2000, p. 17) remark, cited in note [2] of Chapter 1, how 'foreign travel can open linguistic chasms'. Instances include the terms 'new' or 'first-year' teacher and the far softer boundaries between the superficially straightforward categories of 'pre-service' and 'in-service' education. This fact can give cause to reflect more than momentarily on why 'our' ways of seeing the world seem so natural and 'taken-for-granted', as well as allowing us to query their apparent obviousness or necessity. It is to this latter distinction between 'pre-service' and 'in-service' education and where and how induction fits in that we now turn.

In the North American context, there are some boundary crossings that result in undergraduate and 'after-degree' students being in the same education classes together. This is not that sharp a boundary, as many universities do offer in-service courses, as well as there being an increasing number of professional development schools and school–university partnerships. There are many arrangements that blur 'pre-service' and 'in-service' boundaries to a certain extent. However, the participants' status as 'student' or 'student teacher' or 'teacher' is clear, as is their relationship with the institution that is preparing them to be teachers. A student teacher on a teaching practicum placement is not (yet) a teacher in the sense of the profession, nor in terms of the laws and other responsibilities governing school pupils and their education: it is not their class they are working in when on practica in schools.

When we first inaugurated this study, there was uncertainty within our larger research group about whether to include the French PLC2 *stagiaire* year as an instance of induction. Surely, the argument went, this is 'pre-service' education. But the more we discovered about the French system, the clearer we became about the fact that much of what we were seeing elsewhere as induction takes place during this year. A 'norm' with which we started was that 'pre-service' education had some orientation to education and that 'pre-service' teachers did not have the legal status and sanction to work alone with a class over time. That only came with the completion of their programme of study and provisional certification, after which they were 'in service', entitled to teach their own classes and whatever induction was provided began at that point, the next phase. Permanent certification usually followed within a year, or at most two, by which time all induction was then completed.

In France, provisional certification comes with passing a recruiting examination. Despite strong attempts within the IUFM system to frame a two-year 'initial' *formation* as a continuum, one that to our eyes includes both 'pre-service' and 'induction' components, many of the participants in the system do not see it that way. The PLC1 year is not generally seen as 'pre-professionalisation' (and IUFM attendance for this year is optional – some ten percent of mathematics CAPES candidates have not been PLC1s at an IUFM). It is seen as preparation for being *recruited as a teacher*, not as direct preparation for *being a teacher*. Once recruited, a compulsory year of initial *formation* then takes place.

One question we asked involved whether or not the PLC1 year was seen as part of a teacher's initial *formation*: in other words, is the period of *formation* seen as lasting for one year or two? The respondent cited here was the administrative head of the whole PLC1 year for an IUFM.

> It is difficult to reply to your question, but the answer is pretty much 'no' [the PLC1 year is not seen as part of a teacher's initial *formation*]. I will break my answer down into different groups who might have an opinion about this. First of all, administratively it is no: PLC1s are students and not *stagiaires*. From the point of view of the students themselves, it is again 'no'. They consider that their professional *formation* begins at the outset of their being *stagiaire* teachers [as PLC2s]. PLC1 students don't consider that they are being prepared for their profession, only for the competitive recruiting exam.
>
> From the point of view of the *formateurs*, that is the university mathematicians, they do not believe that the short PLC1 *stage* and in general knowledge of secondary education is a relevant element for succeeding at the competitive exam. These mathematicians do not think of themselves as engaged in 'pre-professionalisation'. Nevertheless [in this Academy, but not in all], PLC1s do carry out a compulsory one-week observation *stage* in a *collège* or *lycée*, but many dispensations from this are possible. This *stage* has no effect on competition success.
>
> The situation is slightly different from the IUFM point of view: certain people try to claim at least a minimal link with teaching, in relation to the competition's second oral.
>
> For the *agrégés*, the situation is clearer: the *Agrégation* is prepared for completely within the university; there is no professional part.

Returning briefly to the theme of section 2, namely the translation difficulties around the word *formation*, the period of secondary *formation initiale* is often misleadingly and inaccurately rendered into English as 'pre-service education' – see e.g. Hennequin (1996) or Henry (2000). This, of course, would be at least an oxymoron; they are clearly 'in service' part-time during the entire year that they are engaged in this initial *formation*. But then, in terms of the master/apprentice origins of the term *stage*, the label *stage en responsabilité* also has an oxymoronic quality (apprenticed to myself as the one in charge: there is no *maître de stage,* only a pedagogic advisor?). As the above administrator's comments suggest, a secondary teacher's *formation* arguably only commences with preliminary 'certification' and, currently at least, lasts an entire year.

Lastly, as we ended our study, we were told about reform proposals concerned with further IUFM support for the post-*stagiaire* year (the second year of teaching, currently strikingly different for many from the first). These were initially presented to the Minister of Education in 2001 (and are still unimplemented at the time of writing). Some of the conversations were framed in terms of a 'PLC3 year', which seemed to us quite destabilizing of even the French category distinctions: the boundary between 'initial' and 'continuing' *formation* would become blurred, for these 'PLC3' teachers would have permanent certification and would have been assigned to a specific Academy, and not to an IUFM. And, from our point of view, this continuing support, viewed as induction, would have transcended the frontier of permanent certification.

Cornu comments (he spoke in English and so used the terms 'pre-service' and 'in-service' directly):

> The other major point in the report was about the third year, the possibility of a third year. So there is a debate. Should we call it the third year [PLC3], or call it the first year of practice, of professional practice. I think that we must call it the third year, for several reasons. The main reason is that I want the IUFMs to be in charge of the third year and if we say, "the first year of professional practice", the Inspectors will take it. So it's necessary to say that it's the third year.
>
> The idea was two things. First, to try to establish real articulation between in-service and pre-service *formation*, with activities which are just in between, which belong to pre-service *formation* but which are preparatory to the spirit of "Yes, I need to be trained all my life long", which is not the case with most of the teachers.
>
> As a second point, there are things in teacher education that you cannot acquire or understand if you have not strongly encountered a first practice. So we would like to consider that there are things that you cannot … you have to wait for one year before you can do these kind of things.
>
> So the idea was to say that all new teachers in this year, in this third year or first year, they are teachers so they must teach. They have a duty, eighteen hours per week, usually, generally. We said that one sixth of this time could be devoted to *formation*. So we proposed three hours per week. In fact, we proposed not three hours of *formation*, but that we lessen their duty by three hours per week, which gives them an amount of hours to spend for training. The problem is, there are in France about 22,000 new teachers every year, so reducing duties by one sixth for each means 3,500 posts. Financially, this is the problem. And we do not have these posts. So the first idea which was proposed in my first report was to increase

the duty they have, the part of duty they have in the second year at the IUFM, just to finance that. But it was rejected mostly because the second year is very heavy. They have a lot of things to do. So now we have the problem that everybody is in favour of this third year, because we designed what the content could be, but the minister says, "Yes, but I have no way to finance this third year". So we do not know what will happen.

The issues are complex and, at base, economic. The need to strengthen new teacher induction is widely felt (politically and educationally). Administratively, Cornu felt, any 'PLC3' work must be seen as initial *formation* still. But his comments on this remind us of the continuing power of the Inspectorate in terms of their evident control over the functioning of permanently certified teachers. Once again, the institutional complexity needs to be grappled with. Cornu went on:

When, two years ago, the minister said, "IUFMs are now in charge of continuing *formation*", this should have changed our initial *formation*. Which is not the case. We didn't change anything for a lot of reasons. It invites us to consider *formation* on a very long term, and rethink *formation* from the starting point of initial *formation*, but with this perspective of it continuing on. There are three official texts from the Ministry describing the *compétences* of teachers. If you look at these texts, you can see that no teacher in the world is able to do such. It's a lot. It's a very good programme for life-long *formation*. So we would like to consider it as a life-long process. And the third year is crucial for that.

In the first year, all our students are students in their subject. "Oh yes, perhaps I will be a teacher. Yes, I need some pedagogical and professional *formation* but I don't know why exactly." Suddenly, in the second year, they forget their subject, and they say, "Oh, I am a teacher. I am a professional." In the first year, we have the problem of increasing their professionalism. In the second year, we have the problem of keeping some disciplinary activities, because they certainly think that they have ended their studies. And so we would like to have them continuing to think in their subject. And then the third year, they move to full professionalism, but we say, "You should keep the spirit, the curiosity of a student, the willingness for new knowledge, for learning new things. This curiosity, if you don't have it for all your career, you cannot pass it to your pupils." This is the point.

The whole force of this chapter has come from the presumption that the PLC2 *stagiaire* year is the first full year of being a teacher, despite the conventional English term 'full-time teacher' carrying certain presuppositions. Our making this presumption reminds us of the power of the local understanding of identity in induction. Secondary *stagiaires* have passed a recruiting

257

examination and are no longer students: they are *stagiaire* teachers. They are teachers, working for their permanent certification. *Stagiaires* are allowed to (and many do) join the professional teachers' union; teaching in France is a highly unionized profession. At the end of their *stagiaire* year, they have gained one year's seniority in the system. Even if they have to repeat their *stagiaire* year, they have still earned one year's seniority in the system for this first year, even though they have not yet been granted tenure. *Stagiaires* are fully paid as teachers because they are teachers: what is so strikingly different to us is what they are directed and expected to do with their time during this first year of teaching.

8. What Is Valued by the System

Induction in France currently is not just about a centralised system, one in the process of re-forming itself. Nor is it simply about ambiguous and fluid boundaries both engendered and drawn upon in order for the system to function, but that may generate turbulence. It is also very much about what might be called 'disciplining' the teacher. There is a close relation between what is valued generally by the system (which might be termed 'disciplinary power') and the nature of what a new teacher is being inducted into. Those who have achieved in the discipline are rewarded and the requirements of induction are only the first formal reminders of the power of the discipline and the centrality of subject matter to the act of secondary-school teaching.

We talked with three *stagiaires* in the fall term about their experiences over the school year so far and asked them about the work they were doing for the professional memoir. Two of them (Monique and Georges) pointedly teased a third (Stéphane):

> Monique: Ah, here we have an example of inequality [laughter].
> Stéphane: I, in fact, don't do one.
> Monique: Because he is an *agrégé*. And he didn't want to do one when he didn't have to.
> Georges: They are [mathematically] better than us, they are better paid, they have [to teach] fewer hours and they don't do a memoir.
> Monique: They are getting themselves used to working less during this [*stagiaire*] year, that's why they don't do the memoir. I call a spade a spade.

This short extract encapsulates a number of themes we have presented throughout this chapter. There is a hierarchy among secondary teachers between the uncertified, the certified and the *agrégé*. And as was mentioned in the earlier discussion of the Inspectorate, there are systemic privileges available in terms of both the number of weekly contact hours to be taught and the salaries paid to those with higher subject-matter qualifications.

Without doubt, and despite the changes of the past decade, the core valued commodity of the system is still detailed, technical mathematical knowledge of a very high order. And, in the French system, what is valued is frequently rewarded. The CAPES recruiting examination, and even more so the *Agrégation* recruiting examination, requires an extremely strong mathematics preparation. Even in the PLC1 year when preparing for the CAPES, we were told there is generally little emphasis by many of the instructors on thinking about this mathematics pedagogically (though there are some notable exceptions, particularly from the *didactique* community involved with initial teacher *formation*). There is considerable disagreement as to what extent a pedagogic orientation and knowledge about the teaching of school mathematics provides an advantage in succeeding in the oral part of this examination. But attempts to reform the nature of the examination even slightly to increase the relevance of schools to it meet massive entrenched resistance from many in the university sector and elsewhere.

Within the year spent as a *stagiaire* teacher, attention is given to the nature, design, selection, purpose and rationale of classroom mathematics tasks. Increasingly, at least parts of such PLC2 courses at some IUFMs are being taught by *formateurs* who have themselves undergone some education in *didactique des mathématiques*. But the value of *stagiaires* themselves being explicitly taught elements of this separate but related discipline is far less agreed upon. The interesting aspect of *didactique* is the extent to which it is able to establish itself not as a rival *savoir* to mathematics, but as a *savoir* that is part of the discipline, and hence also valued by the system.

In France, being and becoming a secondary teacher are combined at the same time, conjoined throughout the PLC2 year. At the point of entry, secondary *stagiaires* are judged and see themselves as fully-fledged mathematically (even though some *formateurs* wish them to continue to work to improve their understanding further). But in terms of being a teacher, they are judged to require more: *formation* – to us, induction. In consequence, these *stagiaire* teachers both are and are not fully-fledged mathematics teachers. The new system which was put into place a decade ago in a sense institutionalises this uncertainty, this ambiguity with regard to *stagiaire* status and self identity.

As outsiders looking for new teacher induction, we can certainly see the PLC2 year as induction, even though it is not framed as such in France. Insiders, especially IUFM insiders, look at the same policies and practices and see only initial *formation* and a hoped-for continuity that the PLC designation hints at. However, that sense of continuity is across a specific boundary (the CAPES or *Agrégation* recruiting examinations), one that creates its own difference. Once on the far side of this frontier, the *stagiaires* themselves (and the *formateurs* who listen to their complaints) experience the ambiguity of their position every week – between being at the IUFM and being in their classroom, between their allocated role in one *stage* and the other. Once certified, they go their own way and are not forcibly institutionally framed again.

But many of these ambiguities are not created by this new system; they simply serve to highlight them. For all new teachers, everywhere, need to make that transition from student to teacher (to cross that difficult river that must be crossed, in Blanchard-Laville's pregnant image), whether it is expected of them in an instant or over a more prolonged period of time (as in France), whether it is institutionally supported or intentionally or inadvertently hindered.

The changes that the past ten years in France have wrought, and which are slowly working their way through the entire system, will take another thirty years to complete. When this has happened, assuming no intervening perturbations or more major political upheavals, where continuity and common experience permeate the whole with regard to both becoming and being a secondary mathematics teacher. But some of the ambiguities we have sought to capture and describe, because they transcend the specifics of the system, may still remain.

Acknowledgements

Necessarily, for work of this kind, we are enormously grateful to many French colleagues and other informants in IUFMs, in IREMs and in the Inspectorate for their generosity in meeting with us – individuals who in many instances spent considerable time talking and responding to our questions about their work and system. In particular, we wish to thank Michèle Artigue, Claudine Blanchard-Laville, Bernard Cornu, Bernadette Denys, Colette Laborde, Claire Margolinas and Aline Robert for significant orienting conversations at various stages in our work. We equally wish to thank those teachers, both *stagiaire* and certified (whether pedagogic advisors or not), who allowed us into their classrooms and meetings. Finally, we are very grateful to Nathalie Sinclair and Carolyn Wagner for assistance with some real-time interpreting and extensive audiotape transcription.

Chapter 6

Guiding the New Teacher:
Induction of First-Year Teachers in Japan

Michael Padilla and Joseph Riley

1. Yoko Matsubara's First Year

What a stressful day for Yoko Matsubara. In the eighth month of her first year of teaching, she still has much to learn – about teaching, about her pupils and about herself. She cannot spend much time thinking about these issues now, because she must prepare for the many visitors coming to her classroom. This afternoon, her guiding teacher, a supervisor from the pre-fectural in-service center, the principal, vice-principal and several teachers from her school will visit her classroom to watch her teach a science lesson. In addition, two American educators will be in attendance. And after the lesson they want to interview her. What could she possibly tell them? Yet, because her principal has asked her to co-operate, she has agreed.

Yoko accepted this teaching job in Nikko, a small city in a mountainous area about 100km north of Tokyo. She did so with enthusiasm last April 1, the start of the Japanese school year. Nikko is a ninety-minute train ride from Tokyo and Yoko's upper secondary school, the only one in the city, is culturally a great distance from the cosmopolitan sophistication of the Tokyo she is used to. Nikko is renowned for its historical temple and pris-tine mountain lake. Its clean environment and the opportunities for fresh air and exercise draw many city dwellers. Yoko misses her friends and fam-ily, but the opportunity to get a full-time teaching job was too good to turn down. With Japanese families having fewer and fewer children, there is a decreasing demand for teachers. Yoko knows the competition for teaching jobs is fierce, with only one in twenty getting hired. She is the first new science teacher at her school in twelve years, so considers herself lucky.

At the start of the school year, her principal, Mr. Nakanishi, informed her that she would have both a reduced teaching load and would be assigned guiding (mentor) teachers, as part of an induction program for new teachers. She was relieved to participate in the induction program,

E. Britton et al. (eds.), Comprehensive Teacher Induction, 261–295.
© 2003 *Kluwer Academic Publishers. Printed in the Netherlands.*

because she did not feel well prepared. The program is to include an in-school component, supervised by the guiding teachers, and out-of-school work at the prefectural in-service center. As part of the induction program, Yoko's workload is twelve hours of teaching per week, not the normal sixteen or seventeen hours. She has three preparations and five classes: physics (six hours/week), chemistry (two hours/week) and integrated science (four hours/week). A part-time teacher, a recent university graduate who has not yet taken the prefectural teacher certification test, has been hired by the school as an additional instructor for this year to compensate for her reduced load.

Yoko knows she will be forever indebted to Mrs. Nishi, her primary guiding teacher. Without her advice and counsel, this initial year would have been much more difficult. A biology teacher by training, Mrs. Nishi has twelve years of experience. Because of her duties as guiding teacher, Mrs Nishi's teaching load for this academic year has also been reduced, to ten hours per week. The school principal chose Mrs. Nishi because of her considerable experience in teaching science, but Yoko is additionally appreciative of her warmth and understanding. She found she can be open with Mrs. Nishi, knowing she will understand: it makes everything easier. While there is a schedule of topics to be discussed, Yoko knows Mrs. Nishi has been particularly working on her confidence: it is hard to be really confident while having so much to learn. She also helps with teaching technique and Yoko feels she needs more of a repertoire to keep pupil interest high.

Yoko Matsubara has also had other help during this year. Due to Mrs. Nishi's lack of experience as a guiding teacher – and her subject expertise being in biology and not physics – a second general guiding teacher has been appointed, although Mrs. Nishi remains the primary support for Yoko. The second guiding teacher is the school leader for curriculum and instruction and already has a reduced teaching load of twelve hours a week because of these duties. In addition, because Yoko is the only physics teacher in the school, arrangements were made to connect her with a group of ten area teachers who meet twice per year on Saturdays specifically to discuss physics teaching.

The two guiding teachers, with help from the principal, planned Yoko's induction program, using both Monbusho (the Japanese Ministry of Education, Science, Sports, and Culture – the national agency in charge of educational policy [1]) and prefectural models and guidelines (Japan is structured into fifty prefectures). The schedule seemed daunting when Yoko and Mrs. Nishi first reviewed it: how could they ever accomplish so much? But Yoko now realizes that its main function is to ensure coverage of important topics. They do not keep to it rigidly, but refer to it as a guide.

Yoko was a physics major from a prominent teacher education university in Tokyo. She remembers her education coursework as too theoretical and her student teaching experience, while only three weeks in length, as her most valuable training. Today's lesson is on sound waves, but her physics coursework does not seem quite so relevant or useful now in teaching these upper secondary pupils. At her university, the students learned in one step, but here at this school, it feels like it takes ten steps for pupils to learn. This is not the type of secondary school where pupils go on to university. Thus, teaching here is much more challenging.

Yoko has learned a lot during the last eight months. Both guiding teachers have begun to treat her more independently – more like a colleague. Although Yoko and Mrs. Nishi do not discuss physics very much (Yoko knows more about physics), they typically work together to solve classroom problems, often talking about what pupils do or do not know and how to motivate them to learn more. But they do not attend each other's classes. Both teach chemistry classes, each teaching different parts of this subject, and they team-teach all four hours of integrated science. Yoko is the main teacher and Mrs. Nishi assists her: after every class, they discuss what has occurred.

While Yoko considers the in-school portion of the induction program to be the most useful and practical, she also participates in many out-of-school activities. There are sixty new teachers in the prefecture this year, including thirteen science teachers, four of whom teach physics. In the first term of the school year, the group met on Thursdays, listened to lectures and discussed problems the new secondary teachers were having. While the lectures were not too practical, talking to other new teachers proved a relief, as all admitted they were experiencing many similar problems. During the summer, they had had three day-long sessions on new teaching techniques held at a youth camp. But the best part about the camp was the chance to be with other new teachers. Now they meet once a month. Recently, they visited a program for the disabled, which helped Yoko further realize the diversity of people, some of whom cannot do things most others can. It allowed her to understand her own pupils better.

Today's lesson, with all the visitors present, is not that unusual. Three times per year, Yoko teaches a public lesson when many of the school's teachers attend. This form of in-service education allows both new and more experienced teachers to receive feedback from their colleagues. For new teachers, the prefectural supervisor usually attends at least one of these sessions. Even when schools have no new teachers, many use this method of public teaching to refine lesson plans and to promote discussion of teaching, with an experienced teacher teaching a 'model' lesson.

In preparation for today, Yoko has written and re-written her lesson plans. She has practiced teaching the lesson with one of her other classes and modified the lesson with the help of both of her guiding teachers. She even called a physics teacher from a neighboring school whom she knew from university and he helped her improve her lesson plans and prepare the lab materials. She is nervous, but feels the process and the feedback will be helpful.

Yoko is also thinking about the culminating 'action-research' project that is required of all first-year teachers. It will be about 30–40 pages in length and is to be handed in to the prefectural education office (though no formal feedback on it will be provided). Given the nature of her pupils, she has decided to explore the development of lessons that successfully motivate pupils, especially those not oriented toward science. Last month, she took pupils to the botanical garden to have them draw plants. Today's lesson involving a slinky, if successful, will also comprise part of her project.

Six months later

It is the second month of the new school year and Yoko is no longer a first-year teacher: she is now on her own, with no formal support. Japanese parents would not tolerate for long having their children taught by someone who is not considered an accomplished teacher. Mrs. Nishi, her primary guiding teacher, has moved to a new school, a typical practice in Japan, where periodically moving from one school to another is believed to improve the teaching of individual teachers and the school system as a whole. Yoko's teaching load this year has increased to sixteen hours per week: she has four preparations and six classes, with most classes meeting for either two or three hours per week.

This morning, Yoko is teaching an elective physics course to eight pupils (only one of whom is female). They are discussing last night's homework assignment – two problems, one related to velocity and distance, the other dealing with a time–distance graph. She begins by lecturing about similar problems they have encountered previously. After discussing pupil answers to the problems, she introduces today's lesson about motion with a change in velocity, explaining the concept but only introducing the term 'acceleration' later in the lesson.

When the lesson is finished, she has a free period and begins to think about the class and what the pupils learned. She knows she is not asking enough questions of pupils and, instead, employs direct methods of instruction too often. But she has not had time to work hard on what she sees as weaknesses. She feels that maybe only half her class understood the concept of acceleration, but is not sure what evidence she has for this belief.

She has not yet figured out how to use pupil work to determine how well pupils learn. After further analysis, she plans to re-teach the lesson using review and repetition of the concept, as well as limiting the amount of material she covers.

In reflecting back on her experiences as a first-year teacher, Yoko is grateful it is over. She knows she is certainly not yet as good a teacher as she needs to be. But she is thankful that the stress of the first year is finished: there is a great gap between being a university student and being accepted as a competent teacher. She is appreciative that Mrs. Nishi took care of her very well and misses her. Throughout the first year, they developed a close, collegial relationship to the benefit of both. But Yoko also knows it is good for her to be on her own now, so she can become more independent.

Yoko Matsubara appreciates the variety of experiences she has had – visiting many institutions and facilities and having many lectures from a wide variety of people. In retrospect, these proved more helpful that she initially thought because they broadened her understanding of education and her perspective on the community. Today, she has many new mentors, having discovered that most of the school's teachers believe it is their responsibility to help her to become successful.

2. An Overview of Japan's Educational System

In order to understand the nature of the induction system in Japan, it is important to have a sense of the wider educational system into which the teacher is being inducted as an adult member. The organizational framework of Japan's schools aligns closely with that of the United States, a result of the U.S.-mandated educational reforms during the post-war administration of General Headquarters.

However, Japan has a highly centralized system of educational governance. Compulsory public education in Japan begins at age six with enrollment in first grade and extends to age fifteen at the end of ninth grade. The nine years of compulsory education include six years of elementary school and three years of lower secondary school. At the end of ninth grade, pupils take examinations for competitive entry into three years of upper secondary school.

Educational reform after World War II introduced a common general education into the elementary grades, including study of the Japanese language, mathematics, science, life environment studies, music, art, handicraft, homemaking, physical education, moral education and special activities. Arithmetic is studied in all elementary grades for about 150 hours per year, while science is taught beginning in grade three for 70–95 hours per year. The curriculum of the lower secondary school includes Japanese language, mathematics, science, social studies, music, fine arts, health and physical education, industrial arts or homemaking, moral education, special activities and elective subjects. Approximately 105 hours are dedicated to both mathematics and science each year.

While this curriculum is quite similar to that experienced in many western countries, it should be noted that "schooling in Japan is a unique cultural process" (Shimahara, 1991, p. 273). From pre-school through to upper secondary school, teachers are expected to enhance the moral and expressive abilities of pupils through "character development, moral sensitivity, and habit formation promoted through ritualism and collective activities in the context of *shudan seikatsu* [group life]" (p. 273). Shimahara identifies the central role of moral education in the school course of study at all levels as one of the three prominent areas of responsibility which define the work of teachers, the other two being the curriculum and special activities.

Class size at all grade levels is limited to less than forty, with most classes we observed having between thirty-five and forty pupils. One teacher is assigned for all subjects in the elementary grades, teaching every period on most days (Kinney, 1998). In lower and upper secondary schools, one teacher is assigned to teach various courses within one subject area, such as science, often to different grade levels.

About 95 percent of the pupils who finish compulsory education go on to upper secondary schools or technical schools. Upper secondary schools offer general (academic) and vocational courses of study. About three-quarters of pupils choose the general courses. Japanese upper secondary pupils study the Japanese language, geography and history, civics education, mathematics, science, health and physical education, art and homemaking. The general academic course provides pupils with choice between a humanities or science emphasis.

Changing demographics and societal expectations continue to shape the landscape of Japanese educational reform. The number of elementary school pupils, for example, has declined by 36 percent in the period from 1981 to 1999 (Monbusho, 1999). Beginning in 1992, the Monbusho initiated a slow decrease in the number of compulsory school attendance days, also moving from a six- to a five-day week. This action resulted from a growing national concern that the 'school career' had become too major a value in Japanese society. As the number of children in the family decreased, the parental focus on and expectations for their child's future intensified, often resulting in both the parents and the child becoming too school-centered. According to the Monbusho, the move from the traditional schedule is intended to enable the family and community to assume a more balanced role in the character building of children, by also emphasizing experiences outside school.

Pupils must pass an entrance examination, administered by the prefecture, in order to enter upper secondary school. Private and national schools administer their own separate examinations. Admissions are determined by a combination of entrance examination scores and lower secondary school transcripts, and there is enormous competition to get into high-quality, upper secondary schools. Similar competitive examinations are taken at the end of upper secondary school, in order to achieve admission into university. Both examinations greatly affect the teaching techniques and curriculum of the third and final year in both lower and upper secondary schools.

There is considerable pressure on pupils to do well on these exams and this usually entails much memorization. It is not uncommon for Japanese pupils to attend regular school during the day and then go to a privately run *juku* (an after-school school or 'cram school'). Good *juku* (seen as those whose pupils are admitted to high-ranking schools) are often financially very successful. Because of the high levels of safety in most Japanese cities (despite recent highly publicized crimes), pupils are allowed to go to and from school on their own, often traveling by train and bus for an hour each way. Upper secondary pupils often do not arrive home from their studies until well after dark.

3. Pre-Service Teacher Preparation in Japan

What does pre-service teacher education look like in Japan? What kinds of courses and experiences do new teachers bring to their first year of teaching? Because the teacher education programs we have studied across Japan must follow guidelines set down by the Monbusho, they are basically similar. In a previous project (Riley *et al.,* 1998), we studied two multi-disciplinary, national institutions and two institutions (called *gakugei*) primarily focused on teacher education. All have separate elementary, lower and upper secondary school teacher education programs.

Coursework

Coursework in all teacher education programs falls into five broad categories. The *common core* includes a broad range of liberal arts courses including language, health, humanities, social sciences and the sciences. Students are required to earn twenty-two to forty units in this category. Those enrolled in lower and upper secondary school programs (where the structure is so similar we report them together) identify a major content

267

focus and take between forty-eight and fifty-six units in that subject. In addition, they enroll in fourteen to eighteen units of general educational methods, including coursework in teaching methods and foundations.

Depending on the institution and level of program, lower and upper secondary students take a science methods class of two-to-four units. A capstone *student teaching* experience earns four-to-six units of credit. All students are required to write a *graduation thesis*, which is usually done in the student's major content field, e.g. science. One unit is given for fifteen class sessions of forty-five minutes each.

In elementary teacher education programs, the common core, student teaching and graduation research are similar to that of secondary programs. Students take fewer units in a major content area, such as mathematics or science, and relatively more units in educational methods (elementary pre-service teachers take approximately thirty-six units of methods across all subject areas), including a two-unit course in science methods.

In comparison with North American teacher education programs, there is a somewhat heavier concentration in Japan on science content for elementary (twenty-four units) and lower secondary (forty-six-plus units) pre-service students and a strong concentration for upper secondary students. All education students take at least one course in moral education and another in extra-curricular activities. Graduation research projects or theses are required for graduation from all programs.

School experiences and student teaching

Most students in the programs we studied engage in only a few hours to, at most, a few days of classroom observation before commencing student teaching. At one typical major national university, students generally experienced ten hours of school observation during their second year (five hours each semester), with two hours at the elementary grades and four hours at each of the lower and upper secondary levels. During their third year of study, education students were involved in peer teaching in university classes, but had no school experience. Student teaching at all institutions studied takes place during the final year for a two- to four-week period.

To understand this limited amount of exposure to actual K–12 classrooms, it is necessary to explore the Japanese "attached schools". These are nationally-funded schools associated with universities. The stated main purpose of the attached school is to facilitate research on education relating to teacher training and provide a venue for training undergraduate students to be teachers. (Teachers in the attached schools are expected to do research at least one day per week. This is generally applied – teachers seeking better ways to improve instruction at the school.)

However, attached schools are often the *only* schools in which students get school experience of any kind. In addition, because of the present scarcity of teaching positions in Japan, many students specialize in two areas or levels (e.g. lower *and* upper secondary school science or elementary *and* lower secondary school). These students must have a second student teaching experience. Thus, attached schools frequently can be overrun with student teachers. One that we visited (with 467 pupils in total) had seen 130 student teachers during the school year. This factor is a serious limitation to the possible amount of student school experience.

Most attached schools are elementary and lower secondary schools, although some upper secondary schools are also designated as attached schools. Entrance examinations are required for pupils wishing to enter attached schools and pupils at these schools tend to exhibit more motivation and ability compared with pupils in city and prefectural schools. Even though attached schools are associated with a particular university (and the principal is often a professor from the university), very little collaboration exists between faculty of the two institutions. This has lead to a significant barrier and a subsequent lack of respect.

The two- to four-week student teaching assignment is scheduled twice a year, in October and June, and student teachers are assigned to the attached schools in cohort groups. They sometimes live in specially prepared dormitories on the attached school campus (if it is located far from the university) or in nearby housing. Three to six student teachers (averaging three or four) are assigned to each co-operating teacher. Instead of being involved in all activities in the classroom, student teachers spend most of their time observing. At most, individuals (and sometimes groups) prepare about one lesson to teach each week, spending a great deal of time and energy in crafting these lessons (Tippins *et al.,* 2000). One pair of students who team-taught a lesson we observed told us:

> We spent five hours putting the lesson plan together. We had very
> little help from our co-operating teacher. He was too busy.

After teaching the lesson, all student teachers and their co-operating teacher hold a seminar in which the lesson is dissected and critiqued in detail by all observing it. Participation in this analysis is considered an important part of their professional growth. Typically, after listening to the analysis of those who had observed, those who taught the lesson give a self-reflection. At the end of the student teaching period, one student in the school is selected to teach a lesson and is observed and critiqued by all the other student teachers and co-operating teachers in the attached school, as well as the university supervisor. Often this is the only day a college or university professor observes student teachers in these schools.

We once observed a very crowded classroom on one of these 'study teaching' days with forty upper secondary pupils and thirty-four student teacher observers. This lesson analysis process is very similar to that encountered by both new teachers in their induction year (such as Yoko Matsubara was preparing for) and experienced teachers throughout their career. Both Yoshida (1999) and Stigler and Hiebert (1999) view these lessons and their subsequent public analysis as the core activity of in-school teacher education (*konaikenshu*); they represent an important aspect of a teacher's in-service work in Japan.

When we interviewed students and recent graduates of teacher education programs, we found a marked negativity about the value of their teacher education programs in Japanese universities. This finding concurs with Wray (1999), who asserts that pre-service teachers do not rate highly the courses in their teacher education programs. One recent graduate told us: "There wasn't enough time on the practical side, even though some of the courses were helpful philosophically". We also found that students did not regard their education professors' knowledge of K–12 schooling and teaching highly.

Historically, Japan has employed what has been termed an 'open' approach to science teacher certification, which means that anyone who majors in science is eligible to teach in the secondary schools, provided they take the required education coursework and have had a student-teaching experience. The 'open door' approach to science teacher preparation reflects a heavy emphasis on content, which may also account for the need to design and implement a national induction program with an emphasis on pedagogy. Moreover, most pre-service students majoring in science are able to complete both coursework in their major and all certification requirements within a four-year academic program. This can only be accomplished if the program is relatively light in pedagogy and partially accounts for the limited nature of field experiences (1–10 days) and student teaching (2–4 weeks).

4. Becoming a Teacher

Teaching in Japan is regarded as a high-status occupation, a dignified profession. Being a teacher in Japan carries with it respect and honor and the label *sensei*. This term carries a high degree of regard, and is considered an esteemed salutation. Japanese teacher salaries generally match the high esteem of the profession. In compliance with the law, "special measures have been taken so that public school teachers receive a higher salary than general public officials" (Monbusho, 2000, p. 94).

In 1998 (the most recent data available), teachers earned from 195,000 to 469,000 yen (US $1,625 to US $3,900 [2]) per month for twelve months, plus a bonus equal to 5.2 months of salary. In addition, teachers are also eligible for extra allowances for dependents (27,000 yen per month for a spouse and 2 children), housing (up to 27,000 yen per month) and transportation (up to 50,000 yen per month), among other benefits (Monbusho, 2000).

Using these figures, a mid-salaried teacher with a spouse and two children, a maximum housing allowance and a moderate commute would make over 660,000 yen (US $55,500) per year. Of course, this does not translate straight-forwardly, because of cost of living and other differences. However, most Japanese families of teachers whom we talked to can afford to live comfortably given this level of salary and benefits. Thus, teaching is a financially secure and much sought-after profession, especially since many Japanese companies no longer guarantee to provide a job for life (Kinney, 1998).

To be eligible for a teaching position in Japan requires a teaching certificate, which is awarded by prefectural boards of education and is valid for the lifetime of an individual. Certification granted by any one prefecture can be used to teach throughout Japan. Each prefecture independently administers the certification exams, which are difficult and many do not pass on their first attempt. Teacher qualification tests are difficult.

> Only one of four applicants for public school teaching pass these difficult written examinations, skill tests, and interviews; of these approximately 40 percent only pass them on their second or third attempt. (Wray, 1999, p. 321)

The certificate is designated in three classes:

- *second-class,* which requires completion of a junior college course of study and is valid only for kindergarten, elementary and lower secondary teachers;
- *first-class,* which requires the completion of a bachelor's degree, is valid for all grades and is required for upper secondary school;
- *advanced,* which requires a master's degree.

To be eligible to apply for a first-class teaching certificate, one must finish a university program with forty units of subject content and nineteen units of pedagogical content. To be eligible for a second-class certificate, one must take twenty units of subject content and fifteen units of pedagogical content. Most Japanese teachers today hold a first-class certificate, although it is becoming more common to obtain a master's degree.

> For certificate holders to actually teach at a public school, they must first pass the Teacher Employment Selection Test, held by boards of education in all prefectures and selected cities. After passing this test, certificate holders are employed as teachers. Standard certificates are valid indefinitely, and certificate holders are permitted to

take the Teacher Employment Selection Test as many times as they wish during their careers. The boards of education carry out a multifaceted evaluation of the applicant's skills, qualifications, and suitability for a teaching position. Evaluation methods are diverse and include written tests of general education and specialized knowledge in the applicant's subject specialty; skill tests in areas such as physical education, fine arts and English conversation; essay tests (most of which question the applicant's dedication to education and awareness of related issues); interviews; aptitude tests; and evaluation of a candidate's past participation in extracurricular and volunteer activities. (IAPD, 1995, pp. 126-127)

Due to the dramatic decrease in the school population, competition among certified teachers to obtain a teaching job is also extremely intense. It is not uncommon to have ten to thirty-five times as many applicants as there are positions to be filled.

To increase their opportunities in the job market, as indicated above, many students prepare themselves for both elementary and lower secondary certificates. Many others spend years teaching as a part-time or temporary teacher before procuring their first regular teaching position. *Part-time teachers* are those teaching one or more classes, but not carrying a full-time load; *temporary* teachers are those teaching a full load, but who are not on permanent contract.

Others teach in private schools, which do not require a teaching certificate. It was therefore unsurprising that many of the new teachers we interviewed, told us they had prior teaching experience, with one stating he "had been a teacher for several years, but not a permanent one". Despite the fact that many 'new' teachers actually arrive with prior teaching experience, all who are in their first year of teaching in public education must undergo the induction year activities.

In fact, both part-time and temporary teachers are a necessary component of any system in which individuals go on sick, study or maternity leave or temporarily perform duties of being a guiding teacher. The Monbusho promotes the part-time system, stating that it can:

> diversify and invigorate formal education [...] by enabling schools to employ members of the community with expert knowledge [...] regardless of whether they possess a teacher's certificate. (Monbusho, 1999, p. 31)

Moreover, part-time teaching serves as an important training ground for many of Japan's new teachers. Many of the teachers hired to fill in for the reduced loads of the new teacher and guiding teacher are temporary teachers. Part-time and temporary teachers are typically not eligible for the more than five months of bonus pay and are, therefore, a way for a school to save money.

History of the beginning teachers' induction training system in Japan

> Traditionally, newly employed teachers have been helped to adapt
> to their new situations by the informal support of the other teach-
> ers in the school. This climate of support can be found in almost any
> type of organization in Japanese society, where it is the responsi-
> bility of the senior members of a group to ensure that the junior
> members adapt successfully. (Nohara, 1997, p. 100)

However, this informal system began to be viewed as insufficient. Japanese
teachers typically face larger class sizes (around forty pupils) than teachers
in western schools and have complicated and diverse responsibilities related to guidance and their subject teaching. Moreover, because Japanese
pre-service teacher education was viewed as highly theoretical and lacking
in sufficient practical experience, Japanese school officials as early as the
1960s began to realize the need for further training, especially for new
teachers. While well prepared in their content fields, most beginning teachers simply were not prepared to deal with the pupils, with the academic
demands of society or with the "large numbers of parents, who are usually
considerably older and may be from different backgrounds than the
teacher" (Nohara, 1997, p. 99).

To deal with these needs, many Japanese school boards began to offer
special in-service programs for first-year teachers.

> With partial financial support from *Monbusho*, [many] Boards of
> Education conducted ten-day training sessions for newly appointed
> teachers. (Nohara, 1997, p. 101)

These new teacher in-service programs varied widely, with many spread
over the course of the first year with a focus on observing other teachers'
lessons. Neither the quality nor content of these programs was monitored,
however, nor did all school systems engage in new teacher mentoring.

In 1971, a special Japanese government report called for:

> a systematized and planned program while the teacher is on a trial
> [first-year] basis. (TTC, 1972; as cited in Shiina and Chonin, 1993,
> p. 43)

While no immediate action regarding the induction of first-year teachers
was taken as a result of this proposal, it did cause policy makers to think
about the issue. A renewed effort to start an in-service training program for
beginning teachers was made in 1986 by the National Council on
Educational Reform. The report states:

> It is vitally important that it [the program] assist the newly-appoin-
> ted teacher to enter new fields of teaching. For this purpose, efforts
> will be made to cultivate actual leadership and a sense of mission

for the newly-appointed teachers in national and public elementary, lower and upper secondary schools (NCER, 1986; as cited in Shiina and Chonin, 1993, p. 43)

The report suggested that during the first year of teaching, in-service activities would take place under the guidance of an experienced teacher, with leadership of the program being assigned to the school principal.

We interviewed Dr. Masami Maki, the Deputy Director-General of the National Institute for Educational Research, who chaired the Monbusho committee that created the Japanese induction program. Dr. Maki spoke candidly about the history of the program and the needs it was attempting to fulfill. He pointed out that Japanese teachers are "not intending to leave the profession: this is their career".

Thus, the program's primary purpose was not teacher retention, but to improve teaching and ultimately pupil learning. He also noted that students graduating from university had very little practical experience and that their pre-service training in general was inadequate because it was too theoretical. The Monbusho understood that "changing pre-service education would not be easy"; thus, there was a need for some type of induction program.

As a result of the National Council on Educational Reform proposal, the Monbusho launched a trial test of an induction program during 1987 and 1988. Following this trial, the Monbusho published several models and examples which schools might "use as references to arrange annual training plans". Maki observed:

> the prefectures [prefectural boards of education] and designated cities [city boards of education] were expected to develop 'training system implementation basic outlines' and annual plans for the training system's implementation.

In addition, local boards of education were expected to complete their own in-service plans for new teachers, using the prefectural and Ministry outlines (Shiina and Chonan, 1993). The system had been:

> introduced in graduated stages by type of school, beginning with the 1989 school year. Since 1992, it has been in effect for all schools of the elementary, lower-secondary and upper-secondary levels, as well as for schools for the blind, the deaf and the otherwise specially-needed. (Maki, 1993)

Maki additionally made the following points during our discussion.

- Every school is not capable of or eligible for operating a new teacher program. In the case where a school is not suitable, an opening for the new teacher is created at a suitable school.

- Ten years ago, there were many new teachers, up to 40,000 per year. "There were so many new teachers, it was hard to find suitable mentors." Now with the decrease in birth rate, only 10-12,000 new teachers per year are needed. This makes the program much more manageable, both fiscally and otherwise.
- When the program was created, there were no models available. Therefore, a committee of university professors and teaching professionals worked for over six months to determine the program.
- The debate still rages "about whether these [induction] activities should be part of the pre-service or in-service components". The original idea that the induction program should be "one link in the program of in-service training" endures today, however.
- Since its inception, the program has garnered good evaluation results. Both student teachers and the schools seem to like and appreciate it.

5. Characteristics of Today's Beginning Teacher Induction Program

The Japanese model for induction of new teachers involves a substantial commitment of resources. The minimum number of days designated for in-service is set at ninety by the Monbusho, with many schools requiring more. Each new teacher is assigned an experienced teacher as mentor or 'guiding teacher'. The guiding teacher and the new teacher are both given reduced teaching responsibilities. Using Monbusho, prefectural and local outlines, a plan for the year is devised by the principal and guiding teacher that best fits the local conditions of the school (Monbusho, 1991).

The typical program includes several types of in-service opportunities.

- In-school training – this involves working with the guiding teacher as well as others in the school. This component requires about "two days per week and a minimum of sixty days per year".
- *Outside-school training* – this involves training at the in-service centers located in each prefecture and select large cities, often necessitating an overnight stay some distance from the local school. The outside-school component is about "one day per week or a minimum of thirty days per year".

The Monbusho divides the content of the induction program into six broad categories.

- *Basic knowledge* gives new teachers a broad view of the school and schooling and includes topics such as "current conditions and problems in school education", "goals of school education", "education on anti-discrimination" and "teachers' mental attitude". Much of this component takes place outside the school.

275

- *Classroom management* involves methods of organizing and managing the classroom and pupils. It includes topics such as "enhancing the classroom environment", "creating classroom communication", "enhancing home visits" and "preparing report cards". Much of this category is done in school.
- *Subject guidance* involves the planning and analysis of classroom teaching. It includes topics such as "understanding school children in the classroom", "enhancing of educational materials research", "enhancing individual elements of instruction" and repeated "class-room observations" by the guiding teacher. This component occurs primarily within the school.
- *Moral education* involves the planning and teaching of moral educa-tion. Activities include producing a "guidance plan for moral educa-tion", "enhancing moral education" and classroom observation by the guiding teacher. Such topics are taught both in- and out-of-school.
- *Special activities* include after-school sports and clubs, in which most Japanese teachers take an active role. Topics in this category include "enhancing school events", "guidance practice for school events" and "guidance practice for club and circle activities". Topics in this category are taught both in and out of school.
- *Pupil guidance* is the last category and involves influencing pupils in groups and/or individually. Topics include "teacher–pupil relation-ship", "understanding pupils", "enhancing educational counseling" and "praising and reprimanding pupils". Topics in this category are taught both in- and out-of-school.

Structural latitude and variation in implementing the program

Japanese educators have flexibility within the constraints of an overall pol-icy. All school districts are encouraged to use the Monbusho outline as a starting point for designing their own program outline (sixty days work in-school and thirty days out-of-school as proposed by the Monbusho). Because of the limited amount of information that can be inferred from the outline, it is not included in this chapter. A copy for elementary and lower secondary school teachers can be found in Nohara (1997). Every school we visited that had a new teacher was able to show us its outline and every school, when asked, stated that the program was locally created. But, as with the in-service center materials, we found little difference in what was described on paper across the schools we visited. Nor was this plan, in our experience, followed in a step-by-step fashion. Rather, it seemed to be a tentative outline of potential subject matter – topics which may or may not be discussed. What took precedence was the need of the individual first-year teacher. One guiding teacher frankly told us that the "informal is more important than formal".

Likewise, most in-service centers, whether at the prefectural or city level, have prepared materials available to guide the thirty days of out-of-school training. These materials highlight the specific topics to be covered and who is responsible for the training.

Common to all grade levels
> The Miyazaki prefecutre
> Race issues in the Miyazaki prefecture
> Management rules in public schools
> Basics of study guidance
> What moral education in school should be
> The basics in understanding pupils and children
> Treatment of integrated study
> Health education
> The information-oriented society
> Audo-visual aids
> Environmental education
> Education in international understanding
> Constructing class lessons
> The role of schools in life-long learning
> Understanding handicapped children

Lower secondary school
> Construction and implementation of curriculum
> Special activities
> Class management
> Guidance of specific subject matters (Japanese Language, Social Studies, Mathematics, Science, Music, Fine Arts, Health and Physical Education, Industrial Arts and Home Making, and Foreign Languages)

Figure 1: Sample of topics in the induction program for the Miyazaki Prefecture (1999)

Figure 1 lists a sample of topics common to all grades and those specific to lower secondary school included in the Miyazaki Prefecture outline. Note that all new teachers, regardless of grade level, are taught many of the topics together. Most of the topics listed in prefectural or city in-service guides across the country are similar. One center official told us:

> There is a centralized system in Japan. We all have a common structure and this center does the same in general as the others. But we have local needs.

These local needs play out in numerous ways, including special topics to be covered or special local resources to be visited. In some cases, both the prefectural and city in-service centers, as well as the school district, negotiate to determine who is responsible for which part of the out-of-school training. In one case, the local district was responsible for eleven days, the prefectural center for fifteen days and the city center for four days. Who took which responsibility depended on local capabilities and resources.

In addition to the list of in-service topics at every in-service center, some also published their own detailed guidebooks. In Kumamoto, a twenty-chapter, locally produced guidebook is available and we were seriously told by an official, albeit in a joking manner, "This is the bible for a new teacher!" The contents of each chapter of this unique new teacher resource are briefly detailed in Figure 2. The same official also shared a book for the guiding teacher that was locally created. (More will be said about the outside-school component of the program in a later section of this chapter.)

Ch. 1	Purpose, goals and content of the beginning teacher training program
Ch. 2	Mental attitude as a teacher, including laws and regulations
Ch. 3	The objective of education
Ch. 4	School management, including classroom management
Ch. 5	School curriculum, including course of study planning and evaluation
Ch. 6	Teaching subject matter, including how to devise a syllabus, more on planning and raising the academic achievement of pupils
Ch. 7	Moral education
Ch. 8	Special activities
Ch. 9	Special education
Ch. 10	Race issues in education
Ch. 11	Guidance, counseling and pupil discipline
Ch. 12	Guiding pupils to either academic or vocational programs
Ch. 13	Health education
Ch. 14	Information education, including the use of computers
Ch. 15	Education in remote rural areas
Ch. 16	Use and role of the school library
Ch. 17	Promotion of life-long learning
Ch. 18	Social education
Ch. 19	Environmental education, including identifying and grappling with environmental issues
Ch. 20	Education for international understanding

Figure 2:   *Contents of the Kumamoto Prefecture in-service center induction guidebook*

While the teaching load of new teachers is relatively consistent throughout Japan, there was some variability from district to district. Normally, a new teacher's teaching load is set at 75 percent of the conventional of 16–17 hours/week in upper secondary and 20–23 hours/week in lower secondary. In a few cases, however, a new teacher teaches the normal number of hours. The availability of resources is the largest determining factor regarding teaching load.

Many administrators are imaginative in maximizing resources. For example, new teachers in a prefecture are often grouped at one school because of the good reputation of the school. This allows enough funds to hire an additional temporary teacher to fill in for the new and guiding teachers. An astute administrator can accomplish several objectives with the funds that come for induction, including substantially reducing teaching loads.

In addition, since Japanese teachers are commonly moved from one school to another every three to six years, it is not unusual for a teacher to be moved from one school to another just to become a guiding teacher. Nor is it odd to create an opening at a particularly strong school just to accommodate a new teacher or in one that has a strong teacher.

The in-school training component

The in-school training involves substantial work, approximately sixty days per year, with an assigned mentor called a 'guiding' teacher. The guiding teacher works together with the school principal or vice-principal to create a detailed in-school schedule of activity. More importantly, the guiding teacher is the one who is responsible for the growth and development of the new teacher. The in-school component is considered by many to be the most important aspect of the induction program.

The guiding teacher

The guiding teacher is the key to success in the Japanese system. While the principal is technically responsible for new teachers and their induction, it is the guiding teacher who makes or breaks the experience. Over and over, we heard new teachers speak about their gratitude to their guiding teacher, as Yoko did in the opening vignette. When we visited during Yoko's second year of teaching she simply stated, "She took care of me very well". Others clearly acknowledged that they "learned a lot" from their guiding teachers, with one new teacher indicating, "If I had lacked this guiding teacher, it would have been a very serious problem".

In discussing the importance of her job, a guiding teacher observed that two new teachers dropped out of teaching a few years back because they could not communicate well with their guiding teacher or with other teachers.

She admitted that the possibility of failure drove her to strengthen and cement a positive and productive relationship with her beginning teacher.

Given their central role in the induction process, it would be instructive to explore several questions about guiding teachers. How are guiding teachers selected? What professional and personal characteristics help them to succeed? What professional development is provided to those who become a guiding teacher? Perhaps, most importantly, just what does a good guiding teacher do to help a new teacher? Does the guiding teacher mentor alone or is there a role for other teachers in the school during the induction period? Do guiding teachers perceive professional growth benefits to their role or is this just a different and short-term job?

Procedures for selecting guiding teachers vary widely and are often idiosyncratic to the prefecture or even school. There seem to be no formal guidelines and no one could give precise criteria for selection. Typically, the decision-makers (sometimes school system officials, at other times the principal) seek an experienced teacher who is widely considered to be a good teacher. As we visited various schools throughout the country, we found the two most important criteria for guiding teacher selection are whether there is a subject matter match with the new teacher and the experience/reputation of the guiding teacher.

One principal said, "I believe subject matter background and attitude of respect for others are very important". Another stated that selecting "the leader with the greatest experience in the subject matter is crucial". In yet another school, the principal declared:

> In general, the guiding teacher is either the vice-principal or an experienced teacher. This school has two vice-principals and one has science experience, so he was selected as the guiding teacher.

(The position of vice-principal in a Japanese school is filled by one who has attained a high level of achievement and usually carries with it duties as curriculum leader for the school.)

Sometimes teachers in a prefecture are moved from one school to another in order to create an opening in a desired school, one that has teachers with the appropriate characteristics. At other times, a temporary teacher is hired who has matching qualifications. Mrs. Morishita, the guiding teacher described in the first vignette below, was a retired teacher who took on this responsibility. She was well known in the district as excellent and worked three days per week as a guiding teacher.

Two teacher vignettes

(a) *Learning to communicate with his pupils.* When visited at his upper secondary school in Chiba, in the greater Tokyo area, Mizorigi-san

(Mr. Mizorigi) was in his eighth month of his first year of teaching. After a quick orientation to the school from the principal, we observe a lesson on pulleys. There are nine or ten other teachers and administrators in attendance. They have taken the opportunity of our visit to schedule just such an observation. He has materials prepared, including a poster that describes the problem. He calls the pupils up to his desk to discuss the poster and all pupils cluster around him and seem to listen. They are well behaved. During the lab itself and the ensuing discussion, pupils respond fairly well.

Mrs. Morishita (a 31-year veteran teacher who is serving as a guiding teacher for the fourth time in the last five years) helps him during the lesson by going from group to group, interacting with pupils and asking questions. She seems to get round to all the groups, while he gets bogged down with only a few. He stays up in front of the class, except during the lab work, and although he seems outwardly expressive, he makes no eye contact with pupils. After a short discussion, he collects the pupils' worksheets and the lesson ends.

In discussion afterwards, I ask him about his progress in general. He observes that at the beginning of the school year, "my style wasn't suitable for public school". He explains that he graduated from a private high school and university and his three years of teaching were also in private high schools. "I need to understand how children think and how they feel." At the suggestion of other teachers in the school, he tried to spend extra time with pupils during breaks from classes and after school, but soon found it took too much time. "A teacher needs to understand pupils by playing with them after lunch. I tried this and then stopped. The students did not react well to this change. Now I am again doing it and they like it."

The next year during the second month of school (May, 2000), we visited him again to observe another lesson. Again some eight to ten observers are in the classroom. This lesson on chemical reactions is visibly problematic: neither pupils nor visitors can figure out his intended purpose. Over lunch, a dissection and analysis of the lesson ensued. He is embarrassed, acknowledging that the lesson was too complicated.

Mrs. Morishita, his former guiding teacher who was in attendance as a courtesy to us, tells him, "In today's lesson, the pupils didn't know what the purpose or question was. You need to be more clear." She continues her feedback by talking about the pupils lack of engagement. The feedback was given with much empathy and concern for his professional development. Following her lead, each person in the room took an opportunity to give him feedback. All were extremely encouraging.

The vice-principal recalls that he analyzed the lesson beforehand and told Mizorigi-san that it would not work. He predicted there would be technical problems and that pupils would not understand. "But you worked hard on this lesson for a long time. You tried it on a group of students last week and it failed. I suggested you try another lesson, but you wanted to show you could do it." It is apparent that he is both supporting his efforts and chastising him for not listening.

The session lasts about one hour after which Mizorigi-san must return to his classroom. The observers who remain briefly discuss his progress among themselves. While critical of his lesson and disappointed because he has not grown as fast as they would like, they all remain positive about his future. Later, our translator tells us that it is their job to see that he does not fail and they will do what is necessary to ensure that this occurs.

In some cases, when an exact subject-matter match between the new teacher and mentor cannot be made, a second "subject-matter guiding teacher" is selected. In a school in southern Japan's Miyazaki Prefecture where there were two new teachers, one in science and one in social science, a guiding teacher was chosen who had social science expertise. That individual served as the general guiding teacher for both and as the subject-matter guiding teacher for the social science teacher. A science teacher was then selected to work as the science guiding teacher. In yet other cases (such as that of Yoko Matsubara discussed in the opening vignette), special help is sought for induction-year teachers when necessary. Since there was no other physics teacher in the school, Yoko was connected to a physics study group in the district.

There is little special training available for those who become a guiding teacher in the Japanese system. While guiding teachers attend three meetings over the period of the year (either in Tokyo or at prefectural in-service centers), these meetings are focused primarily on program goals and the teachers' responsibilities, with only some attention paid to methods of mentoring the new teachers.

Mrs. Morishita reported that she discussed "how you help the new teacher" and she listened to a lecture from a previous participant on how to mentor at the Chiba Prefecture. But she was hoping that there would be "more discussion next time because we had a lot of questions". This comment comes from an experienced, four-time guiding teacher. Moreover, a guiding teacher in the Miyazaki Prefecture told us that if there are two guiding teachers working with a new teacher, it is not uncommon for only one of them to attend such meetings. In general, we found that most of the guiding teachers we talked with recommended more in-depth training for mentors.

> (b) *Dilemmas in being a guiding teacher.* It is Monday morning toward the end of May, the second month of the school year, and Mrs. Nakayama reads over her notes from her last visit with the new teacher.

She is thinking about what to do next with Mr. Yoshi Hamata. "How do I help?", she murmurs to herself, all the time thinking that this is a much more difficult assignment than she first thought it would be. While her teaching load is reduced, her feeling of responsibility to the school and her colleagues is putting a lot of pressure on her. An accomplished teacher of lower-secondary science with twelve years experience, she is confident in her ability to help pupils learn their science well. In asking her to take on this responsibility, the principal explained, "What is vital is your experience and beliefs about what is important in teaching". But this new assignment is an undeniable challenge.

Yoshi Hamata is a fine new teacher who has had more than two years of experience as a part-time teacher. Yet he does not seem to understand some of the basics of teaching that come naturally to Mrs. Nakayama: such things as knowing how to attend to the learning of all pupils, communicating with pupils and planning lessons that will help pupils learn. But what are some reasonable ways to give Yoshi feedback and not, at the same time, destroy his confidence? Luckily, he is eager and willing and he knows his science content. At least there is no problem with that. "I wish I had more training. I wish I could talk to others who are guiding teachers. I need to know how they are working with their new teachers."

Unfortunately, there has been no training for Mrs. Nakayama. She knows that there is an up-coming meeting of guiding teachers at the prefectural in-service center, but her colleagues tell her to expect only a few speeches and not much that is useful. "Maybe I can talk to other teachers before the meeting if I arrive early."

Looking back at the notes from her last meeting with Yoshi, Mrs. Nakayama compares what she believes his needs are with the topics on the official outline. She prepared the outline from a prefectural model with the help of the school principal. But this was before she knew what Yoshi's actual, specific needs would be. Now she knows that it is unrealistic to deal with the goals of education or health and hygiene issues, both on the list. Instead, she recognizes that Yoshi needs help with classroom management and with understanding how children think. Fortunately, these two topics are also on the official list. She makes a professional decision to ignore some topics because of his needs.

This week Mrs. Nakayama will help Yoshi Hamata prepare a special lesson for his upcoming observation by a prefectural in-service center staff member. She will also observe two lessons, discuss these with him and teach one of his classes while he observes another science teacher, known for strong classroom organization. These are strategies that seem of use. She and Yoshi will also spend a lot of time talking – about children, classroom management and other topics. This appears to help Yoshi understand and it gives him confidence, a very important aspect of becoming a teacher Mrs. Nakayama senses. He has made a lot of progress in his first two months and a loss of confidence this early in the year would be a disaster.

As she leaves the teacher's workroom, a warren of desks where teachers plan and work together, Mrs. Nakayama has a short conversation with an experienced science teacher, who asks about Yoshi. The teacher offers his help and this makes Mrs. Nakayama very happy. "If all the others help this way, maybe this won't be so difficult after all."

Just what does the guiding teacher do to help new teachers? Where do the responsibilities start and end? Answers to these questions were more difficult to determine. Most often when asked this question directly, guiding teachers referred to the official program outline or gave a general response. One teacher said, "Growing a new teacher successfully is my [most] important task" in the induction program.

Guiding teachers were clearly responsible for all subject matter and general teaching-related issues. How this responsibility was carried out varied considerably. Some activities included team-teaching with new teachers, visiting and observing their classes, having meetings with them, communicating through reflective journals and having the new teachers observe them and other teachers in the building teaching. There was no one model that was either suggested or utilized. Instead, it seemed that the pair followed a pattern that fitted their personal and professional needs and abilities as well as the time constraints.

The following are some of the major themes of the informal, in-school work undertaken by guiding teachers to accomplish the goals for the induction program.

Assist in understanding pupil thought and behavior

'Understanding pupils' is one of the first foci of help the guiding teacher provides. Because of the new teachers' lack of experience in schools, most guiding teachers believe they must work intensively to help new teachers understand and communicate with pupils as soon as possible. "At first, we worked on the understanding of children", declared one guiding teacher. Another indicated that communication with pupils is the most important assistance she can give a new teacher. When visiting classrooms, she looked for communication and the general relationship between the teacher and pupils.

Others suggested to new teachers that they spend as much time as possible with pupils during after-school sports, to help them better understand both the pupils and their issues. It was clear from all guiding teachers that this was the one area without which a new teacher would not make progress. Our discussion of the new teacher Mr. Mizorigi highlighted and exemplified the challenges he had with 'understanding children'.

Support in becoming confident in their work

In many cases, building confidence in the new teacher was seen as the main over-riding focus of the guiding teacher's work. A guiding teacher from Miyazaki Prefecture felt that, "Monitoring children's understanding was the best training for building the confidence of new teachers". Yoko Matsubara's guiding teacher told us, "About fifty percent of the pupils have learning difficulties, so I must work on her confidence. In spring [near the beginning of the Japanese school year], there were many times when she lost confidence." It is clear from these comments that bridging the gap between university and public school teaching or between part-time teaching and a full-time, regular job is a difficult one. New teachers in Japan find the job overwhelming, especially at first. Keeping the new teachers positive about themselves and about teaching is critical, especially in the first few months.

Help to deal with and plan for classroom management

Widespread disruptive behavior in general is not a large problem in Japan: pupils do not frequently challenge teachers or regularly misbehave in Japanese schools. Even under these somewhat desirable circumstances, new teachers recognize that their organization, task directions and other overt actions directly affect classroom learning. This aspect of classroom management is a major focus of the first months of teaching. On several occasions, we observed lessons in which the new teacher ignored a large number of pupils while discussing with a few or gave confusing directions (e.g. Mr. Mizorigi) that were never corrected, even though pupils were obviously confused. After two years teaching experience, one teacher we visited said that now he was better able to:

> observe all the children. The most important thing [the induction program helped me with] was classroom management. Ms. Okada [the guiding teacher] especially helped me with getting pupils to attend at the beginning of class.

Assistance in planning and teaching lessons

Clearly, both subject-specific and general help with the planning and teaching of lessons is a major part of the in-school experience and was a vital element in the interactions and discussions of those we interviewed. In Japan, writing a good lesson plan is a valued art and teachers often spend days and even months refining a lesson. New teachers frequently plan lessons with help from the guiding teacher and ask for teaching suggestions and input on lesson plans, as in the case of Mr. Mizorigi. They then try out the lesson with one or more classes, using what they learn to revise the plan again. Many of the new teachers' action-research projects that we viewed consisted of lesson plans designed to accomplish specific goals.

Most guiding teachers gave considerable help to new teachers in teaching techniques, but the specific type of help varied considerably. Almost all (including Mrs. Nakayama) observed lessons, giving feedback both orally and in writing. Some guiding teachers taught sample lessons or allowed the new teacher to visit in her classroom and observe. In one school, a guiding teacher said:

> Generally, we meet several times per week. I visit his classroom and he visits mine. Approximately two periods a week we discuss plans and other issues. For another two hours we discuss the six topics on the program outline.

Another stressed that, in his school, "Most [new teachers] teach by themselves. They observe many demonstration lessons of veteran teachers, but they teach by themselves." Yet others team-taught with the new teachers. An important part of Yoko Matsubara's work was team-teaching with Mrs. Nishi and the discussions that followed each lesson.

One new teacher we interviewed in Kumamoto Prefecture told us that all her classes were either team-taught or observed by her guiding teacher. She acknowledged this may have been excessive:

> I feel insecure and strange [with this arrangement] because I am always observed, but I get support too. I guess this is both good and bad, but this [system] does allow me to study the best ways to teach.

The demonstration or 'study teaching' lesson, a traditional Japanese method for improving teaching described earlier, is a formal public lesson, which is observed and then subjected to a critique by colleagues. All new teachers typically teach two or more demonstration lessons in their first year, with the lessons being viewed by prefectural administrators, the guiding teacher, the school principal/assistant principal and other teachers in the school.

New teachers prepare for these lessons for several weeks, often planning what they believe to be innovative and exciting lessons. As was the case with Yoko Matsubara, it is very common for the lesson to be tried out with one class of pupils and then modified prior to the group visit. The guiding teacher usually plays an important role in providing feedback during the preparation process.

Over the years, we have observed this 'study teaching' method utilized during student teaching, the induction year and by experienced teachers who wish to improve their teaching. In Mr. Mizorigi's feedback session, comments were made that directed him to be clearer in giving directions, to show more passion for teaching and to continue to plan more engaging lessons.

Despite the fact that the lesson needed much improvement, all the participants in the analysis conveyed a sense of compassion for the new teacher and strong encouragement for his improvement. Other sessions we have observed were quite direct (and sometimes felt unpleasant to us) in their criticism of the lesson. Yet, the method is so universal that everyone experiences it and all seem to see its wisdom and believe in its efficacy. In fact, several teachers and administrators we talked to about the technique emphasized that a critical factor is that the lesson be criticized, not the teacher.

Mentor in performing homeroom duties

'Homeroom' duties in Japanese schools are an important part of a teacher's responsibilities. Typically, a Japanese teacher is assigned a group of pupils and she or he is "responsible for the academic work of the pupils, for contacting parents and for out-of-school activities". One new teacher said that homeroom is an opportunity to learn "about the pupils and how to talk to them about their feelings and accomplishments in school and in club sports".

A vice-principal from the Kumamoto Prefecture listed the duties of a homeroom teacher as follows:

- discussing a pupil's progress when the parents visit the classroom and observe their child;
- meeting personally with parents and the principal at least once a year to discuss their child's progress;
- visiting the home of each of the pupils at least once a year;
- meeting specially with parents and principal to discuss serious problems that might arise.

While the list helps in understanding homeroom duties, it does not describe the entirety of the responsibility. Simply put, a homeroom teacher is responsible for the academic and personal progress of her or his pupils during the year. This responsibility is taken so seriously that new teachers are only gradually introduced to being a homeroom teacher. In one case, when we visited a second-year teacher, he had not yet fully taken on homeroom duties. We were told that he was "still the vice-homeroom teacher. This allows him to practice again."

Support from the entire school community

Generally speaking, it is the responsibility of the whole school to ensure that a new teacher succeeds. Teachers and administrators believe that it reflects badly on them should a teacher fail. In fact, very few fail. Everyone in the school makes every effort as a group to ensure that this does not happen. As Yoko Matsubara observed about her second year, she had many mentors now – the other teachers in her school.

One guiding teacher from Miyazaki Prefecture indicated that teachers are proud to have a new teacher at their school and want to make the new teacher proud of being there too: therefore, they help the new teacher whenever possible. A guiding teacher noted, "All the teachers in the building feel responsible to provide help and they do so. It's not just my job." This notion that each individual has a responsibility to the group and that the group is similarly responsible for all the individuals is common in Japan. All three vignettes, about Yoko Matusbara, Kazu Mizorigi and Yoshi Hamata, exemplify this. When asked about mentors in her second year, Yoko Matsubara flatly stated, "[The school] has a lot of experience [in supporting new teachers]".

Benefits to the guiding teacher

There is undoubtedly some sense of honor in being selected as a guiding teacher, as only the most experienced and respected teachers are chosen. When we asked directly about his, however, most guiding teachers demurred, preferring to talk about the new teachers. We could ascertain no financial benefit for being a guiding teacher and many acknowledged that the duties entail a lot of extra work.

One teacher said point blank, "It is too much work. I did not want to be guiding teacher." While typically being assigned a reduced teaching load (usually 50–60 percent of normal), the added responsibilities of ensuring the success of the new teacher can weigh heavily, as was mentioned by Mrs. Nakayama.

The most important and plausible advantage of being the guiding teacher is the professional growth that occurs. When asked what she learned from the experience, Yoko Matsubara's guiding teacher, Mrs. Nishi, exclaimed with a laugh that she had learned, "I am old!" Then, after a short reflection, Nishi-san added, "This has been a good experience and [it allowed] me to think more about teaching and teaching materials". Another teacher when asked whether being selected was an honor, responded by saying:

> Maybe. But to be a guiding teacher is an opportunity to learn more
> [...] and to reflect on it.

The out-of-school training component

The out-of-school training usually occurs at a local or regional in-service center and typically encompasses thirty days per year. New teachers can work with other new teachers from different schools. Much of the training occurs in one-day sessions, but at least one event requires an overnight stay.

In-service center activity

Most out-of-school activity occurs under the guidance of a city or prefectural in-service center (only larger cities have sufficient resources available to support an in-service center, which are generally well-funded). Such a center usually consists of a rather large building, well staffed with specialists in most disciplines and dedicated to the in-service development of local teachers. The out-of-school responsibilities are frequently shared by city and prefectural in-service centers.

At one center in the Shizuoka Prefecture, we toured modern dormitories that could house up to 150 teachers, which is not at all unusual. Beyond the induction year, all Japanese teachers must participate in Monbusho-sponsored in-service programs five, ten and twenty years after their induction program is completed. Specialists at the centers, who are usually among the region's best teachers and who have been promoted to the in-service center, provide these courses. They spend much time preparing in-service courses and activities.

The intent of the out-of-school component of the induction program is to expand the perspective of new teachers. As one Monbusho official told us, "Teaching by its nature narrows the mind over the years. [The induction] program helps to broaden [new] teachers' understanding." An in-service center specialist added, "All training is not teaching related. The overnight experiences offer an opportunity to study the community." Still another explained that the in-service center's role was to "broaden the [teacher's] experience".

In-service centers involve new teachers in activities such as visiting the programs of special-needs pupils (who are segregated in most Japanese schools) or understanding vocational programs. As has already been discussed, in-service centers have the freedom to design specific activities within the general Monbusho model. The Kumamoto City In-service Center prides itself on an intensive component in which new teachers from various disciplines teach lessons that are open to critiques by other first-year teachers. Almost universally, in-service center supervisors visit each new teacher at least once during the induction year to view and comment on a lesson. Most centers also use local resources like science centers or botanical gardens as a focus for training. When the new teacher is attending such sessions, either the guiding teacher or vice-principal will cover his/her classes.

All in-service center programs include partial-day and full-day sessions as well as at least one 2–3-day overnight session. There is little or no subject-specific work undertaken at in-service centers. Only a very small proportion of the activity deals with subject matter that the new teachers actually teach. The most science-related work we found was at the Chiba Prefecture In-service Center that dedicated three of its thirty days to science-related topics. A major reason for this lack of subject-matter focus, already mentioned above, is that new teachers are thought to be sufficiently expert in content upon being hired and their first-year job is to learn about children and how to teach.

At Chiba, we were given a very detailed overview of in-service center activity. Staff members described the typical structure for a one-day session as follows. Such activity is widely generalizable to other in-service centers.

> *Session 1* – Opening lecture by an education expert.
> *Session 2* – Experience with practical tasks related to teaching. These include school safety, health, the environment, CPR or use of computers and are done through lectures and demonstrations.
> *Session 3* – Experiential learning. New teachers are involved in activities like micro-teaching and learning how to group by ability. They work one day with handicapped children and another day with the elderly in a 'care house'. The participants decide on some of these topics themselves and are often grouped by means of the grade level they teach.

In *three-day* sessions, new teachers often stay overnight at a camp, where they cook for themselves. The purpose of these activities is to build team spirit and camaraderie, to teach the new teachers about certain educational support functions and to broaden their experience with the community and all its citizens. Highlights include the following:

- the participants often determine at least part of their own curriculum for this experience;
- experiences are gained through both lecture and experiential learning;
- the new teachers often listen to a lecture and decide on a group project based upon it;
- project groups are often organized across grade levels and subject areas;
- projects often focus on topics like local environmental problems, local history or use of specialized equipment for the handicapped;
- small groups present their findings to the large group using posters;
- social events (e.g. one in-service center had new teachers visit a *sake* factory, an important local industry) and physical activities (e.g. rowing a boat together) are used to foster group co-operation.

The program aboard ship

The Japanese government runs a program that occurs aboard ship, although by no means all new teachers participate. The selection process varies and typically only about 20 percent of new teachers participate in the shipboard program. Some prefectures have instituted a lottery to give all new teachers a chance to go; others report that they send the oldest new teachers. Typically, the program is run during the summer with all participants boarding together, usually near Tokyo. The ship then sails around Japan's many islands, stopping at various ports. In the summer of 2000, the shipboard program lasted nine days, starting in Tokyo, proceeding to Hokkaido (a large northern island), sailing on to Nagasaki (on the southern island of Kyushu) and finishing back in Tokyo.

Not surprisingly, the program was very controversial at first. But new teachers like it very much, because they are able to have sustained contact with other new teachers, many of whom teach the same subject at the same level. Being on board a boat isolates new teachers from other distractions giving them an opportunity to discuss in depth with others like themselves.

The curriculum aboard ship mostly involves cultural activities. A typical program includes lectures from distinguished professors on cultural and social topics in the morning. In the afternoon, the new teachers form groups (often crossing grade levels and subject-matter lines) and determine their own projects and focus. Self-determination of work is considered an important aspect of the shipboard curriculum. Very few, if any, lectures focus on education. The purpose of shipboard activity is to develop a broad-minded teacher, not to train teachers. The boat holds about 400 teachers per sailing, with approximately 1800 teachers having the experience each year. To date, since its inception over one million Japanese teachers have participated in this part of the induction program.

Induction-year research project or portfolio

The Monbusho recommends that new teachers complete an action-research project during their first year. They typically present their results on a periodic basis or at least at the end of the year, usually as part of the out-of-school in-service component. These projects are accumulated in the prefectural in-service offices. It is unclear if others ever utilize these reports, even though in-service officials declare, "They are available for other teachers to use".

However, undertaking them appears to have a profound effect on the new teachers. In the opening vignette, Yoko Matsubara spoke of her project on motivating pupils. Her 30–40 page report included lesson plans, handouts and other materials. Another teacher decided to identify problems she was encountering in her teaching and dedicate her project to finding solutions to them. She eventually focused on five major problems and used a reflective notebook to document how she worked to overcome them.

New teacher stress during induction

Not surprisingly, many of the new teachers conceded that the induction program proved very stressful for them, because of the constant monitoring and the extensive amount of work the program entailed. Most agreed that this was a necessary evil during the first year. This attitude provides some recognition that most new teachers believe they do not have the experience to take over a teaching position without support, due to their limited school experience in pre-service programs. One new teacher said:

> At the beginning of the year, I would compare veteran [teachers] with my class and it was stressful. But the experienced teachers told me to relax.

Another teacher said:

> I wanted to be a teacher, so it was not so much pressure for me.

Still another suggested that there were:

> too many topics [for discussion]. For a new teacher, the most serious problem is what to do the next hour!

One new teacher even broke down crying when she described some of her difficult experiences.

Professional development beyond the induction year

To help put the induction year activities in context, it can be informative to understand other professional development opportunities available to Japanese teachers. Following the induction year, all teachers are required to continue to study and improve their teaching. In-service training formats vary but can be divided into three categories. The first involves self-training, by means of school-based and various professional organization programs. The second consists of system-wide training offered by the national and prefecture education offices, while the third involves university training.

- *Self-training* Teacher-initiated study circles and organization-sponsored study groups provide on-going professional development experiences at the school and prefectural level. The research in these groups blends components of action research with performance assessment: however, little or no quantitative data is collected. Lessons and teaching strategies are discussed and demonstrated. These research lessons are planned by a group of teachers and taught by one of them to a regular class with colleagues crowded around the room taking notes. The objective of the research is to improve instruction. Teacher participation in these research groups is generally voluntary and rough estimates are that from 10 to 50 percent participate (Lewis and Tsuchida, 1997).

- *System-wide training* Compulsory professional development programs occur at prefectural education centers during the fifth, tenth and twentieth year of teaching. These mandated programs, partly funded by the national government, are generally scheduled for one week in the summer. Coursework includes offerings that respond to the expressed needs of the participants. Central workshops are held at the national level for the in-service training of administrators and advisory teachers at the prefectural level. Prefecture boards of education release teachers for study leave at universities, research institutes, private firms and other institutions for long-term training. In addition, the Monbusho sends about 5,000 teachers abroad each year to broaden their international perspective.

- *University-based training* Graduate study plays a limited, although growing, role in teacher professional development. At present, relatively few teachers have a post-graduate degree, with only 6.5 percent of upper secondary teachers reported to have a masters degree in 1990 (Monbusho, 1994). But there has been a growing effort to reform the Japanese graduate school system, including that related to teacher education. This reform has resulted in three universities being specially designated as offering unique programs to appeal to experienced teachers. In addition, as the number of pre-service students declines, many higher education institutions are being urged to 'reinvent' their missions and focus on graduate and in-service education.

6. Program Evaluation and the Politics of Induction

There is wide and strong support for the induction program in Japan. While it is very expensive, it is becoming less so as noted above, because there are fewer new teachers coming into the profession. We were repeatedly told that official program evaluations focused on subjective data from surveys of participants and that they reported very positive attitudes toward the program. However, we never viewed any official evaluation reports. The teachers and administrators we asked to assess the program expressed mostly positive, although somewhat varied, opinions, including:

- strong support for the program's results (the majority of respondents, especially most in-service center and school officials);
- high praise about their own participation in the program (the vast majority of new and guiding teachers interviewed);
- criticism of certain components, especially the in-service center one (many new teachers and some guiding teachers);

- belief that the program entails too much work (a minority of guiding teachers, especially those who did not receive enough recompense);
- condemnation of the program in any form, perhaps for political reasons (a small minority, often those associated with the unions who oppose many official programs).

Formal evaluation of the induction program is considered to be weak by some, because it consists solely of participant perceptions. They complain because there is no hard pupil achievement or performance data that addresses program outcomes. The Monbusho is dedicated to correcting this perceived deficiency, but has not proposed any solutions as yet.

Most new teachers believe that the in-school component is much more valuable than the out-of-school one. As seen above, some, in fact, question the worth of the out-of-school work. In contrast to this is the strong belief held by in-service center officials that out-of-school activity is an important and perhaps crucial aspect of new teacher development. It is instructive to see how Yoko Matsubara in the opening vignette changed her opinion of the out-of-school component as she matured in the profession during her second year of teaching. There is a widely-held belief (accepted by new teachers as well as others) that informal and unplanned aspects of the out-of-school program (e.g. compassion from other teachers and conversation among new teachers, especially) are more important than the formal program components themselves.

The many political issues related to the Japanese induction program are also worth mentioning. While some officials admit that a second year of induction might be beneficial, they believe that this is impossible because most parents want their children to have an experienced teacher, not a declared newcomer. As the Monbusho official in charge of the national program observed, "Within one year, the new teacher must become an expert. But there are too many things to learn in this short time." When asked whether he thought the program, therefore, should be extended to two years, he rather forcefully said "No! New teachers, if given a two-year program, will not be viewed by the public as an expert quickly enough. Parents do not want a first-year teacher for their children." He also acknowledged that a two-year program would be too expensive.

The historical power struggle between Nikkyoso (the Japan Teacher's Union, hereafter the JTU) and the central government has also had an impact on the national induction program. The tension, which resulted when the Monbusho shunned the JTU in the post-occupation era, has limited the union's acceptance of the induction program (Beauchamp, 1991). Much of the JTU's initial resistance could be seen as a predictable reaction to the central government's mandate for a national program.

These concerns have given way to a gradual recognition that the induction program meets the needs of the schools and the new teachers. The JTU's lingering apprehensions center on the government's role in shaping the thinking of the entry novice teacher during the induction process. Only a little over 30 percent of new teachers joined the union in 1996, which is a direct threat to union influence and effectiveness. The JTU has experienced a dramatic decline in general membership from 90 percent in 1960 to 59 percent in 1992 (Kinney, 1998). Sato (1992) claimed that the JTU has lost power and the ability to influence policy because of these decreases. Others (e.g. Okano and Tsuchiya, 1996) report that the JTU has been forging a new relationship with the Monbusho by building a gradual partnership in recent years. For a recent general account of teachers' unions and the politics of education in Japan, see Aspinall (2001).

7. Concluding Remarks

Japan has created and nurtured an induction program that is alive and healthy. It serves to introduce new teachers to the culture of teaching, while educating them in many of the practical skills of the craft. It also serves as a form of professional development for those chosen to be guiding teachers. One major reason for the initial introduction of such a system in Japan was the relative weakness of pre-service programs, which traditionally have valued excellence in content over teaching knowledge.

While successful in what it aims to do, the program does not solve all of Japan's teaching problems. Kinney (1998) quotes one principal as saying about Japanese in-service education in general (and, by inference, about the induction program in particular) that it "is a big 'systems way' that teachers are trained. It would be nice if that were all that was needed" (p. 197). Clearly, the induction program is not all that is needed, but it is a successful first step toward improvement.

Acknowledgements

The authors would like to thank many colleagues in Japan who helped in setting up appointments and school visits, as well as performing translations. Individuals who greatly facilitated our work include: Yasushi Ogura from the National Institute for Educational Research in Tokyo, Hideo Ikeda from Hiroshima University, Yoshisuke Kumano from Shizuoka University, Genzo Nakayama from Kumamoto University and Manabu Sumida from Ehime University. In addition, our thanks to Terry Woodin and Joan Prival of the NSF who shared their data from a 1999 field trip to Japan to study teacher preparation.

Chapter 7

Making Sense of Induction:
Looking across International Cases

We began this book with a claim that induction represents a phase and not simply a program. In arguing for recognizing induction as a unique period, we are reminded of the lessons of Aries (1996) and others about childhood. That research demonstrated how 'childhood' came to be constructed as a category during the nineteenth century, created in part to go against a then-prevailing view of a child as simply a 'little adult'. This was done in order to argue for a protected period in the life of the young human, where particular things both should and should not happen. Yet, nowadays, childhood has become a 'natural' category.

Consider as well the construction of the concept of 'adolescence' (Hall, 1904). That term, an even more recent construct than 'childhood', spawned a set of scholarly questions, professional associations and specialists to pursue them, and has had among its institutional consequences the creation of the modern middle and high school (or lower and upper secondary school). But, today, most lay people take the notion of adolescence as simply describing a particular period in a person's life, with its distinctive characteristics, dilemmas and needs.

It is possible to see 'induction' as a comparably constructed category, equally signaling a specific phase in the life-span of a teacher, one that brings with it unique challenges, requirements and needs. We are aware of the danger of seemingly equating a category involving young people (either childhood or adolescence) and a phase of an adult profession ('beginning teachers'). Nevertheless, we feel that the comparison is worth making. It is also noteworthy that some recent French writing refers to *stagiaire* teachers in terms of their being "the adolescents of the profession". [1]

In stepping back from the individual cases reported in this book, it is easier to see that, like those early advocates constructing childhood or adolescence as a differentiated category, we too have suggested, perhaps imposed, a category on a diverse collection of individual practices, orientations and assumptions. Certainly, this set of cases highlights significant differences in practices, policies and assumptions about induction.

E. Britton et al. (eds.), Comprehensive Teacher Induction, 296–336.
© 2003 *Kluwer Academic Publishers. Printed in the Netherlands.*

The local terms we have taken as equivalents for what we have consistently termed 'induction' are themselves somewhat different from one another, each bringing in varying connotations, while locating the practice and programs in somewhat different terrain. French educators talk about the *formation* of new teachers, of *formateurs*, 'pedagogic advisors' and *stagiaires* all participating in this one 'shaping' process, a notion used in other civil-service professions. The metaphors associated with 'forming' contrast with the language of 'advice and guidance' and 'buddy teachers' that animates discussions of induction in New Zealand.

Yet both the French and the New Zealand frames differ from the connotations associated with the common Chinese terms used in induction: of new teacher 'training' and 'masters' 'guiding' 'new' and 'young' teachers. Finally, the Swiss-German terminology is yet again distinct. Like France, it draws on general professional language used for other occupations as well: as such, the word *Berufseinführung* (literally "a leading into the profession") is closest to the Latin etymological roots of the English term 'induction'. But, although both are abstract nouns, the German word draws attention to the fact that 'induction' does not indicate into what one is being inducted, while 'beginning teacher induction' privileges the *who* rather than the what.

While we have used the term 'induction' unproblematically throughout this book, we can see a need to be more cautious, to ask further questions. What, in fact, does occur in the learning of beginning teachers? When is this period of time? What is assumed as a goal? What are the sources for such assumptions and who is assumed to be pivotal to this experience? From examining the cases, we see not just different terms and meanings, but strikingly different practices and arrangements connected to them.

Beginning teachers in Switzerland are offered opportunities for collegial counseling, co-operation and reflective practice – dimensions of teaching seen as essential for new teachers to develop early in their careers. 'Induction', for these teachers, is about developing the whole person, as the extensive emphasis on counseling attests. Novices beginning to teach secondary school mathematics in France, on the other hand, enter the profession through a year-long process that moves them firmly into a disciplinary culture of teaching. There, the process of 'induction' is centrally defined and organized to mold beginners into the profession of mathematics teaching.

Japan provides yet another contrast, having as a central goal broadening the teacher from the narrow disciplinary focus of pre-service education. The organization of teacher education there, especially its emphasis on content knowledge, leads many to assume that the first-year teacher needs guidance from more experienced practitioners in ways that can not only support the beginning teacher but also improve pupil learning.

For New Zealand teachers, 'advice and guidance' is also at the heart of 'induction', but the means of 'advising and guiding' are organized in eclectic ways that provide help to the beginner from many sources, of many kinds and in varied locations. While senior teachers are crucial in supporting the newcomer, the role for 'buddy teachers' reminds us of the strong local school culture of support that is at the heart of New Zealand's approach. Finally, the influence of culture comes through particularly clearly in the Shanghai case, where 'induction' can be seen as the process of entering a public culture of teaching. Whether support comes from within the school, the district or via other sources, it socializes new teachers to a shared language of teaching, habits of mind and norms of practice.

The contrasts are vivid: these cases collectively exemplify varied approaches to induction, allowing us to ask questions and consider perspectives on induction itself, and on teacher learning more generally, that we might not otherwise raise. In Chapter 1, we asserted that we need not conceptualize induction by presuming a deficit model: that is, induction need not be thought of as simply 'filling in gaps'. But what, then, is it? And how do these cases provide new lenses for understanding and asking questions about our developing notion of induction?

We have been impressed by the varied goals and purposes, structures and logics of induction internationally. Yet, we also recognize some striking similarities, despite the very different contexts in which that induction takes place. This mixture of similarity and difference forces us to re-examine our original questions and ask more fundamental ones. As our work proceeded, we came to realize how where we stood shaped our initial specification of what was important but also helped us reframe our questions as we learned how induction takes place in other cultural settings.

An initial question about what induction is (or looks like) became transformed into an examination of why induction exists. Secondly, rather than assume in some unquestioned way the target audience for induction ("Isn't it obvious?" we might have thought), we now realize it is also important to ask whom induction serves. And from asking about how to do induction, our question shifts to asking what 'the curriculum of induction' is. Finally, instead of focusing on the roles of participants in induction, a question that predominates in the North American literature, we now ask where knowledge about teaching resides, whose knowledge it is and how it is articulated.

In this concluding chapter, we explore these four main questions. We hope that their examination will encourage a rethinking of familiar assumptions about entering teaching, about becoming a professional and about systems which support teacher development and learning.

1. Why Induction?

For many, the motivation for an international look at induction might be a desire to understand what induction looks like in different contexts. In our study, our operational concerns at the outset, mirrored in Chapter 1, were focused on understanding induction as a period, phase and process. However, undergirding any induction program, and manifested in its approach, is a combination of values, assumptions, theories and goals. Although these may remain implicit, they are nonetheless central, for they provide a frame within which one can then explore other questions. Understanding what and how induction occurs requires that we first examine these elements upon which it rests.

Philosophies drive induction policies and practices, even if they do so in unspoken ways. Across the contexts we studied, the philosophies of induction were strong and distinctly different. The language associated with induction – how it is named, what its participants are called – hints at some philosophical differences. In this sense, induction can be seen as a reflection of a culture's assumptions both about how teachers learn about teaching and what teaching itself involves.

But induction is not simply this. We note in Chapter 1 that induction can also been seen as a response to a (sometimes unarticulated) problem. For example, in many contexts, policymakers and educators claim that induction programs might reduce teacher attrition in the early years. Another, very different 'problem' might entail surmounting teaching's complexity: is teaching considered too dynamic and complex to be mastered before one actually takes institutional responsibility for one's own class(es)? Some systems create induction programs with this problem foremost in mind. These and other problems – some reflecting perceived failures in the educational system (weak teacher education, low recruitment, high teacher turnover, etc.) and others reflecting assumptions about inherently complex practices (teaching, learning to teach, etc.) – become the genesis for induction (see Bolam, 1995).

Clearly, these different induction systems serve to define the problem that induction is to solve. Finally, the culture of teaching (within individual schools, within the larger formal school system and within society at large) helps to shape what the 'problem of induction' is – and, therefore, how policies are conceptualized – and how that problem is to be approached. Induction is thus not just programmatic activity, but embedded cultural practice, as we discuss later in this chapter (see also Alexander, 2000).

The detailed information we collected from each site confirmed what we had found during our initial selection process: the uniformly strong value given to induction within the countries containing the cases. In each setting, induction is assumed to be important and valuable. Exploring the values ascribed to induction leads us to consider the broad range of goals we see across induction programs in the five cases. We pursue these two issues – the value of induction and its goals – in the discussion below, before concluding this section by examining further the fundamental role of culture in shaping both what and how a beginning teacher learns to teach.

Valuing induction and induction practices

Participants at each site in our study viewed induction as a distinct phase in a teaching career, one that demands particular (sometimes unique) experiences, opportunities, relationships and support. While the working out of the particular system that flows from this stance requires a complex architecture of policies and programs, the foundation on which the structure lies – the rationale for induction as a practice or policy – appears to be fundamental and not readily open to question. Yet the strength of these fundamental views is pivotal to the created approaches to induction.

Arguments for induction

Induction in these sites is valued for different reasons, but in all cases occurs as a kind of act of faith. In fact, viewed through a North American researcher's lens, only one of the countries we studied – Switzerland – even comes close to evaluating its induction programs at a system level. Indeed, some countries take it as a given that beginning teachers need support and guidance in their first year or two of teaching. This is the case for New Zealand at the policy and resource level, where for twenty-five years the national government has paid for 20 percent release time for beginning teachers to support their participation in induction activities primarily at their schools. Induction activities are valued in their own right and supported without much check on what services are provided by individual schools: Advice and Guidance plans, which each school creates, are not reviewed for quality, much less any of the proffered induction activities evaluated.

In both Shanghai and Japan, where the actual classroom experience provided to pre-service students preparing to become teachers is very limited, induction programs are seen as an absolutely critical component for honing the teaching skills of novices. The purpose is to ensure that every individual entering the profession will be helped to succeed in becoming a highly proficient teacher. The Japanese Ministry of Education has collected some survey information based on self-report that documents the generally favorable attitude toward induction-program offerings by participants and providers alike. Shanghai's municipal administrators have not undertaken systematic evaluation of the impact of induction. In fact, in neither of these sites does induction depend on evidence of its success. Rather, it is assumed that the breadth of skills, knowledge and dispositions required for teachers to be able to support high achievement in pupils requires guided learning *in situ.*

France represents yet another view, for there the current induction system was created almost at a stroke to help 'form' (and reform) the profession and proved to be in marked contrast to the earlier Inspectorate-based, post-recruitment 'induction' process. One of the primary original purposes for setting up the IUFMs, with their one-year special professional development period for beginning teachers, was to recruit more people to the teaching profession. (Two others were to increase the professionalisation and status of elementary teachers and to make the teacher education system more uniform.) The IUFM reform slogan was "recruit more, form better". Even though the first part of this goal has broadly been accomplished [2], it has become axiomatic that teacher development needs to be improved.

The Swiss cantons studied offer still another reason for valuing induction; they argue for the importance of supporting the development of the new professional amidst personal and professional transition. Yet the Swiss cantons also stand out among the sites with respect to evaluation of their induction offerings. Lucerne continuously gathers evaluative information on the practice groups; Zurich does the same with respect to its mandatory induction course and counseling services. However, this information gathering is largely in the mode of research and formative evaluation, undertaken in order to improve what the cantons are offering and to decide what to emphasize. This is done in order to meet the needs of the beginning teachers rather than to evaluate the enterprise itself. It very much fits the spirit of 'reflective practice' with respect to induction activities themselves and to reflective practice encouraged in science teaching. Thus, evaluation activities are designed to provide information relevant to the local goals of induction: developing teachers as both professionals and individuals. Solving the 'problem' of retention is not the purpose of induction in Switzerland, nor in fact is it in any of the sites we studied. This is so even though in Switzerland there have been periods of problems with retention of the teaching force.

More generally, it appears that, while the genesis of a particular program or policy may differ, there is an almost universal belief that induction is important. The view that it contributes uniquely to forming teachers and their profession is, for the most part, widely shared, even without consistent effort to collect data to document this. Induction is not simply or primarily to decrease teacher turnover: instead, in these sites, it stands as a key juncture of learning, growth and support. Induction occupies a special place, looking both backward to pre-service teacher preparation and forward to the career of teaching, with its challenges of becoming and being a teacher (Feiman-Nemser, 2001). While deeply affected by what both these directions entail – as with childhood or adolescence – the induction moment, so say these sites, requires its own particular attention. It is not primarily about fixing a problem. It is about building something desirable – a teacher, a teaching force, a profession, a kind of learning for pupils in schools.

Induction reflects broader values

What is deemed important, of course, reflects the particular values of any setting that creates an induction program. It is not surprising, given that induction is embedded in a larger system of schools, teacher education, civil service, and so on, that it takes on and typically supports those culturally determined values. Hence, while the belief that induction is important is found strongly in each of the sites, these sites make manifest very different orientations towards the 'problem' of induction.

Thus, for example, Switzerland's long tradition of direct democracy gets reflected in the ways in which beginning teachers in that country have a strong voice in determining not just in which activities they will participate, but the content focus of discussions within them. A second thread that runs throughout the Swiss approaches, varied as they are, is the emphasis on personal growth and the assumption that this occurs, in part, through reflection. This thread resonates with strong psychological traditions found within a country that produced both Jung and Piaget.

A contrasting but equally compelling example can be found in France. There, where mathematics takes pride of place in schools, the induction of mathematics teachers similarly moves mathematics pedagogy powerfully to the center of beginning teachers' work; the attention to mathematical didactics occupies center stage. However, there is no officially enshrined pedagogy. What there is is a cultural valuing (though not uniform) of teachers preparing and teaching their own *cours*, an assertion of individual teacher autonomy, in the face of a nationally-specified base curriculum.

A final, and yet again contrasting, illustration comes from Shanghai. Like France, the induction of mathematics teachers takes on a significance that reflects the privileging of mathematics (along with Chinese language and foreign language) in the hierarchy of school subjects. Yet, for beginning mathematics teachers, while the mathematics curriculum and its teaching and learning form the focus of their attention, the organization of induction is best understood not in terms of subject matter but in terms of more pervasive cultural norms about community. Unlike the Swiss emphasis on developing the individual, induction in Shanghai relies on collectivist and public approaches that inculcate a shared language and mutual goals among teachers.

In short, one cannot consider induction without understanding the assumptions, values and orientations of the broader culture it serves. Why induction is valued in any place is a function of what else is valued, as well as how the 'problem' of induction is perceived and defined. Nonetheless, there are interesting similarities across our studies when one asks what induction is to achieve.

Broad goals

In any given setting, the original motivation for developing and investing in induction programs may have been quite specific. Thus, in Japan, it became clear that teachers' pre-service education, with its very brief exposure to actual K–12 classrooms, did not prepare them to face the realities of school, pupils and their parents: hence, special interventions were deemed necessary. In Lucerne, two visionary individuals, observing the stress under which beginning teachers labored, instituted group meetings where these teachers could engage in mutual problem solving focused on their practice. Beginning in 1973, this developed into a formal induction program and now includes practice groups, individual and group counseling, training for group leaders and counselors, special induction courses, reciprocal classroom observation followed by discussion, and more (Vogel and Vogel, 1996). Several other cantons have since instituted similar induction programs. [3] In New Zealand, providing resources for induction in the form of free time for beginning teachers has long been in place, unchallenged, with the original explanations lost in the mists of time.

But no matter what the origins of induction practices were, we observe key patterns with respect to the goals of induction. First, they are broad and robust. In each site, policies and practices aim not at a single dimension of a teacher's development, but at many. Furthermore, each site targets significant, complex issues in teaching rather than offering shorthand recipes and quick orientations. The focus – whether on nurturing reflection, developing a curriculum critique or teaching-analysis skill, or deepening understanding of diverse pupils, for example – concentrates squarely on what one might think of as building blocks of teaching.

Second, there is a rather remarkable congruence in terms of large categories around which effort is invested: improving teaching quality and personal development. Clearly, not all countries address these goals with the same degree of emphasis, in part depending on the experiences beginning teachers have had in their pre-service education. Yet these categories, and aspects within them, seem to have meaning for several sites. It is, we think, noteworthy that other potential goals for induction – using it to filter out weak teachers, for instance – do not figure in these cases. The fact that we do find convergence across these sites around two broad goals speaks in part to what it is teachers need to learn early in their careers, as well as to the complexity of developing one's teaching practice and professional identity.

Improving teaching quality

Across our sites, the support given to new teachers involved significant attention to improving the high quality of teaching. Of course, how quality teaching is defined and verified, and what approaches are thought as best to assist a novice in reaching this goal, varied. Yet each place had worked out induction programs that in their enactment made clear that 'teaching quality' comprised a range of complex skills and understandings: building on prior preparation, focusing on instruction, developing skills for management and establishing constructive relationships in schools.

Complementing teacher preparation. There is significant difference in the content and learning opportunities offered by pre-service education in our cases, and this informs the charge given to induction. For example, Swiss educators recognize that pre-service education provides repeated experiences in the field and, combined with university didactics coursework, beginners have already had extensive exposure to issues related to what Lee Shulman and others have termed 'pedagogical content knowledge' (Shulman, 1987; Wilson, Shulman and Richert, 1987). That particular domain, therefore, is not a prominent feature of induction work in Switzerland.

Contrast that with Japan or France, where the extremely limited time in the field is influential in determining the kinds and amount of attention this receives within induction programs. But even though the Swiss beginning teacher has had much professional preparation prior to taking on formal teaching status, induction nevertheless has to engage with the challenge presented by a gap between school reform and the reform of teacher preparation curricula. In short, induction in each case makes some effort to take into account prior experiences and training of beginning teachers.

For several countries, induction experiences focused, among a variety of goals, on remedying these perceived shortcomings. In France, where pre-recruitment education focuses almost entirely on subject-matter learning, beginning teachers have little knowledge of the structure of mathematics teaching and, therefore, of what instructional strategies to use with pupils. Thus, roughly one-third of their first teaching year is devoted to professional development, dealing with both subject-matter-specific didactics and general pedagogic and foundational knowledge. Another example is provided by Japan, where pre-service education's emphasis on university-based content preparation restricts time in schools. Hence, induction activities are given considerable time (some ninety days during the first teaching year) to guide teacher learning during immersion in the classroom. And in New Zealand and Switzerland, where science teachers are expected to teach integrated science courses, new teachers may not have had sufficient disciplinary preparation in one or more of the requisite sciences. Some induction offerings attempt to address this difficulty.

Enhancing the quality of instruction. While programs did offer opportunities for new teachers to build on the knowledge they had developed and extend the limited experiences they had gained in pre-service preparation, in no site was this the sole aim of induction. In addition to addressing such 'gaps', the induction programs we investigated aimed to enhance the quality of instruction for, as Sharon Feiman-Nemser (2001) notes:

> New teachers have two jobs – they have to teach and they have to learn to teach. No matter how good a preservice program may be, there are some things that can only be learned on the job. The pre-service experience lays a foundation and offers practice in teaching. The first encounter with real teaching occurs when beginning teachers step into their own classroom. Then learning to teach begins in earnest. (p. 1026)

While new teachers cannot possibly be fully prepared, no parent, teacher or policymaker wants to sacrifice the learning of children who have new teachers. Thus, a critical challenge in supporting new teachers involves enhancing their instruction in the here and now, while also providing them with opportunities to learn and grow. But this also indicates limitations on the period of time all are willing to accept the label of 'novice'.

Even when pre-service education includes a balance of learning disciplinary content, learning about teaching and learning, and classroom experience, beginning teachers still need and want help as they face the challenges of achieving the goals of the mathematics or science curriculum in the middle grades. In Shanghai, for instance, the emphasis of the induction program is for beginning teachers to understand the 'important' points of the mathematics curriculum and to learn, through intensive lesson planning and 'public' lesson teaching, how to work with points that are viewed as 'difficult' for pupils to learn. Local educators argue that, despite an introduction to instructional concepts and activities in pre-service preparation, only when teachers actually start teaching can they develop firmer pedagogical content knowledge and see how it may be used.

A major Shanghai induction activity, therefore, is the 'public' lesson, carefully prepared by the novice teacher and open to critique by experienced teachers and district administrators. Through the preparation and presentation of such lessons, beginning teachers wrestle with decisions about how to teach particular content, receive a range of feedback on their ideas and approaches and have the opportunity to connect principles of teaching, learning and subject-matter knowledge to particular instructional actions. They also get to see the consequences of their decisions and actions in their own classrooms. This extended process, and its connection to the particulars of a lesson, allows beginners to dig in deeply and gain insight that they could not have acquired if divorced from a classroom or separated from pupils' learning and curriculum trajectories.

In Switzerland, though not 'public' in the same way as in Shanghai, critiques of observed classroom lessons also focus not only on content of the lesson, but also on topic presentation, the use of teaching aids, the arrangement of groups, responses to individual pupils, and the like. There, despite lengthy teacher preparation which offers prospective teachers rich opportunities for acquiring pedagogical content knowledge and extensive time in the field, induction advocates assert that only when one is in complete charge of a classroom do the broad range of complex skills and their dynamic interplay related to instruction come fully into play. Learning in the moment about how to teach in the moment, once one is a fully-fledged teacher, stands as a prominent goal in each of these two sites.

The professional memoir in France offers an instructive contrast to the immediacy of in-class learning that is so central in the Swiss and Shanghai induction approaches. The professional memoir is designed in fact not to thrust the beginning teachers into the classroom, but rather to require them to stand back from the immediacy of their new job. Yet, enhancing instructional quality is one of the goals of the memoir. One rationale for this approach claims that, in order to work successfully 'between theory and practice' (Artigue *et al.*, 1998), *stagiaire* teachers need regularly to be somewhat removed from 'the clamour of the immediate' – to use Corry's (1970, p. 33) telling phrase, albeit one made in quite another context.

It is not that some things can only be learned *on* the job, but instead learned *with* the experience of the job as a resource and *with* the analytic distance that the disciplined memoir requires. Just as Cochran-Smith and Lytle (1999) argue for knowledge not only 'for practice' and 'in practice' but also 'of practice', so the French approach assumes that beginning teachers can construct crucial knowledge of practice. They are to do so, however, not on their own, but with supported space and intellectual resources outside of the classroom, in pursuit of a significant task. This is so that they can work "in the spirit of research", to recall Bernard Cornu's interview phrase. In France, teacher induction frames novice teachers as teacher–researchers of their own practice to some degree, something apparently seen by the system as an important part of the professional work of teachers.

The range of demands for classroom teaching is such that beginners can benefit from support in many aspects, not always those involving direct classroom instruction. One such example of becoming better versed in effective classroom practice is the appraisal of pupils' work and their developing competence. This is so especially in a country like Switzerland, where no externally developed assessments are required to evaluate pupil performance in the middle grades. This, then, becomes a focus of induction support for novice Swiss teachers.

Managing classroom instruction and working with pupils. Another important aspect of enhancing beginning teachers' instruction involves helping them learn to manage classrooms. Shanghai educators stress the importance of learning 'basic routines' during the induction years, where this is seen as distinct from learning how to craft lessons to teach specific content. This aspect of becoming an accomplished teacher is almost impossible to address in any meaningful way in pre-service education, even when practice teaching is a considerable component of the program.

Not until teachers have full responsibility for a class or set of classes do they have to attend to the minute-by-minute decision-making entailed in teaching. Also, in some settings there are demands on teachers not fully levied against student teachers in their practice teaching: for example, managing classroom behavior, keeping order and dealing with disciplinary problems.

As a beginning teacher in Zurich observed:

> After all, I could walk away from the class after my six weeks [of practice teaching], now I have to take full responsibility for all my pupils for the whole year. Then, I didn't care who spoke up or who didn't; now I have to know whom to call on, who needs more time, who needs encouragement.

Related to this is the goal of helping beginning teachers attend to individual pupils, an important instructional goal in several countries and a difficult task for any novice teacher to accomplish. As Bertila, a novice in Bern, explained, it is hard to figure out how to pay attention to individual children: "I can't be everywhere – monitor everything". Her concern about the need to learn how to manage instruction for all the individuals in the class was echoed by a French novice who recalled being criticized by her pedagogic advisor for her inability to manage instruction for all of the pupils in her class:

For instance, the first time she came to see me, I spent a little bit of time with two pupils who were having major problems, doing [geometric] constructions with them. And she told me that, during the time that I spent with these pupils, the rest of the class drifted and that I should have let those two drop by the wayside, as I didn't have time to concern myself with them to the detriment of everyone else.

Establishing constructive relationships to support instruction. The first three sub-goals related to teaching quality discussed above all focus directly on the classroom. A fourth common focus of induction in many of our sites involved helping beginning teachers learn how to develop constructive relationships with others outside of the classroom, in the service of instruction. Whether it is parents, other school colleagues or district resource people, teachers need to be able to work with other adults (often older and more experienced than themselves) in ways that support their instructional efforts and pupil learning. For New Zealand and Shanghai teachers, much activity in the induction year encourages the new teacher to see and approach colleagues in their department and building as resources.

Beginning teachers in France, during their weekly, half-day, non-disciplinary sessions at the IUFM, work with other subject teachers. They have the opportunity to develop ways of working across customarily strong subject-matter boundaries, to see teachers as members of a common profession, connected as members of allied but distinct 'tribes', to use the word of one of the mathematics *stagiaires*. In addition, New Zealand beginning teachers get guidance during their school-based Advice and Guidance sessions on working with parents. Switzerland also gives prominence to the need for beginners to learn how to develop relationships with parents, something especially important in a system run by local communities.

All of these goals – addressing the need for further or different experiences, enhancing instruction, strengthening classroom management and class-based work with pupils, and building adult relationships – may involve emphasis on curricular choices, both of subject matter and of curriculum materials. Ways of engaging these possibilities include: lesson planning; assessing pupil understanding and achievement; learning, marshaling and using various instructional techniques and technologies, such as organizing group work, using different questioning strategies, working with graphing calculators or computer software such as spreadsheets or dynamic geometry; building on pupils' knowledge; dealing with misconceptions.

These examples – and many more discussed within each chapter – illustrate the range of objectives addressed by the induction practices and activities we observed. All also remind us that the complexity of teaching comes in part from its situated quality: as a practice in and of the moment, with different and changing learners and the unique dynamic created by a teacher combining learners and content. (See King, 2001, for a discussion of mathematics teaching as jazz improvisation.)

Personal support and development as a teacher

Becoming a teacher is not only a matter of learning how to work with pupils and content in classrooms. Learning to teach also means locating oneself as a teacher – in an organization, in a system and as a person. What status does one have as a novice? It is certainly different in Shanghai from in France. While each setting we studied emphasized goals related to improving teaching quality, support providers also worked to help beginning teachers develop beyond their classrooms, often with the assumption that this was essential to their success inside classrooms. This attention to personal and professional development appears to have three distinct components: orientation to the school site and administrative practices of the jurisdiction (for example, the district in Shanghai, the canton in Switzerland, the Academy in France), personal support and enculturation into the teaching profession.

Orientation to the school site and local practices. Although practice teaching, where it is emphasized, may have introduced prospective teachers to one or more school sites, each school is likely to differ somewhat in resources, personnel and administrative procedures. Beyond the school, there are system procedures to be learned about also. In New Zealand, since the schools themselves are charged with induction activities, the orientation to the site is a natural component of beginning teachers' guidance, although its quality and focus are likely to vary considerably. In Switzerland, schools share responsibility for this aspect of induction, although implementation is quite variable and often accomplished informally through colleagues. The practice group helps with orientation to a given canton's administrative procedures and mandates, such as the amount of homework to be assigned at a given grade level.

In Shanghai, school orientations typically are important first activities and introduce the novice to the local school culture and its way of connecting to its environment (parents, the district, and so on). In France, pedagogic advisors offer some orientation to the specifics of school life and the school principal receives IUFM funding to provide information about the educational system to beginning teachers, even if this task is often delegated in various ways. Yet, in part, because there is no expectation of stability in school appointment between a teacher's first and second years, the day-long orientation that is offered to *stagiaires* at the IUFM right before school starts in September focuses on practicalities of teaching, rather than on specifics of local administration.

Personal support. Personal support is particularly prominent in Switzerland, where it is provided both through the practice groups and through individual and/or group counseling. It includes balancing time demands, both inside and outside the classroom; stress management; teaching versus non-instructional demands levied by colleagues or administrators; maintaining physical and mental health; giving one's best to teaching and the school while maintaining one's outside responsibilities and recreational activities. In France, each Academy has a workplace doctor solely for teachers and provides access to voice therapy – and there are a number of other instances of institutional acknowledgement of and provision for the stress and particular demands of teaching.

We also observed personal support extended through the informal teacher-to-teacher interactions in New Zealand, during the regularly scheduled coffee breaks and lunches. Beginning teachers in Shanghai, although busy, do not describe themselves as harried – but they nevertheless express deep appreciation for the wide range of personal support extended to them. Mentors and others in Shanghai's schools reach out to new teachers not only with advice, but also with food, recreation and other personal support in an effort to help the new teacher "love teaching". Developing a positive attitude to being a member of the profession is a major goal of Shanghai's induction.

Enculturation into the teaching profession. The enculturation of new teachers takes many forms, according to a given country's culture of teaching and the status of the teaching profession. It may include developing appropriate relationships with other teachers (both in one's school and beyond), collegiality and teacher collaboration, as well as acquiring an understanding of what a classroom, say for teaching science, might or should look like. As one novice biology teacher in Switzerland said, "I get new ideas about how to present a topic from my colleagues when we meet in the biology preparation room and chat informally about what works with seventh and eighth graders". Generally, participation in school-based, non-teaching activities such as curriculum planning, excursions (prevalent as an important component of schooling in New Zealand, Switzerland and Japan) and coaching of sports or other club activities also are part of school culture that novices need to learn about.

They also need to begin to understand teachers' relationships to administrators within the school and beyond, as well as relationships to pupils, their parents and the community. In Bertila's practice group in Bern, for example, we see the care given to helping novice teachers plan for their first and subsequent formal and informal meetings with parents. In New Zealand, Sarah and the other first-year teachers in her school receive specific advice from their Advice and Guidance head on how to write progress reports for pupils and their parents.

In some countries (e.g. Japan and France), union membership or professional subject association activities also are important. In France, some branches of the mathematics teachers' association APMEP organize activities for 'new' teachers, including those teachers returning to their 'home' Academy following their initial assignment(s) in another part of the country. Enculturation can also include learning the norms for continuing teacher development, such as a certain percentage of compensated time to be invested by all Swiss teachers in professional development.

Learning to teach as cultural activity

While we did find similarities in induction goals across the cases, which speak to induction's particular qualities and needs, we also found important differences. Just as Stigler and Hiebert (1999) argue for recognizing the powerful ways in which teaching may reflect 'cultural scripts', our analyses suggest that learning to teach is likewise a cultural practice. Induction is very much determined locally.

How the induction phase is defined (for example, literally, for how long a beginning teacher is deemed to be 'new'), what various markers of the transition to 'full' teacher status are, what the 'problem' of induction is framed to be and what the goals for teaching are – these are all culturally defined. Similarly, the forms that get drawn on to provide or embody this 'induction' are themselves culturally created: coffee breaks and department meetings in New Zealand, 'public' lessons in Shanghai, the professional memoir seminars in France. Consider, for example, the different emphases of the Swiss and Shanghai induction programs.

In Switzerland, the choice to work with a counselor is the novice's. In fact, privacy and confidentiality are seen as important dimensions to the development of the beginner. Feedback on classroom observations is provided only when requested and is carefully designed to support the teacher. Even though collegiality among teachers is encouraged, running throughout the Swiss stories are assumptions about individuality and autonomy within the development of a school community.

These contrast notably with the collectivist orientation towards teaching which imbues induction in Shanghai. New teachers there, in being asked to teach a 'public' lesson, are being asked something that any teacher would be expected to do: in that, there is continuity. That others get to see your practice is, thus, not a marker of novice status, a marker of still becoming – on the contrary, it is a mark of being a teacher. While the specifics are tailored to meet the needs and possibilities of the beginner, the assumption that all teaching is public – and can and should be shared and discussed – is widely held in schools. In fact, the 'public' lesson is not solely for the benefit of the individual beginning teacher who is teaching it, but can support the learning of others as well – especially other young teachers. But it additionally provides opportunities for learning how to make and render a public critique of another's practice.

Thus, induction practices hint at significant cultural differences in how teaching is defined – here, as an inherently public or private practice. In France, Switzerland and New Zealand, regardless of cultural norms of collegiality, teaching is essentially understood as a private domain. One may create one's own *cours*, as many French teachers do (or at least claim to do), or work closely with departmental colleagues to develop curriculum plans, as in New Zealand. But the act of teaching in these settings involves teachers typically shutting their doors behind them, working within their own rooms (even if that room is only theirs for some portion of each day). In France, this is seen as aligned with the first of the three national canons: liberty, equality and fraternity.

Collegial talk and peer observation may be present, but often in ways that reinforce the novice's distinct status. Novices have opportunities to learn about teaching through talking and sharing resources and in each of these sites they have opportunities to work with a mentor. Switzerland also provides opportunities for mutual observation by and of more experienced teachers. Nonetheless, there is not the widespread assumption, nor conventional practice, of practicing teachers observing each other. [4] This private orientation towards the act of teaching not surprisingly shapes what novices are inducted into. For example, in New Zealand, it is more common for novices to be observed by a mentor or advisor, rather than observe that mentor or other experienced teachers. While novices are observed, a marker of their different status as beginners, the experienced teacher is not, or is to be observed chiefly by novices, looking on the experienced teacher as a teacher of teachers. In all three countries, observation is connected to a phase of learning and the beginner's peripheral and often provisional status within the profession.

However, in Japan and Shanghai, teaching itself is viewed as a public activity, open to scrutiny by many. Induction welcomes the beginner into that process and practice. In Shanghai, this is reflected in induction strategies for beginning teachers which include many regular opportunities for novice teachers to observe their peers, their mentors and other teachers in their school, as well as in other schools. No special arrangements need to be made, for schools and teaching are organized to allow for such open observations. In fact, it marks them as a teacher that they are allowed to attend. Similarly, demonstration lessons are given both by novice and experienced teachers; these are followed by debriefing sessions, where the observers collectively but supportively critique the lesson plan, instructional techniques and successes or failures of the lesson. In addition, teaching competitions for new teachers (which parallel the larger teaching competitions among more experienced teachers) train beginners to discuss and demonstrate their approaches to instruction to outsiders. Induction in both Shanghai and Japan foreshadows a public-ness about teaching that persists long after a probationer gains permanent teaching status. But it also reflects the notion of a special induction phase, in that there are different foci, criteria and expectations for 'new' teachers taking part in these events.

Our data suggest that the way teaching is viewed along some continuum of public–private affects the purposes and approaches of induction. But this continuum is only one aspect reflecting the broader, cultural assumptions about the nature of teaching. Subject-matter cultures also shape induction, with France and Shanghai providing especially clear instances. As noted, in France, the cultural primacy of mathematics positions it at the center of most of the induction activity for beginning secondary mathematics teachers. Furthermore, an approach to mathematics education which gives prominence to *didactique* leads to a corresponding emphasis on this in some Academy induction programs. In Shanghai, the dominant version of mathematics education, even in the face of reform, lays special emphasis on the curricular building blocks of 'important' and 'difficult' points. Engaging with these distinctions thus becomes central to the work of induction.

For New Zealand science teachers, the subject-matter shift to integrated science makes it important for beginning teachers to have assistance in thinking through the teaching of this 'subject'. While New Zealand's induction has a relatively weak subject-matter focus when compared with either France or Shanghai, it does nevertheless attend directly to this dimension of learning to teach. And it is worth noting that the combination of science teachers traditionally working without a textbook, in a strongly 'hands-on' science culture with a broad range of required scientific knowledge (in grades eight and nine) places a particular burden on new science teachers in New Zealand.

Similarly, cultural approaches to professions generally influence what induction into teaching entails. In both Switzerland and France, general notions of professional practice – such as the preparation of a memoir – affect what comes to be expected of the beginning teacher. In short, culture powerfully shapes not only what induction is but, more fundamentally, both *why* it is seen as important and *what* newcomers are being introduced to. It helps both define the 'problem' of induction and significantly serves to determine how that problem is approached.

2. Whom Does Induction Serve?
Who Is (or Gets to Be) a New Teacher?

Asking *why* induction exists helps us recognize crucial aspects of learning to teach and its inherently cultural nature. Asking about those who are defined to be beginning teachers helps us understand *who* is to be served by the induction system.

What is a 'beginner'?

Why ask this question? Surely induction, by its very nature, has an obvious target? The range of responses in France, Switzerland, Shanghai, Japan and New Zealand suggests just the opposite. In fact, in several countries, 'beginning' teachers are not necessarily 'new' to the profession. [5] These definitions vary by place and help us understand how even the concept of 'beginning teacher' is socially constructed. The story of France points up complications in making clear distinctions between pre-service, induction and in-service education. It suggests that we should not assume that 'initial' *formation* is necessarily 'pre-service', that 'in-service' is the same as 'continuing' *formation* or that there is such a clean boundary between them.

Why, in a particular context, are such distinctions made? What does this imply about deeper assumptions about the profession, about entering it and about learning the practice of teaching? Consider, for example, when a person is deemed to be a beginning teacher versus a teacher in preparation. Very wide differences among countries' educational systems make it impossible to craft internationally consistent definitions of when a person is one rather than the other. However, for all our sites, we can at least say that all the formal subject-matter preparation that teachers will undergo occurs prior to assuming a teaching position.

But if one looks at *when* teachers learn *how* to teach school mathematics and science (pedagogical content knowledge), commonality vanishes. In New Zealand and Switzerland, formal learning of subject-specific teaching methods is completed during teacher preparation. In Shanghai, it begins there but continues intensively on the job, while in France and Japan, most of such learning takes place while also teaching, by means of organized programs or activities – though in France, much of such learning is not primarily in the school, the site of actual practice.

What about practice teaching? New Zealand and Swiss teachers have extensive practice teaching experiences during their preparation. But student teachers in Japan and Shanghai have had only two or eight weeks of practice teaching, respectively. In France, there is very little, if any, school observation let alone teaching practice prior to recruitment as a teacher via the CAPES examination and none prior to the *Agrégation* examination. (For some high in the national recruiting examination hierarchy, such familiarity with schools is considered a distracting irrelevance.)

French first-year teachers, however, spend a third of their time at teacher education institutions while receiving full pay and status as a first-year teacher in the system. Also while receiving full pay, novices in Japan and Shanghai spend about a half day a week in courses run by their school districts and New Zealand teachers are supposed to spend a fifth of their time in school-based professional development programs specifically organized for them. Yet, first-year teachers in all the countries studied are regarded as teachers, although ones with provisional status. However, it is important to remember that in Shanghai first-year teachers, as yet, have no rank, while in France novices are earning a year of seniority (along with its accompanying mobility points) – both of which are retained even in the unlikely event they subsequently have to repeat their *stagiaire* year.

Educational systems differ greatly in when and how they prepare teachers for various aspects of teaching, as our brief discussions of pre-service teacher preparation in these cases suggest. The level of effort of the induction programs studied is explained in part by formal teacher preparation. But educational systems with more comprehensive preparation programs (in New Zealand and Switzerland) recognize that even comprehensive preparation programs cannot fully equip novices for the job. Further on-the-job learning opportunities are provided through induction programs.

Assessment of beginning teachers versus development and support

Closely related to the matter of how societies determine who is consi-dered a new teacher is the issue of selectivity in and for the profession. In our earlier discussion of goals, we noted that one approach systems can take towards induction is to see this as a crucial moment for winnowing out those not suited for teaching. The sites we studied do not see this as a key function of induction, even though in all cases teachers in the induction year(s) are formally considered probationers with respect to permanent certification.

Across the five countries, we observe a range of practices with respect to formal assessment during the first year or two of the novice's teaching and the decision whether this individual should be retained in teaching. In two of them, the maximum number of teachers to be recruited (in France) or certified (in Japan) in a given field in any one year is fixed by the relevant national ministry. For these countries, the decision point comes at the recruitment stage. For other countries, the decision point comes earlier, during an individual's college or university preparation.

315

In France, the CAPES, an almost entirely content-based examination, is the normal acceptance route to becoming a secondary teacher. Only as many are accepted as the national ministry decides in relation to the number of jobs forecast to be available (bearing in mind anticipated numbers from the other two main routes in, the internal CAPES for those already in the civil service and the *agrégation* recruiting examination): hence, the pass mark varies from year to year. However, since teaching is a civil-service job (and therefore very secure), there are currently many more candidates than are accepted (a significant change over the decade since 1991 when the IUFMs were formally created). However, the number of teachers who are actually granted permanent certification is exactly known only at the end of the *stagiaire* year.

In Japan, only as many new teaching licenses are awarded as there are jobs available, as determined by the Ministry of Education (*Monbu-kagakusho*). A license is necessary to enter the teaching profession. Because teaching is an honored and well-rewarded profession, and because the child population has been decreasing in Japan, there usually are many more applicants than needed – up to 10 to 35 times as many as get licensed.

The central planning that characterizes selection to the profession through examinations and licensure in France and Japan is more muted in Shanghai. There, significant selection takes place as one enters the pre-service phase. There is no examination as one moves from pre-service to employment. Once novices enter the teaching profession, the whole emphasis of induction is on helping them succeed in becoming highly skilled teachers, rather than selecting more of them out. Essentially, there are no 'failures', with the very rare exception of an individual who has not met the formal course-taking requirements of the district. [6]

In Switzerland, during the first year of their pre-service education, students must pass a rigorous content exam in their chosen specialty and are evaluated on their early student teaching performance. In one canton's university, one-third of potential candidates were weeded out at this point or chose to leave on their own. In Zurich, novice teachers in lower secondary schools (grades 7–9) are not eligible for a permanent teaching contract until they have completed the mandatory four-week induction course, but there is no formal evaluation of their performance different from that of other teachers in any of the cantons we studied. Induction activities such as practice groups and individual counseling, to the extent that they deal with evaluation, are focused on the novice's own performance appraisal and motivation to stay in the teaching profession. [7]

Clearly, when selection occurs and on what basis varies in each of these sites. In fact, the approaches within sites have also changed over time. The

sites we studied likewise have different attitudes toward combining evaluation with support and development of the beginning teacher, one of the
persistent challenges in designing induction programs and policies. Perhaps
at one end of the spectrum is Switzerland, where induction policies and
procedures have been deliberately separated from the evaluation of teachers. Evaluation is done for all teachers by school board members, who have
no induction responsibilities. Evaluation of the school is done by the
canton's inspectorate.

In clear contrast to that approach is New Zealand, which does not separate evaluation from induction activities at all. The individual most
responsible for providing Advice and Guidance, usually the department
head within the school, also evaluates the novice teacher, as does one of the
administrators (the principal or vice-principal), who may also have some
induction responsibilities. However, it is very rare that beginning teachers,
dubbed 'provisional' during their first two years, are not awarded permanent status at the end of this period. At worst – and this happens very rarely
– they may remain with provisional status for a third year. There are no
examinations required at any stage specifically for entering or remaining in
the teaching profession.

The end of the beginning: induction in the career time-line

When and how one ceases to be a beginning teacher is, of course, formally
a function of the assessment or inspection system created for teachers. But
the analysis of the approaches held by systems within these five countries
speaks to the constructed nature of the teacher career time-line. In some of
these sites, passing from probationary to permanent status marks the end of
the induction phase and moves the teacher into the ranks of all other teachers: New Zealand provides one such example.

In Shanghai, on the other hand, completing induction does not mark
the same end as that experienced by the New Zealand teacher, nor a
launching into the same new beginning. Rather, in a system which sees
'new' (that is, first-year) teachers as formally distinct from a larger category of 'young teachers', permanently certified but who are still early on in
their careers, beginning teachers in induction look forward to entering a
phase quite different from that of their New Zealand counterparts. For
these Shanghai 'young' teachers, continued support, competitions and the
like are seen as needed to support particular learning goals.

Likewise, current institutional discussions in France about continuing
support for 'new teachers' beyond the *stagiaire* year are on-going and
detailed, even if, at the time of writing, there is no formal 'application text'
(texte d'application) from the national Ministry of Education specifying pre-

cisely what is to be done. How this continued support is seen and framed will be interesting in light of the boundaries between 'initial' and 'continuing' education in France (even if the IUFMs are now positioned to be in charge of both).

If, as Feiman-Nemser (2001) has suggested, one sees induction as a Janus-faced doorway looking both backward and forward, opening in or out, it is important to recognize that when new teachers complete induction and what they head towards differ in different settings. These differences have potentially profound effects on the profession in each context, as well as on the nature of induction itself.

As this discussion points out, induction is inherently a definitional activity. It determines who is considered a beginner, when that 'beginning' commences and when the period ends. Our cases demonstrate that there is not a single, obvious answer to these questions, but also that the answer has consequences for the nature of teaching and learning about teaching.

3. What Is Induction? What Is the 'Curriculum of Induction'?

We next turn our attention to a third question, "What is induction?" Each site has, in effect, a *curriculum* vision that links what teachers are to learn – the goals – to activities designed to help them learn. We might then talk about a 'curriculum' of induction to highlight the educative dimension of induction and the thoughtfulness of the approaches we have studied, all of which have learning and growth at their heart. In examining this curriculum, we need to ask about the what, when and how of induction. [8]

What is to be learned?

As the discussion in section 1 of this chapter suggests, there is unusual, broad cross-national agreement about what teachers need to learn in their first several years of teaching, and the help they need to do so. The goals for beginning teacher induction, as enacted in the sites we studied, remind us that learning to teach is complex, demanding and time-consuming. Even in settings like Switzerland, where extensive teacher preparation occurs that provides a solid grounding in both subject specialization and pedagogy, there is the assumption that a beginning teacher, even one with prior classroom experience (e.g. as a substitute teacher) needs opportunities to learn.

What is it that teachers need to learn? Although the specifics, and how they are described, vary by country, the induction goals in the study countries speak loudly to the importance of developing knowledge and skill in:

- effective subject-matter teaching;
- understanding and meeting pupils' needs;
- assessing pupil work and learning;
- reflective and inquiry-oriented practice;
- dealing with parents;
- understanding school organization and participating in the school community;
- understanding self and current status in one's career.

This list reminds us forcefully of the demanding nature of teaching as a practice. Each site, in making these the prominent goals for induction programs, suggests a theory of teacher development: these are matters that cannot be fully mastered in advance of taking on responsibility as a classroom teacher, but at the same time they are aspects of teaching in which novices must gain competence early on in their careers. This implicit claim about induction argues for the need to recognize it as a unique phase in a teacher's career, one that demands energy, attention and support.

Varied practices to support learning

If these are the goals of the induction curriculum, then what are the activities used to achieve these goals? For the most part, they are closely connected to practice: the opportunities to learn *in situ* create possibilities teachers could not otherwise have.

Variation within programs

We saw many and varied practices involved in induction – school-based Advice and Guidance discussions and out-of-school seminars in New Zealand; taking courses at the IUFM and assisting in a second school in France; counseling, observation, seminars and courses, *Standortbestimmungen* and practice groups in Switzerland; a menu of possibilities both in and out of school in Shanghai that includes 'open' lessons, school-level and district-level mentoring, teaching competitions, school orientations, district seminars, subject specific hot-lines, and more.

In fact, variation is seen to be a critical characteristic of the induction curriculum. Beginning teachers, these programs believe, need a range of different approaches – different formats and different teachers – to support the broad range of learning and development required of novices. The degree to which the novice has choice within this range varies, from Switzerland's highly individualized program arrangements to France's approach, where beginning teachers chiefly get to exert overt choice through the topic they select for their memoir. [9]

319

Patterns in the varied practice: locations for action

Even with such variation, we were nonetheless intrigued by patterns in the induction practices we observed. One way to explore this is by analyzing *where* an activity occurs and *with whom*. Much of the induction activity we documented occurs close to the site of beginning teachers' practice. New teachers observe and are observed, mentors and occasionally others discuss individual lessons, teachers are encouraged to talk about particular pupils. Falling within this category are at least three kinds of activities that we found widely across the sites: mentoring, peer-group activity and reflective work.

In every site, there is the opportunity (in most, the requirement) that a beginning teacher work one-on-one with an experienced teacher. Certainly, it is intriguing that the terms used to describe this role vary by site and associated with the terms are different connotations. The words used in Shanghai have a strong lay feel to them – 'guiding teacher', 'old teacher' or 'master' (and they imply a counterpart, one being led, a 'disciple' or a 'new teacher'). France has its pedagogic advisors, with a title that suggests the focus of their work, in contrast to New Zealand's Advice and Guidance advisors, department heads and 'buddy' teachers who together might be seen as taking on different mentor-like roles.

Yet despite the linguistic variation, there is a shared underlying assumption that one does not learn to teach (or become a teacher) alone. Experience helps – and one can tap into that collective experience of the profession through close contact with a more experienced teacher. The experienced other has something unique to offer and intense relationships, born of bringing novice and experienced teachers together, are common.

In addition to the work of mentors, support providers across these cases created regular opportunities for novices to share, discuss, plan, investigate and vent with other beginners. Just as across cases we see the implicit value of experience, we also see that site participants treat induction as an opportunity to develop collegial relationships with peers – in this case, with other novice teachers. In so doing, they are also valuing the trading and sharing of experience of the here-and-now rather than solely relying on situations where novices can contact past experience in the form of 'older' teachers.

Peer observation, peer reflection, joint inquiry projects (such as the French professional memoir which is not only permitted but in some Academies encouraged to be carried out in pairs or even trios) all reinforce this idea. But 'peer support' is structured variously and deployed for quite different ends both within and across cases: peer support is not peer support is not peer support.

The Swiss practice groups offer perhaps the clearest example of the attention and value given to such connections (adult learners as problem solvers), with a strong counseling focus. In New Zealand, the school-based Advice and Guidance meetings, one of that setting's key induction practices, provides a peer forum, while regional Advisory Service meetings serve broader groups of novices beyond beginning teachers from within a single school. These horizontal relationships matter, but in order to have them serve institutional ends, these groups are all facilitated.

But also recall the comment by one French beginning teacher about the importance of 'the tribe' (who gather regularly at the IUFM during the *stagiaire* year for both facilitated and unfacilitated contact). After the induction year, it was drawing on these informal contacts for support that seemed attractive to these *stagiaires*, rather than making use of the possibility of a new pedagogic advisor in the Academy to which they were moving.

A final activity close to the classroom focuses on reflecting, inquiring, researching self and others. At several sites, leaders and support providers also expect that beginning teachers are developing a reflective stance, personally and/or professionally. The *Standortbestimmung* undertaken in Switzerland exemplifies the importance Swiss educators give to the personal in teacher development. The professional memoir typifies the French interest in teachers developing analytical and reflective skills which they can bring to bear on aspects of their own emerging practice, including – in the case of mathematics – task design and the use of pedagogic resources.

Learning outside one's own classroom is a second major locus of activity. Even though in all sites beginning teachers can take part in activities that center on their classroom and school (such as work with a mentor), each system also provides opportunities for beginners to participate in activities out of school: regularly visiting another teacher's classroom through the 'accompanied practice' as well as the IUFM-based work and the memoir in France, the occasional seminar in New Zealand, the practice group in Lucerne, even as far-ranging as the teacher cruise ship in Japan. This pattern raises interesting questions about the locus of knowledge that most supports teacher learning early in the career. Clearly, schools provide foundations as sites for learning, but the approaches of these systems seem also to suggest that learning need not be restricted, and in fact can be amplified, by participating out of one's main teaching context.

Location is not all: we must also consider learning over time. Using the lens of curriculum to take seriously induction as a process of learning, what about the timing and sequence of opportunities. The case studies suggest induction takes time for making necessary arrangements, establishing relationships, linking beginning teachers to effective instructional practices and curriculum, and more. Supports for teachers and accompanying opportunities for teacher learning in their early years are neither easily nor quickly offered.

We note both a frequency and intensity in induction activities in each setting. The total number of hours is significant: Shanghai beginners are committed to a minimum of 100 hours of induction activity, although we consistently observed novices engaged in more intensive induction. French first-year mathematics teachers, one could argue, have their entire week arranged to support induction – with a day and a half at the IUFM, solo teaching of a single class in one school throughout the entire year, developing and presenting a professional memoir, and supporting and observing weekly at another school (for some twelve weeks in a block during the year). Weekly AG meetings, coupled with a range of other activities, constitute 20 percent of a beginning teacher's schedule in New Zealand – all focused on supporting the beginner – in intent, if not always in practice.

In Japan, the out-of-school induction component alone involves ninety days. Even in Switzerland, where choices made by the beginning teachers create what we might think of as individualized programs of induction, the time commitments are still great, regardless of the teacher's decisions: twenty-four hours, for example, devoted just to practice group sessions, up to thirty-five hours of counseling or a four-week course in Zurich, not to mention the longer list of options new teachers have when seeking professional support and development.

Just as important, perhaps, is that any single activity is, for the most part, a sustained one. Working with a mentor, constructing a professional memoir, participating in a practice group all involve repeated interactions over a substantial period of time, where there is the opportunity to develop relationships, dig into a topic, consider alternative views and gather and explore data. Finally, we hope it is clear how centrally important time when not teaching as well as time when teaching is as an enabling condition for induction and the teacher learning that is at its heart.

Substantive foci: activities with an educational purpose

One danger in simply listing induction goals is that the *form* of the activity appears to be the important thing. But the actual substance of these activities, diverse as they are, is significant. Induction – in whichever case – encouraged beginning teachers to think deeply, often collectively, about specific aspects of teaching.

Novices engaged with hard issues they faced in their own classrooms: the challenges of planning, the design of pedagogic tasks, the management of educational settings for learning, the dilemmas of assessment, and so on. Induction created opportunities for teachers early in their careers to work in targeted ways on elements of their own practice, broadly conceived.

The focus of the activities demonstrates the complexity of teaching, whether it is consistently on mathematics instruction, as is so much the case in France, or more wide-ranging, as in New Zealand. The practice group in Switzerland, as discussed in the guiding document Dossier 40A (EDK, 1996), illustrates this particularly clearly. There the assumption is that what needs to be worked on – that is, the focus for induction – arises from practice. The problems of practice are rich ones and the challenges for the beginner are both unique and acute.

Such an assessment of the requirements of beginners, when combined with assumptions about teaching as a complex practice, means that the focus of induction is less one of sharing techniques and more one of encouraging problem solving as a necessary skill for teachers. The wide-ranging conversation, reflection and guided discussion at the heart of the Swiss practice group foster this skill. Not surprisingly, the induction programs we observed were thus themselves complex, both in the individual activities and in their combination.

This complexity also raises one of the challenges associated with induction. Induction can be seen as a process of enculturation into a practice. It brings newcomers into an established community. Yet induction is not only about reproducing existing practice. As the France case vividly portrays, it also has the possibility of creating a new version of the profession. Induction systems need to establish an appropriate balance between supporting new teachers' entry into an established community with conventional practices and helping them develop new kinds of teaching that advance pupil learning more effectively – not an easy feat.

Going beyond formal policy

In each site, induction, as experienced by the beginning teachers themselves, comprises far more than the formal activities mandated by policy. Induction from these novices' perspectives benefits from a combination of informal interactions, sometimes made possible through special induction structures (such as the creation of a cohort group under the auspices of the IUFM in France).

Informal interaction also occurs independently of induction program activity (as in the case of the New Zealand coffee breaks, staff interactions in the science preparation rooms in Switzerland or at lunch and other breaks during the IUFM-based days in France). In other cases, informal connections even continue after the induction period or program has formally ended, as in the continuation of a practice group in Switzerland on the teachers' own time after the induction year.

4. Who Provides the Needed Knowledge and Activities? Whose Knowledge Is It? Where Does It Reside?

By asserting that induction is fundamentally about learning particular kinds of knowledge and acquiring certain skills at a particular point in a teacher's career, we have to confront the problem of who can provide this knowledge. Where is the knowledge that new teachers are to acquire? Such a question is a transformation of the more common attention (at least in North America) to delineating the roles and responsibilities of participants in induction. We need to get beyond a superficial concern about roles to recognize the inevitable tensions and complexity that lie at the heart of the induction enterprise.

Each of the studied sites aims to tackle ambitious induction challenges required of teachers, including engaging with learning tasks that involve a high level of effort, such as deepening novices' pedagogical content knowledge. These challenges therefore draw on varied types of knowledge, coming from multiple providers and shared or developed through a broad range of activities. Because these settings argue that induction involves going *beyond* support (Feiman-Nemser *et al.*, 1999b), such complexity is a given.

Induction offers a particular challenge, one which entails a transition from university to K–12 schools and from being a student to being a professional or civil servant. This means that any induction program has to deal with the issue of multiple institutions (universities, schools, etc.) and multiple actors (mathematicians, teacher educators, administrators, teachers, parents, pupils, etc.). Since the purposes and cultures of these institutions and groups are at times so very different, one default would be to leave the transition to individual novice teachers and let them grapple with how to make it. This transition and emergence of teacher identity is in sharp focus in France, due to the fact that it takes a full year, with switches in and out of these different positions every single week. In other settings, this transition happens at a particular moment. Blanchard-Laville (2000a) has written of the *stagiaire's* uncomfortable psychic position of being the 'in-between' (*l'entre-deux*) as being highly significant in the *formation* of French teachers.

But the sites also illustrate what happens when policies and programs try to stitch something together to make that transition more seamless. Below we ask about the kinds of providers who hold the knowledge deemed vital for novices and who support them in developing it in themselves. Who are induction providers and where are they located? What sort of system allows them, collectively, to contribute to the learning of their beginning teachers?

Multiple providers

The range of goals each site aims to achieve requires complex and sophisticated knowledge, housed in different locations. In each system, beginning teachers interact with several kinds of professionals who employ a wide variety of activities. The systems cannot charge one person with all the induction activities to be carried out, because no single individual could have the range of experiences, expertise and personal qualities required for addressing everything a beginning teacher requires (or is deemed to require). Therefore, multiple providers are necessary. And it is worth recalling that in virtually each case, individuals and institutions not specifically targeted at the first-year teacher provide additional support for the beginners' learning.

Induction in each system assumes that the knowledge needed is close to the classroom, arising from practice. There was variation, even within a site, in terms of grounds for selecting support providers. Knowledge of the subject matter, expertise in teaching or an ability to communicate professional understandings figured in many cases. But regardless of the selection criteria, providers always included either current practitioners (as mentors, pedagogic advisors, Advice and Guidance co-ordinators, buddy teachers) or leaders deeply grounded in classroom teaching, with some themselves still engaged in teaching part-time.

But knowledge for beginning teachers is not only seen as craft knowledge, passable from teacher to teacher, but as a theoretically informed body of understanding – for example, of adult learning (such as in Switzerland) or *didactique* (as in France). As one Shanghai district provider explained:

> I help them [new teachers] use theoretical knowledge of education and psychology for them to see its relevance to these problems. Many new teachers [...] don't know how to reflect on their teaching. And if you can't reflect, you can't improve. And without that, they lose the resources they need to make headway.

The knowledge seen as needed across all the sites combines this breadth of close understanding of the particulars of classrooms, pupils and instruction with equally clear insight into general principles, abstract concepts and analytic lenses for teaching. This range of knowledge is almost inevitably located in different individuals and institutions.

Delicate balance of providers

Thus induction requires many participants. The detailed specification of who is involved in induction is, in fact, a sometimes controversial issue, since it touches on questions of authority and expertise. The debates over the status of the IUFMs in France represent one such instance of this, as do the controversies over the Colleges of Education in Shanghai. In each setting, there has had to be a working out (often a continual one) of agreements about whose knowledge is the relevant knowledge for beginning teachers. In some settings, such as Switzerland, those engaged in induction bring expertise not simply as teachers, but as individuals whose authority comes from special training, as didacticians, practice group leaders, supervising (or monitoring) teachers, and so on.

Induction entails a unique dance between theory and practice. It must be grounded in practice, yet it requires (so say its advocates in these sites) the perspective of research away from immediate practice, which allows formulation and discussion of general principles, theories and abstractions. Hence, as we noted earlier, induction activities occur in many sites, in and out of school. Each of the case chapters illustrates how these activities involve not only experienced teachers in schools, but those in universities, colleges, district offices, special institutions and elsewhere who can offer a different perspective. They are in a position to share knowledge and facilitate conversation and insights that might not otherwise occur, given the press of teaching, the 'clamour of immediacy' mentioned earlier, especially in the beginning years.

Yet, when it works, this very mix, this elegant dance relies on a balance among participants, who need to recognize the limits of their own contribution and the benefits of the contributions of others. Not surprisingly, in some of our cases, we heard stories of the delicacy of these arrangements. Even when induction works well, participants may not equally value the contribution of others. But neither does it work in some idealized fashion. Instead, politics, history and economics may render more vulnerable the position of some participating in this dance.

Consider the debate in France about the degree of *didactique des mathématiques* to be included in *formation* and whether it is appropriate to be teaching this analytic knowledge explicitly to beginning mathematics teachers. A somewhat similar dilemma occurs for teaching research staff at the district level in Shanghai, who see themselves trying to support new teachers in recognizing the importance of having a teacher–researcher stance in relation to their practice. These district providers see themselves somehow caught between the schools and the universities, seen as too distant from the one and not sufficiently research-oriented by the other.

These are not new issues in Shanghai, but as reforms have moved the rest of professional development increasingly into higher education, such delicate relationships are more tenuous. Finally, France's history with induction demonstrates the complexity of having generations of teachers (and participants and providers in induction) with very different personal experience of and assumptions about how one becomes a teacher and therefore what kinds of shaping support are needed.

Thus, we see that creating induction programs is not solely about defining the relevant knowledge for new teachers and ascertaining who holds that knowledge. There is also an institutional question: how does this knowledge get located institutionally? In some of the cases, sites have created distinct units (housed in free-standing institutions) whose responsibility it is to provide induction: Switzerland offers perhaps the best example of this. In others, induction is added to the existing work of institutions: New Zealand's induction rests heavily on the work of local schools. The variation we saw in the seriousness of effort given to school Advice and Guidance plans and their implementation may well reflect tensions in schools, when this added responsibility cannot be undertaken with sufficient energy or resources.

5. Induction as Complex Systems: Articulation and Co-ordination

Despite the variation in the cases, it is clear that induction is not simply the provision of a single activity, offered by one individual or one institution. This is not, for example, induction understood simply as mentoring. Induction in each of these sites must be seen not so much as a practice but rather as a system. As one of our project advisors, Gary Sykes, commented:

> What is notable is that these places have sophisticated, multi-faceted induction. Their depth, complexity and variety are startling. Policymakers in countries with less ambitious induction view it as a single, isolated practice or program, instead of the systems seen here.

With so many professionals involved in developing beginning teachers, the induction systems have designs that delineate the roles of different induction providers (articulation) and schedule activities in a systematic way (co-ordination). All systems at least specify clearly the contributions of different participants and some of the systems actively co-ordinate the activities, as in the case of the Advice and Guidance co-ordinators in New Zealand schools.

Policies as funded mandates

The complexity of these systems is supported by policy that is robust and authoritative. The national or regional levels of these induction systems have established requirements and provided the resources needed to carry them out. In several cases, these systems started at the top. The national or state government forcefully launched the system in relatively short order. But the governments also set flexible policies, leaving it to other levels of the system to flesh out most details.

All of these changes came with some resources or required lower jurisdictions to do something that meant they would have to allocate resources. France's system places some of the costs for induction in the relatively-recently created IUFMs, but also requires Academies to locate two placements for each new teacher and at the same time funds these new, part-time (in the classroom) teachers as full-time civil servants, as full-time teachers. Japan mandates prefectures to provide in-service events and courses, provides a reduced load for beginning teachers and funds guiding teachers. Shanghai's Municipal Education Commission created an induction plan that requires contributions and resources – time and personnel – from both schools and districts. Switzerland's induction creates courses, counseling on demand and practice groups, specially designed for new teachers, that address problems arising from the novices' classroom experiences.

In none of these sites is induction something that was created *ad hoc*, haphazardly or entirely from the grassroots. Even in places where the genesis of the current induction program originated with visionaries (like the Vogels in Lucerne) or in some long-standing local practices (as in Shanghai), high-level support, structural commitments and resources were instrumental in induction becoming institutionalized as it is today in each of these sites.

Japan, arguably the best-known of induction systems internationally, experimented as early as the 1960s with school boards attempting to offer programs for first-year teachers. But these early efforts were not system-wide, nor monitored for quality or content. The program as it is known today only really took hold once the Ministry of Education launched a pilot program, developed alternative models and argued for a commitment nationwide.

Moreover, in none of these sites is induction seen as a resource-free activity. Most major induction providers in the system have some kind of support for what they do, rather than simply being required to add another function to their existing workload. This means that induction becomes (or is) a part of their teaching, not extra to it. (In Switzerland, some providers do this work full-time and are paid for it full-time.) The same is true for novices: induction is, in fact, part of the core, remunerated work-load of beginning teachers.

For beginning teachers in France and New Zealand, a lightened teaching load creates space for induction activities. It is a fully-paid part of their job as a new teacher, not something additional to it. (Swiss novice teachers

328

are granted only a small percentage of time for their induction activities and, for Shanghai teachers, induction is part of their job but also on top of their already full-time job.) Induction is not just a period of time, but a process of learning during a specific phase of their teaching – part of *being* a new teacher.

Involving every level of the educational system

Just as salient as the presence of high-level support for induction is the way, in each of these sites, that induction as a system involves multiple levels. Every level of the educational system actively addresses induction. At a minimum, each level sets policies that foster induction, rather than impede it. Each site also has multiple levels actively involved in providing induction. Recall Figure 6 from Chapter 2 (p. 70) that depicts the three levels (municipal, district and school) which interact with an individual teacher's induction. Switzerland's Dossier 40A recommends, "Three parties should carry some responsibility: the school, the teacher training institution and institutions for continuing education" (EDK, 1996, p. 103). Programs form a coherent and co-ordinated system, using multiple strategies and activities that are well articulated. Optimally, a clear division of labor and co-ordination of effort exists among multiple providers across different levels of the system.

Dynamic systems and their accompanying challenges

Although some of these systems started relatively quickly, within only one to three years from passage of a policy, they have had to change in order to adapt to changes in education during the 10–25 years they have been institutionalized. New Zealand's history, one of the longer of those featured in this book, demonstrates ways in which induction programs can change. Similarly, the gradual development of Japan's program since initial discussions in the 1960s and early 1970s suggests that creating induction programs takes time. Designing and implementing a comprehensive induction program is not something that can be done well quickly.

This dynamic characteristic of induction programs is particularly clear across the three Swiss cantons we studied, for each has developed along somewhat different time-lines, creating its own constellation of specific practices. In Lucerne, for example, the practice group first became established for elementary school teachers but is now mandatory for all lower secondary teachers as well, and strongly recommended for upper secondary teachers. And as schools assume more responsibility for induction activities, including mutual classroom observations, the practice groups are able to cut back on some of the logistically more complicated activities. This enables them to concentrate on the critical aspects of the group meetings, including the capstone group *Standortbestimmung*. In both Zurich and Bern, the emphasis of the induction program has shifted over the last five years from supervision and evaluation of novice teachers to guiding and counseling on demand.

One of the challenges facing induction is the need to balance the desirable goal of it having some stability and institutional strength with an equally important commitment to responsiveness and adaptability. For induction to work as a system, rather than as an always-changing collection of *ad hoc* practices, it must work through institutions which commit some energy and human resources to it: that requires time. Moreover, for induction to serve the learning of teachers, as well as the broader demands of the profession and the schools, it must regularly reinvent itself, potentially redefine its goals and reshape its practices.

We see this challenge in the ways in which induction has worked out in some of the sites. Shanghai, for instance, has established an impressive institutional machinery to support induction. Yet there is the danger, as those in Shanghai described to us, that professional development generally, as it has moved to a mandated, modular approach, becomes something teachers *have* to do, rather than *want* to do.

The pieces of the modular puzzle which make up Shanghai's induction system are not all equally vibrant in each community, district or school. There is certainly the possibility that the beautiful grid which lays out an articulated system for induction – and helps give it its systematic qualities – may have cells within it that are more formal than real or rich with learning possibilities for the novice.

We have argued throughout this book that practices cannot be understood separately from their cultural contexts. Indeed, induction rests not only on a system of policies and structures which support a given set of practices, but also on an enabling context that make it possible. Shanghai, once again, offers a good example. There, the orientation towards viewing teaching as a public act, as well as the collectivist orientation within the society at large, facilitate programs of support for new teachers. In fact, when Shanghai's formal induction policy was created, it codified certain practices that had long been present informally in many schools in the city.

Yet even in places where induction does not emerge organically from long-standing practice, contexts can support needed policy and new practice. France's system of teacher assignment might be one such example. With the goal that beginning teachers have the opportunity to learn and work in their own class, in another class in a different school and in an academic setting, scheduling could be a nightmare. Yet the network of relations and shared goals among the schools, the IUFM, the Academy and the Inspectorate make it possible for this division of time to succeed without leaving *stagiaires* badly caught between the demands of multiple 'teachers'. Both New Zealand's and the Swiss *Gymnasium* laboratory technicians offer another example of aspects of the school context that facilitate induction of beginners into a culture which values 'hands-on' science for pupils.

Not surprisingly, we also saw clear evidence that strong leadership played a vital role in the birth and development of some of the induction systems. For example, Bernard Cornu served on the original 1989 Bancel Commission which led to the establishment of the IUFM system and, in 2000, was one of a committee of two making reform recommendations to the national Ministry of Education. It is not a cultural coincidence that Cornu's own area of expertise is mathematics. In Switzerland, the Vogels, though less politically central, have been philosophical parents of induction, playing as important a role there, as did Cornu in France, in developing a vision of why induction needs to exist, what it should include and how it should be provided.

6. Some Concluding Thoughts

One of the striking things about the word 'induction' is the passive feel that the term suggests. The verb 'to induce' is transitive: either I induce something or I induce someone either to do something or into doing something. But it also raises the possibility of self-induction: I can induct *myself* into something, and to some extent, we argue, this is always the case. Harking back to the opening words of this book, we claimed that induction, at some level, always happens: the new teacher always starts teaching.

Induction practices must be understood not in isolation, but as reflections of a 'philosophy of induction' which any setting necessarily has, even if tacit or only poorly articulated. In the context of teaching mathematics, French mathematician René Thom (1973, p. 204) has claimed, "In fact, whether one wishes it or not, all mathematical pedagogy, even if scarcely coherent, rests on a philosophy of mathematics".

We believe this to be true for induction as well and the cases demonstrate both the power and distinctiveness undergirding the philosophical foundations of each of the systems studied here. It is one core reason why we assert that induction practices can only be understood in context and why we therefore caution against the simple adoption of any specific practice that might be found in this book. As with an iceberg, much of what 'comes with' any particular practice is either poorly visible or completely invisible beneath the surface, stemming from deeply held beliefs and values.

331

Varied technical meanings of the word 'induction'

Especially related to this book's context of mathematics and science teaching, the word 'induction' has a number of differing, specific meanings. Rather than them being seen as interfering or contradictory, however, there is enough of a common core to enrich our view of induction practices in teaching.

Dictionary definitions of *induction* imply it to be a causal, productive process, to produce an effect or outcome. For instance, in a birth context, one can *induce* labor, which in this instance means bringing something about by artificial means. (This suggests that certain deliberate means might be employed to bring about a desired end. Medical usage reminds us, however, that the notion also may contain certain unwished-for ends, e.g. having to treat a stress- or allergy-induced disorder or a doctor fearing surgery might *induce* a heart attack in a patient.)

In electromagnetism, various means can be employed to *induce* an electrical current or a magnetic field. This is usually done by means of simple *proximity* to another body with this characteristic already present (without physical contact), though often other actions need to take place for something to be successfully induced. (This calls to mind bringing a mentor teacher into proximity with a novice, for instance via mutual class observation.)

In mathematics, *induction* refers to a proof technique. It provides a means for 'going beyond' the particular, the specific, and arguing for certainty about what must be the case, even for situations that have yet to be examined directly and specifically. It relies on certain assumptions about the set of whole numbers as an entity, which provide the context for this proof practice. One can argue inductively, but one cannot *induce* in mathematics. What this proof technique produces is knowledge about a situation beyond that which can be directly observed. (This suggests the possibility of teachers gaining an understanding of and confidence in their ability to see beyond the immediate here and now, whether to the future of the specific class in front of them or to other classes yet to come.)

Finally, in chemistry, there is also the term 'induction period', one of whose dictionary definitions is as follows:

> an initial period in some chemical processes (esp. free radical reactions) during which the rate of reaction is very slow. It may be attributed to a variety of causes, e.g. the presence of inhibitors or the dependence of the process upon minimum concentrations of intermediates which must be produced first. (Webster, 1988, p. 494)

(This notion serves for us as a strong reminder that, when it comes to 'assessing the effectiveness' of induction programs anywhere in the world, many of their effects may not yet be detectable, while they may nonetheless still be present and active.)

Tensions: practical and conceptual

At the beginning of this chapter, we noted that it is we who have imposed the category of induction on the systems and practices involved with teaching, teacher development and the production, management and reproduction of teachers and teaching in diverse settings. None of the places we studied actually use the term 'induction'. But, nonetheless, we feel it legitimate to frame their practices using this construct.

Throughout this book, there has been the implicit claim that these are local renderings of a more general phenomenon. However, this runs the risk of doing some violence to the particular practices and the intentions that lie behind them, as well as to the cultural and contextual connections between practice and intention. Yet, there are benefits from taking this perspective as well. In bringing these diverse practices together, we shake up our assumptions of the boundaries of the term – what induction is, who is inducted into what, how, when, by whom and, of course, why.

The cases illustrate that, as we have claimed, induction is inherently complex – both in the content of its work and in the institutional arrangements required to execute that work. The resulting tensions and challenges are not so much solvable as able to be managed (Lampert, 1985). The very complexity of induction – its inevitable connecting of different institutions and resources – adds to the depth of the challenges.

We summarize here the tensions identified and discussed earlier in this chapter. One category relates to *roles and boundaries.* The comprehensive nature of induction that addresses broad goals for teacher learning inevitably requires many participants. But this then raises issues of responsibility, roles and institutional boundaries. A detailed reading of the case chapters reveals a range of ways institutions in specific sites and settings have chosen to address this tension, yet all suggest that this is a tension that cannot be resolved, only managed.

As the IUFMs take on responsibility for providing all continuing education, their role is being transformed. Providing some support beyond the *stagiaire* year may also pull at the French boundary between 'initial' and 'continuing' *formation*. For the Shanghai district providers who feel caught in the middle, neither academic enough to be welcomed by higher education, nor grounded enough in daily practice to be considered a true insider by school people, boundaries are visible.

In Switzerland, recent changes make more obvious the potential faultlines associated with multiple institutions involved in induction. Until recently, the *Seminars* (teacher training 'colleges') had been training the elementary teachers in many cantons. The general idea for the German-speaking cantons is that teacher training will now be done at the professional schools (the *Pädagogischen Hochschulen*) that are affiliated with or housed within universities. [10]

Beside potentially positive effects, we suspect these changes may lead to some deleterious ones as well. For example, this might lead to breaking the close tie between pre-service education and induction we observed in Zurich, where the pre-service Seminar faculty also provide counseling and courses for the beginning elementary teachers whom they had taught as students a year or two earlier.

A second kind of tension we see involves sites in *solving (or at least resolving) the content problem.* The nature of induction, and the focus of much of the learning which is the goal of the process, involves sorting out how (and when and where) learning content and pedagogy and their interaction should be addressed.

This dilemma is managed differently, as our cases demonstrate. Some, like in parts of Switzerland, place virtually the full burden for pedagogical content knowledge preparation on pre-service education, while other places, notably France, make this part of the unique role of the induction phase. In all cases, these are answers that suffice, not solutions, as beginning teachers still must work out in daily practice what it means to teach specific curricular content to their pupils.

A third kind of tension we observed is related to whether induction serves *to preserve the status quo or to help transform teaching, teachers and the profession.* In some sense, systems of induction inevitably try to do both: enculturing new teachers into existing professional communities, while preparing these teachers to be the next generation (often, as for instance with the use of new technology in France, with novice teachers in the vanguard).

Yet, how sites stress one of these goals over the other clearly varies. New Zealand's Advice and Guidance system seems well crafted to support the new teacher's fitting into the schools. In fact, that is one of the overt goals of the program. That contrasts with the ways in which IUFM-based induction for French secondary mathematics teachers is, in effect, starting to re-shape mathematics education, changing both notions of what a teacher needs to know and how one enacts this knowledge.

How these dilemmas are managed has consequences, as our cases illustrate. The choices each site and setting makes for what it values (within the scope for choice that the educational context and its history allow), where it lays its stress and what it ignores play out in myriad ways – for what novices have opportunities to learn, for how much induction can bring together disparate communities, as well as for transforming teaching and/or supporting the *status quo.*

In summary

We end this book with a brief recap of what, for us, are some of the 'important' and 'difficult' points about induction. The cases make clear that induction grows out of and is both shaped and facilitated by its context. But as distinct as each of these contexts is, there is also, as we have argued here, a set of themes that resonate powerfully across these cases. We are, of course, hesitant to generalize from these five cases to other contexts. But we also believe that by considering them together, we can begin to think in new ways about induction and systems that support learning for beginning teachers. Just as our initial questions were transformed by what we saw, heard and experienced, so examining these cases encourages us to see induction in new and multiple ways.

As Feiman-Nemser (2001) has observed, induction can be seen as a phase, not simply a program. As a phase, it brings certain unique needs and opportunities. It is also a period of time, like adolescence, one with boundaries that are socially and culturally constructed, but clearly marked off. Connected to time, it also takes time. We are reminded of the aphorism that 'teaching takes place in time, learning takes place over time'. And induction is centrally about teachers learning *about* teaching while they themselves are engaged *in* teaching.

Induction programs have the fundamental possibility of being about teacher learning, not just teacher 'support' (however that is framed and construed – see Feiman-Nemser *et al.*, 1999b) – or even teacher 'needs' (see Blanchard-Laville, 2000b). There are things that can only be learned once one is fully engaged and responsible within a classroom, whether learned in the classroom itself or by means of taking 'a step back' from that practice. Induction is essentially a process of learning, one connecting learning activities to a complex set of goals.

Induction certainly need not be solely about filling gaps. It should not come from a deficit model of either the novices or the educational system from which they emerged, but from seeing the beginning teacher as both a professional and a learner. Blanchard-Laville (2001) writes of a teacher's 'pupil-self' and 'teacher-self' and the at-times uneasy cohabitation of the two, especially within the beginning teacher. At the same time, induction (and the novice teachers' learning) needs to be understood in terms of the trajectory of what precedes and what follows (Feiman-Nemser, 2001).

For induction to work across a system, it needs to be understood *as a system*. The complex requirements for beginning teachers' learning necessitate the involvement of many different providers, with distinct knowledge and contributions. Their co-ordination supports more productive induction, which in turn requires coherence of policy.

At its foundation, induction has definitions, problems and values. Who beginning teachers are, what they are deemed to 'need' (and who decides), what teaching is – all these serve to determine what 'induction' can become and, partially at least, how it is experienced. But these most fundamental questions and aspirations (and the dilemmas that accompany them) are often left unexamined. Their answers, however, are not predetermined nor limited to a single option. That they are socially constructed leads to induction's complexity but also to the possibility for change.

In spite of its complexity, induction is important to many people. There is concern around the world about this phase of teachers' careers. This book allows us not to find answers, but to re-examine things – not just specific induction practices and policies, but the deep and significant bases upon which they rest. Our hope is that, in any given context, those responsible for induction will find possibilities for responding in new, more creative ways to help their beginning teachers learn what they need to know to help their own pupils learn more effectively.

Acknowledgements

We owe a particular debt of gratitude to Sharon Feiman-Nemser, whose work on conceptualizing and studying induction has considerably shaped our thinking about this chapter, our study more widely and the power of understanding induction as being fundamentally about teacher learning.

Appendix A: Notes on Data Collection

The following brief descriptions of the data collected in each of the five countries discussed in Chapters 2–6 provide further documentation for each case. In each setting, multiple fieldwork trips allowed the research team to gather data from many sources, as well as to benefit from repeated contact with individuals. The schedule of trips also made it possible for interim analysis to occur that informed subsequent data collection.

Our goal of developing rich cases meant that intensive fieldwork, opportunities to verify findings and the commitment to having plural perspectives on induction in that site were present in each case study. At the same time, our orientation towards developing case studies meant that the timing of data collection, the specific locations and types of informants consulted, and the particular activities observed and analyzed necessarily varied with each site. Thus, the details listed below illustrate the case-specific variations in data collection and approaches within the overall framework followed by each of the individual studies.

Data collection in Shanghai

Chapter 2: *Entering a Culture of Teaching* draws on data collected during 1998-2000 in Shanghai. That work took place in four stages, with data collection trips in May 1998, May–June 1999, October 1999 and May–June 2000. Correspondence, telephone interviews and reading of documents preceded each field trip, while analysis followed each and led to refined foci for each subsequent trip.

Preliminary fieldwork began in May 1998. Our interest was in learning about approaches to and new directions in professional development. To that end, Paine spent two weeks in Shanghai in May, 1998, interviewing and observing in schools. She was accompanied for part of the work by Yanping Fang, at that time a researcher at the Shanghai Academy of Educational Sciences. Paine, who speaks Chinese and conducts interviews without translation, had already done extensive study of teaching and teacher education in China and had, previous to this study, worked with colleagues in Shanghai in an international study of mentoring. Fang, a native of China and an experienced researcher at the Shanghai Academy, came with experience in research in different regions of China, as well as work with local Shanghai schools. We interviewed and observed teachers and lessons in six schools; conducted additional focus group interviews of teachers and professional developers from across Shanghai; interviewed education researchers, teacher educators, and administrators at in-service institutes and both teacher education universities; interviewed key municipal education policy people. This preliminary trip helped identify induction issues as part of broader policies related to teacher development and it provided opportunities to meet and interview key policy leaders involved in Shanghai educational reform.

As our induction study formally commenced later that year, we began investigating the possibility of a case in China with exploratory research that involved reading documents, corresponding with knowledgeable insiders in China and Hong Kong, and conducting lengthy and repeated phone interviews with a policy official at the Ministry of Education and a key policy researcher in Shanghai. On the basis of this work, and drawing on the prior 1998 work, we then designed our study in Shanghai.

Three trips of two weeks duration each occurred in May 1999, October 1999 and May 2000, with analysis of data in between that helped us refine our data collection requests. Two researchers (Paine and Fang, Paine and Pimm respectively) conducted work in the first two trips. A team of three researchers (Paine, Chazan and Fang) participated in the third. Pimm and Chazan, both mathematics educators, were involved as part of the project team at Michigan State University and had analyzed translated interview data, examined videotapes and studied preliminary analyses Paine and Fang had developed before they went to to the field. They speak no Chinese, and in Shanghai they worked with and through interpreters who were also mathematics educators, as well as Fang. During each fieldwork trip, some of the interviews and observations would involve all project researchers jointly, while at other times we divided up activities and interviewed or observed alone (or with the assistance of a translator).

In addition to the collective fieldwork, Fang remained on in Shanghai for additional data collection following both the May 1999 and May 2000 trips, conducting an additional month of fieldwork each time. Fang's work included extended observations and interviews in a single school each year, so that she was able to spend four weeks shadowing a small number of teachers each visit, videotaping and audiotaping her interviews and observations, which were subsequently shared with the project team.

The data collection gradually moved from using what might be thought of as a wide-angle lens on teacher development generally, teacher induction and teacher preparation, to an increasingly more focused gaze. We began by trying to learn about the formal policies, the range of induction programs and activities, and the nature of mathematics teaching in schools. While each trip always involved some interviews focusing on policy, mathematics education and the range of induction programs, we were able over time to identify particular practices on which we concentrated some data collection effort.

Thus, as we came to learn about their role in new teacher development, we sought out opportunities to investigate and observe 'open' lessons, lesson preparation groups and teacher research groups, teaching competitions, and district induction and professional development activities. Similarly, as we heard about the importance of curriculum analysis to the development of teachers' knowledge and skills, we developed more targeted interview questions about this work, how teachers learn to do it, and how schools, university teacher education programs, and district induction activities support it. We also sought out curriculum developers to understand their vision of the curriculum and their assumptions about how teachers use and come to understand it.

Over the course of 1999–2000, we interviewed 30 new and young teachers (a category in Shanghai that describes teachers in their first five years of practice), as well as 45 other, experienced teachers who serve as mentors or play other roles pivotal to the life of new teachers and the school. During that time, we observed 29 classes in 21 schools. We also had the opportunity to interview 22 school-level administrators and 39 district-level administrators and professional development providers. While our initial exploratory work exposed us to a wide range of districts, we decided early on to concentrate our data collection on four districts: Pudong, Songjiang, Xuhui and Zhabei. We wanted to concentrate our time in a relatively small number of districts, so that we could get a fuller understanding of how a district deals with induction and to capture some of the range of activities within a single district. With a limited number of districts, we could navigate in ways that allowed us repeated access to the same people and institutions.

We chose these four, after much consultation with insiders in Shanghai education and our own fieldwork in these and other districts, in order to capture some of the range of educational, economic and demographic contexts that inform induction. Over the course of our fieldwork, we were able to make at least two different trips to each of these districts and their Colleges of Education (centers of professional development), and in some cases repeated trips to schools in each of these districts. We were able to observe induction-related and other in-service activities in three districts and interviewed participants about them in each. Each visit also included interviews, many repeatedly, with officials at the Education Commission. In addition, we surveyed 275 teachers from five schools in each of five districts about teaching, teacher development, teachers' work and lives.

We concentrated on learning about induction practices and policies from the perspectives of those most involved – new teachers, those in schools who support them, district personnel and relevant central level officials. But because we knew we needed to understand the intersection of induction policies and programs with the life of middle schools, mathematics teaching and its reform, we also spent time speaking with teachers and administrators not directly involved in induction work but able to help us understand the context in which new teachers are learning and the systems of provision in professional development.

We made repeated visits to the two universities primarily involved in preparing secondary school teachers and providing in-service for experienced teachers, interviewed 20 mathematics faculty and university-based education researchers and observed a few classes. We also benefited from the support of researchers at Shanghai's Academy of Educational Sciences, with whom we met on each visit.

We audiotaped most interviews and videotaped many of the lessons we observed. All interviews were transcribed and through a process of deliberation, individual interviews were chosen for translation. All interviews and observations were written up, with notes shared among the project team, and analytic memos were developed about particular activities, events, and lessons, as well as mini-case studies of individual teachers, mentors and professional developers. We translated key documents – curriculum frameworks and guidelines, teacher reference materials and textbooks, induction policy documents – and developed summaries and pattern analyses of others, especially Chinese and specifically Shanghai research on teaching, mathematics education, school reform and the role of the *banzhuren* (or class director). As a team, we identified particular videotapes, interviews and documents to discuss together; these discussions helped inform the on-going analysis of the broader set of materials, as well as the foci and activity for later field trips.

Our fieldwork was valuably supported by efforts of our Shanghai collaborators to gather documentary materials for us in advance and after individual trips. Schools also provided us with much documentation – including policy statements, mentor/novice agreements, teacher evaluations, videotapes of their teaching or professional development activities and teacher research they had produced. Our analysis was also informed by prior work that both Paine and Fang had conducted separately.

Data Collection in Switzerland

The study on which Chapter 3: *Co-operation, Counseling and Reflective Practice* draws was carried out in three stages: an exploratory field visit of eight days in May/June 1999 three weeks of fieldwork in November 1999 and confirmatory fieldwork of ten days in March 2001. Each visit was followed by an analysis stage, synthesising field notes and writing analytical memos, and discussion by the project principals and staff. In addition, a number of key documents were collected, translated and summarized to feed into the case. These include, among others:

- program descriptions and syllabi for teacher education from several Swiss universities;
- *Teacher Education in Transition* (2000) – a 350-page monograph (No 14 in a series developed by the Lucerne teacher center);
- structures and programs of several centers for continuing teacher education;
- course descriptions and schedules for induction-related offerings by the cantons and teacher centers;
- evaluation reports and data on induction programs in Lucerne and Zurich;
- an inter-cantonal guide to induction policies;
- an individual school induction program from Basel;
- a monograph on the practice group and *Standortbestimmung* in Lucerne;
- the grade K–9 cantonal curriculum guidelines from Bern, St. Gallen and Zurich, including the integrated grade 7–9 science/social issues curriculum;
- the curriculum plan, resources and teaching materials, teaching strategies, and assessment recommendations for *Mensch und Umwelt*, an integrated K–6 science/social issues course in Lucerne;
- the new Lucerne University catalogue – an open university;
- background material for observed didactics classes;
- booklets for beginning teachers (Lucerne);
- a research monograph and reports on Swiss pupil performance in science in TIMSS.

May 31–June 7, 1999: exploratory visit

Based on preliminary telephone conversations, Edward Britton and Senta Raizen (who speaks German and French) visited four German-speaking cantons (Bern, Lucerne, St. Gallen, and Zurich) and one French-speaking canton, Geneva. Individuals interviewed included staff and heads of centers for continuing teacher education, cantonal ministry officials, and staff and faculty in teacher training institutions (both primary and secondary). Raizen also collected information and interviewed university faculty from a fifth German-speaking canton, Aargau.

Mary Ann Huntley then analyzed the information from the exploratory visit to identify key features of teacher education and induction practices in Switzerland. The findings from this analysis and a review of the field notes led to the choice of three cantons, two with well-established but differing induction practices (Lucerne, Zurich) and one with a variety of voluntary programs (Bern). We decided not to do further work in Geneva because of similarities to French practices, which comprise the focus of a separate case study in this book.

November 8–26, 1999: Field Work

Raizen conducted some 45 interviews and observations in the three selected cantons. For most of these, she was accompanied by Christine Wassmer, a bilingual (German/English) graduate student at Bern University, who helped record some of the observations and transcribed many of the recorded interviews. The types of data Raizen collected in Switzerland fall into the following categories.

1. *Observation of didactics courses* (combining content and methods). These courses were for aspiring lower secondary teachers, often with follow-up interviews with the didactics teacher. Didactics classes were observed in Zurich in the following fields: chemistry, conducting demonstrations and experiments; mathematics, teaching eighth-grade algebra; physics, evaluating computer-based lessons; evaluating a grades 7–9 human biology lesson; archaeology, the neolithic age (the Oetztal iceman); nature study, orientation in space.
2. *Observation of other courses.* Mathematics course for upper primary school pupils and student teachers, with a master teacher observing (Zurich); course in "NMM" (*Natur–Mensch–Mitwelt,* i.e. Nature, Man and the Surrounding World) for re-entering or substitute teachers (Bern); intensive course for mentors of *Gymnasium* practice teaching (Bern).
3. *Observations of student teacher practica and beginning teacher classes.* Lower secondary: geometry, pre-algebra, human biology, taught and discussed by master teacher and two student teachers (Zurich); mathematics instruction, fifth grade, beginning teacher (Zurich); math/space instruction, sixth grade, beginning teacher (Zurich); tenth-grade lesson on global warming and greenhouse gases/effect, *Gymnasium*, beginning teacher with mentor observer and post-lesson discussion (Lucerne); biology lesson, ninth grade, *Gymnasium*, beginning teacher (Lucerne); geometry lesson, eighth grade, also eighth grade biology lesson by same beginning teacher, *Gymnasium* (Lucerne); seventh grade biology lesson, student teacher practicum in *Gymnasium* – part of the course for mentors (see above) (Bern).
4. *Interviews with beginning teachers and student teachers.* Two beginning teachers, one in second year, one in third year, grades 7–9, math/geometry; math/science/environment (Zurich); beginning teacher, grades 5–7, (Bern); three upper primary beginning teachers, two observed in classrooms (Zurich); beginning *Gymnasium* teacher, grades 7–9, observed teaching biology and math (see 3. above) (Lucerne); group of student teachers in a mathematical didactics class (Zurich); another group of student teachers (Zurich).

5. *Observation of practice groups.* Counseling with group of beginning teachers (Bern); *Standortbestimmung* with group of beginning teachers (Bern).

6. *Interviews with heads of induction programs, mentors, counselors.* Jacob Manz, Bern, head of induction; René Meier, Zurich, head of lower secondary teacher induction; Claudio Zzing, Zurich, induction and counselor for primary teachers; Werner Schüpbach, Lucerne, head of induction for *Gymnasium* teachers – grades 7–12/13; Monica and Fritz Vogel, with practice group leader Eva Briggeli-Grimm, Lucerne, head and staff for primary and lower secondary (non-*Gymnasium*) teacher induction; Anni Heitzmann, leader of course for *Gymnasium* mentor teachers (see 2. above) (Bern, Aargau); Daniel Räber, *Gymnasium* mentor (Lucerne); Madlena Cavelti, *Gymnasium Prorectorin* (vice-principal) for math/science (Lucerne); *Seminar* teachers and also counselors in charge of induction (Zurich).

7. *Cantonal interaction and general.* Interview with U. Kramer, EDK, Swiss Conference of Cantonal Ministers of Education (Bern); Observation of cross-Canton meeting and decision making (Olten); Interview with Erich Ramseier, Bureau for Educational Research (Bern).

March 11–22, 2001: Confirmatory Field Work

The practice group plays a large part in the induction activities of two of the cantons studied, and they are advocated in Dossier 40A (EDK, 1996) for all cantons. However, the first field work did not allow for sufficient observations of practice groups, and none in Lucerne, where this practice is most mature. Therefore, Raizen revisited Lucerne mainly for observing practice groups and *Standortbestimmung* discussions, and also to conduct more interviews with beginning teachers.

1. *Observation of four practice groups.* Two separate groups with different leaders of beginning middle school teachers, nine participants in each group; a group of eight lower primary beginning teachers; a group of eight grade 5–6 beginning teachers.

2. *Observation of Standortbestimmung (status determination).* Two individual sessions, one with a primary teacher, one with a lower secondary teacher; two sessions as part of two of the practice groups observed as listed in 1. above.

3. *Interviews with beginning teachers (all on an individual basis).* In-depth interviews with two beginning teachers from each of the two middle school practice groups observed (four teachers in total); shorter interviews with three beginning teachers from a third observed group.

4. *Classroom observations.* Ninth-grade biology class taught by beginning teacher, with mentor observation and subsequent mentor feedback and

discussion; seventh-grade science class (a double period to allow for both lecture and lab), lower track (*Realschule*), taught by a science specialist, followed by interview.

5. *Observation of professional development.* Course in *"Mensch und Umwelt"* (Man and the Environment) for teachers re-entering the profession.

6. *Interviews and discussions on induction and teaching conditions.* Several interviews and discussions with Fritz and Monika Vogel and Gabrielle Schorno on practice groups, induction, and professional development in Lucerne; review and comments by Vogels and Schorno on draft of the Swiss case study; attendance at meeting of education officials from Central Swiss cantons on working conditions of teachers.

Data Collection in New Zealand

Chapter 4: *Help in Every Direction* draws on substantial amounts and varied types of data from New Zealand, acquired between 1999 and 2001 over nine person-weeks during three visits. Britton collected data in all visits and was joined by Raizen for the first.

We addressed the heart of the study in the second visit, that is, understanding how schools design induction programs and carry them out. The secondary schools visited were of almost every socio-economic level as designated by the national Ministry of Education, including deciles 1 and 10, and most levels between them. All schools were urban or suburban schools and located in the metropolitan areas of Auckland (8 schools) and Wellington (7 schools). During 4–12 hours at each school, we interviewed 24 beginning teachers: 7 first-year science, 7 first-year mathematics and 10 second-year science. We also interviewed 32 people who supported these new teachers: the 15 primary mentors of the 15 beginning teachers (11 department heads and 4 senior teachers), 10 induction program co-ordinators (Advice and Guidance Co-ordinators, usually assistant principals) and 8 laboratory technicians for science departments. We had informal conversations with dozens of additional faculty and administrators while in the schools.

The central investigation into induction in the second visit was made possible by our first visit, when we delved into national induction policies and determined how to identify schools known to have good induction programs. To understand induction policies, we collected documents from and interviewed staff at the Teacher Registration Board, Ministry of Education and the Post-Primary Teachers' Association (secondary teachers union). Teacher induction specialists at Ministry-funded centers for professional development services in the Auckland and Wellington regions

Visit	Main Research Foci	Major Types of Data
1st	national induction policies	collected documents; interviewed education policy-makers
Apr. 1999	national science curriculum	collected documents; interviewed science education experts
2 weeks	teacher preparation	collected documents; interviewed faculty and observed classes at three institutions
2nd	school induction programs; activities	visited 14 schools recommended as having good induction programs
Oct. 1999		interviewed 24 1st and 2nd year teachers and 32 induction providers
3 weeks		informally interviewed dozens of additional faculty and administrators
3rd	science teaching	observed 15 1st and 2nd year teachers at five schools
May 2001	science department curricula	interviewed faculty, reviewed documents, inspected resources at five schools
2 wceks	regional induction support	observed and surveyed 70 1st year teachers at four regional workshops

identified schools they knew to have good induction programs and arranged schedules for interviewing staff there in our second visit.

We also observed four one-day workshops that these specialists held for beginning science teachers in their regions. We used a questionnaire and informal interviews to ask participants about the induction program at their schools. So, while our visits to the recommended schools shed light on good induction programs, the regional workshop participants gave insights into induction programs of more widely-varying quality, because they came from schools having induction programs that were excellent, poor and in-between.

Also in the first visit, we explored this question: What is New Zealand teacher preparation like, and what are its implications for induction of science teachers? We interviewed a total of 20 faculty and administrators and observed classes for 10 courses (mostly science methods) while spending 3 days at three major teacher preparation institutions: Auckland College of Education, Auckland University, and Wellington College of Education.

In our final research visit, we deepened our understanding of typical teaching in New Zealand, in order to better appreciate the teaching practices and science curriculum into which beginning science teachers are being inducted. In our first visit, we had become familiar with the national science curriculum. In this last visit, we observed 15 science classes taught by 15 teachers at 5 schools of varying sizes and pupil populations. We also examined the course guidelines, curriculum materials and instructional resources that these teachers' science departments made available. Listed below are the types of documents collected and analyzed during the the course of the study.

Induction

- Teacher Registration Board publications;
- secondary teachers' union publications;
- schools' Advice and Guidance program descriptions, course outlines and handouts;
- schools' orientation books for new faculty;
- the MOE's Teacher Performance Management System;
- schools' teacher performance appraisal forms;
- national Advisory Service outlines and handouts for new teacher workshops;
- higher education outlines for courses on supporting beginning teachers.

Teacher preparation

- institutional brochures and program descriptions for secondary teachers;
- course descriptions, applications for admission to secondary program, course outlines, handouts and applications for student teaching;
- student teaching guidelines and forms for evaluating student teaching.

Science curriculum

- national curriculum standards for integrated science, biology, chemistry, physics;
- course outlines, lesson plans and textbooks at science departments;
- science teacher magazines.

After each field visit, we transcribed the interviews, all of which were recorded. Mary Ann Huntley analyzed interviews and we reviewed documents and observation notes to produce analytical memos. Analysis was enriched by gaining the perspectives of all project researchers during one or two meetings held between each data collection. Project researchers and advisors provided feedback on drafts of this chapter.

Data Collection in France

Chapter 5: *Being and Becoming a Mathematics Teacher* draws on data collected 1999–2002 in France. The work took place during four visits: November 1999, March 2000, October, 2000 and March, 2002 totalling a little over one calendar month. Telephone and e-mail communication as well as document reading preceded each trip, while transcription, analysis and extensive discussion followed each return. The first two trips and the last one were undertaken by Pimm alone, who conducted interviews in French, while the third involved Pimm and Chazan, accompanied by Nathalie Sinclair (then a mathematics education doctoral student at Queen's University, Ontario, Canada) in the role of translator for Chazan.

The first visit involved orienting discussions and interviews with a number of mathematics education figures based in IREMs and/or IUFMs, gaining a clearer sense of a national picture as well as identifying and visiting two Academies to explore the possibility of more detailed visits and interviews to take place subsequently. An initial interview was carried out with the director of one IUFM, as well as with the associate director in charge of continuing *formation*. At the other Academy, a presentation regarding the project was made to a cross-disciplinary research group of *formateurs*, as well as preliminary interviews being undertaken with two mathematics *formateurs*. A day was also spent with the group of mathematics *stagiaires* during their disciplinary *formation* day, making observations and fieldnotes and engaging in informal conversations.

In addition, many Ministry of Education documents (such as information about the CAPES recruiting examination or the *collège* national curriculum), mathematics teacher education books (such as Artigue *et al.* (1998) on the professional memoir or Hébert and Tavignot (1998) on extensive *stagiaire* reports on their *stages de pratique accompagnée*), as well as general internal IUFM brochures and material prepared for pre-CAPES students and *stagiaire* teachers were obtained during this initial visit.

The second visit was to a single Academy, designed to fall at the time of the second IUFM *formateur* visits to mathematics PLC2 *stagiaires* in their *stage en responsabilité* classes for a formal lesson observation and follow-up discussion. (Permission for videotaping each lesson was obtained from the individual *stagiaires*, the schools and the IUFM.) Ten such visits were made to both *collège* and *lycée* classes in schools in a variety of locations within the Academy: urban, suburban and rural. Each lesson observation was followed by an hour's discussion with the *stagiaire* (of these six out of the ten pedagogic advisors were also present). These subsequent discussions were predominantly led by the *formateur*, but with Pimm asking a variety of questions towards the end. They were audiotaped with everyone's agreement.

In addition to these school visits, an audiotaped interview was conducted with a mathematics IPR in her office in the *Rectorat*, and another with the director of the IREM of the Academy in its university mathematics department setting, as well as with three other IUFM mathematics *formateurs*. A second disciplinary *formation* day was spent with the group of *stagiaires*, some of whom had additionally been visited in their schools during this visit. The opportunity was also taken during this visit to review a considerable number of previously submitted professional memoirs from the IUFM library, as well as various French mathematics education journals and periodicals (e.g. *Recherches en Didactique des Mathématiques, Repères, Petit x, Grand N* (the *lycée* counterpart to *Petit x*) and the *Bulletin* of the APMEP).

The third visit (Pimm, Chazan and Sinclair) included five days spent in Paris as well as five more at one of the main Academies under study. The Paris part of the visit involved interviews with two *formateurs* at the Paris IUFM, one with the head of the Paris IREM, another with two other *formateurs* from another Academy (who were visiting the IREM), one with a teacher at a Parisian *lycée* and one with an Inspector-General for mathematics.

We also took the opportunity to attend a day meeting of the national *didactique des mathématiques* seminar, at which a number of focused informal conversations were held. Finally, a group of eight ex-*stagiaires* from one of the two focal Academies met with us and their former IUFM *formateur* (who had come to Paris for the *didactique* meeting) to discuss their post-*stagiaire* experience of being a certified teacher teaching mathematics in the outer Paris suburbs. This two-hour discussion was videotaped. Later on in this visit, Pimm and Chazan visited one of the focal Academies for five days, which allowed ten *stagiaires* to be interviewed at the IUFM, either individually or in small groups, as well as a number of professional memoir seminars (held with *stagiaire* pairs) to be observed. We also conducted five interviews with IUFM mathematics *formateurs* (both *enseignant–chercheurs* and *professeurs associés*) and two IUFM directors (one was visiting the other).

The fourth visit was brief (only three days in length) and more opportunistic than planned. Pimm conducted interviews with the *formateur* in charge of the non-disciplinary *formation* half-day for the IUFM and with a new IPR for mathematics (a former *lycée* teacher in the Academy who, the previous year, had been a *stagiaire* Inspector, prior to receiving tenure in this new position). Pimm also made two school observation visits to two ex-*stagiaires* from the previous year who had stayed within the Academy and subsequently interviewed them. Finally, he participated in an APMEP-sponsored afternoon event held at the IREM, welcoming those mathematics teachers new to the Academy. They included teachers with four or five years experience who were returning to the Academy as well as a couple of newly-certified ex-*stagiaires* who had been able to stay within the Academy where they had received their PLC2 *formation*. This occasion took the form of a panel presentation comprising a representative of the regional branch of the APMEP, a mathematics IUFM *formateur*, the director of the IREM and an IPR for mathematics, followed by an informal social.

In general, the data on which Chapter 5 is based took the form of video-taped, audiotaped or hand-written observer records of both events which would have taken place anyway (e.g. the disciplinary day sessions at the IUFM, the class lessons, the post-lesson discussions, the above-mentioned APMEP welcome) and events that were made to occur for the study (most obviously the extensive interviews). In addition, considerable documentary material (e.g. books, journals, brochures, Academy *formation* plans) was collected.

Data Collection in Japan

The prefectures we visited included: Tochigi (north of Tokyo), Chiba (sub-urban Tokyo), Shizuoka (between Tokyo and Nagoya), Hiroshima (in southern Honshu), Kumamoto (on Kyushu island in southern Japan), Miyazaki (also on Kyushu). We visited and discussed the induction program with the following individuals employed in these institutions:

- twelve new teachers from nine public schools in the above-named six different prefectures who were undergoing or had undergone the induction program;
- the guiding teachers assigned to most of these new teachers;
- the principals or vice-principals in charge of overseeing the in-school portion of the induction programs in the nine different schools;
- officials at five prefectural or city in-service centers, in order to discuss their role in the induction program;
- the Monbusho official responsible for the induction program, in order to discuss program goals, procedures and evaluation;
- the Monbusho official who chaired the committee that created the induction program in the late 1980s.

A native speaker of Japanese who was also very familiar with Japanese education to each interview always accompanied us. Questions in the interviews included those which addressed details of the induction program, the assessment of program effectiveness, details related to teaching in Japanese schools (e.g. workload, in-service opportunities), and teachers' general and specific views on teaching (including philosophy of teaching). When possible, we observed the new teachers teach one or more lessons and recorded instructional techniques, pupil activity, pupil reactions to learning tasks and general classroom atmosphere. In order to get a sense of how the new teachers change over time, we visited four of the teachers a second time in either their second or third years of teaching. We also interviewed a successful third-year teacher to get a perspective on how she thought the induction program had contributed to her success. All interviews with officials, new teachers, their principals and guiding teachers were recorded in field notes, which were transcribed, coded, then edited and checked for accuracy with our Japanese education experts. Portions of documents relevant to this study were translated into English at a later date.

The authors of this chapter are not Japanese, but Americans who have spent considerable time in Japan studying science education at various levels. We have visited and traveled about the country on sixteen separate occasions for periods varying from one week to three months over a duration of fifteen years. In addition, we have hosted numerous Japanese educators in our department at the University of Georgia, four of whom have spent sabbatical leave with us ranging from six months up to a year. Some of our research resulted from the three National Science Foundation collaborative research grants in which we participated. We have observed in dozens of schools and read numerous books and journal articles on Japanese culture and education. While our knowledge is incomplete, we are quite familiar with Japanese schooling, traditions and customs.

For this particular project on induction we spent a total of seven weeks in Japan solely focused on learning about induction. We visited schools and talked to individuals who were knowledgeable about the Japanese induction program. The above list describes the places we visited, the types and numbers of individuals we interviewed, the arrangements we made for translation and the types of questions we asked. Despite the methodological and other safeguards and precautions, interpreting both national policy and how it is implemented in various schools is difficult, especially in a country like Japan. Even though we are serious students of Japanese schooling, we are experienced enough to understand the limitations under which we worked (see Tippins, Kemp and Ogura, 2000, for more on these ideas).

First, as with any cross-cultural research, language is a serious barrier. We do not speak Japanese. Though we had very able translators, we are not fully confident that we understood all of the nuances being communicated. Also, in Japanese culture, certain things are not said to visitors. Thus, whether the new teachers and guiding teacher were directly and completely answering our questions needs to be asked. In some cases, they seemed to 'pull their punches': that is, they answered questions with accurate responses, but did not volunteer any problems with the system. Yet, because we visited so many classrooms, in so many parts of the country and had so many different translators (at least six), we have confidence in the descriptions in this chapter.

Appendix B: Swiss Induction Practices by Canton

As depicted in Figure 1 (overleaf), each of the three cantons we studied offers a variety of induction help, but they do so in differing proportions and with varying emphases. We noted that the three cantons are re-examining their pre-service education structures (as are all the German-speaking cantons), particularly at the primary level, but to some extent at the lower secondary level also. This will obviously affect induction programs since, in varying measure, the pre-service education institutions have considerable responsibility for providing induction experiences.

The planned reorganizations also are likely to affect the currently free-standing centers of continuing professional teacher development. It is certain, however, that induction and beginning teacher support services will receive greater rather than lesser emphasis, will become more institutionalized (for example, in Bern) and will continue to shift in emphasis more to advice and assistance rather than evaluation.

Lucerne

This canton has the most comprehensive and mature model of an innovative induction program. It is for beginning teachers at all levels (other cantons' programs often being limited to primary and lower secondary education). The program explicitly rejects a deficit model of beginning teachers. New teachers are assumed to be fully educated and professional. Collaborative work and reflection are the main goals, with the needs of adult learners in mind.

The main vehicle for Lucerne's induction program for teachers of grades K–9 is the required, reflective *practice group,* constituted of five to seven beginning teachers and facilitated by a trained leader. Within this organizational structure, beginning teachers have an opportunity to address problems that arise out of their immediate practice; they also engage in *mutual classroom observations,* discussion of each other's teaching and that of more experienced teachers, and in their own *Standortsbestimmung* ("determining where I stand").

Counseling is available on demand; both the classroom observations and counseling generally involve the practice group leader. Yet another aid consists of a *series of booklets* developed by the induction center and provided free to beginning teachers (see below). *Courses* also are available, but not emphasized for beginning teachers, although practice group counselors are expected to engage in continuing education specific to their responsibilities. The Lucerne program also is accompanied by *yearly evaluations* by

351

	Bern K–9	Lucerne K–9	Lucerne 7–12[1]	Zurich K–9
Practice group	**	***	**	~
Courses	*	*	~	***
Counseling	**	**	X	**
Standort- bestimmung	***	***	***	X
Mentoring	~	**	***	~
Classroom observation[2]	*	***	***	*
Informal support	*	*	**	*
Program evaluation[3]	+	+++	?	++
Mentor/Counselor training[4]	++	+++	+++	++

Legend:

X   unavailable   +   present

~   available, but weak   ++   frequent

*   voluntary, frequently used   +++ extensive

** funded, scheduled at request of beginning teacher(s)

*** obligatory, officially scheduled

[1] *Gymnasium*, grades 7–12.

[2] Classroom observations are part of counseling in Bern and Zurich; part of the practice group in Lucerne, K–6; and part of mentoring in Lucerne, *Gymnasium*.

[3] Lucerne conducts evaluations of its induction programs for K–6 and 7–9 teachers every year. Zurich has carried out research on its induction programs for K–6 teachers. Bern has evaluated its summer planning course.

[4] Obligatory for practice group leaders K–9 in Lucerne and for counselors in Bern; voluntary for *Gymnasium* mentors in Bern and Lucerne; obligatory for practice teaching mentors (grades 7–9) in Zurich.

Figure 1: Overview of induction activities in three cantons

participating beginning teachers and counselors, as well as by the induction staff. Occasional outside evaluations are conducted by external university faculty and graduate students.

At the *Gymnasium* level (which includes grades 7–9), *mentoring* is the main form of support for beginning teachers. Mentors also are expected to take special courses to prepare for this role and to continue honing their mentoring skills.

The Lucerne concept dismisses certification or oversight as a goal for the induction program and emphasizes independence from the educational authorities. Yet there is evaluation of teachers' work, though it is self-evaluation or formative evaluation given in confidence and for the purpose of further development. Though the schools are involved to some extent, especially so at the *Gymnasium* level, the teacher education institutions are not. The Lucerne model expects a lot of novice teachers: in addition to a full teaching load, they are expected to invest time in their practice group – the counterpart to experienced teachers taking further courses or other professional development.

Responsibility for the induction programs rests with special induction staff housed in the canton's free-standing Center for Teacher Professional Development. A whole floor of a large building is devoted to the induction program for K–9 teachers, including an impressive library and media center. The canton supports the Center and staff, as well as substitute teachers for practice-group sessions that meet during school time, including classroom observations.

The following titles are illustrative of the booklets provided free to beginning teachers by the Center for Teacher Professional Development in Lucerne. (Booklets dealing with science are briefly summarized below.) Each booklet is about fifty pages long, amply illustrated with teachers' experiences and pupil comments, and provides many teaching suggestions and other tools for the beginning teacher. The booklets are available to all other teachers by subscription.

- *Transitions* (May, 1994)
  The start of the new school year is addressed.
- *Today is Tomorrow already Yesterday* (1997)
  This booklet deals with the time pressures that beginning teachers experience.
- *Of Angels and Asses* (December, 1998)
  The booklet deals with the spiritual development of children.
- *Forest Time – Experiencing Nature* (April, 1999)
  This booklet contains stories, dances, songs, as well as material for teaching pupils to observe, record and report their findings from excursions to parks, nature preserves, zoos, etc. The various teaching

suggestions are interleaved with discussions of child development and pupils' acquisition of an understanding of their natural surroundings. Art, music, writing and science are integrated.

- *The School as a Just and Caring Community* (October, 1999)
  The booklet deals with school and classroom climate to further effective learning by all group members.
- *The Four Elements: Air, Water, Earth, Fire* (Four booklets: 1995–2000)
  Air discusses weather, weather observation and pollution; it also includes a number of experiments, e.g. on photosynthesis, generating smog, volume and mass of gases, and air as a carrier of balloons and airplanes. There are sections on teaching children how to breathe deeply (which the teacher is shown how to demonstrate) and how to deal with a child with asthma. Relevant poems and songs are interspersed with teaching suggestions. The religious and secular development of the notion of air is treated also. Similarly, *Water* selects from folklore and mythology; natural and environmental science concepts (e.g. the water cycle, distribution of water across the earth's surface, pollution, conservation); art, poetry and song; vocabulary; and crafts to suggest appropriate learning and project activities. *Earth* and *Fire* are treated similarly.
- *How Teachers and Parents Can Work Together* (January, 2000)
- *Humans and Their Environment* (August, 2000)
  This integrated course for grades 1–6 deals with content from the natural sciences and social studies. The themes from the natural sciences include plants/animals/ecology and human effects on the environment, matter and its properties, magnetism and electricity, energy and its transformations, weather, human anatomy, health and nutrition, vision and hearing, pollution and conservation. Connections to the pupils' social surroundings are made. The booklet includes many teaching strategies, from games to pupil investigations and the use of various instruments, pupils' self-evaluation and teacher assessment. Learning to learn is a major objective of the course. Numerous reference sources are provided, as well as transition strategies to the science fields taught in grades 7–9.
- *Expectations and Assessment* (December 2000)
- *Checklist for the Start of School* (Spring 2001)

Zurich

Induction has also long been institutionalized in Zurich. Historically, there are two origins to the program. First is the concept that induction is part of a teacher's initial preparation; teachers do not get final certification until after two years of actual teaching practice and induction activities. Second, since the canton has a lay inspectorate, the responsibility for induction has traditionally rested with the teacher education institutions, which employ the advisors charged with induction. In the past, these advisors played the same role as official inspectors in other cantons, since they also had responsibility for evaluating both novice and experienced teachers. The advisors experienced constant tension between evaluating the beginning teachers and assisting them, particularly since they were charged with making final judgements on the novice teachers after the two-year induction period. Partly as a result of this tension, the counseling and support functions have by now been completely separated from the evaluative function.

The main component of the current induction program is the *obligatory four-week course* (three weeks for primary teachers) to be taken toward the end of the beginning teacher's second year of teaching. Also available is *voluntary counseling* (in place of the previous obligatory classroom observation and evaluation by the advisor), which is provided when requested by the beginning teacher. Both the course and the counseling are supported by the canton: formation of and participation in practice/reflection groups is optional.

Similar to the induction services for primary school teachers, which are lodged in the *Seminar* that also provides their pre-service education, the Zurich office responsible for induction of middle-school teachers is located in the same K–9 school that also provides the didactics courses for prospective middle-school teachers. The individual responsible for induction is part of this school's leadership team. (The induction responsibilities make up 50 percent of his job, taking up 11 periods or 22 hours; he teaches *Sportsdidactics* for the other half of his job.)

Currently, the counselors are much concerned with improving their own competence in giving advice, since continuing development of novice teachers is one of their main responsibilities. Because the counselors are so tightly linked to the beginning teachers' pre-service institutions, a striking feature of the Zurich program is that the induction activities are closely coupled to the teachers' pre-service experiences and that essentially the same 'language' is spoken both in pre-service and in induction.

Bern

As yet, Bern does not have any institutionalized induction programs. Responsibility for induction rests with specially designated staff within the canton's free-standing Center for Continuing Professional Teacher Development. Although to date the Bern induction programs are largely voluntary, the legislatively mandated program is to start in 2004, with responsibility split three ways: preparatory institutions are to provide 60 hours; the schools employing the beginning teachers are to provide 60 hours; the professional development institutions in the canton are to provide 60 hours.

At this time, Bern offers voluntary *practice groups* facilitated by trained counselors, *individual counseling* when requested by the beginning teacher and an individual (or small-group) *Standortbestimmung* for every beginning teacher, all largely subsidized by the canton. A number of *courses* also are available at no or low cost to beginning teachers, particularly the popular summer course to plan for the following year of instruction. There is disagreement, however, whether certain activities ought to be mandated or whether beginning teachers, like their senior colleagues, should simply select activities most meaningful to them using their five percent allocation of professional development time, in addition to choosing from the various activities financed by the canton. However, the canton is concerned about the costs of professional development in general and the need to raise more money as the demand grows: for example, by charging teachers Sw. Fr. 100 (US $60) for a one-week course.

Appendix C: The French *Mémoire Professionel*

This appendix offers a translation of one Academy's detailed advice to its *stagiaires* about memoirs and then provides a comparable set from another (Reims Academy) given in Artigue *et al.* (1998). But before turning to these, however, we start by offering an interview observation from Claude Comiti about the results of a research study (Comiti *et al.,* 1999) exploring among other things variation in memoirs across subject discipline and Academy:

> The main result we found was that the differences [between the memoirs in different disciplines] depended on several factors that interacted with each other, one of which comprised the epistemology of the discipline. For instance, the type of memoir in history: history, on the epistemological level and that historians themselves say, is a matter of the truth, truth that one knows about. Therefore, history memoirs are very different from memoirs in, for example, physics, chemistry or biology, which are experimental sciences with experimenters attending to different elements again from those present in mathematics memoirs. So here there is already the role of the epistemology of the discipline counting for something.
>
> And then there will of course be the orientations of each IUFM involved, drawing on institutional texts but local [rather than national] ones. And there is also the role of *didactique* in the geographical location. For instance, in Grenoble, we have a very strong tradition and a very big community, concentration, of didacticians: mathematics, physics, chemistry, biology, French, geography. While in some other IUFMs, it is the opposite, the first didactician is 100km away. Obviously, all this will have an influence too.

This provides clear instance where the question of wide variation within a given system (ostensibly determined by a centralized national directive) arises. The practice was originally decided on, loosely framed and broadly specified by the official text. It was decreed into existence. But it was also interpreted according to more local considerations within individual IUFMs that shaped practice from one year to the next.

Written notes presented to the new PLC2 students concerning the professional memoir in one study Academy

Goals and purpose of the professional memoir

Conceiving and preparing a professional memoir is something one encounters nowadays in almost all professional *formation* (engineers, nurses, etc.).

The purpose of a professional memoir is to establish a link between theory and practice, which is why it comprises an essential element of all means of *formation*. In their professional practice, practitioners come across many problems which, due to lack of time, they are unable to study. As for novices, when they stop studying they have theoretical knowledge whose practical import they sometimes underestimate. The professional memoir provides an opportunity for carrying out some work which joins these points of view together. The *written* nature of the memoir is an indispensable aid for the elaboration of structured thought, while the *oral* presentation allows its value to be displayed to others.

Memoir seminars

Depending on the number of *stagiaires*, we will arrange two or three memoir seminar groups, which will operate in parallel and have a broad theme of study of which you will be informed on Sept. 9th. Each *stagiaire* will decide upon one seminar which will influence in part the choice of his or her memoir topic. At the outset (the first three sessions), the task will comprise the sharing of the work of reading and bibliographic research dealing with the broad theme under study; then the topics will be chosen. Next, the *formateur* in charge of running the seminar will suggest several individualised follow-up tasks to the already-constituted memoir groups, and the seminar sessions will consequently be used to advance the study of the theme collectively. At the end, the *formateur* in charge of running the seminar will be the IUFM mathematics department representative at the oral presentation of the memoirs from his or her seminar.

Choice of topic

Choosing the topic will become clearer during the first month of *formation*, but specification of the topic will be in the process of becoming more refined throughout the first term. The memoir seminar, even if it identifies a theme, will not specify topics, that is to say the questions each of you will study. Proposed questions should start out from reflection arising from professional practice of the teaching of mathematics. As the theme of the memoir needs to be chosen quickly (up and running in October), the limited practice of the *stagiaire* during the first few weeks in school is not always sufficient to do so. A wide call has been made to the PLC2 group of the mathematics department to collect possible ideas for topics, which will be given to you in the seminars. Of course, you can also suggest a topic that is close to your heart.

We will prefer the development of collective proposals (two or possibly three students [*étudiants*]).

The memoir director (le directeur de mémoire)

The professional memoir is subject to a double shaping: that by the memoir director and that by the memoir seminar. The seeking out of a memoir director will be carried out jointly by the *stagiaire* and by the leader of the relevant memoir seminar.

The memoir director is usually a practising secondary schoolteacher and most of the time is not the pedagogic advisor [something not widely the case]. The role of memoir director is to be interested in the work of the *stagiaire*, to be in some sense his or her first professional point of call for discussions. They should not substitute for the *stagiaire*, nor be a specialist on the chosen topic, rather they should simply keep an eye on the work and give an opinion, especially during the experimental phases. They should also set up a working timetable with the *stagiaire* and remind the *stagiaire* of this. The leader of the appropriate memoir seminar is available to the memoir director to help him or her carry out the task.

[There then follows advice on the written form of the memoir, including bibliographic style for referencing to be followed and a reminder to make sufficient records at the time of the on-going research activity. A maximum of thirty pages to be used and, because of abuse in previous years, a maximum of twenty pages of appendices.]

Advice for the oral presentation of the memoir is as follows

The presentation is *individual*. Each is to present what is dear to his heart from the work on the memoir. In contrast to the written text, the oral form allows a more individual manner of expression to be used to indicate the relevance of the memoir work for future practice. The presentation is to last 10–15 minutes, followed by questions from each member of the panel for 20–30 minutes. It is strongly recommended you use appropriate audiovisual technology and particularly an overhead projector.

The evaluation panel comprises: the memoir director, the leader of the relevant memoir seminar and one other person depending on the topic of the memoir. The presentation is public, anyone can take part: questioning by the panel, on the other hand, will be carried out in a more confidential setting. The panel values four elements: for the written version, form (correct language, presentation) and content (interest of the topic, relevance of the study); for the oral presentation, quality of the argument and the manner of expression.

The panel award the following categories of mark: very good, good, quite good, pass and fail (not validated).

Reims Academy Memoir Advice

[The following is a translation of pages 15–19 of Artigue *et al.* (1998), *Between Theory and Practice: the IUFM Professional Memoir in Mathematics* which sets out the Reims IUFM mathematics group's setting and orientation of their PLC2 *stagiaires* to the memoir. The publication of this book can itself be seen as an attempt to share practice across IUFMs and Academies, by making public both their processes of framing and support and examples of the 'best' of their *stagiaires* work. Certainly, within a given Academy, *stagiaires* can see examples of past years' memoirs, but this publication marks a further step in the process of the objectification of the memoir as a text object in the public domain.]

I The framing text of the memoir

1. Goals of the professional memoir
The memoir is an *important* element in the means of second-year IUFM *formation*. In conjunction with the various other elements of this *formation*, it should more specifically:

- allow you to better articulate the theoretical and practical contributions of the *formation*;
- help you to gain a certain distance from the everyday class in order to engage, in relation to a restricted topic, in a deeper analysis of how your pupils are operating and your own practices;
- alert you to what constitutes a research step (formation of a question, bibliographic research, hypothesis formation, creating a setting to study the questions, carry out and collect the data, analysis and interpretation, going back to the initial questions) and help you in this way to make use of the already existing research work on the teaching and learning of mathematics.

The memoir is usually prepared in pairs. We can, however, accept memoirs prepared individually or in threes, if justified.

2. The topic of the memoir
You will be the one to determine the topic of your memoir. Quite varied types of topic can be conceived: analysis of pupil conceptions in a particular domain; spelling out, carrying out and analysis of a teaching sequence on a given topic with specific goals; analysis of using new technology in teaching; study of teaching techniques, processes of evaluation, ... But we hope that, apart from a suitably justified exception, that every memoir will contain an experimental part involving students. This experimental part can be based on teaching sessions, questionnaires, interviews, ... the means being chosen dependent on the questions that you want to study and the constraints under which you must work.

3. Preparation and carrying out of the memoir
The memoir can take place over a six-month period from November to April. It is structured into different phases.

(a) Specification of the memoir
(November – beginning of January)
A preliminary group preparation session is arranged in November. This meeting is devoted to the initial framing of the memoirs:

- introduction to goals, expectations, timetable and physical preparation, presentation of possible sorts of topics and the associated implementations based on memoirs carried out in previous years;
- setting up the pairs and reflection in pairs on possible topics;
- discussion about these topics and appointing of *tuteur mémoir;*
- inventory of requests, notably biographical.

At the end of this session, you will pursue the specification and planning of the memoir, in pairs and in consultation with your memoir tutor. You may also, of course, seek the advice of your tutor, even if he is not your memoir tutor, your pedagogic advisor, your colleagues. This work will mainly become more solid by a index card (*fiche*) specifying the proposed memoir, to be handed in in January following the second joint preparation session for the memoir.

This index card 1, the rubric for which is given below, should be handed in in duplicate (one copy for the tutor and one for the person in charge of the memoirs). It mainly asks you to make more precise the topic of the memoir, the question or questions being studied, the expanded plan to study these questions, the data you anticipate collecting, the organisation of the likely time needed to carry out the project.

In addition, for the second session, each group should prepare a joint presentation of the project and the work already carried out (ten minute presentation, max). Based on the comments and advice given to you, following the *fiches* being read and the oral presentations, you will then move rapidly to produce the definitive outline of the problem setting and the proposal.

(b) Carrying out the proposal, analysis of the data, write-up
(January – April)
This phase is essentially overseen by the memoir tutor. A final joint preparation session will be organised in March. It is dedicated more precisely to questions of analysis and interpretation of data and the preparation of the memoir write-up. For this session, which is a group work session under the lead of the memoir tutors, you should prepare a second index card (given below) to be handled as the one before and bring all the documents you will use.

(c) The memoir as 'product'

What is expected as a result is what is made more explicit in this paragraph. It goes without saying that it is a question here of providing general suggestions to be adapted according to the specific subject dealt with.

We are expecting a memoir which provides:

1) The problem setting of the work undertaken

> Which questions did you explore and why?
> How was (or were) the starting question(s) refined and constrained and finally modified so as to reach the definitive topic?
> Which research or other work did you rely upon?

2) The method chosen for the work

> Here it is a question of responding to the following questions in a justified manner:
> Which way did you specify for carrying out the questions(s) posed and why?
> Which data did you choose to collect?
> How did you handle and analyse them?
> Here again, you will make more precise the final alterations that occurred giving reasons.

3) The detailed presentation and *a priori* analysis of the teaching sequences, questionnaires and/or other instruments developed for working on the memoir.

4) A synthetic description of what was actually done.

5) The way of handling, the analysis and the interpretation of the collected data making reference, of course, to the questions being studied.

6) A conclusion which:
   - returns to the original questions: how has the work undertaken led to elements of a response to the questions posed? What are the limitations? How might it possibly go forward?
   - tries to specify more globally what the study has brought you, as a teacher.

7) A bibliography, briefly annotated, if not already done so in the main text. The written version of the memoir should be typed (it is of course strongly advised that you use a word processor, as changes and corrections are much easier to make) and including a summary abstract.

It should be prepared in a clear and concise style. It should be about 30 pages, appendices excluded. For memoirs prepared in pairs, the main text can be prepared together, but in this case each member of the pair is asked to add, at the end, a part which deals with a personal reflection on the work that has been undertaken.

4. Assessment of the memoir

This assessment will depend on both the written product and the oral submission. For this oral submission, which is individual, you have 15 minutes to present your work, showing its structure, what you found out, the conclusions you came to and questions which arise at the end of the work. You will then be asked questions by the examination panel [*le jury*] which is made up of two people.

II *The memoir index cards [Les fiches mémoire]*

Index card 1

This index card is to be structured according to the following rubric:

Pair:
1. Memoir topic.
2. Questions foreseen by the memoir.
3. Why have you asked these questions?
4. Have you any idea of possible responses: if so, which ones?
5. Projected scenario of studying these questions (different stages of the work, goals and content for each phase, outline timetable).
6. Envisaged data to be collected.
7. Bibliography used so far.
8. Particular problems met. Questions to the formateurs.

Index card 2

This index card is to be structured according to the following rubric:

Pair:
1. Actual topic of memoir.
2. Proposed title.
3. Possible development of the problem setting since index card 1 with reasons.
4. Possible development of the scenario since index card 1 and why.
5. Present state of the study.
6. Data actually collected.
7. Handling and analysis of data collected (both anticipated and that actually carried out).
8. Proposed plan for the memoir.
9. Problems encountered, questions for the *formateurs*.

Notes by Chapter

Chapter 1

[1] We list Shanghai rather than China here because our research was, in fact, a study of Shanghai as its own educational system. We chose to study Shanghai because of its long and rich history of induction practices and programs. In our preliminary explorations, we did interview national educational policy makers and researchers in China and that work informed our site selection. As Chapter 2 demonstrates, we situate Shanghai within the broader Chinese national political–cultural context. However, throughout this volume, we refer to Shanghai as if it were the name of a country, in part acknowledging its administrative autonomy.

[2] Literary critic Hugh Kenner (2000), in his book *The Elsewhere Community*, has written engagingly about the traditions of the European 'Grand Tour' and, more significantly, about the continuing importance of journeying after knowledge (to travel is to learn, what we do not yet know is to be found Elsewhere, such pursuit is a way of seeking entrance to what he terms 'the Elsewhere Community'). Kenner underscores the importance of on-the-spot informants acting both as guides and interpreters, to enable one to see past the surface, yet notes how "foreign travel can open linguistic chasms" (p. 17).

Elsewhere, however, does not necessarily connote Other and, as suggested earlier in this chapter, we consciously sought to avoid the common danger of constructing Others in the course of comparison – the unfortunate tendency of certain earlier generations of tourists and some early schools of comparative education.

> One of the most long-standing of these [traditions of comparative education] has been that of 'travelers' tales' – descriptions of educational practices in other countries. Frequently such descriptions became the basis for inducing changes at home. (Altbach and Kelly, 1986, p. 3)

Mindful of this possibility, we undertook to establish our work through peers and colleagues, in order to emphasize a common community as well as a sense of elsewhereness. Kenner's examples are literary, but our international work on induction, engaging with widespread Elsewhere Communities, contains a number of these same key elements. In particular, the intent of such focused travel, to learn both about the world and about ourselves, is identical.

Chapter 2

[1] In addition, Dan Chazan, Violetta Lazarovici, David Pimm and Jian Wang have each contributed to the case study, through data collection, data analysis or both.

[2] All words in double quotation marks and in extended quotations are direct translations of our informants' words. At times, the translation may read somewhat awkwardly in English, but in these cases we wanted to stay close to the literal meaning of the original phrases, even if the phrasing was unfamiliar to native English speakers. Words in single quotation marks include technical terms of the system, such as 'important' and 'difficult' points or 'open' lessons' – see below.

[3] Throughout this case, we refer to Li Mei as 'Teacher Li', as she would be called by her colleagues and pupils at school.

[4] In this chapter, 'open' lessons (*gongkaike*) are also referred to as 'public' lessons, since a literal translation of the term allows both interpretations.

[5] We did find in our interviews that, in ordinary conversation, school people more often used the more inclusive term 'young teacher' and discussed 'new teachers' as part of that larger category, even though formally in the eyes of the system these are two distinct categories. However, in this chapter, our use of the terms 'new' and 'young' teachers respects these category boundaries: they are the technical designations of the system.

[6] We will also sometimes refer to new teachers as 'beginners' or 'probationers', the latter referring to a distinction sometimes made by our interviewees between 'new teachers', who are participating in 'probation training', and all other teachers, who have received full teaching status or 'teaching credentials' (*zige zhengshu*) and who have been approved for a professional rank. (New teachers are not entitled to any rank.)

[7] In some populous districts, such as Pudong (which was one of our focal districts), there are intermediate levels that function as sub-district units and deal directly with schools in much the way other districts do. But the most common arrangement is for the district to serve as the sole organizational intermediary between Shanghai's Municipal Education Commission and the individual school.

[8] We choose the translation 'lower secondary' for *chuzhong*, literally 'early middle'. The term has within its structure an implicit connection to upper secondary (*gaozhong*), literally, 'high middle school'. And in both levels of secondary school being named literally as 'middle school' (*zhongxue*), there is an implicit connection to what precedes and follows it ('small school' for elementary and 'big school' for university).

[9] Social practice activities include field-related experiences in the community, such as going to an agricultural community for a week to experience agricultural labor (and to help with the harvest).

[10] The Municipal College of Education, no longer a free-standing institution in the wake of recent reform of Shanghai's higher education system, had for years been the leading in-service institution for the city, providing degree and short-term courses to teachers and district-level faculty.

[11] A fourth area for training is mentioned but given much less prominence. This is related to a standard teachers must reach (and be assessed on) concerning good *putonghua* (or Mandarin), the official national spoken dialect.

[12] One municipal official explained that most mentors do not have subsidies because of several factors:

> First, old teachers mentoring new teachers show a kind of dedication. They should help selflessly. They have to have this spirit. Second, being mentors, they have a sense of honor. It is a recognition of a mentor's ability. Third, it is part of a senior-ranked teacher's work responsibility to offer guidance for new teachers. For middle-ranked teachers, experience of mentoring is taken into account in the evaluation for professional promotion. Fourth, mentoring is continuing education. For those who not only provide mentoring but do research on mentoring experience, they receive credit towards satisfying their professional development requirements.

[13] Zhabei #8 Lower Secondary School, a school we visited, is one such training site. It offers a weekly mathematics workshop on problems of teaching for teachers from eighteen

schools in the district as a form of continuing education that can satisfy municipal requirements for courses taken.

[14] Traditionally, Shanghai's higher education system has included single purpose institutions: teacher training universities, agricultural schools, engineering institutions, and so on. One type of institution, comprehensive universities, is distinctive for not being so bounded in its institutional charter, yet until the newest reforms, these institutions were unable to prepare teachers for pre-college-level teaching.

[15] This description does not do justice to the variation across the two institutions, the changes each has experimented with over recent years and the complexity of each of these categories. But for the larger argument of this case – that pre-service education leaves the new teacher with particular strengths and weaknesses – these details may not be significant.

[16] The table, compiled from documents gathered from the university, reflects the general arrangement of time for mathematics majors intending to be lower secondary school teachers. The exact amount of time for practica continues to shift, but at the time of our data collection it was eight weeks. Prior to that, for only one year as an experiment, the practicum was a full semester in duration. Traditionally, lower secondary teachers have undertaken the shorter-length practicum that is currently in place. In addition to these courses listed in the table, there are also other general university-wide requirements and electives outside one's field.

[17] This statement does not capture the variation we saw in our visits to schools, as some schools experimented with their own curriculum reforms.

[18] The teachers' union is one such feature standard in the school organization of any school in Shanghai. Our informants never mentioned the role of the union as having a significant direct impact on the learning of beginning teachers and thus we do not give prominence to its discussion here. But teachers we interviewed did confirm that a school's union leader holds an administrative leadership position, while union committee members are ordinary staff without special administrative roles. The union monitors the administration of the school and its compliance with state policies, takes part in policy-making for the school and is especially concerned about teachers' welfare and benefits.

[19] We did hear some limited variation. For instance, one new teacher, Ms. Pan, described her lack of enthusiasm for being in the office and her preference for the quiet and isolation of working in a borrowed space elsewhere in the school building.

[20] That teachers are necessarily spending a great deal of time with others does not mean they develop shared ideas, think of themselves primarily in collective terms or view themselves as members of a tight-knit community. We did find teachers who talked in this way and research by others (see Ross, 1993, for example) reinforces this view. But we did meet a much smaller number of young teachers who clearly chose to present themselves rather as loners (like Teacher Pan) or as independent actors working against the grain (like Teacher Liu – another teacher we observed and interviewed).

[21] These comments resonate with Vygotskian notions of assisted performance (Vygotsky, 1935/1994), although it should be noted that no one ever made such a direct reference.

[22] See Ma (1999) for more discussion about what 'knowledge points' are, how they connect to the content of the curriculum and how teachers view them.

[23] The standard Chinese term for what we would call *observing* a lesson, is 'listening' *(tingke)* to a lesson.

[24] Public lessons (*gongkaike*) are widely used and, as a general category, includes several different forms, distinguished chiefly by their purpose. The most common term and most general is a 'public' lesson, yet sometimes public lessons are 'demonstration' lessons (when an expert teacher is demonstrating a particular technique or approach). Some are termed 'research' lessons, in which some aspect of teaching will be studied by the teacher-presenter and those observing. New teachers would not be candidates to present either of these latter types of lessons, but they would certainly have chances to observe them. For new teachers, the standard 'public' lesson form is the 'report' lesson, in which, after teaching a lesson, they are expected to provide a critique and reflect publicly on their own work.

[25] In almost all cases, we heard about novices having mentors. Beyond this, there was tremendous variation in terms of which induction-related activities were mentioned when we asked about what contributed to beginning teachers' learning. But virtually all new teachers we interviewed (with one exception working in a particularly challenging school context, with many new teachers and few area resources) reported multiple sources of support.

[26] We thank Sharon Feiman-Nemser for her help in getting us to think about the ways in which a common, highly-specified curriculum both narrows the range of things novices have to attend to at one and the same time, while additionally sharpening the focus of what those helping them – in both pre-service and induction programs – address.

[27] This concern in Shanghai indirectly connects with philosopher Alfred North White-head's (1925) trenchant observation that:

> I will not go so far as to say that to construct a history of thought without profound study of the mathematical ideas of successive epochs is like omitting Hamlet from the play which is named after him. [...] But it is certainly analogous to cutting out the part of Ophelia. [...] For Ophelia is quite essential to the play, she is very charming – and a little mad. Let us grant that the pursuit of mathematics is a divine madness of the human spirit, a refuge from the goading urgency of contingent happenings. (p. 26)

[28] This is the economically poorest district in our sample. Formally, this district is actually a county: the district used to be rural and is also the least cosmopolitan site in our sample. It is our suspicion that the district does not have confidence that all schools have the capacity to do mentoring well and so they provide these district-level mentors in an attempt to increase the likelihood that the mentoring policy is properly enacted.

Chapter 3

[1] See section 3 on Teacher Education in this chapter and the glossary for an explanation of 'didactics' education.

[2] It is very common for Swiss teachers to be teaching part-time, especially females. Of the four other teachers in Bertila's practice group, only one was teaching full-time. Note that Bertila's reduced teaching load is *not* a function of her being a beginning teacher: rather, she is employed at about 72 percent time.

[3] Parent meetings are mandatory for grades 1 and 2, because pupils get no report card in these grades. After that, parent meetings follow the established custom of the school, but generally are voluntary. They are again mandatory in grade 6, because of the teacher's role in recommending transition and placement for grade 7.

[4] For a summary of the study's data collection, see Appendix A on p. 340.

[5] The fourth Swiss language, Romansh, is spoken in one canton together with French.

[6] The attainment of Swiss pupils in science as measured by TIMSS is instructive. While only at the mean in Population 3 specialist physics, Switzerland was in the highest band for the Population 3 science literacy test. Many of the tasks for this test were linked to everyday life, mirroring science instruction in the Swiss schools, which is very problem-oriented. Evidence for the effects of the Swiss privileging of mathematics comes from the PISA results (OECD, 2001), an international assessment in reading, mathematics and science conducted in 2000. Swiss fifteen-year-olds scored among the highest eight of twenty-seven OECD countries in mathematics, but were only in the average range in science.

[7] For a full discussion of the needs for upgrading teacher education at the elementary level, the reasons for the proposed changes and the changes already under way, see Schärer (2000).

[8] About one-third of the candidates studying to be lower secondary teachers at Bern University are currently elementary school teachers. Advancing their careers in this manner is attractive because of the higher pay commanded by secondary teachers. Their program lasts three years and concentrates on upgrading their subject-matter knowledge in mathematics and the sciences, with fewer education and didactics courses and only one three-week culminating practicum. However, these candidates may drop out because they did not pass the content exam. About 50 percent of those failing the content examinations elect to try again, but the majority of these still fail for a second time.

[9] Results for the 1995 TIMSS performance assessment demonstrate that eighth-grade Swiss pupils in the German-speaking cantons do very well in carrying out experiments, making observations, etc., scoring second out of nineteen countries (Harmon *et al.,* 1997). This goal of the Swiss lower-secondary science curriculum seems to have been achieved.

[10] The ministers of education of the cantons or their representatives meet periodically to take up cross-cantonal educational issues. The meeting in 1995 took up the question of induction of beginning teachers. Dossier 40A (EDK, 1996) resulted, a key document for Swiss induction practices in that it lays out general guidelines for good induction programs; it also summarizes induction activities in the various cantons. Documents produced by the cantonal ministers are not binding, but they are very influential and carefully crafted to make adoption of recommendations feasible across all the Swiss cantons.

[11] As we go to press, Fritz Vogel has retired. He has turned over the leadership function to Monika Vogel and two long-time practice group leaders.

[12] Teacher pay in the canton of Lucerne is one of the lowest in Switzerland and recent changes have made attaining the top salary level very difficult.

[13] We were told by university science and didactics faculty that insufficient science knowledge is a problem in lower secondary school (grades 7–9) as well, particularly for physics and chemistry.

Chapter 4

[1] The vignette about Sarah is drawn from interviews with a particular first-year teacher. Sarah is a pseudonym, as are all other names used in this chapter. The many types of support in Sarah's day actually occurred over several days, but for simplicity are described within the frame of a single day. Based on the interviews with Sarah and more than thirty other beginning teachers in fifteen schools, the support in the vignette could have occurred in the course of a single day.

[2] We use the term 'grades' and identify schools' grade levels as treated in the international description of the New Zealand educational system by New Zealander Bob Garden (1997) in the TIMSS Encyclopedia. In New Zealand, the terms 'years' or 'forms' are used rather than 'grades'.

[3] The national Ministry of Education identifies the average socio-economic level of the pupil body at every school in New Zealand using a scale of 1 to 10, with decile 10 schools serving the most advantaged pupils. The decile ranking of a school is widely known and referred to by school staff and parents. For example, it was common during interviews for teachers to begin describing their school by citing its decile level. Higher decile schools supplement their Ministry funds by asking parents for 'voluntary' annual contributions, which can be in amounts of hundreds of dollars per pupil at prestigious schools.

[4] This area is roughly equivalent to the U.S. state of Colorado.

[5] Particularly entrepreneurial principals have successfully enrolled fee-paying pupils from other countries. For example, some wealthy families of Japanese pupils who were unsuccessful in passing entrance exams to prestigious Japanese high schools send their children to New Zealand high schools. Some New Zealand schools we visited had dozens or even more than a hundred foreign pupils paying $7,500–11,000NZ per year.

[6] For additional description of the educational system and/or analysis of the impact of changes in it during the 1990s, see Ministry of Education (1995), Moskowitz and Kennedy (1997), Olssen and Matthews (1997), Garden (1997), Thrupp (1999), Fiske and Ladd (2000) or www.inca.or.uk

[7] Secondary teachers rarely pursue a Masters degree; the University of Waikato in Hamilton runs the most substantial masters programs in science education, as well as the only Ph.D. program in the country.

[8] The generality of the recent requirements for establishing a teacher preparation program and the lack of a strong system for judging the appropriateness and quality of the established program's specifics has led to concerns about the effectiveness of some new entrants, but mostly regarding new elementary programs (Gray and Renwick, 1998). In one instance, the body that oversees registration of teachers learned that a cohort of graduates had been permitted to take elementary teaching positions without completing a semester or even more of the preparation program.

[9] Rejections have been higher lately because of insufficient English proficiency among applicants who have come to New Zealand from non-anglophone countries.

[10] Teachers' college science is generally well aligned with school science for grades 11 and 12, when most schools offer specialist science courses in biology, chemistry, and physics taught by teachers with a specialty in that subject.

[11] Some beginning teachers also mentioned that, when meeting or telephoning peers from their teacher preparation program, they discussed what kinds of support they were receiving in their different schools. In Sarah's story, for example, she and her friend Glenda who graduated from the same teacher preparation program spoke about their Advice and Guidance programs.

[12] As of 12/23/01, the U.S.$. equivalents of these salaries are $15,000 for beginning teachers and a maximum of $20,000 for experienced teachers.

[13] The elementary school teachers' day requires a quite different allocation of the release time. The time typically is split between novices and their supporting teachers, enabling them both to be temporarily free of their classes so that they can confer. In secondary

schools, administrators try to maximize the synchronization of novices' free periods with their supporters' free periods.

[14] While national officials often used the term 'Advice and Guidance program', few school personnel immediately recognized the term. They usually referred to their efforts merely as the 'new teacher support program' or similar. However, we use the terms 'Advice and Guidance program', 'Advice and Guidance co-ordinator', etc. in this chapter as a convenience.

[15] The government mostly plans to continue these registration stages and procedures when it replaces the Teacher Registration Board with an Education Council in 2002. This new teacher-dominated body will, additionally, play a more active role in appraising teacher education programs.

[16] The Treaty of Waitangi was signed in 1840 by the British colonial administrators and by representatives of the tribes of the Maori people, the indigenous people of Aotearoa (New Zealand). It was largely ignored for 150 years, but has now been given legal status with the result that bi-cultural aspects of education are now given much more attention. The implications of the Treaty are expected to be understood and implemented by teachers and therefore considerations of the Treaty form part of teacher education.

[17] We observed fifteen first- or second-year teachers' grades 8–10 integrated science classes in five schools.

[18] On the other hand, we heard of a few instances where beginning teachers under-reported their interactions with support providers. The latter related such detailed accounts of meetings and conversations with novices that we checked back with the novices, who concurred with their mentors' accounts and said they had just failed to recall as many details when originally asked.

[19] A single political party (National) has led the national government during 1989–1999, launching its *Tomorrow's Schools* initiative in 1989 and creating major educational changes up until 1999. The Labor party, which took office in 1999, is generally not reversing the structural changes of the prior decade, but is pursuing further changes more incrementally.

Chapter 5

[1] Roughly 80 percent of French schools are public, the remainder private and mostly religious in orientation. To qualify for state funding, private schools need to follow the same syllabi and timetables as public schools. The considerable majority of private schools are state-contracted in this way, which leads to a considerable national homogeneity with regard to curriculum.

[2] A *collège* is a state lower secondary school, consistently comprising grades six to nine throughout the country. We have used North American grade levels throughout this chapter: in French secondary schools, grade 6 is comparably called 'the sixth', but the labels then proceed to decrease in countdown mode, so grade seven in France is called 'the fifth', grade eight 'the fourth', and so on. Grade eleven is called 'the first' and grade twelve 'the terminal'. The four years of schooling in the *collège* are divided into three 'cycles': the first of 'observation and adaptation' for the newly arrived grade sixes, the middle one of 'consolidation' for grades seven and eight (where many *stagiaire* teachers working in *collèges* are placed) and the final one of 'orientation' for grade nine, at the end of which pupils go either to a academic/technological *lycée* or a vocational one.

[3] The exception to this arises if a teacher has successfully passed a higher teacher recruiting examination, known as the *Agrégation*, which moves them both to a higher salary scale and

reduces their teaching load to a contractual fifteen hours per week. See sections 3 and 4.

[4] French secondary schools have counsellor positions known as CPEs *(Conseillers Principals d'Education),* who also deal with more major discipline difficulties as well as many school administrative functions (such as attendance and chairing *conseil de classe* meetings – see note [6]).

[5] Mathematics classes are not necessarily taught each day at the same time. Additionally, the constraints on a *stagiaire's* time are well-known throughout the school system and are taken into account when timetabling their teaching for the academic year.

[6] This is a formal institutional meeting with legal status and has representatives of both parents and pupils present (who are sworn to absolute confidentiality), grades are discussed and comments made on each pupil. It is presided over by a CPE – see note [4] above.

[7] This use of 'North America' here interestingly includes francophone Québec in Canada where, despite very strong cultural and linguistic links with France, the usage of the terms *stage* and *stagiaire* are quite different, and refer to student school-based practica.

[8] The French word *formation* is also used to denote 'adolescence', which connects to a subsequent discussion presented at the outset of Chapter 7.

[9] The comparable middle-level civic structure of the country to the Academy is called the *département* – there are some ninety plus in mainland France – each headed by a *Préfect*, the official representative of the Interior Ministry. Geographically, each Academy comprises a collection of *départements*, usually three or four. With only two minor exceptions, each *région* – a historic, higher-level civic grouping of from two to eight *départements* – also combines a small collection of Academies, so these are virtually nested structures. However, the word 'regional' in the term Regional Pedagogic Inspector (IPR – see later in this section) actually refers to 'Academy' and not 'region' in this civic-geographic sense.

[10] The majority of our study took place in two Academies, with interviews with a number of other informants connected with others. Because of between-Academy variation, many of the features we discuss, unless otherwise specified, cannot necessarily be assumed to be national practices, but simply possibilities permitted within the national framework specification.

[11] Teacher moves throughout the educational system are determined by a complex system of rankings and points: there is a national seniority scale that determines comparability rankings when applying to move between teaching jobs. This provides an instance of an attempt to implement visible 'equality' when organising teacher moves within a single system. Points are primarily awarded for years spent in any civil service position (not just in teaching), for being married (to someone who cannot easily relocate) and for having children.

[12] It is the national-level General Inspectorate who are responsible for inspecting *stagiaire* and certified *agrégé* teachers, though they can and regularly do delegate their authority in this regard to the relevant subject IPRs within an Academy.

[13] There are eleven increments on the main secondary teacher salary spine. An inspection, generally undertaken once every five years or so, places a teacher anew into one of three categories with regard to the rate of passing to the next step: being classified into the top category (roughly fifteen to twenty per cent of inspections) provides an increment every two years, while being judged as falling in the middle category results in a salary step being taken every three years (roughly sixty per cent of teachers inspected) and the bottom one provides for a pay step every four years (the remaining roughly fifteen to twenty per cent inspected).

The level 1 for a CAPES–admitted teacher is about 7000FF a month for twelve months (after all taxes and social security deductions) and the level 11 salary is about 13,000FF a month. (the parallel levels for those teachers who have passed the *Agrégation* starts at about 9000FF per month and rises to about 19,000FF monthly). Other factors affect a teacher's initial placement on the salary scale (such as years of experience as a non-teaching civil servant), but once you have been initially placed, inspection is the key route to more rapid financial advancement. The scale is, however, uniform (though there are some exceptional levels available above the top of the scale). Another systemic reward is the allocation of a teacher's contact hours and a third is a combination of reduced teaching hours and a different salary scale as a result of passing the *Agrégation* examination, either as an initial or internal candidate. However, neither of these last two rewards results from a school inspection.

[14] Some fairly new teachers who wish to return sooner to a particular Academy (often the one where they are from and likely were *stagiaires*) are accepting these 'replacement' teacher positions, in order to speed the process of return from the North of France and their first permanent positions. One mathematics IPR commented on her experience of such returning mathematics teachers:

> In order to get back here quicker, I think it is necessary that they accept being appointed to the Academy as what we call 'replacement teachers'. They get back to the Academy after three years, no more. So they are still new teachers.

[15] A wide range of school subjects is compulsorily studied in the *collège*, including in grade seven: French (4 to 5.5 hours per week), mathematics (3.5 to 4.5 hours), English (3 to 4 hours), Science-Life-Earth (1.5 to 2 hours), Physics-Chemistry (1.5 to 2 hours), History-Geography-Civics Education (3 to 4 hours – including topics such as equality and solidarity as well as political institutions), Arts Education (Plastic Arts and Music) (2 hours) and Sport (3 hours). The school day runs from 8am to 5pm every weekday (apart from Wednesday afternoons which are free throughout the country) as well as Saturday morning. (Usually grades six and seven meet either for Wednesday morning or Saturday morning for classes, whereas grades eight and nine will likely have classes on both mornings.) However, like their teachers, pupils are not required to be on the school premises either if they have more than an hour's gap between classes or after their last class, and are able to leave school (usually to go home), provided the school has a record of their parents' permission.

[16] There is some significant differentiation by function among *lycées*, in terms of an orientation either towards vocational or general academic/technological education. But exploring the nature of this differentiation falls outside the scope of our study.

[17] This follows the general pattern of French reforms in education (particularly in terms of revisions to the national curriculum), which is that experimental variations are permitted in some locations for one year prior to a planned system-wide change, variations which feed information into the full national change the subsequent year.

[18] In one of the Academies we studied, of the twenty-eight mathematics *stagiaires* in a particular group we met, there were sixteen with *collège* placements and twelve teaching in *lycées*. All of the *lycée stagiaires* were in accordance with the guidelines in having a grade ten class. But in the *collèges*, while there were four with a grade seven class and seven with a grade eight class, there were also three teaching sixth grade and two in ninth grade classes.

[19] A recent published collection (Hébert and Tavignot, 1998), based on 300 reports written by mathematics *stagiaires* about observations in their pedagogic advisor's classes during this *stage*, documents a wide variety of practices seen from the novice's point of view. Much

is made of the invitation 'Come into our classes' which forms the title of the book, a some-what uncommon invitation at least as judged by the tenor of the book's introduction written by two IUFM *formateurs*. The preface by an Academy Inspector, who of course has the insti-tutional right to go into classes to observe, underlines the mixed reception ('warmth, reti-cence or even resignation', p. 7) she had received in more than a thousand classroom visits. The range of organizing themes – the conduct of the class, the behaviour of the pupils, ped-agogic practices and rather special classes ('weak' and 'difficult' classes, sixth grade) – as well as the detailed descriptions provide a wide-ranging introduction to the preoccupations and foci of interest of first-year secondary mathematics teachers.

[20] In 1999, an insider enquiry was carried out by seven IUFM-based academics looking back at the professional memoir and how it functioned in five Academies in the areas of mathematics and the physical sciences and, occasionally, in other disciplines (Comiti *et al.,* 1999). Some of these Academies had the same framing across all subjects, whereas others varied by particular subject, but one of the things they document and comment on is how varied the interpretation of the memoir requirement was and how different the roles it was made to play in teacher *formation*.

[21] There is also the journal the *Bulletin of the APMEP* (a single, national association of public institution teachers of mathematics from pre-kindergarten to university level), the journal of the French mathematics society and the journal *Repères* published for and by the IREM network.

[22] The French term *banlieu*, although referring geographically to part of a large city that in English would be called 'suburb', has little in common with it in terms of socio-economic imagery or reality. Many large urban areas, especially in the North of the country and par-ticularly Paris, have sizeable areas in these *banlieux* of concentrated poverty, poor housing, high unemployment and substantial recent immigration. In contrast, the centres of cities (again accurately referred to as 'inner city' in purely geographic terms) are frequently the most desired locations to live, with the corresponding most bourgeois and academic schools. Many *stagiaire* teachers' first permanent positions will be in one of the urban *banlieux*.

[23] In response to a question about why in the age of photocopiers, pupils were not simply handed *le cours,* at least in their teacher's version, an IUFM *formateur* replied:

> Photocopied material can be very demotivating for pupils, and teachers
> find themselves solely in the role of commentator, which is very difficult to
> bring to life. At the point at which the teacher is dictating, the pupil can still
> ask questions (something which is frequently the case) and the fact of being
> required to write it himself [or herself] involves him in some way. But pre-
> prepared copies prevent the teacher from taking into account his sense of
> pupil difficulties or any other idea which comes to him from interacting
> with the class. He is trapped to a certain extent. [...] For teaching, there is
> no 'the method', there is no 'the best *cours*', because you must always be
> convinced by what you are doing at the moment and that you could do it
> better.

[24] In various quotations and comments made in this chapter, there has been the impres-sion of a binary divide between 'discipline' and 'pedagogy'. This is unfortunate, as it is clear that *didactique des mathématiques* provides a third position, and not one simply part-way between 'discipline' and 'pedagogy'. Seeing these three elements as verticies of a triangle opens up the scope for tensions between any pair (all of which exist), as well as a way to consider tensions within the triangular system as a whole.

Chapter 6

[1] In 2001, the name of this Ministry changed from Monbusho – the Ministry of Education, Science, Sports and Culture – to Monbukagakusho – the Ministry of Education, Culture, Sports, Science and Technology (MEXT). Details can be found on the English language web site of the Ministry:

> http://www.mext.go.jp/english/index.htm

As this book goes to print, Japan has just launched a significant, comprehensive reform of its educational system at both the elementary and secondary school levels.

[2] The conversions were made at the rate of 120 yen to $1.00 US.

Chapter 7

[1] As Blanchard-Laville (2000a) observes:

> All these elements indicate that, for us, the time period of *formation* is to be understood as 'a time period of professional adolescence' and just as the question of adolescence has not been an object of study for psychoanalysts for very long, equally the question of the 'adolescent passage' in the professional setting has not been greatly studied up until now. (p. 181)

[2] This is demonstrated by the statistics for recent years on the large applicant pool and the small percentage of accepted candidates. (The existence of the IUFMs was not necessarily solely instrumental in achieving this goal; increased salaries for teachers and changed economic patterns, with unemployment rising in other sectors, no doubt also helped significantly.)

[3] Dossier 40A, which concludes with recommendations intended to guide induction in all the cantons, makes the case for a specific version of induction. Below is a summary of some of that document's major points:

- induction should take as its starting point the daily conflict-laden situations faced by novice teachers;
- the central goal should be improvement in the complex decision-making required and understanding of professional development methods – not supervision and selection;
- the main vehicle should be the collaborative and reflective practice group, assisted by experienced advisors;
- the period of induction should be a year: more than that keeps the novice teachers unnecessarily in dependency. This year should be conceived as a separate phase, not an extension of pre-service education, nor part of subsequent further training. (EDK, 1996, pp. 100-102)

[4] The Lucerne cantonal *Gymnasium* is an exception here, but the observation there is one-on-one, not the large public event that characterizes public lessons in Shanghai and Japan.

[5] Even though they are not necessarily new to teaching, in Switzerland, Shanghai and New Zealand, it is assumed that there are still issues that these teachers need help with, that the 'beginner' still needs to develop familiarity with local practice.

[6] Even in cases of problems, it is more likely that first-year teachers will have their probationary period extended than that they will be summarily discharged from teaching.

[7] The case is different for grades 7–9 *Gymnasium* teachers (in Lucerne only); they are evaluated both by their mentors and the *Prorector* in charge of their subject specialties, who then decides whether they will be offered a permanent position.

[8] We do not intend to suggest, in using the term 'curriculum', that there is a single, uniform program in place, nor that this program is created by or through one agency or institution. Also, in talking about a 'curriculum of induction', we do not want to ignore the power of the many informal aspects of school and professional life which supplement the formal induction experiences of new teachers.

[9] There is also usually some negotiation of what happens during the subject-specific day at the IUFM and a certain degree of choice of modules taken at certain points of the year during the non-subject-specific time allocation.

[10] For a full discussion of the needs for up-grading teacher education at the elementary level, the reasons for the proposed changes and the changes already under way, see Schärer (2000).

Glossary of Terms

Chapter 2 Shanghai

Ban – class; the group of pupils who take their classes together and share a common classroom. Over the course of the school day, their different subject teachers will come to their classroom to teach them their classes.

Banhui – class meeting; a regular feature of Chinese school life. Class meetings are occasions when a *ban* (class) of pupils meet in their classroom during the school day with their *banzhuren* (class director) for a period or more to discuss isues involving the class. These class meetings might, for example, focus on discussing study habits, planning some class event, praising outstanding performances or behavior, and so on. Like subject teaching, class meetings can also be 'open' to outside observers, and novices learning how to be *banzhuren* are expected to give 'open' class meetings.

Banzhuren – class director; a subject teacher who also has responsibility for overseeing and supporting the learning and growth of a class (*ban*) of pupils. *Banzhuren* are responsible for much extra-curricular activity, as well as being aware of how each pupil is doing in all his or her classes. They also serve as the key person in handling problems related to discipline or behavior.

Basic education – grades 1–9, which are compulsory.

Beikezu – lesson preparation group; the group of teachers who teach the same subject and grade level. This group meets regularly to plan lessons, discuss curriculum, and design and analyze assessments.

Chenggong jiaoyu – literally 'success education; a comprehensive reform approach in Chinese schools which has curricular, teaching, assessment, and administrative implications. Originally developed in a Shanghai school, and now more widely taken up both within Shanghai and across China more generally, this approach rethinks traditional assumptions which guide teaching and learning. One of its principle advocates, Liu Jinghai, describes the philosophy of the reform as follows.

> Every person has the potential for success, has the desire or need to become successful and can develop his originality and approach to success. [...] Through educational reform, students' negative self-concept can be transformed and their intrinsic motivation for self-study fostered in ways that allow them to become successful learners and prepare them to be successful members of society. (Liu, 1994)

The reform challenges deficit assumptions and practices related to learners and encourages teachers to work from where pupils are, rather than where externally mandated curricula might suggest, in ways that allow pupils to experience success, build confidence and begin to take on responsibility for an interest in their own learning, while continuing to raise expectations for them. The reform gained attention and popularity in part because it originated in work with low-achieving schools serving pupils typically seen as 'at-risk'.

Chuzhong – junior secondary school; literally, 'early middle'. These schools now serve sixth–ninth graders.

Daoshi (more often, *zhidao laoshi*) – mentor/advisor.

Fenpei – job allocation; the approach used in earlier periods for finding employment. This involved a central (municipal or provincial) plan which matched employer and job seeker. College and university graduates were assigned positions based on needs reported by institutions throughout a region. This allocation system has now been replaced by a labor market in which job seekers directly apply to employers.

Gaozhong – upper secondary school (grades 10-12).

Gongkaike – open or public lesson. 'Open' lessons are lessons taught by a teacher to a class of pupils, with observers in attendance. Typically, an open lesson involves a public debriefing or discussion following the lesson.

Guanjian – hinge point; something in the curriculum – specific and key pieces of understanding, strategies or solution methods –- identified as central to pupils overcoming a difficult aspect of the content in order to understand an important idea.

Gugan laoshi – backbone teacher; teachers who play a leadership role in the life of the school or who exert influence on other teachers.

Huibaoke – report lesson; a version of an 'open' lesson taught by first-year (beginning) teachers, with the purpose of evaluating the first-year teacher's teaching. Attending and participating in the session would be school administrators, including principals, mentor teachers and other key teachers in the school.

Jiaowuchu – Teaching Program (office); the section of the College of Education responsible for its programs or curriculum.

Jiaoxue sixiang – teaching philosophy; a term referring to the orientation, stance or philosophy one brings to one's teaching.

Jiaoyanshi – Teaching Research Section; the division within a district's College of Education responsible for stimulating and leading district research activities related to teaching. A College of Education always has a Teaching Research Section, which includes specialists in each subject area.

Jiaoyanzu – teaching research group; the group of all teachers in the school who teach the same subject area. This group meets regularly to discuss issues related to the teaching and reform of curriculum and instruction in that subject area, and it organizes 'open' lessons in the school and facilitates teachers attending 'open' lessons in other schools.

Jinyan xing de mofang – experiential imitation; mentoring which simply encourages the novice to duplicate the techniques of the mentor.

Nandian – difficult point; ideas or points in the curriculum that tend to prove difficult for pupils to grasp or master.

New teacher training – see *xin laoshi peixun*, less commonly called, "education for entering the profession" (see *ruzhijiaoyu*).

New teacher – see *xin laoshi*.

Peixunbu – Training Section; a district's College of Education may be organized into sections which include a Training Section, which is the home for those running professional development for teachers in the district.

Putonghua – literally 'common language', Mandarin; the official language of China and hence the official language of instruction in Shanghai schools.

Qingnian laoshi – young teacher; officially, a teacher in their first five years post probation, although often people use this term to refer to any new or young teacher in their first many years of teaching.

Ruzhijiaoyu – induction; literally, 'education for entering the profession'.

Shuoke – talk lesson; a variant on 'open' lessons, a kind of précis of a lesson that a teacher would give not to pupils but to an audience of other teachers or experts. In a talk lesson, the teacher explains why he or she chose to teach the content chosen, describes the goals for the class and outlines the methods and processes to be used.

Suzhi jiaoyu – usually translated as quality education; a reform of the 1990s, quality education shifts schooling away from a traditional focus on academic achievement, which tended to concentrate instructional effort on preparing only a portion of the pupils, the strongest ones, for success on competitive examinations; instead, quality education is intended to support all pupils' growth and learning – cognitive, but also social, personal, and vocational.

Xin laoshi – 'new teacher' is the literal translation of this term, used to refer to inductees. These teachers are considered probationary teachers.

Xin laoshi peixun – induction; literally, 'training of new teachers'. Induction programs for first-year teachers, mandated at the municipal level by the Shanghai Municipal Education Commission and requiring all first-year teachers to work with a mentor at their school and to take part in some combination of activities organized by their district.

Young teacher – see *qingnian laoshi*.

Yubeiban – preparatory class; sixth grade, which only relatively recently was moved from being part of elementary schools to being housed in junior secondary schools.

Zhidao laoshi – literally, 'guiding teacher'; the term often used to refer to mentors.

Zhongdian – important point; ideas in the curriculum which are seen as most basic and/or crucial for the knowledge structure of that field.

Zhongxue – secondary school, literally, 'middle school'; this term encompasses both junior secondary and senior secondary school.

Zige zhengshu – qualification, certification; qualifications for, in this case, a teacher, that certify the person has the appropriate level of training for the level of work he or she undertakes.

Chapter 3 Switzerland

Begleiter – literally 'companion' or 'escort'; used formerly in Zurich as the main form of mandatory induction: an experienced counselor who observed, provided advice and evaluated the beginning teacher.

Berufseinführung – a leading into the profession; the Swiss term for induction. Relevant programs are provided for novices in all professions, not just for beginning teachers.

Canton – a Swiss state; there are 26 cantons making up the Swiss Federation. Educational policy is made at the canton level.

Continuing education – all teachers are expected to spend a certain amount of their working time (generally five percent of their work hours, i.e. 90 hours total over a year) on continuing education and professional development. A distinction is made between:

(a) education to provide greater depth for the current teaching level;
(b) education resulting in an additional diploma that allows teachers to move to a higher (and better-paid) teaching level, e.g., from upper primary teaching (grades 4–6) to lower secondary teaching (grades 7–9).

Counselor – in Lucerne and Bern, the leader of a practice group, usually specifically trained, also available to provide individual advice or counseling as demanded by beginning teacher or (rarely) requested by an inspector at the behest of a parent or the school leadership. In Zurich, experienced teachers or senior advisors are available to provide individual assistance as requested by beginning teacher. The service is free in all cantons for a specified number of counseling sessions.

Didactics – the art and science of teaching; one to two years of didactics courses are required of all grade 7–9 teachers to prepare them for the teaching profession. There generally are two types of courses:

(a) theory, e.g. cognitive and educational psychology, development of children and adolescents, evaluation of one's own teaching;
(b) how to teach specific subjects, course sequences, and topics, e.g. evaluating curricular units on force and motion, distillation in chemistry, use of the canton-wide middle school mathematics textbook series.

Gymnasium – élite-track leading directly to university entrance; pupils who graduate from the *Gymnasium* are allowed, without any further examinations, to study any subject at any Swiss university. Generally, the *Gymnasium* starts in grade 10 (grade 7 in Lucerne and a few other cantons). About 15 percent of a given cohort generally attend the *Gymnasium* and they are prepared for it in middle school. Governance and organization follow the university model rather than the community school model.

Inspectorate – office of school inspectors under the canton's ministry of education; generally education professionals, but sometimes lay as in Zurich. The inspectors carry out evaluations of teachers and schools based on school visits and act as the canton's liaison with parents and the community.

Lower secondary school – grades 7–9, traditionally organized into three tracks; *vocational/technical* (a minority – larger in the countryside than in the cities – of generally underachieving pupils), middle school (*Mittelschule*, attended by the large majority of pupils) and pre-*Gymnasium* (some 15 percent). The sixth-grade teacher makes the placement recommendations, although parents may dispute these (not a common occurrence) and have the final say, at least in some cantons. A common course of study is required of all pupils at this level, although it varies somewhat in rigor; vocational/technical pupils may take longer to complete it.

Maturität (equivalent to *Matura* in Austria, *Abitur* in Germany, *Baccalauréat* in France and the International Baccalaureat Diploma) – a set of final examinations students must pass to graduate from *Gymnasium*; roughly equivalent to completing the first year or two of a North American college education.

Mensch – the common English translation of this word as 'man' (see below) is misleading, as the German word means 'Human Being' and refers to both men and women.

Mensch und Umwelt; Natur, Mensch und Mitwelt – "Man and the Environment", "Nature, Man and the Surrounding World", the names of the integrated science and social issues courses for grades 7–9 in Zurich and Bern, respectively; the Lucerne curriculum mandates a similar course in grades K–6, but changes to the traditional disciplines (physics, chemistry, biology, geography) for grades 7–12.

Mittelschule – middle school; the grade 7-9 track generally enrolling the majority of the cohort. Some 15 percent of the cohort are enrolled in the pre-*Gymnasium* track (or in *Gymnasium* in Lucerne); this track may be part of middle school or explicitly separated.

Pädagogische Hochschule – an institution for the preparation of elementary and lower secondary teachers; can be compared with a four-year U.S. college or a professional school such as a law school or business school.

Philosophy I – field of university study comprising languages, history, and the social sciences.

Philosophy II – field of university study comprising mathematics and the natural sciences.

Practice Group – in the context of this study, a group of five to seven beginning teachers, usually from different schools, who meet during their first and second year of teaching to exchange and resolve problems they encounter in their practice; reciprocal classroom observations anchor the group's discussions in the realities of practice. The groups are facilitated by a trained leader (see under 'counselor', above).

The groups generally meet for six to eight sessions of three to four hours each (depending on the canton and the desires of the group); the canton pays for substitutes for half the sessions and for the leader. The groups can be continued beyond the induction period; they count toward the five percent time each teacher is supposed to spend on professional development. (In a broader sense, the term applies to all groups of teachers working together, including groups of experienced teachers.)

Primary school – grades 1–6 in almost all cantons (grades 1–5 in Aargau).

Pupils – we use the common German distinction between children and youths in primary and middle schools, who are called *pupils*, and youths in the *Gymnasium, Seminar* and university, who are called *students*.

Prorector – the vice-principal of a *Gymnasium*; depending on the size of the *Gymnasium*, there are a number of *Prorectors* (resembling deans in colleges and universities), each handling a particular set of disciplines, such as the sciences and mathematics.

Realschule – the lowest track for grades 7–9 providing vocational education for technical and agricultural careers.

Rector – the principal of a *Gymnasium*; this position resembles more the position of president of a college, since a *Gymnasium* is organized more like a tertiary than a secondary institution.

School board (school commission) – a lay board made up of prominent community members who govern a school; in small communities, members are elected directly by the people of the community, while in larger communities, they are appointed by the community's parliament. The board has decision-making powers on hiring teachers (although the canton sets salaries), on school expenditures beyond those set by the canton and on school policies. The board also generally has evaluative functions: for example, in Bern, an individual board member visits teachers (including beginning teachers) twice a year to observe lessons and discuss them, if the teacher so desires.

School leadership – carries out some of the functions of a school principal for elementary and lower secondary schools, but has fewer responsibilities as well as fewer rights. Constituted of one or more teachers who advise the school board, based on input from all the school staff. Generally, all the teachers meet periodically (e.g., every two weeks) to discuss school goals, purchases, new materials, problem issues, suggestions to forward to the school board, etc.

Secondary school – comprises lower secondary school (grades 7–9) and upper secondary school (grades 10–12, grades 10–13 in some cantons).

Seminar – a teacher training institution for elementary (grades 1–6) and early childhood teachers; considered an extension of secondary education, since it was possible to start this type of teacher preparation after comple-ting ninth grade; they also provide some professional development and induction services. *Seminars* are due to be abolished within two to three years, with preparation of all teachers shifted to the tertiary level, i.e. either the universities or the professional *Pädagogischen Hochschulen* (four-year colleges – see above).

Standortbestimmung – literally 'a determination of status; a reflection by a beginning teacher, usually with the help of a counselor or mentor, on where he or she stands as a teacher and as a person. They are mandated as part of induction in Bern and Lucerne, and are commonly used in pre-service education, as well as in other professions.

Supervision – a general term for a group of teachers (often beginning teachers) or other professionals (such as social workers), working collaboratively on problems arising out of their practice; the group is facilitated by a leader. *Intervision* refers to similar groups, but ones which are conducted without a facilitator.

Swiss Conference of Cantonal Education Ministers – periodic meetings of the education ministers of most cantons (attendance is voluntary) to address cross-cantonal education issues such as induction programs, expectations and training for school leadership members or the pre-service education of elementary school teachers.

Chapter 5 France

Academy – the regional organisational structure of the Ministry of Education, which within its geographic borders has considerable power and influence over all aspects of K–12 education as well as over practising teachers and teacher education at all levels.

Agrégation – the highest academic level of teacher recruiting examination; it is solely a subject-matter examination (taken after students have gained a subject-based masters degree). It is intended more for those who plan to teach in a *lycée* than a *collège* or in some parts of higher education. Passing and becoming a schoolteacher leads to increased salary and a reduced teaching load (from eighteen to fifteen class hours per week), and you are known as an *agrégé(e)* teacher.

CAPES (Concours au professorat d'éducation secondaire) – one of the main national recruiting competitions for teachers; this one leads to employment in the secondary sector. There are both oral and written papers, and it is only after successfully passing the written papers that you are eligible to take the orals in front of a jury in Paris. If you pass (becoming referred to as a *capétien/capétienne*), you then have been accepted into the teaching profession and are then assigned to an IUFM for the subequent (*stagiaire*) year. Provided you are granted confirmation by the relevant subject IPR at the end of the PLC2 year, you are tenured (*titularisé*) as a teacher in the national system for your entire life.

Collège – lower secondary school, uniformaly covering four grades, six to nine, of compulsory secondary schooling in a free-standing institution; at the end of grade nine, there is an end of junior high school examination, the *brevet*.

Conseiller/conseillère pédagogique (CP) – literally 'pedagogic advisor', a school-based mentor (almost always in the same institution, preferably teaching one class at the same grade as the *stagiaire* teacher) appointed by the relevant subject IPRs in consultation (if they so choose) with the IUFM staff. There is one each appointed for both the *stage en responsabilité* and for the *stage de pratique accompagnée*.

Didactique des Mathématiques (DdM) – A high-level, academic and theoretical approach to the study of issues of teaching and learning mathematics, originated in France during the early 1970s.

DEUG (Diplôme d'études universitaires générales) – A university qualification earned at the end of the second year of unviersity study, following which a greater subject-matter specialisation occurs.

Former/formation/formateur – a key set of terms which have no exact parallel in English; *former* is a verb, and broadly means "to shape" or "to mould", and it is something I can do to someone else (transitive verb) but it is also something I can do to myself (*se former* – reflexive verb). *Formation* is usually translated into English as either 'education' or 'training' (and *formateur* as 'educator' or 'trainer') and it is neither of these and reflects a somewhat different sense of being prepared. The Latin root of the word 'educate' is "to lead out", whereas *former* has more of the sense of something being done from the outside.

Inspecteur/Inspectrice Générale (IG) – These are powerful supra-Academy figures located in the Ministry of Education in Paris: there are 10 IGs nationally for mathematics. They are responsible for managing the national curriculum, the inspection of *agrégés* in their subject as well as being allocated a group of Academies each in terms of general supervision.

Inspecteur/Inspectrice Pédagogique Régionale (IPR) – a significant figure in the Academy structure and hierarchy, responsible for ensuring the national curriculum in primary and secondary schools, teacher inspections and specific fiunctions in relation to *stagiaire* teachers within the Academy. There are subject-based IPRs (at least one per Academy for mathematics, usually more).

Institut de Recherche sur l'Enseignement des Mathématiques (IREM) – literally, Institute of Research on the Teaching of Mathematics (and importantly not *Institut de Recherche sur Didactique des Mathématiques* – see above).

Institut Universitaire de Formation des Maîtres (IUFM) – literally, University Institute for the *Formation* of Teachers; this institution is not a University Institute in the sense of being part of one, in that they are free-standing institutions usually linked with one or more universities in the Academy. These are key institutions in French teacher education at all levels and have recently been ceded responsibility for the organisation and provision of all of the *formation continue* (broadly, in-service education) for the country.

Lycée – upper secondary school, usually covering the three grades from ten to twelve (compulsory schooling ends on reaching age 16, usually reached during the grade ten year); there are various types of *lycées*, including vocational ones as well as more academically focused general/technical ones. At the end of grade twelve, there is a high-stakes examination, the *baccalauréat*, which determines the right to university entrance.

PLC1 (Professeur Lycée Collège year 1) – these are students affiliated with an IUFM who are preparing for the CAPES teacher recruiting examination. Despite the name *professeur* ('teacher') in the label, PLC1s are students – they are not yet teachers and many such students will never be teachers.

PLC2 (Professeur Lycée Collège year 2) – these are new teachers who have just passed the *CAPES or Agrégation* recruiting examinations (see above) and are mandatorily affiliated with an IUFM for their first, *stagiaire* year as a teacher.

Stage/stagiaire – the term *stage* is not an education-specific term; the nearest English term is perhaps 'work experience course' or 'practicum'. *Stages* are evaluated practical periods spent doing the thing that is being learnt or apprenticed, prior to becoming certified. So for instance engineers go on *stages*, as do doctors and nurses, social workers, and so on. A *stagiaire* is simply someone who is undertaking a *stage*. So a *professeur stagiaire* is a teacher on such a *stage*, usually in a school, and in England might be called a 'probtionary teacher' or a 'probationer', as the strong expectation would be at the end of the period of being a *stagiaire* that one would become fully certified (*titularisé*).

Titulaire/titularisé – a general term meaning 'certified' and hence a contrastive terms with *stagiaire*. To become a *professeur titularisé* is to be allocated to a numbered post in a school that is yours until you retire, unless you move school to another such position or you permanently leave the profession. The sense is also there of being 'entitled' to this title of teacher.

References

ACE (1998) *New Zealand Teacher* (Special edition for graduating teachers), December, Auckland, NZ, Auckland College of Education.

Alexander, R. (2000) *Culture and Pedagogy: International Comparisons in Primary Education*, Oxford, Blackwell.

Altbach, P. and Kelly, G. (1986) 'Introduction: perspectives on comparative education', in Altbach, P. and Kelly, G. (eds), *New Approaches to Comparative Education*, Chicago, IL, University of Chicago Press, pp. 1-10.

Ambauen, M. (1998) *Ziele und Wirksamkeit der Berufseinführung aus der Sicht von Primarpersonen.* [Goals and Effectiveness of Induction in the View of Elementary School Teachers, summary by Monika and Fritz Vogel. Lucerne, Switzerland: available from Fritz Vogel, Center for Continuing Teacher Education]

André, B. *et al.* (2000) 'A l'aube du XXIe siècle, les mathématiques n'auraient-elles plus leur place dans l'enseignement secondaire?', *Le Monde,* Paris, p. 8. ('At the dawn of the twenty-first century, might mathematics no longer have its place in secondary school?')

Antin, D. (1987) 'The stranger at the door', *Genre* **20**(3/4), 463-481.

Aries, P. (1996) *Centuries of Childhood* (trans. Baldick, R.), London, Pimlico.

Artigue, M. and Perrin-Glorian, M.-J. (1991) 'Didactic engineering, research and development tool: some theoretical problems linked to this duality', *For the Learning of Mathematics* **11**(1), 13-18.

Artigue, M. *et al.* (1998) *Entre Théorie et Pratique: le Mémoire Professionel de Mathématiques à l'IUFM,* Reims, CRDP de Champagne-Ardenne. [Between Theory and Practice: the Mathematics Professional Memoir in the IUFM]

Aspinall, R. (2001) *Teachers' Unions and the Politics of Education in Japan,* Albany, NY, SUNY Press.

Balacheff, N. (1988) 'A journal: *Recherches en Didactiques des Mathématiques',* in *Keep Up with Teaching in France* (booklet prepared for ICME VI, trans. Pimm, D.), French Commission for Mathematics Teaching (The ICMI Subcommission for France), Lyon, pp. 75-78.

Balacheff, N. (1990) 'Towards a *problématique* for research on mathematics teaching', *Journal for Research in Mathematics Education* **21**(4), 258-272.

Beauchamp, E. (1991) 'The development of Japanese educational policy, 1945-1985', in Beauchamp, E. (ed.), *Windows on Japanese Education,* New York, NY, Greenwood Press, pp. 27-49.

Blanchard-Laville, C. (2000a) 'Le temps de formation', in Blanchard-Laville, C. and Nadot, S. (eds), *Malaise dans la Formation des Enseignants,* Paris, l'Harmattan, pp. 167-184. ['The time period of formation', Unease in the *Formation* of Teachers]

Blanchard-Laville, C. (2000b) 'Au-delà de l'analyse des besoins en formation', in Blanchard-Laville, C. and Nadot, S. (eds), M*alaise dans la Formation des Enseignants,* Paris, l'Harmattan, pp. 45-58. ['Beyond the analysis of needs in *formation*', Unease in the *Formation* of Teachers]

Blanchard-Laville, C. (2001) *Les Enseignants entre Plaisir et Souffrance*, Paris, Presses Universitaires de France. [Teachers between Pleasure and Suffering]

Blanchard-Laville, C. and Nadot, S. (eds) (2000) *Malaise dans la Formation des Enseignants*, Paris, l'Harmattan. [Malaise in the *Formation* of Teachers]

Bolam, R. (1995) 'Teacher recruitment and induction', in Anderson, L. (ed.) *International Encyclopedia of Teaching and Teacher Education* (second edition), Oxford, Elsevier Science, pp. 612-615.

Bourdoncle, R. (1994) 'Educational research in France', in Calderhead, J. (ed.) *Educational Research in Europe*, Clevedon, Avon, Multilingual Matters Ltd, pp. 9-13.

Brousseau, G. (1997) *Theory of Didactical Situations: Didactique des Mathématiques 1970-1990* (Balacheff, N., Cooper, M., Sutherland, R. and Warfield, V. trans. and eds), Dordrecht, Kluwer.

Caillot, M. (2002) 'French *didactiques*', *Canadian Journal of Science, Mathematics and Technology Education* **2**(3), 397-403.

CNDP (1999, revision of 1998 version) *Enseigner au Collège: Mathématiques – Programmes et Accompagnement*, Paris, Centre National de Documentation Pédagogique. [Teaching at Junior Secondary School: Mathematics – Syllabus and Accompanying Material]

Cochran-Smith, M. and Lytle, S. (1999) 'Relationships of knowledge and practice: teacher learning communities', *Review of Research in Education* **24**, 249-305.

Comiti, C. *et al.* (eds) (1999) *Le Mémoire Professionel: Enquête sur un Outil de Formation des Enseignants*, Grenoble, l'IUFM de Grenoble. [The Professional Memoir: an Enquiry into a Tool for the *Formation* of Teachers]

Cornu, B. (1999) 'Training today the teacher of tomorow', in Hoyles, C., Morgan, C. and Woodhouse, G. (eds), *Rethinking the Mathematics Curriculum*, London, Falmer, pp. 195-202.

Corry, J. (1970) *Farewell the Ivory Tower: Universities in Transition*, Montreal, QC, McGill-Queen's University Press.

Darling-Hammond, L. and Cobb, V. (eds) (1995) *Teacher Preparation and Professional Development in APEC Members: a Comparative Study*, Washington, DC, U.S. Department of Education.

EDK (1996) *Berufseinführung von Lehrerinnen und Lehrern – Dossier 40A*, Bern, Schweizerische Konferenz der kantonalen Erziehungsdirectoren. [Induction for Teachers, Swiss Conference of Cantonal Education Ministers]

ERO (2000) *In Time for the Future: a Comparative Study of Mathematics and Science Education*, Wellington, NZ, Education Review Office.

Erziehungs- und Kulturdepartment des Kantons Luzern (1998) *Beurteilung der Lehrperson*, Lucerne. [Evaluation of Teachers, Lucerne Education and Culture Department]

Erziehungs- und Kulturdepartment des Kantons Luzern (1999) *Evaluation der Praxisgruppen 1998/99*, Lucerne. [Evaluation of the 1998/99 Practice Groups, Lucerne Education and Culture Department]

Erziehungs- und Kulturdepartment des Kantons Luzern (undated) *Angebotsmappe der externen Beraterinnen und Berater für Schulentwicklungsprojekte,* Lucerne. [Listing of External Consultants for School Improvement Projects, Lucerne Education and Culture Department]

Erziehungsdirektion Zürich (1991) *Lehrplan für die Volksschule des Kantons Zürich* Zurich, Lehrmittelverlag. [Instructional Plan for the Canton of Zurich, Zurich Education Ministry]

Feiman-Nemser, S. (2001) 'From preparation to practice: designing a continuum to strengthen and sustain teaching', *Teachers College Record* **103**(6), 1013-1055.

Feiman-Nemser, S., Schwille, S. Carver, C. and Yusko, B. (1999a) *A Conceptual Review of Literature on New Teacher Induction* (A report prepared for the National Partnership on Excellence and Accountability in Education), Washington, DC, NPEAT.

Feiman-Nemser, S., Carver, C., Schwille, S. and Yusko, B. (1999b) 'Beyond support: taking new teachers seriously as learners', in Scherer, M. (ed.), *A Better Beginning: Supporting and Mentoring New Teachers,* Alexandria, VA, Association for Supervision and Curriculum Development, pp. 3-12.

Fiske, E. and Ladd, H. (2001) *When Schools Compete: a Cautionary Tale,* Washington, DC, Brookings Institution Press.

Fursman, L. and Visser, H. (1998) *A Survey of New Graduates from Teacher Training Programmes* (School Labour Market Policy), Wellington, NZ, Ministry of Education.

Garden, R. (1997) 'New Zealand', in Robitaille, D. (ed.), *National Contexts for Mathematics and Science Education: an Encyclopedia of the Education Systems Participating in TIMSS,* Vancouver, BC, Pacific Educational Press, pp. 270-278.

Gold, Y. (1996) 'Beginning teacher support: attrition, mentoring, and induction', in Sikula, J. (ed.), *Handbook of Research on Teacher Education,* New York, NY, Macmillan, pp. 548-594.

Gray, A. and Renwick, M. (1998) *A Study into the Effectiveness of Teacher Education Programmes,* Wellington, NZ, Research Division, Ministry of Education.

Gu, L. *et al.* (1997) 'Jinru 21 shiji de zhongxiaoxue jiaoyu xindong gangling (1997-2010)', *Shanghai Jiaoyu* **9**, 7-13. ['Guidelines for mathematics education in elementary and secondary schools upon entering the twenty-first century', Shanghai Education]

Hall, G. (1904) *Adolescence: Its Psychology and Its Relations to Physiology, Anthropology, Sociology, Sex, Crime, Religion and Education,* New York, NY, D. Appleton and Co.

Harmon, M. *et al.* (1997) *Performance Assessment in IEA's Third International Mathematics and Science Study,* Boston, MA, Boston College.

Hatzfield, H. (1996) 'Decentralizing the education system', in Corbett, A. and Moon, B. (eds) *Education in France: Continuity and Change in the Mitterand Years, 1981-1995,* London, Routledge, pp. 164-182. (A translation of Hatzfield, H. (1991) 'La décentralisation du système éducatif, les régions à l'épreuve', *Politiques et Management Public* **9**(4), 23-49.)

Hébert, F. and Tavignot, P. (eds) (1998) *Entrez dans Nos Classes,* Rouen, CRDP de Rouen. [Come into our Classrooms]

Hennequin, P.-L. (1996) 'Mathematics and teacher training in France since 1990', in *L'Enseignement des Mathématiques en France* (ICME 8, English version), Grenoble, French Commission for Mathematics Teaching (The ICMI Subcommission for France), pp. 15-24.

Henry, M. (2000) 'Evolution and prospects of preservice secondary mathematics teacher education in France', *Journal of Mathematics Teacher Education* **3**(3), 271-279.

Herbst, P. and Kilpatrick, J. (1999) 'Pour lire Brousseau', *For the Learning of Mathematics* **19**(1), 3-10. [in English]

Hsiung, S. and Tan, K. (1998) 'Supporting novices through the internet', paper presented at the annual meeting of the U.S. National Association for Research in Science Teaching, Atlanta, GA.

IAPD (1995) 'Teacher training and professional development in Japan' (a sub-report submitted for APEC members by the International Affairs Planning Division of the Monbusho), in Darling-Hammond, L. and Cobb, V. (eds), *Teacher Preparation and Professional Development in APEC Members: a Comparative Study*, Washington, DC, U.S. Department of Education, pp. 113-129.

Ingersoll, R. (1999) 'The problem of underqualified teachers in American secondary schools', *Educational Researcher* **28**(2), 26-37.

IREM (1984) *Fifteen Years for the Institute for Research into the Teaching of Mathematics (IREM)*, Bulletin Inter-IREM ICME V Special, Paris.

Kenner, H. (2000) *The Elsewhere Community*, New York, NY, Oxford University Press.

Kieran, C. (1998) 'Complexity and insight', *Journal for Research in Mathematics Education* **29**(5), 595-601.

King, K. (2001) 'Conceptually-oriented mathematics teacher development: improvisation as a metaphor', *For the Learning of Mathematics* **21**(3), 9-15.

Kinney, C. (1998) 'Teachers and the teaching profession in Japan', in Stevenson, H. (project director), *The Education System in Japan: Case Study Findings*, Washington, DC, U.S. Department of Education, pp. 183-253.

Laborde, C. (1989) 'Audacity and reason: French research in mathematics education', *For the Learning of Mathematics* **9**(3), 31-36.

Lampert, M. (1985) 'How do teachers manage to teach? Perspectives on problems in practice', *Harvard Educational Review* **55**(2), 178-94.

Lave, J. and Wenger, E. (1991) *Situated Learning: Legitimate Peripheral Participation*, Cambridge, Cambridge University Press.

Lewis, C. and Tsuchida, I. (1997) 'Planned educational change in Japan: the case of elementary science instruction', *Journal of Education Policy* **12**(5), 313-331.

Lewis, C. and Tsuchida, I. (1998) 'A lesson is like a swiftly flowing river: how research lessons improve Japanese education', *American Educator* **22**(4), 12-17, 50-52.

Liu, J. (1994) 'Shixian *chenggong jiaoyu*, zhengqu jiaoyuchenggong', paper presented at the *4th International Conference on Chinese Education for the 21st Century*, Shanghai, August. [Implementing 'education of success', striving for success in education]

Lord, B. (1994) 'Teachers' professional development: critical colleagueship and the role of professional communities', in Cobb, N. (ed.), *The Future of Education: Perspectives on National Standards in America,* New York, NY, College Entrance Examination Board, pp. 175-204.

Lu, B. (ed.) (2000) *Yi Tihua: Shifan Jiaoyu Gaige de Sikao yu Shijian,* Shanghai, Huadong Shifan Daxue Chubanshe. [Putting into One System: Thoughts and Practice on Teacher Education Reform, East China Normal University Press]

Ma, L. (1999) *Knowing and Teaching Elementary Mathematics,* Mahwah, NJ, Lawrence Erlbaum Associates.

Maki, M. (1993) 'A case study of induction training for beginning teachers in Japan', paper presented at the OECD–CERI meeting on teacher quality, Tokyo, Japan.

Maki, M. (1999) 'Teacher policies in Japan', paper presented at the Korea–OECD seminar on teacher policy, Tokyo, Japan.

Mansell, R. (1996) *Professional Development of Beginning Teachers: How Does It Work?,* Wellington, NZ, Teacher Registration Board.

Margolinas, C. (2000) 'Relations between the theoretical field and the practical field in mathematics education', in Sierpinska, A. and Kilpatrick, J. (eds), *Mathematics Education as a Research Domain: a Search for Identity,* vol. 2, Dordrecht, Kluwer, pp. 351-356.

MOE (1995) 'Teacher training and professional development practices in New Zealand', in Darling-Hammond, L. and Cobb, V. (eds), *Teacher Preparation and Professional Development in APEC Members: a Comparative Study,* Washington, DC, US Department of Education, pp. 147-178.

MOE (1997) *Science in the New Zealand Curriculum,* Wellington, NZ, Learning Media.

MOE (1999) *Teacher Performance Management: a Resource for Boards of Trustees, Principals and Teachers,* Wellington, NZ, Ministry of Education.

Monbusho (1991) *Basic Outline for the Beginning Teacher Training Implementation,* Tokyo, Ministry of Education, Science, Sports and Culture.

Monbusho (1994) *Education in Japan,* Tokyo, Gyosei.

Monbusho (1996) *The Current and Main Activities of the Monbusho,* Tokyo, Ministry of Education, Science, Sports and Culture.

Monbusho (1999) *The Current and Main Activities of the Monbusho,* Tokyo, Ministry of Education, Science, Sports and Culture.

Monbusho (2000) *Education in Japan,* Tokyo, Gyosei.

Moser, U., Gretler, A., Ramseier, E. and Labudde, P. (1997) 'Switzerland', in Robitaille, D. (ed.), *National Contexts for Mathematics and Science Education: an Encyclopedia of the Education Systems Participating in TIMSS,* Vancouver, BC, Pacific Educational Press, pp. 376-385.

Moskowitz, J. and Kennedy, S. (1997) 'Teacher induction in an era of educational reform: the case of New Zealand', in Moskowitz, J. and Stephens, M. (eds), *From Students of Teaching to Teachers of Students: Induction around the Pacific Rim,* Washington, DC, Department of Education, pp. 131-167.

Moskowitz, J. and Stephens, M. (eds) (1997) *From Students of Teaching to Teachers of Students: Teacher Induction around the Pacific Rim*, Washington, DC, U.S. Department of Education.

Nadot, S. (ed.) (2000) *Formation Initiale: le Livret du Tuteur de Mémoire Professionel 2000-2001,* l'IUFM de l'Academie de Versailles. [Initial *Formation:* the Booklet for Professional Memoir Tutors]

NCER (1986) *The Second Report of the National Commission of Educational Reform,* Tokyo, National Commission of Educational Reform.

Nohara, D. (1997) '"The training year": teacher induction in Japan', in Moskowitz, J. and Stephens, M. (eds), *From Students of Teaching to Teachers of Students: Teacher Induction around the Pacific Rim,* Washington, DC, U.S. Department of Education, pp. 95-130.

OECD (2001) *Knowledge and Skills for Life: First Results from PISA 2000,* Paris, Organisation of Economic Co-operation and Development.

Okano, K. and Tsuchiya, M. (1999) *Education in Contemporary Japan: Inequality and Diversity,* Cambridge, Cambridge University Press.

Olssen, M. and Matthews, K. (1997) *Education Policy in New Zealand: the 1990s and Beyond,* Palmerston North, NZ, The Dunmore Press Limited.

Padilla, M., Riley, J., Bryan, L. and Ikeda, H. (1999) 'Induction of first year teachers in Japan: program description and a case study of two new teachers', paper presented at the annual conference of the U.S. National Association for Research in Science Teaching, Boston, MA.

Paine, L. (1990) 'Teacher as virtuoso: a Chinese model for teaching', *Teachers College Record* **92**(1), 49-81.

Pimm, D. (1987) *Speaking Mathematically: Communication in Mathematics Classrooms,* London, Routledge and Kegan Paul.

PPTA (1999) *Beginning Teachers,* Wellington, NZ, Post-Primary Teachers' Association.

Ramseier, E., Keller, C. and Moser, U. (1999) *Bilanz Bildung,* Zurich, Verlag Rüegger. [Education Results]

Riley, J., Padilla, M., Weiseman, K. and Ikeda, H. (1998) 'Science teacher education in Japan: student teaching and the preparation of preservice science teachers', paper presented at the annual meeting of the Association for the Education of Teachers of Science, Minneapolis, MN.

Robert, A. and Haché, C. (2000) 'Connecting research to French mathematics teacher education', *Journal of Mathematics Teacher Education* **3**(3), 281-290.

Robitaille, D. (ed.) (1997) *National Contexts for Mathematics and Science Education: an Encyclopedia of the Education Systems Participating in TIMSS,* Vancouver, BC, Pacific Educational Press.

Ross, H. (1993) *China Learns English,* New Haven, CT, Yale University Press.

Rousset-Bert, S. (2000) 'Les activités: un thème à retravailler', *Petit x* **56**, 61-79. ['Tasks: a topic in need of further work']

Sato, M. (1992) 'Japan', in Leavitt, H. (ed.), *Issues and Problems in Teacher Education: an International Handbook,* New York. NY, Greenwood Press, pp. 155-168.

Schärer, H.-R. (ed.) (2000) *Lehrerbildung im Wandel: Grundlagen – Ansprüche – Impulse*, Aarau, Switzerland, Verlag Sauerländer. [Teacher Education in Transition: Foundations – Demands – Motivations]

Shanghai Jiaoyu Weiyuanhui (1998) *Shanghai Jiaoyu Nianjian 1997*, Shanghai, Shanghai Jiaoyu Chubanshe. [Shanghai Education Commission, Shanghai 1997 Education Yearbook, Shanghai Education Press]

Shanghai Zhongxiaoxue Kecheng Jiaocai Gaige Weiyuanhui (1998) *Quanrizhi Jiunian Yiwu Jiaoyu – Shuxue Xueke Kecheng Biaozhun*, Shanghai, Shanghai Jiaoyu Chubanshe. [Shanghai Elementary and Secondary Curriculum and Teaching Materials Reform Commission, Full-Time Nine-Year Compulsory Education – Mathematics Subject Curriculum Standards, Shanghai Education Press]

Shanghai Zhongxiaoxue Kecheng Jiaocai Gaige Weiyuanhui (2000) *Mianxiang 21 shiji zhongxiaoxue xin kecheng fangan he ge xueke jiaoyu gaige xingdong gangling*, Shanghai, Shanghai Jiaoyu Chubanshe. [Shanghai Elementary and Secondary Curriculum and Teaching Materials Reform Commission, Framework for New Curriculum Policy and Subject-Specific Education for the Twenty-first Century, Shanghai Education Press]

Shanghaishi Jiaoyu Weiyuanhui Shizichu (1998) 'Guanyu benshi zhongxiaoxue, youeryuan xinlaoshi peixun de yijian, wenjiandi 38 hao', in *Shanghaishi Zhongxiaoxue, Youeryuan Ganbu, Jiaoshi Peixun Gongzuo Wenjian Huibian (si)*, Shanghai, Shanghaishi Jiaoyu Weiyuanhui Shizichu, pp. 75-79. [Shanghai Municipal Education Commission Teacher and Staff Training Section, 'Opinion regarding new teachier training for kindergarten, elementary and secondary teachers in the municipality', document number 38, in Collected Documents on Training Kindergarten, Elementary, and Secondary Administrators and Teachers in Shanghai Municipality (4)]

Shiina, M. and Chonan, M. (1993) 'Attracting and preparing worthy teachers', *Peabody Journal of Education* **68**(3), 38-52.

Shimahara, N. (1991) 'Teacher education in Japan', in Beauchamp, E. (ed.), *Windows on Japanese Education*, New York, NY, Greenwood Press, pp. 259-280.

Shulman, L. (1987) 'Knowledge and teaching: foundations of the new reform', *Harvard Educational Review* **57**(1), 1-22.

Shuxue – Qinianji diyi xueqi (Jiunianzhi yiwu jiaoyu keben) (shiyong ben) (1998), Shanghai, Shanghai Jiaoyu Chubanshe. [Mathematics Teaching – First Semester Seventh Grade (Textbooks for Nine-Year Compulsory Education) (Trial edition), Shanghai Education Press]

Shuxue Jiaoxue Cankao Ziliao – Qinianji Diyi Xueqi (1998) (Jiunianzhi yiwu jiaoyu keben), Shanghai, Shanghai Jiaoyu Chubanshe. [Mathematics Teaching Reference Material – First Semester Seventh Grade (Textbooks for Nine-Year Compulsory Education), Shanghai Education Press]

Stigler, J. and Hibert, J. (1999) *The Teaching Gap: Best Ideas from the World's Teachers for Improving Education in the Classroom*, New York, NY, The Free Press.

Thom, R. (1973) 'Modern mathematics: does it exist?', in Howson, G. (ed.), *Developments in Mathematical Education,* Cambridge, Cambridge University Press, pp. 194-209.

Thrupp, M. (1999) *Schools Making a Difference: Let's Be Realistic!,* Milton Keynes, Bucks, Open University Press.

Tippins, D., Kemp, A. and Ogura, Y. (2000) 'Learning to teach science: the curriculum of student teaching in Hiroshima "attached" schools', *Journal of Science Teacher Education* **11**(3), 189-206.

TRB (1993) *Advice and Guidance Programmes for Teachers,* Wellington, NZ, Teacher Registration Board.

TRB (1997) *Information for Newly-Registered Teachers,* Wellington, NZ, Teacher Registration Board.

TRB (2001) *Handbook: the Registration of Teachers,* Wellington, NZ, Teacher Registration Board.

TTC (1972) *Reformation Strategy to Foster Improvement in Educational Instructors,* Tokyo, Teacher Training Council.

Vogel, F. and Vogel, M. (1996) *Berufseinführung,* Aarau, Switzerland, Verlag Sauerländer. [Induction]

Vygotsky, L. (1935/1994) 'The problem of the environment', in van der Veer, R. and Valsiner, J. (eds), *The Vygotsky Reader,* Cambridge, MA, Blackwell, pp. 338-354.

Wang, J. (1998) *Cong Bashi Niandai Zouxiang xin Shiji,* Shanghai, Bai Jia Publishing House. [From 1980s on to the New Era – Tracing Hot Issues of General Education in Shanghai]

Webster (1988) *The New Lexicon Webster's Encyclopedic Dictionary of the English Language* (Canadian Edition), New York, NY, Lexicon Publications.

Whitehead, A. (1925) *Science and the Modern World,* New York, NY, Macmillan.

Willetts, R. and Williams, Y. (1990) *A Guide for Beginning Teachers in Secondary Schools,* Palmerston North, NZ, Palmerston North College of Education.

Wilson, S., Shulman, L. and Richert, A. (1987) '"150 different ways" of knowing: representations of knowledge in teaching', in Calderhead, J. (ed.), *Exploring Teachers' Thinking,* Eastbourne, West Sussex, Cassell, pp. 104-124.

Wray, H. (1999) *Japanese and American Education: Attitudes and Practice.* Westport, CT, Bergin and Garvey.

Yoshida, M. (1999) 'Lesson study [*jugyokenkyu*] in elementary school mathematics in Japan: a case study', Paper presented at the AERA annual meeting, Montréal, QC.

ZBS (2000) *Mensch und Umwelt: Literatur und Lehrmittel,* Lucerne, Zentralschweizerischer Beratungsdienst für Schulfragen. [Man and the Environment: Literature and Curricular Materials, Counseling Service for School Issues for Central Switzerland]

Zhang, M. (1998) 'Mianxiang xinshiji jinyibu shishi suzhi jiaoyu', *Shanghai Jiaoyu* **9**, 6-12. ['Facing the new era and furthering implementation of quality education', Shanghai Education]

Ziegler, P. (1994) *Sekundarlehrerausbildung an der Universität Zürich,* Zurich, Stutz and Co. [Secondary Teacher Education at the University of Zurich]

Zumwalt, K. (1989) 'Beginning professional teachers: the need for a curricular vision of teaching', in Reynolds, M. (ed.), *Knowledge Base for the Beginning Teacher,* New York, NY, Pergamon Press, pp. 173-184.

Zzing, C. (1999) *Auswertung Befragungen: Berufseinführung 1996-1999,* Zurich, PrimarlehrSeminar. [Questionnaire Analysis: Induction 1996-1999]

Book Contributors and Project Advisors

Book Authors

Edward Britton is currently Associate Director of WestEd's National Center for Improving Science Education. His research foci include analyses of curriculum specifications, materials and assessments and studies of educational innovations. His prior books include *Examining the Examinations* (Kluwer, 1996), *Connecting Mathematics and Science to Workplace Contexts* (Corwin, 1999) and contributions in volumes from the Third International Mathematics and Science Study (TIMSS).

Lynn Paine is currently an Associate Professor in the Department of Teacher Education at Michigan State University. Her scholarly interests focus on teaching and teacher education understood in their social and cultural contexts. Her previous work includes participation in a cross-national study of mentoring in England, the US and China, as well as involvement in a comparative study of the relationships of teachers to the university in France, England and the US.

David Pimm is currently Professor of Mathematics Education in the Department of Secondary Education at the University of Alberta. During much of the lifetime of this project, he was Professor of Mathematics Education in the Department of Teacher Education at Michigan State University. His two previous books were *Speaking Mathematically: Communciation in Mathematics Classrooms* (Routledge, 1987) and *Symbols and Meanings in School Mathematics* (Routledge, 1995).

Senta Raizen has been involved in science education for some four decades. As director of the National Center for Improving Science Education, she has led many science education reform projects and authored or edited a number of books and articles. International volumes include *A Splintered Vision: an Investigation of U.S. Science and Mathematics Education (Kluwer, 1997);* and *Bold Ventures: Mathematics and Science Innovations (Kluwer, 1997)*. She serves in an advisory capacity, among others, to the National Assessment of Educational Progress (NAEP), the Third International Mathematics and Science Study (TIMSS), OECD's Program of International Student Assessment (PISA) and OECD/SRI's SITES-Module 3 project.

Chapter Co-Authors

Daniel Chazan is currently Associate Professor in the Department of Curriculum and Instruction at the University of Maryland College Park and a member of its Center for Mathematics Education. During the lifetime of the project, he was an Associate Professor in the Department of Teacher Education at Michigan State University. He is the author of *Beyond Formulas in Mathematics and Teaching: Dynamics of the High School Algebra Classroom*, published in 2000 by Teachers College Press.

Yanping Fang is currently a Ph.D. candidate in the Department of Teacher Education at Michigan State University. Before 1998, she was on the research faculty of the Shanghai Institute of Human Resource Development under the Shanghai Academy of Educational Sciences in the People's Republic of China.

Mary Ann Huntley is currently Assistant Professor in the Department of Mathematical Sciences at the University of Delaware. Her main research interest involves studying the effects (on pupils and teachers) of NCTM *Standards*-based mathematics curricula, particularly at the middle- and high-school levels. During work on this project, she was a Research Associate at WestEd's National Center for Improving Science Education.

Michael Padilla is a professor and former chair of the Department of Science Education at the University of Georgia. He is presently Associate Dean for Educator Partnerships at UGA. He has extensive international experience, especially in Japan, and has served as PI on three National Science Foundation and numerous US Department of Education grants.

Joseph Riley is a professor of science education at the University of Georgia. His international experience includes: Fulbright Scholar to the Philippines, science education consultant to World and Asian Development Bank projects in Indonesia, consultant to the U.S. Agency for International Development in Egypt and visiting scholar to the Center for the Study of International Cooperation in Education, Hiroshima University, Hiroshima, Japan.

Suzanne Wilson is currently Professor of Teacher Education and Director of the Center for the Scholarship of Teaching at Michigan State University. Three major inter-related strands form the nucleus of her work: teacher knowledge and its relationship to teaching, curricular policy and its relationship to teaching, and teacher learning and its relationship to teaching. Her most recent work, *California Dreaming: Reforming Mathematics Education*, was published by Yale University Press in November, 2002.

Project Advisors

Deborah Ball, Professor, University of Michigan

Rodger Bybee, Executive Director, Biological Sciences Curriculum Study

Sharon Feiman-Nemser, Professor, Brandeis University

Robert Floden, Professor, Michigan State University

Willis Hawley, Executive Director, National Partnership for Excellence and Accountability in Teaching, University of Maryland

David Imig, Executive Director, American Association of Colleges for Teacher Education

Glenda Lappan, Professor, Michigan State University

Jean Miller, Director, Interstate New Teacher Assessment and Support Consortium, Council of Chief State School Officers

Jay Moskowitz, Vice-President, American Institutes for Research

Jack Schwille, Professor, Michigan State University

Gary Sykes, Professor, Michigan State University

Michael Timpane, Senior Advisor for Education Policy, RAND Corp.

Gerald Wheeler, Executive Director, National Science Teachers Association

Arthur Wise, Executive Director, National Council for Accreditation of Teacher Education

INDEX

Academy mathematics Inspector 205, 207, 225
'Accompanied practice' *stage* (*stage de pratique accompagnée*) 226
action-research project 39, 85, 90, 286, 291
activity class (*huodong ke*) 20, 29
advice and guidance co-ordinators 153, 156-158, 169, 171, 173, 174, 176-181, 184, 325, 327, 344, 370
advice and guidance programs 146, 148, 157, 169, 180, 183, 184, 189, 369
after-school school or cram school (*juku*) 267
AG program, *see* advice and guidance programs
Agrégation 203, 209, 215, 218, 245, 255, 259, 260, 315, 316, 370, 372
alignment of college science with school science 151
Asia-Pacific Economic Co-operation (APEC) 10
application text (*texte d'application*) 317
Auckland College of Education (ACE) 149-152, 154, 165,, 192, 345
Auckland University program 149, 150

Baccalauréat 100, 210, 213, 214, 221
backbone teacher (*gugan laoshi*) 24, 31
Bancel Commission of 1989 331
Begleiter 110
Bern canton 121Bern University 94, 100, 131, 139-40, 342, 368
Berufseinführung 16, 83, 202, 297
Bildung 14
bi-weekly after-school meetings 143, 144
buddy teacher 142, 157, 169, 171, 175-177, 185, 192, 297, 298, 320, 325, 354

Canton-mandated counselors 85
CAPES examination 210, 215-218, 241, 247, 259, 260, 315, 347
class advisory meeting (*conseil de classe*) 199

class director (*banzhuren*) 14, 20, 31, 32, 38, 47, 59, 66, 70, 340
class meeting (*banhui*) 20, 66, 67
classroom management 38, 111, 135, 142, 143, 167, 171, 174, 175, 177-179, 197, 228, 229, 276, 278, 285, 308College of Education: Research Section (*jiaoyanshi*) 76
College of Education: Teaching Program Office (*jiaowuchu*) 76
College of Education: Teaching Section (*peixunbu*) 76
Conference of Cantonal Education Leaders 132, 383
Cornu-Brilhaut report 247
culture of schools 26, 298, 309, 310
culture of teaching 20, 49, 66, 69, 295, 297-299, 310, 337
curricular burden on beginning teachers 187
curriculum of induction 6, 8, 19, 240, 244, 298, 318, 375

department heads 16, 142, 144, 153, 155, 157, 159, 161, 165-167, 169-172, 176, 178, 180-182, 185, 187-190, 317, 320, 344
development programs 7, 28, 293, 315
didactics 84-86, 91, 94-96, 99-102, 104, 114, 117, 122, 124, 125, 132, 137-140, 250, 302, 304, 305, 341, 342, 355, 367, 368
didactics classes 84, 95, 96, 100, 114, 341, 342
didactics courses 91, 95, 96, 101, 102, 125, 342, 355, 368
didactics teachers 84, 104, 124, 138, 342
didactique 313
Didactique des mathematiques 228, 240, 241, 243, 244, 259, 326, 348, 373
difficult points (*nandian*) 24, 35-37, 41, 51, 54, 55, 58, 60, 62, 313, 335, 364
district-level mentors 45, 74, 75, 367

East China Normal University 33, 34, 77, 81

399

education for entering the profession
    (ruzhijiaoyu) 25
Education Review Office (ERO) 148,
    149, 157, 158, 163, 165
educational policy 10, 12, 81, 262, 364
enculturation into the teaching profession
    310
examination panel 195, 363
experiential imitation (*jinyanxing de
    mofang*) 71
extra-curricular roles 152, 154

facilitated peer support meeting 178,
    180, 183
field experience 99, 270
financial incentive/salary 155, 191
formal/informal observations 170, 174-
    176
formateurs 16, 197, 198, 200-202, 204-
    206, 209, 211, 212, 215, 222, 224-
    229, 232-235, 240-242, 244, 245,
    248-250, 252, 253, 255, 259, 260,
    297, 347-350, 363, 373
formation 14, 15, 18, 108, 121, 163, 194,
    197, 200-208, 210-212, 214, 217,
    219, 222, 224, 226, 229, 231-238,
    240, 241, 243-257, 259, 266, 297,
    314, 324, 326, 333, 347-349, 355,
    357, 358, 360, 371, 373, 374
French education system 204, 207, 247

General Inspectorate 207, 245, 371
German-speaking cantons (Bern,
    Lucerne, Zurich) 15, 92, 93, 112,
    113, 333, 341, 368
goals for induction 2, 40, 46, 304, 319
Graduate diploma programs in secondary
    teaching 149
group life (*shudan seikatsu*) 266
guiding teacher (*zhidao laoshi*) 288
Gymnasium 86, 92-94, 100-102, 104-
    106, 113, 117, 121, 126-128, 130-
    132, 137, 138, 140, 331, 342, 343,
    352, 353, 374

head of department (HOD) 155, 170,
    176, 177
hinge points (*guanjian*) 35, 377
home visits, enhancing 276
homeroom duties 174, 178, 180, 287

important points (*zhongdian*) 35, 51, 305
individual counseling 111, 114, 115,
    121, 122, 135, 316, 356
individual *Standortbestimmung* 115,
    119, 133
induction as a developmental phase 111
induction as complex systems:
    articulation and co-ordination 327
induction as period of time 4
induction curriculum 319
induction policies 6, 8, 11, 16, 25, 26,
    29, 32, 69, 70, 72, 74, 80, 138, 149,
    158, 182, 193, 299, 317, 330, 340,
    341, 344
induction providers 2, 16, 38, 145, 324,
    327, 328, 345
induction responsibilities 137, 317, 355
induction services 16, 94, 122, 132, 136,
    137, 173, 298, 355, 382
induction support 38, 70, 76, 122, 126,
    134, 158, 173, 307, 345
induction system 2, 5-7, 10, 14, 16, 18,
    25, 32, 81, 115, 137, 138, 155, 191,
    195, 247, 250, 265, 299, 301, 314,
    325, 327, 328, 330, 331
induction year 25, 68, 75, 170, 272, 287,
    289, 291, 292, 307, 308, 315, 321,
    323
induction, dictionary definitions of 332
initial *formation* 202, 211, 212, 232,
    250-252, 254, 255, 257, 259, 314
initial teaching conditions 2, 185, 190
in-school competitions 41
in-school teacher education
    (*konaikenshu*) 270
in-service center 261, 262, 265, 276-
    278, 282, 283, 289, 290, 293, 294,
    349
in-service education 77, 201, 263, 293,
    295, 314
Inspectorate 110, 113, 118, 120, 121,
    203, 206, 207, 210, 221, 245, 250,
    257, 258, 260, 301, 317, 331, 354
inter-cantonal guidelines for induction
    113, 341
IUFM *formateurs* 198, 209, 222, 224-
    226, 229, 233-235, 242, 247, 249,
    253, 347-349, 373

IUFM system 206, 211, 236, 244, 245, 254, 331
IUFM, place and role 210
IUFM-based and school-based tasks 231

Japan Teacher Union (JTU) 294, 295
Japanese Ministry of Education, Science, Sports and Culture 262, 300, 316, 374
job allocation *(fenpei)* 34

Kumamoto Prefecture 286

laboratory (lab) technician 141, 142, 164, 166, 167, 169, 172, 190, 331, 344
lesson planning 36, 38, 50, 98, 102, 111, 133, 135, 188, 305, 308
lesson preparation group *(beikezu)* 21, 23, 37, 40, 42, 47, 51, 9, 69, 61, 66, 339
Lucerne induction system 115
lycée 198, 199, 203, 205, 209, 216, 217, 221, 227, 228, 235, 239, 241, 242, 245, 249, 255, 347, 348, 370, 72

master *(maître de stage)* 35, 46, 201, 320
mathematical teaching culture 195
mathematicians 122, 214, 216, 229, 242, 255, 324, 331
mathematics education 9, 35, 51, 56-58, 61, 75, 197, 198, 243, 313, 334, 338, 340, 347
mathematics inspectors 205, 207, 216, 221, 222, 225, 245
mathematics reform in Shanghai 24
mathematics *stagiaires* 197-199, 206, 213, 221, 206, 213, 219, 221, 223-225, 227, 234, 235, 236, 241, 308, 347, 372
Mathematics Teachers Association (APMEP) 311
mathematics teaching 6, 18, 21, 44, 50, 55-58, 67, 75, 197, 206, 220, 221, 236, 251, 297, 304, 309, 338, 340, 342
memoir director 234, 359
memoir seminars 311, 348, 358, 359

mentoring 1, 5, 30, 32, 39, 41, 43, 47, 66, 70-74, 83, 111, 113, 117, 126, 127, 129, 131-134, 170, 191, 273, 282, 319, 320, 327, 337, 352, 353, 365, 367
mentors 1, 2, 12, 13, 19, 23-25, 31, 38, 41, 42, 46, 48, 49, 63, 66, 70, 71, 73-75, 78, 84, 100, 117, 126-129, 132, 168-170, 183, 196, 224, 275, 279, 282, 287, 312, 21, 322, 325, 342, 343
middle grades 16, 18, 93, 105, 145, 187, 188, 305, 307
middle school 83, 92, 94, 102, 105, 106, 127, 340, 365
middle-school *(Mittelschule)* teachers 85, 94, 95, 104, 105, 114, 125, 343, 355
Ministry of Education 92, 154, 159, 162, 187, 203, 205, 206, 212, 217, 222, 225, 236, 237, 244, 248, 249, 252, 317, 328, 331, 338, 344, 347, 369
Ministry of Education in China 33
Ministry of Education in France 204
Ministry of Education in Japan 262, 300, 316, 374
Ministry of Education in New Zealand 146, 148
Mittelschule 16, 92, 94
Miyazaki Prefecture 277, 282, 285, 288, 349
Monbusho 262, 266, 267, 270-276, 289, 291, 293-295, 349, 374
moral education 265, 266, 268, 276-278
multiple providers 324, 325, 329
multiple stakeholders 25, 69, 71

national curriculum standards for science 186, 346
national induction policy and guidance 149, 158, 193, 344, 345
National Science Curriculum 151, 162, 193, 344, 345
national teacher conferences 175, 181
new teacher training *(xin laoshi peixun)* 27, 113, 219
New Zealand education system 146, 158, 192, 379
North American assumptions 5

North American dichotomy of 'pre-
    service' and 'in-service' education
    200
North American teacher education
    programs 268

open lessons 60, 61, 63
paid release time 153, 154, 156, 158,
    191
pastoral responsibilities 180
pedagogic advisor (*conseiller
    pédagogique*) 196, 199, 200, 206,
    208, 209, 220-226, 230, 234, 235,
    238, 239, 241, 247, 248, 252, 253,
    255, 260, 297, 307, 309, 320, 321,
    325, 347, 359, 361, 372
pedagogical content(s) knowledge 36,
    46, 152, 304
pedagogical strategies for science
    teaching 173, 302, 306, 314, 324,
    334
peer observation 39, 312, 320
peer support 169, 174, 175, 178-180,
    183, 191, 320
peer-support meetings 174, 178, 183
performance management system 160,
    186, 346
personal support 309, 310
Philosophy I 84, 94, 124
Philosophy II 84, 94, 95, 105, 124
physical education 29, 120, 265, 266,
    272, 277
'PLC1' year 213, 218, 235, 254, 255,
    259
'PLC2' year 213, 214, 229, 236, 259,
    383
'PLC3' year 247, 256
Post-Primary Teachers' Association
    (PPTA) 147, 153, 155, 158, 159, 187,
    191, 193, 344
practice group leaders 103, 104, 113,
    114, 116, 119, 139, 140, 326, 343,
    351, 352, 368, 374
practice groups 83, 87, 106, 111-119,
    121, 124, 130-136, 138, 139, 301,
    309, 310, 316, 319-323, 328, 329,
    341, 343, 344, 351-354, 367
practice teaching experiences 84, 151,
    314
practice-teaching sessions 84, 99, 151

preparation class (*yubeiban*) 28
pre-service education 17, 22, 26, 31-36,
    76, 94, 110-112, 119, 123, 134, 137,
    139, 150, 255, 274, 297, 303-305,
    307, 316, 334, 355, 366, 374
principal 23, 38, 67, 68, 127, 130, 152,
    154, 159, 175, 178, 209, 221, 225,
    253, 261, 262, 269, 274-276, 279-
    281, 283, 286, 287, 295, 309, 317
private schools 148, 158, 272, 370
process of enculturation 3, 323
professional development activities 104,
    339, 340
professional development centers 193,
    339
professional development course 75, 138
professional development institutions
    112, 355
professional development opportunities
    120, 170, 181, 292
professional development programs 7,
    28, 171, 293, 315
professional development services 147,
    191, 344
professional ethics 30, 32
professional knowledge 45, 59, 67, 159,
    160, 202, 250
professional memoir (*le mémoire
    professionel*) 195, 197, 198, 200,
    202, 204, 209, 219, 220, 228, 230-
    234, 240, 241, 243, 246, 251, 258,
    306, 311, 320-322, 347, 3348, 357-
    360, 373
professional practice 45, 159, 184, 201,
    229, 231, 256, 313, 358
professional schools 93, 104, 334
program evaluation 97, 98, 158, 293,
    352
Prorector 127, 375
prospective teacher 5, 7, 17, 32, 35, 96,
    99-104, 147, 151-154, 188, 189, 306
providers 2, 4, 12, 16, 34, 35, 38, 46, 48,
    79, 145, 157, 168, 169, 172, 174, 180,
    181, 185, 192, 250, 300, 309, 320,
    321, 324, 325, 327-329, 333, 335,
    337, 345, 370
provisionally registered teacher (PRT)
    148, 158, 170, 184, 189
public conversation 41, 50, 58, 59, 62,
    63, 66

public lesson (*gongkaike*) 40, 45, 47, 62, 65-67, 263, 286, 305, 306, 311, 312, 365, 367, 374
Pudong district 73, 75
pupil's homework 49, 63, 197, 199
pupil's motivation 143, 160

qualification (*zige zhengshu*) 203, 204, 206, 210, 259, 271, 272, 280
quality education (*suzhi jiaoyu*) 55, 56

Realschule 342
rector 205, 207, 208, 212
regional pedagogic inspectors for mathematics (IPR) 196, 207, 208, 221, 348, 349, 371, 372, 383
regional science advisors 169, 173, 177
regional workshops for beginning science teachers 146, 157
Reims Academy 357
replacement teacher 208, 209, 372
report lesson (*huibaoke*) 39, 48, 66, 67, 73, 367
Research Institute on the Teaching of Mathematics (IREM) 202, 242

school administrators 12, 36, 67, 148, 185
school board 92, 110-112, 125, 150, 273, 317, 328
school certificate exams 147, 152
school education 94, 205, 209, 237
school leadership 112, 113, 120, 121
school science courses 149, 152, 161, 186
school science curricula 145, 188
science methods courses 151, 268, 345
science classroom 98, 164, 166
science courses 142-145, 150, 152, 161, 163-167, 182, 186, 187, 188, 305, 369
science education 9, 123, 166, 182, 350, 369
science preparation 150, 323
science teaching 6, 10, 18, 157, 166, 301, 332, 345
second-year teachers 24, 144, 154, 156-158, 168, 171, 180, 182-184, 239, 287, 370
self-reflection 62, 119, 122

Shanghai Academy of Educational Sciences 340
Shanghai Municipal Education Commission 328, 365
Shanghai Teachers' University 22, 33-36, 50, 81
Shanghai's formal induction policy 29, 32, 69, 330
Shanghai's Municipal Education Commission 328
Shanghai's teacher competition 41, 43, 46, 66, 67, 70, 313, 319, 339
socio-economic levels of the pupil 145, 151, 245, 369
Songjiang district 73, 74
stage 15, 201, 202, 219, 221, 222, 226, 227, 231, 255, 260, 371, 372
stagiaire teachers 4, 194-196, 200, 208-212, 213-225, 231-239, 241-243, 249-251, 255-259, 266, 296, 302, 308, 309, 331, 338, 347, 370, 373
stagiaire week 219, 220
stagiaire's stage en responsabilité 220-222, 224, 231, 233, 255, 347
Standortbestimmung 15, 112, 113, 115, 118-120, 122, 127, 132, 139, 321, 330, 343, 352, 354
Standortbestimmungen and practice groups in Switzerland 15, 112, 115, 118-120, 122, 127, 132, 133, 139, 319, 321, 330, 341, 343, 352, 354
student teachers 100-102, 125, 126, 131, 132, 134, 151, 158, 254, 269, 270, 275, 307, 314, 342
student teaching 7, 22, 81, 100, 125, 131, 136, 263, 268-270, 287, 316, 346
subject-matter preparation 34, 95, 314
substitute teacher 15, 87, 118, 125, 137, 144, 159, 181, 318, 342, 353
success education (*chenggong jiaoyu*) 75subject-matter mentor 38, 74
supervision 124, 131, 158, 201, 330, 374
support programs 146-148, 152, 153, 156-159, 183, 184, 189, 191, 370
support providers 157, 168, 169, 174, 177, 180, 181, 185, 192, 309, 320, 321, 325, 370
Swiss cantons 109, 113, 133, 138, 301, 329, 344, 368

Swiss Conference of Cantonal Education
    Ministers 343, 383
Swiss induction philosophy 109

talk lesson (*shuoke*) 39, 42
teacher development 4, 6, 10, 18, 24, 30,
    31, 33, 73, 75-77, 294, 298, 301, 311,
    319, 321, 333, 338, 339, 351, 355
teacher education 9, 12, 16, 22, 33-36,
    79, 91, 93, 94, 100, 112, 119, 123,
    137, 197, 200, 202, 208, 211, 242,
    256, 267, 293, 297, 299, 301, 302,
    337, 341, 367, 368, 370, 375
teacher *formation* 204, 205, 208, 210,
    211, 214, 236, 248-251, 259, 373
teacher learning 4, 5, 26, 43, 46, 50, 54,
    58, 59, 69, 73, 80, 219, 249, 298, 305,
    321, 322, 333, 335, 346
teacher preparation 2, 4, 7, 10, 11, 13,
    17, 32, 36, 46, 76, 84-87, 93, 95, 111,
    123, 139, 146, 149-152, 180, 188,
    200, 203, 267, 270, 295, 302, 304,
    306, 314, 315, 318, 338, 345, 346
teacher preparation institutions 11, 94,
    153, 169, 175, 192
teacher preparation programs 1, 100,
    149, 152, 153, 155, 173, 174, 180,
    189, 369
Teacher Registration Board (TRB) 148,
    149, 152, 156-159, 184, 193, 344,
    346, 370
teacher unions 153
teacher's career 4, 7, 13, 217, 317, 319,
    324, 336
teacher-pupil relationship 178, 276
teaching competition 24, 39, 41, 43, 46,
    66, 67, 70, 313, 319, 339
teaching reference materials 50, 51, 54,
    58, 70
teaching research group (*jiaoyanzu*) 21,
    23, 37, 38, 40, 42, 47, 54, 59-61, 66,
    67, 69-71, 78
teaching research section (*jiaoyanshi*)
    26, 27, 39, 76
teaching research section group
    (jiaoyanzu) 21, 23, 37, 38, 40, 42, 47,
    54, 59, 61, 62, 66, 67, 69, 70, 72
technical/vocational schools 92, 105,
    106

textbooks 20, 27, 50-54, 58, 60, 63, 96,
    98, 144, 164, 165, 187, 217, 233, 239,
    240, 242, 313, 340, 346
TIMSS 10, 341, 368
training of counselors and mentors
    130training section (*peixunbu*) 26, 27,
    31, 71, 76
tribe 228, 234, 236, 308, 321, 370
two-year induction period 124, 355

understanding pupils 47, 48, 276, 277,
    284
University Institutes for the Formation of
    Teachers (IUFM) 197, 204, 211
university mathematicians 216, 255

Versailles IUFM 234

Wellington College of Education (WCE)
    149, 150, 151, 154, 192, 345
workshops 32, 43, 70, 73, 76, 153, 169,
    173-176, 228, 229, 246, 293, 345, 346

Xuhui district 76

young teachers (*qingnian laoshi*) 24, 37,
    40, 42, 48, 60, 61, 62, 67, 71, 72, 74,
    73, 161, 297, 312, 317, 339, 365, 366

Zhabei district 75
Zurich 83, 84, 91, 93-96, 100, 105, 106,
    110, 112, 117, 119, 122-125, 132,
    134, 135, 137-140, 301, 316, 330,
    334, 341, 342, 352, 354, 355